Information System
Development and Op

R G Anderson FCMA, MInst, AM(Dip), FMS

Information systems development and operation

PITMAN PUBLISHING
128 Long Acre, London WC2E 9AN
A Division of Longman Group UK Ltd

First published 1989

© Longman Group UK Ltd 1989

British Library Cataloguing in Publication Data
Anderson, R.
     Information systems in development and
     operation.
     1. Offices. Automated information processing
     systems
     I. Title
     651.5'9

ISBN 0-273-02997-5

Typeset, printed and bound in Great Britain

Contents

iv

Preface

The speed at which information technology is developing is having a great impact on business operations and administration in both the public and private sector. Evolving technology has expanded the subject of data processing to information processing and system design to system or information engineering. This Study Revision Pack covers all topics associated with modern office automation, including information systems and related information technology. The Pack has been written specifically to meet the examination requirements of the ACCA 2.7: Information Systems in Development and Operation examination, but is also an up-to-date and informative source of reference for all other students of related subjects.

Facts are presented in a logical way to cover all aspects of the new ACCA syllabus, including the nature and use of information systems , from systems theory to hardware and software requirements for specific systems needs. Particular emphasis is given to those topics which have frequently occurred in recent examination papers. These include: system design strategies, system testing, the prevention of unauthorised access to files, databases and computer centres; establishing procedures for ensuring the accuracy of data entering a system; the distinction between logical and physical system design; the type of screen dialogue suitable for senior management and for other employees; system and program specifications and matters relating to traditional and structured design methodology; distinguishing between the three types of computer; the type of processing technique required for different applications; the information needs of top, middle and supervisory management; considerations to be taken into account in the selection of a computer; local area networks; and differences between centralised and distributed processing. Students who work conscientiously through the Pack and who attempt to provide solutions to the range of review and self-test questions will be as well prepared for the examination as it is possible to be.

R G Anderson

Spring 1989

Acknowledgments

British Telecom: for provision of information and photograph of Prestel CitiService screen display and information relating to other Telecom and Prestel services.

D.J. Buttrey acting on behalf of Apple Accounting Ltd: for the loan of manuals relating to Apple Macintosh Accounting packages including nominal, purchase and sales ledger. Also provision of photographs illustrating windows in a multi-tasking environment; graphics illustrations and of a desktop publishing system including a scanner.

Cadbury Ltd: provision of illustration of EAN bar code.

Comshare Ltd: provision of details relating to Commander Executive Information Systems (EIS).

Computer Associates: provision of details relating to Supercalc 3.

IBM United Kingdom Ltd: for various photographs illustrating their current computer range.

Intelligent Environments Ltd: details in respect of decision support software.

Microsoft Ltd: for the provision of details relating to the Excell spreadsheet and various illustrations of screen displays. Also details relating to MS-DOS.

Midlands Electricity Board: supply of optical mark meter reading sheet.

Oracle Corporation UK Ltd: details relating to SQL Forms and other literature and illustrations relating to their reporting and other systems.

Penn Communications acting on behalf of Ashton-Tate: for the provision of a photograph illustrating a screen display of Ashton-Tate's Framework II spreadsheet. Also for photographs showing screen displays of dBASE IV and illustrations of dBASE III PLUSE Screen Painter.

System C Ltd: details relating to their program generator software.

Work Sciences Associates: details regarding their Priority Decision System.

1 Systems theory 1

1.1 Introduction

The principles of systems theory should always be considered when developing any business system, whether manual, computerised or a combination of both. These underlying concepts need to be built into such a system (particularly as most business systems are information systems). An information system must take account of a number of factors, such as the *delay factor*, which can have an adverse effect on the achievement of business objectives; the effect of *buffeting* on the behaviour of systems; the need to attain a state of balance in system performance (*homeostasis*); and the effect of *noise* and *redundancy* on management reports and aspects of communication theory. All of these elements need appraisal to ensure a system has the necessary ingredients for the level of performance required. Other factors which must also be considered are dealt with in Chapter 2.

1.2 Concepts

Systems theory provides the scientific principles and concepts which may be applied to the study of systems of all types. Within this Study Pack the term embraces all types of business system, both manual and computerised, routine processing applications and management information systems. Systems theory is based on knowledge obtained from the study of the behaviour of systems when subjected to random influences from various environmental sources and under varying operational circumstances. Such knowledge enables the future behaviour of systems to be predicted to some extent.

The behaviour pattern of systems is, therefore, obtained from systematic studies and simulations. What may appear to be very different systems on the surface often have similarities to which normal systems theory applies. Consider, for example, commodity stocks in a warehouse — the stocks need to be controlled by an efficient stock control system to avoid stock shortages and duplicated stock allocations. In the same way, a tour operator dealing with package holidays needs to control some 'object': in this example, it is necessary to control the various package holidays to avoid shortages, which lead to loss of profit, on the one hand, and duplicated allocation of holidays on the other. Such systems must be designed to overcome operating problems which may arise due to environmental influences, often dealt with as a result of feedback (dealt with in Chapter 2) and effective communication.

1.3 Delay factor

1.3.1 Time-lag between physical event and information flows

If as a result of feedback unfavourable deviations are detected and action taken to eliminate them, the ultimate result will depend upon when the action was effected. Careful consideration must be given to the time-lag between a physical event and the information flows informing the effector of the event. For instance, if an unfavourable production output is detected and action is taken too late to alter the situation, then it is out of phase because the state of the system has probably changed in the meantime and action is taken to remedy a situation which no longer exists. This is referred to as the *delay factor* and such circumstances cause systems to hunt or oscillate around the desired state (*see* 1.6).

In the cirumstances outlined, if production fails to meet the desired target, action can be taken to increase production but if the necessary adjustment is delayed it is possible that, in the meantime, production has taken an upward swing. The result of the delayed action to increase production tends to increase production even more, perhaps to a greater level than is warranted by the previous shortfall.

An adjustment may be effected to reduce production but by this time production may have taken a downward swing and the delayed action decreases production below the desired level thereby amplifying the situation.

1.3.2 Amplification and damping

The principles outlined show that if action to remedy a situation is delayed then the result achieved is of a positive feedback nature, whereby deviations are amplified instead of being damped down. What was meant to be negative feedback becomes positive feedback.

1.3.3. Practical example

In order to demonstrate the above principles and concepts Table 1.1 outlines the actual production output in five different weeks, the delayed information flow in respect of each week's output, the *corrective* action taken and the resulting output. The table should be studied in conjunction with Fig. 1.1.

Table 1.1 Result of the time-lag between physical event and information flow

Week 1	Week 2	Week 3	Week 4	Week 5
Normal output -200	Normal output +200	Normal output -400	Normal output +800	Normal output -1600
	Information received for week 1	Information received for week 2	Information received for week 3	Information received for week 4
	Corrective action +200	Corrective action -400	Corrective action +800	Corrective action -1600
	Adjusted output +400	Adjusted output -800	Adjusted output +1600	Adjusted output -3200

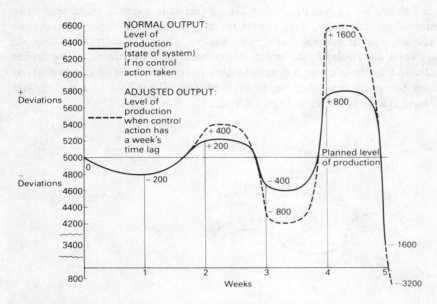

Figure 1.1 Effect of time-lag in an oscillating system

1.4 Timeliness

Other aspects of the timing of information flows and the resulting action may be related to the preparation of annual accounts and the balance sheet of a company at the end of the financial year. These are, of course, historical and, although delay in their preparation should be minimised, no action can be taken to remedy the situation disclosed even if the facts are available within one day of the year-end. The operations for the year are complete and what is done is done as it were. Recognition of this situation has led to the development of periodical short-term accounting reports, statements and statistics. This involves reporting on events as soon after the conclusion of an operating control period as is feasible, so as to effect adjustments to the situations being controlled, either to eliminate adverse variances or to take advantage of favourable conditions.

It is important to appreciate that the best possible type of information will not affect control without a human or automated controller to effect adjustments to the systems being controlled, based on the information provided. The time factor must be considered with regard to its importance in achieving the degree of control required. For example, if information in respect of scrapped production is not reported early enough, no remedial action can be taken to stop production and to remove the cause of the scrap. It becomes necessary to introduce quality controllers to monitor the quality of production at strategic locations in the production processes. By this means, production may be stopped when it is discovered that the acceptable level of quality is not being achieved. Quality control charts are normally employed for monitoring the quality of production. By this means, corrective action may be taken to remove the cause of the scrap and so ensure that production achieves the desired level of quality (the desired state of the system).

1.5 Random influences

Business activities hardly ever achieve a steady state as they are subjected to random influences from both the internal and the external environments. This causes results, or the level of performance, to fluctuate above and below the average or normal state. For example, stocks of materials attain an overall average level, but vary on a day-to-day basis, which is a normal state of affairs. It is extreme variations which must be controlled, as these cause a system to *hunt* or *oscillate* around its standard or normal state, corrective action being effected as a result of feedback. The effect of negative and positive feedback in an oscillating system is shown in Figs. 1.2 and 1.3.

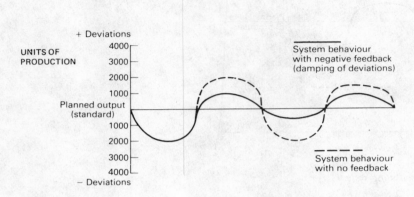

Figure 1.2 Effect of negative feedback in an oscillating system

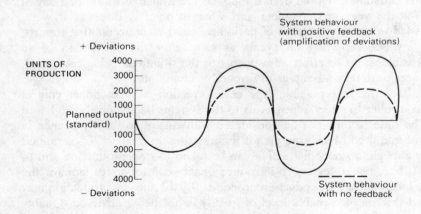

Figure 1.3 Effect of positive feedback in an oscillating system

1.6 Buffeting

Unusual disturbances to a system's behaviour are caused by *buffeting* and this results in fluctuating system states, i.e. a tendency to hunt or oscillate and deviate from the desired course. For example, a strong cross wind on a motorway will buffet a motor vehicle, causing it to deviate sharply from the desired direction. The driver of the vehicle must apply corrective action to remedy the effect of the cross wind, usually by the application of negative feedback, i.e. steering in the opposite direction to the wind.

1.7 Homeostasis

Systems, to be effective, must maintain a state of balance, which requires the elimination of unnecessary hunting or oscillating. The term *homeostasis* may be defined as the process of holding steady or balancing the output of a system, i.e. the *controlled variable*, despite disturbances and buffeting. It is the process of restoring a system to its desired state when subjected to changing environmental conditions (*see* 1.5).

In a stock control system, unusual variations in demand and supply may be interpreted as disturbances to normal behaviour. Safety stocks are integrated into the system to overcome this situation, but in the case of extreme variations the stock control parameters (reference input) may require modification to allow for changing trends.

1.8 Response time

This term is usually used in the context of computing systems and is a measure of the time elapsed from making a request for information to the time it takes for the computer to respond. A clerical information system may react too slowly to requests for information which is one of the reasons why MIS are ofter computer-orientated. In real-time systems a computer must respond to changing circumstances as they occur in order that the system may be effectively controlled.

1.9 Communication

Before defining specific aspects of communication and noise in the narrow sense of everyday business activities, it is important to appreciate the wider concepts involved in communication.

All systems contain the element of communication, especially closed-loop systems providing the basis of feedback. Communication may therefore be defined as the provision of information on which to base a decision to control the state of a system.

1.9.1 Elements of communication

The elements of communication may be described by an example from telecommunications: a wireless operator using a morse key transmits messages to a distant location where they are received by another wireless operator who records the messages.

The elements of such activities are as follows.

(a) *Information source*. Originator of message wishing to convey information to another person.
(b) *Message*. Details of situation on message pad.

(c) *Transmitter*. Wireless operator transmitting message by means of morse key connected to transmitting set.

(d) *Signal*. The signal produced by the transmitting set when the morse key is depressed.

(e) *Receiver*. Wireless operator receiving message by means of a receiving set and earphones and writing message on a message pad.

(f) *Information destination*. Despatch message to addressee.

1.9.2 Elements of communication in cost control system

In order to relate the elements of communication outlined above to a business environment, a cost control system is used as an example: it is desired to communicate the incidence of scrap production to the cost control system.

(a) *Information source*. Inspector responsible for informing cost office of scrap production.

(b) *Message*. Details of scrap recorded on scrap notes (source documents).

(c) *Transmitter*. Distribution of scrap notes by messenger service.

(d) *Signal*. Delivery of scrap notes to cost office.

(e) *Receiver*. Cost clerk receiving scrap notes.

(f) *Information destination*. This may be the cost clerk receiving the scrap notes, or the cost controller after the cost clerk has processed the scrap notes.

1.9.3 The noise element in communications

Noise is a telecommunications term which indicates the presence of unwanted signals in electrical and electronic devices. In the context of data communication, noise is any disturbance to the transmission of the required signal which causes the signal being received to differ from the signal transmitted, perhaps due to interference caused by static. In the business context, this implies that as the effective control of business is dependent upon accurate information, the incidence of noise is likely to distort the information being received by either the controller or the effector. Consequently the state of a system may be misinterpreted as a result of the distorted information, and incorrect action to remedy the situation may be applied.

In general terms, noise alters the content of a message received from that which is meant to be conveyed. This situation can arise simply by misinterpretation of the context of a message, the use of terms not understood by the recipient (jargon), the presence of static on the line during a telephone conversation, too much padding in a report which tends to hide the essential facts, and inadequately worded communications.

1.9.4 Redundancy and the noise factor

The element of redundancy is often incorporated into communications to overcome the problem of noise. Redundancy refers to the addition of bits, characters or digits to ensure that messages are received correctly or that the correct record is being processed. Examples of redundancy are as follows.

(a) The spelling-out of a value in addition to presenting it in the normal way, i.e. £20 (twenty pounds).

(b) The inclusion of a parity bit (binary digit) in addition to the bit combination of a character in coded form. The parity bit is an additional 1 bit which is included in character codes encoded on magnetic media for either data transmission or data transfer in computer operations. The parity bit is inserted automatically by the data preparation equipment, and is for the purpose of checking that data is being transferred or transmitted free of corruption. A 1 bit is added to ensure that the 1 bits accord either to an even number count or to an odd number count, depending on the mode in use.

(c) Quite frequently in computer data processing applications, check digits are used to ensure the accuracy of stock numbers and account numbers prior to processing. A check digit is a number which is added to such numbers for the purpose of producing a *self-checking* number. A check digit has a unique mathematical relationship to the number to which it is added. The editing routine of a computer program performs check digit verification and data is rejected as invalid when the check digit derived is any number other than the correct one. In effect, a check digit is a redundant character.

1.9.5 Redundancy and management reports

Redundancy incorporated in management reports tends to overshadow the essential facts. For example, a complete listing of cost-centre budgeted and actual expenditure, although conveying all the facts, does not in fact convey a clear appreciation of the situation directly. The manager concerned is required to establish the significance of each of the items listed by going through the list item by item comparing each budgeted and actual expenditure amount to determine those which require his immediate attention.

If reporting is restricted to items with significant variations of actual expenditure from budgeted expenditure, then a greater impact is made and the recipient of the report can speedily respond to the situation disclosed. In the complete listing indicated above, the significant details were not highlighted and in fact the essential requirement, the disclosure of variances, was not included. In such a case, the control system is inefficient, as a complete listing in such a case is an obstacle to the clear understanding of the situation.

Review questions

1 Specify the nature of systems theory, stating its importance to the development of business systems.

2 Define the meaning of 'delay factor'.

3 What is the effect of random influences on the behaviour of business systems?

4 Homeostasis may be defined as the process of maintaining a systems output at a steady state. Discuss.

5 What is 'response time'?

6 What is meant by the term 'noise' in the context of business systems?

7 Discuss the term 'redundancy' in a systems context.

2 Systems theory 2

2.1 Introduction

The principles of systems theory and their importance for the development of systems of all types has been stated in Chapter 1. This chapter outlines other important concepts relating to systems theory and describes the various types of system, their relationships and their operational characteristics. This provides an appreciation of the nature of the various systems, which is important for understanding how such systems function and the types of situation to which they are relevant. The chapter also explains the nature of control systems and underlying concepts such as the 'exception principle', Pareto Law, threshold of control system, control interface, cybernetic control process and the nature of feedback.

2.2 Classification of systems

2.2.1 Mechanistic and organismic systems

A *mechanistic* system or organisation structure is rigid in construction and is designed to operate on the basis of standardised rules and regulations which restrict its ability to react to its environment. If non-standard situations arise the system many not be able to deal with them, which causes a complete breakdown of the system. Computer systems which have been designed in an inflexible manner can be said to be mechanistic.

It is well known that stable conditions do not exist in business for long and mechanistic systems, as we have seen, are limited in dealing with this. An *organismic* system or organisation structure, on the other hand, is geared to respond to environmental influences and is able to redefine its objectives according to the prevailing circumstances. It accomplishes this by an efficient reallocation of resources and retuning of the system to the new circumstances.

2.2.2 Deterministic systems

One type of mechanistic system is the *deterministic* system, which performs effectively when input is invariable and so output can be predetermined. In general, this type of system enables the output generated from specific inputs to be predicted without error. This equally applies to a computer program. Business and economic systems do not come into this category, however, as they are highly unpredictable.

2.2.3 Probabilistic system

Business and economic systems are of a *probabilistic* nature as they are subjected to random influences from the internal and external environments. Their state cannot be predicted precisely; it is only possible to assess their *probable* behaviour. The state of such systems can therefore only be defined within specified limits even when they are subject to control, because stocks of raw materials, parts and finished goods, for instance, are influenced by changes in demand and variations in supply. Stock control systems are implemented to detect and control such variations on a probability basis.

Similarly, production activities are subjected to random variations in respect of manpower availability and level of productivity achieved, machine breakdowns and material supply, etc. Production planning and control systems are implemented to detect and control such variations in order to minimise their effect on the achievement of desired states.

The quality of production also varies randomly due to inconsistency in the quality of raw materials, human error and faulty machine operation. Quality control systems are designed to detect and correct such situations. At a higher level, top management cannot be sure of the outcome of any specific strategy as it is not certain what actions will be taken by competitors, suppliers, customers and the government in the future. This depends upon the vagaries of the international economic climate and market trends at any point in time.

In general, probabilistic systems are of a stochastic (random) nature. It is not certain what outputs will be achieved from specific inputs because it is not possible to ascertain what events will occur outside the direct control of a system.

2.2.4 Adaptive (self-organising) system

This type of system is dynamic as it responds to changing circumstances by adjusting its behaviour on a self-organising basis. The system alters its inputs as a result of measuring its output. It attempts to optimise performance by monitoring its own behaviour.

Computerised systems such as stock control are often adaptive as changes in demand are sensed and responses are speedily implemented to change the state of the system and so avoid the following.

(a) Overstocking and the related consequences of high average stocks, which increase the investment in stocks over the desired level; increased interest on capital; increased depreciation due to prolonged storage; increased obsolescence due to a complete fall off in demand; and increased costs of storage facilities.

(b) Stock shortages, which generate loss of orders or disrupt the flow of production, causing under-utilisation of resources, under-absorbed fixed overheads and loss of profits on units not produced and/or sold.

A computerised stock control system can also adjust the re-order level as a result of changes in demand and so avoid re-ordering materials unnecessarily. If this did not occur, then in a situation of reduced demand, a replenishment order may be automatically placed, which would increase the level of stock to an even higher level than required (*see* (a) above).

In the event of increasing demand, a failure to adjust the re-order level would mean that the program would not replenish supplies in accordance with the new circumstances and stock shortages would occur (*see* (b) above).

2.3 Control

2.3.1 Definition of control system

A control system may be defined as a *control loop* superimposed on other systems which have different purposes, e.g. the production system is controlled by the production *control* system. The purpose of a control system is to detect variations in the behaviour of a system so that signals can be communicated to the appropriate manager, who is then in a position to effect changes to the system so that it can achieve its objectives despite changes in environment or random factors. Many administrative systems are control-orientated but they do not necessarily effect control directly — this is the prerogative of the manager concerned (*see* Figs 2.1 and 2.2).

2.3.2 Basic elements of control

Control in business systems consists of the following elements.

(a) *Planning*. The determination of objectives, or parameters: standard time for an operation, level of production activity required, level of sales required, expenditure allowed, performance level required, etc.

(b) *Collecting facts*. The collection and recording of data in respect of: actual time taken, level of production achieved, level of sales achieved, expenditure incurred, actual performance level, etc.

(c) *Comparison*. The comparison of objectives with actual results for the purpose of indicating variances from planned performance in the various spheres of business operations, and informing the relevant manager of significant deviations (variances).

(d) *Corrective action*. Action is taken by the relevant manager (effector) to maintain a state of homeostasis (system stability) or to revise plans (*see* 2.4.2).

2.3.3 Control based on the exception principle

Control is often based on signals collected relating to deviations from planned performance. This is referred to as *management by exception*. This concept is extremely important to business control as it allows management to grasp essential facts more speedily and to correct adverse trends much sooner, owing to the fact that only *significant* factors are reported on. Time is thus saved on compiling reports and redundancy of information is eliminated. More detailed control schedules waste time collecting uninformative data and filtering essential requirements, slowing down the process of corrective action. In fact, corrective action may not be taken at all as it is very easy for a manager to overlook essential facts in the hurly-burly of daily routine.

Examples of control techniques using the exception principle are budgetary control and standard costing. Budgetary control compares actual with budgeted results periodically for the purpose of reporting to the relevant managers significant variances for their attention. While budgetary control is used for controlling overall business results, the control of costs relating to products in respect of direct material and direct labour is achieved by standard costing.

2.3.4 Control and the Pareto Law

An important factor for effective control is the application of the *Pareto Law* which, in general, states that many business situations have an 80/20 *characteristic*. This means that 80 per cent of the value of items in stock can be represented by 20 per cent of the high-value items. Therefore, the degree of control necessary to manage stock may be reduced by concentrating control on these 20 per cent high-value items, especially for controlling the total value of items held in stock. Less rigid control procedures may be applied to the remaining 80 per cent of the items which only account for 20 per cent of the total value.

Similarly, key production materials and parts may consist of 20 per cent of the total range held in stores, therefore tight control must be applied to these items, which should reduce the number of failures to report crucial stock situations, especially if the importance of the 20 per cent is stressed sufficiently and independent checks applied to the stock records, perhaps by the stock controller or auditor.

2.3.5 Threshold of control system

The measurement of a systems output by a sensor is the most important element of control because it is the point at which control begins and is, in fact, the threshold between the physical system and the related control system. For example, the output from the factory is measured and used as a basis of control by the production control system.

2.3.6 Control interface

The communication of data from a physical system to its related control system is a means of connecting the two systems and may be defined as the *control interface*. Interface may be accomplished by strategically sited data collection devices, forming a factory data collection system. The data is then communicated to a computer for processing. The communication device is in fact the interface in this instance. In a more basic system the provision of source documents, such as progress tickets, to the control system serves the same purpose and may be classified as the control interface.

2.3.7 Requisite variety

Business systems consist of combinations of interrelated variable elements and it is the number of such elements which creates difficulty in designing effective control systems. The number of elements is a measure of a system's inherent variety and the greater the number of elements, the greater the degree of complexity.

A control system needs to be designed with the same degree of variety as the system it is to monitor, in order to allow for all possible conditions likely to arise in the operation of the system. This is a very important feature of control systems, particularly so with regard to computer-based systems, as the range of variety must be fully catered for, so far as it is economically viable to do so: programs must contain the necessary instructions for processing data according to its classification or significance.

Before coding a computer program for a specific application a *program flowchart* is normally prepared which itself may be based on a *decision table*. The decision table is compiled to ensure that all conditions relating to data, and all necessary actions relating to such conditions, are taken fully into account during processing. The flowchart is a means of representing in graphic form the logic of computer operations. It indicates the *flow* of control and establishes how the desired results can be achieved. A decision table is therefore an aid in the preparation of a flowchart which is, in its turn, an aid to program coding.

These factors are particularly relevant to computerised exception reporting applications, such as automatic stock re-ordering and credit reporting.

The effectiveness of control is dependent upon the extent to which the variable elements in the system to be controlled have been predicted and, if not included in the computer program (when relevant), are catered for by other secondary control procedures.

2.4 Cybernetic control

2.4.1 Definition of cybernetics

The subject of cybernetics is important for control systems of all types and the basic concepts apply equally to business control systems and to man and machine systems. Cybernetics may be defined as 'the science of communication and control in man and machine systems'. The term is derived from the Greek work *kybernétés*, the derivative of the Latin word *gubernator*, which in English may be translated as *governor* or *controller*.

2.4.2 Cybernetic control process

The cybernetic control process is identical to the process of control based on exception reporting, i.e. management by exception. The basic elements of the cybernetic control process may be analysed as follows (*see* Fig. 2.2).

(a) *Reference input*. The use of resources is planned to achieve a defined objective(s) and appropriate control parameters are established to assist this achievement. The parameters are referred to as reference inputs.

(b) *Sensor (measurement of controlled variable)*. Operations are undertaken and output is measured by a sensor, which indicates the actual state of the system, i.e. the magnitude of the output signal. The measured output is referred to as the *controlled variable*. A sensor may be a mechanical, electronic or manual data recorder, depending upon the nature of the system being controlled.

(c) *Feedback*. The output signal is then communicated by the process of feedback to the control system.

(d) *Comparator*. The comparator compares the output signal (the actual state of the system) with the desired state (the reference input). The difference between the two states is a measure of the variance or error. A comparator may be a control clerk (stock control clerk, cost clerk, budgetary control clerk), an automatic device in a machine or a computer program.

(e) *Error signal*. The error is signalled (communicated) to the effector.

(f) *Effector*. The effector adjusts the controlled variable by modifying the input of resources, perhaps to increase or decrease the level of production in accordance with status of the error signal, + or −. This action is to modify the behaviour of the system to achieve the reference input and obtain a state of *homeostatis* or system stability. The effector may be a manager or supervisor in the case of business systems or an automatic device in a process control system.

(g) *Modification of reference input*. It may be found that the reference input of a system is inaccurately defined, invalid or out of date and requires to be modified to conform to the true situation.

2.5 Feedback

2.5.1 Features of feedback

An important feature of information systems is *feedback*, which is the communication of a systems-measured output to a comparator for the detection of deviations (errors).

Automatic regulation is not usually possible with business systems as the deviations from a required performance must be observed by a human being in the control system or by a computer program. Action to achieve the desired state of homeostasis (*see* 1.7) must be taken by a manager after being notified of the deviations from the required state of the system. If the controller of the system fails to observe the deviations, then no effector action can take place. Even when deviations are noted and communicated, an effector may fail to take the appropriate action.

Feedback is essentially an output signal causing error signals to be generated as the basis for adjusting the input to a system which, in automatic control systems, is achieved by an inbuilt control mechanism.

2.5.2 Negative feedback

Most business control systems are *negative* error-actuated systems as the actual behaviour of the system is compared with the desired behaviour and the differences are detected as positive deviations (errors) and action is effected in the opposite direction to counteract them. For example, if the actual output from a production system is lower than the planned output, the difference between them would be detected as an error below standard. Corrective action would then be taken to increase output to the desired level, necessitating an adjustment in the opposite direction to the error — an increase in production. Negative feedback is therefore appropriate in business systems when actual results move unfavourably from the desired standard. Examples are:

(a) overspending on budget;
(b) failure to meet sales targets;
(c) failure to meet production levels;
(d) customer exceeds credit level.

The signal(s) which modify the behaviour of a system is not feedback but the result of feedback.

2.5.3 Positive feedback

The characteristics of some types of system are such that the detected deviations need to be amplified. The process of amplification in telecommunications is defined as 'a unidirectional device which creates an enlargement of a waveform'.

Amplification applies to servo-mechanisms whereby a small manual force is detected and amplified to achieve a defined purpose. For example, a small manual force applied to aircraft controls is detected and amplified to the force necessary to adjust the control surfaces.

If unfavourable deviations detected in business systems were amplified, corrective action would not be achieved as the errors would be amplified and cause the systems to deteriorate until they went completely out of control.

In situations causing favourable deviations in business systems there is a case for their amplification or an adjustment to the control parameters. For example, if a lower-priced material was used in production instead of the standard material at a higher price, then the material cost of production would be lower. This situation assumes that the alternative material is suitable for its purpose and may be considered for further use thereby amplifying the deviations. For policy reasons it may be considered prudent to maintain the original standard for a while. Alternatively the parameter (standard) may be amended immediately, in which case the deviation will disappear completely and will not be subjected to amplification as the desired state of the system has been modified.

Positive feedback is therefore appropriate in business systems where the actual results are better than the set target. Examples are:

(a) sales exceed target;
(b) costs are reduced below target without undesirable effects.

2.5.4 Feedforward

The error signals generated by a system are usually used to adjust the current input to a system to utilise resources more fully and to achieve system objectives. The error signals may be noted over a period of time by a monitoring process and used as a basis for planning future system resources. This approach ensures that the historical trend or inherent behaviour of a system is allowed for when establishing control parameters for future operations.

2.6 Open-loop system

2.6.1 Basic characteristic

The basic characteristic of an open-loop system is that it does not contain the element of feedback. Without feedback, a system does not provide for the sensing of measured outputs for comparison with the desired outputs. Such a system does not therefore contain the element of control at all.

2.6.2 Example of open-loop system

A basic type of open-loop system could be a domestic hot-water system without a thermostat – there is no automatic regulation of the water temperature; the heater has to be switched off manually when the desired temperature is attained. If the heater is switched off prematurely then the desired temperature is not reached or, if the heater is switched off a little late, the temperature of the water is too high.

Such a system would not be effective in critical situations within a business. Control of stocks by such a system is not feasible; storekeepers would have to report stock shortages as they occurred which, of course, is a little late in the day to obviate the consequences of such circumstances. In addition, excessive stocks may not be noted until the year-end stocktaking by which time it is too late to take effective action to minimise losses when the excess stocks are written off or disposed of below cost. Open-loop systems are thus not desirable in business systems.

2.7 Closed-loop system

2.7.1 Basic characteristics

An essential element of a closed-loop system is the communication of measured outputs to the control system — feedback. Such a system is defined as *closed-loop*, which is a basic requirement of cybernetic systems.

Many closed-loop systems are self-regulating as they contain a built-in control mechanism, for example the thermostat in a domestic water-heating system.

Business systems containing integrated control systems performing continuous monitoring activities are also closed-loop systems as they contain the essential element of feedback (*see* Figs 2.1 and 2.2).

2.7.2 Automatic closed-loop business systems

Computers are widely used for business data processing applications and the computer programs often contain in-built control functions. For example, a stock control application includes the processing of a transaction file and the updating of the stock master file for the purpose of calculating the new stock balance for each item in stock (*see* Fig. 2.1).

The program may also provide for the comparison of the actual quantity in stock with the maximum permissible stock and print out an *excess stock* report for management control. The program may also incorporate automatic stock re-ordering whereby the actual quantity in stock of each item is compared with the re-order level. When the balance in stock is equal to, or less than, the re-order level a re-order list may be printed which is despatched to the purchasing department for the placing of purchase orders. Alternatively, a purchase order may be printed by the computer directly which would reduce the lead time for the replenishment of supplies.

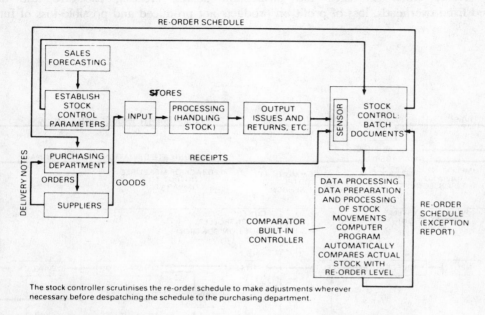

Figure 2.1 An automatic computerised closed-loop stock control system (outline only)

If however, the balance in stock is greater than the re-order level no action is effected and the computer continues with the basic routine. The program may be defined as a built-in controller and the computer system a closed-loop system, as the actual state of the system is compared with the desired state and exception reports automatically printed (error signals).

It is essential to incorporate safeguards in this type of system which can take the form of a manual override to the action indicated by the computer program. In this way abnormal random situations not built into the computer program can be dealt with. If, for instance, there is a sudden increase or decrease in demand or supply, managerial intervention is necessary to avoid the consequences of excessive stocks on the one hand and shortages on the other. It is also necessary to modify the parameters of each item held in stock to provide for changing trends so that stock re-ordering is effected on the basis of current and not historic circumstances — only in this way can stock shortages and excessive stocks be avoided.

2.7.3. Manual closed-loop business system

Manual control systems are widely used in business and providing they contain feedback, may be classed as closed-loop systems. Indeed, to be classed as a control system at all feedback must be incorporated (*see* Fig. 2.2).

With regard to a manual stock control system, a stock control clerk is required to observe the stock status of each item, usually when updating the master record with current transactions, and trigger off the re-ordering procedure as necessary. However, through lack of concentration or interruptions, the clerk may fail to observe items which require to be re-ordered and no action will be effected to replenish supplies for stock requirements. This is the danger of a manual control system, as human beings are not infallible.

Failure to take action either to reduce excessive stocks or re-order supplies may have drastic consequences. In the first instance, excessive stocks lock up capital unnecessarily and increase interest charges, stock handling costs and the cost of storage facilities. On the other hand, failure to obtain supplies may create stock shortages and production delays, creating excessive idle time, under-absorbed fixed overheads, loss of profit on products not produced and possible loss of future orders.

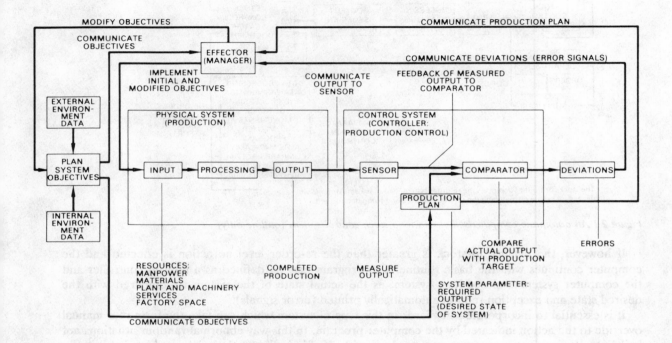

Figure 2.2 A manual closed-loop production control system illustrating cybernetic concepts

The solution to such a problem may be the employment of conscientious clerks who fully understand the consequences of their failure to report on situations requiring action. The incorporation of checking facilities such as random or spot checks may also provide the means of detecting previously unobserved situations.

2.8 Systems and subsystems

2.8.1 What is a system?

A system is a set of interrelated subsystems which when combined serve a defined purpose and achieve a specified objective. For example, a car is a system designed for the purpose of travelling from point A to point B, which is capable of being done at a particular speed and rate of fuel consumption — its objectives. The objectives consist of defined performance parameters built into the design of the car. The car's performance rating is a matter of cost — a budget car has a relatively low top speed but a reasonable rate of fuel consumption. A performance car on the other hand has a relatively high top speed but a high rate of fuel consumption. The actual performance in terms of both speed and fuel consumption is affected by environmental conditions such as the prevailing speed limit, traffic density, road works, accidents, driving ability and personal choice of speed of travel. The several subsystems of a car — the total system — comprise the power unit, the transmission system, the fuel injection system, the electrical system and so on. The car is controlled by a driver in the same way that an aircraft is controlled by a pilot. The operation of the car may be assisted by power steering or automatic gear changing and the operation of the aircraft is assisted by servo-mechanisms and computerised controls such as the automatic pilot.

2.8.2 What is a business system?

A business system has similar characteristics and is constructed in a similar way to any other type of system. Specifically, a business system consists of a combination of processes designed for a specific purpose, perhaps to prepare insurance renewal premiums, and to accomplish a specific objective(s) which may be defined as the production of insurance renewal premiums by a stated date at a given cost with a defined use of resources. Many business systems are designed to serve the needs of a specific functional activity while others are integrated to provide a more efficient larger system as discussed below.

2.9 Subsystem relationships

Several subsystems may be combined to create a more efficient integrated system forming a larger subsystem. If several integrated subsystems are combined a very large system would result which ultimately would embrace the business as a whole, thus becoming a total system. Such a total system is an ideal rather than a practicality due to the difficulty of identifying the many cause and effect relationships which exist in the real world. The cost of developing such a system would also be beyond the resources of many businesses. In addition, if one part of the system malfunctioned all of the related subsystems would cease to function. Computer application packages go some way to attaining the ideal integrated system because the various modules are directly related and can be interfaced allowing data from one to be passed to the other. A computerised integrated order processing system, for instance, consists of several highly related subsystems. When orders are received (order handling) the credit status of the customer is determined (credit control). If this is satisfactory the stock position is assessed and if sufficient items are in stock, either for a part order or for the complete order, the stock records are updated (stock control) and a back order report produced for shortages (order control). Orders are assembled for despatch in the warehouse (despatching) and the goods despatched are charged to the customer (sales invoicing). The value of the invoice is recorded in the customer's account (sales accounting), and when the customer pays the amount is also recorded on the customer's account (sales accounting) and the bank account (cash accounting) and so on. A conceptual model of an integrated order processing system is shown in Fig. 2.3, which illustrates the inputs, the processes including those for testing the status of customer credit and stock availability, the files used and the outputs produced. The model does not intimate the use of a computer but merely illustrates the logic of the system.

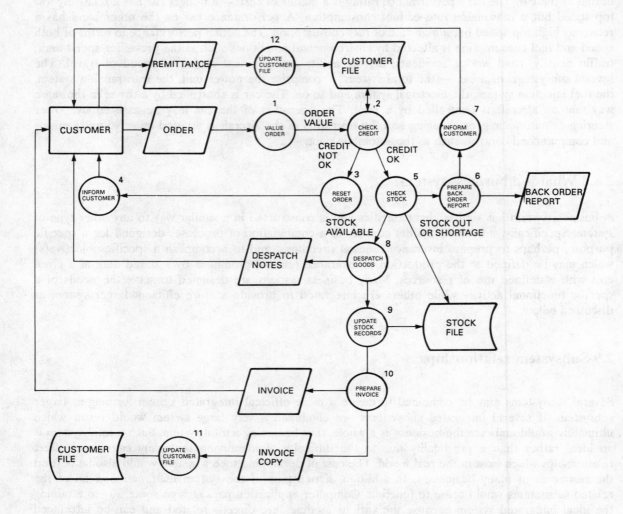

Figure 2.3 Conceptual model of integrated order processing system

2.9.1 Input/output relationships

In many cases systems have a *direct* relationship where the output from one is the input to another, even though they may be administered as separate systems. Input/output relationships are the basis for integrating systems to take advantage of administrative efficiency. For example, the output from an order handling control system provides input for updating the finished goods stock and customer accounts in the sales ledger.

2.9.2 Open systems

Open systems (as opposed to closed systems) are those which *interact* with their environment, either for the collection of information on which to base strategy, or for conducting business transactions with suppliers, customers, the general public, internal departments, trade organisations, etc. Such systems adapt to changes in the environment in order to survive, which requires speedy reactions to changes in market trends, competition, etc.

2.9.3 Closed systems

These are systems which do not interact with their environment either for the exchange of information or business transactions. Such systems are completely self-contained and thus business systems do not conform with this categorisation.

Note: Do not confuse open and closed systems as indicated above with open-loop and closed-loop systems — these are control systems (*see* 2.6 and 2.7).

2.9.4 Control relationships

Control systems are often separately structured from the systems which they control; for instance, the production control system controls the production quantity and the quality control system controls the quality of production. In a similar manner, the cost control system controls the cost of production, and so on. These control systems are basically administrative systems for monitoring the results and modifying the state of the physical systems to which they relate.

2.9.5 Coupling and decoupling of systems (integration and disintegration)

If systems are over-integrated they may become too complex to understand and operate: if one part of the system ceases to function correctly this may cause the system as a whole to deteriorate. This creates unacceptable delays and disruption to those parts of the system (subsystems) which as a result are unable to function.

When systems are decoupled it is usually easier to administer them as they become less complex and more flexible. Decoupling may recreate the former situation whereby systems existed separately on a functional basis but were coordinated by the chief executive for the achievement of overall objectives. Each functional subsystem thus has more independence even though they are still interrelated in reality, but loosely connected for administrative convenience. Each functional executive must apply initiative to achieve functional objectives but must cooperate with the various subsystems and so avoid sub-optimisation.

Sub-optimisation results when a department operates in its own best interests, regardless of conflicts with company objectives. For example, a production manager gears production resources to achieve the highest possible production levels over a period of a month. However, the sales department complains that it is not receiving a balanced mix of products throughout the month and those products special to customer requirements are always behind schedule. As a result the company loses customers for these products. The production manager will have to compromise by programming resources (manpower, machines, space, etc.) more frequently to produce lower levels of a variety of products. The efficiency with which systems are coordinated thus plays a large part in success or failure.

Students should note that the introduction of a computerised, company-wide database encourages the development of integrated systems within an organisation. This is one of the advantages of databases (*see* Chapter 9).

Review questions

1   Define the nature of mechanistic and organismic systems.

2   Distinguish between a deterministic and probabilistic system.

3   An adaptive system is dynamic as it responds to changing circumstances by adjusting its behaviour on a self-organising basis. How does it do this?

4   What are the basic needs of a control system?

5   What are the basic elements of the cybernetic control process?

6   Define the meaning of the terms negative and positive feedback.

7   Specify the nature of 'feedforward'.

8   State the characteristics of open-loop and closed-loop systems.

9   Indicate the precise meaning of the following terms:
     (a)   system;
     (b)   business system;
     (c)   subsystem.

10   Distinguish between open and closed systems

11   What is meant by coupling and decoupling in the systems context?

3 Data

3.1 Introduction

Data is the term used to describe the primary element of any business system. Data relates to the details of business transactions which are often recorded on source documents to maintain a record of an event and subsequently used in data (information) processing systems for producing information for administrative needs, business control and decision making. In many instances details are input directly into a computer without first being recorded on source documents. It is important to appreciate that data is required for all business transactions and it flows to wherever it is needed in a business because many systems, known as subsystems, are related to one another and the output from one subsystem is often required as input by another. The many ways in which data can be collected or 'captured' are discussed in this chapter. Some data elements (the smallest unit of definable data) require to be coded for identification and reference purposes during processing — these are referred to as *key fields*. Data also needs to be validated before being accepted for processing, which is dealt with in Chapter 15.

3.2 Data defined

In the context of data processing, data may be defined as details of business transactions which are unprocessed. After data has been subjected to processing operations it is converted into useful information. The terms data and information are often used synonymously, but this is not strictly correct as information is *derived from* data. Data is the *input* element and information is the *output* element of a data processing or information processing system (*see* Fig. 3.1).

3.2.1 Data characteristics and types

The smallest unit of definable data is known as a *data element*; examples are supplier name, customer address, catalogue number, item description and quantity in stock, etc. Data elements need to be specified precisely, giving the name of the element, the number of characters it contains (size of the element), the type of character, whether alphabetic or numeric, and the range of values for validation purposes to ensure that data is correct before being processed. Data elements are also referred to as *attributes* or *fields*. A data element is technically the logical definition of data, whereas a field refers to the physical data *within* the element, e.g. the data element *quantity in stock* is the name of the element which stores the *actual* quantity in stock. Other terms used to define a unit of data are *data item* and *variable*.

The types of data with which a business is concerned may be categorised as follows.

  (a) Data relating to social, political and economic factors.
  (b) Data relating to the performance of competitors.
  (c) Qualitative and quantitative data regarding levels of performance, costs, overheads, profits and

losses and cash flows.

(d) Organisational data relating to manpower levels, the span of control and responsibilities of managers.

(e) Reference data such as stock control parameters.

Certain types of data are common to most businesses, particularly those relating to payroll, purchasing, stock control and production planning, but other types of data are specific to a particular type of business. One would not expect to find the same type of data in a bank, insurance company, travel organisation or building society as would be found in a manufacturing organisation.

Data is stored in a record to provide a running account of the status of the specific *entity*, usually defined as something tangible, whether it is stocks of items in the stores, employees' tax and earnings or the credit card status of customers. Examples of data relating to specific businesses and systems include those outlined below.

System: Stock control
Entity: Stock record
Data element/attribute/field:
(a) part number, stock number or catalogue number;
(b) quantity issued from stores to various departments;
(c) quantity received into stores from suppliers;
(d) quantity returned to supplier;
(e) quantity returned to stores from various departments.

System: Payroll
Entity: Employee record
Data element/attribute/field:
(a) employee number;
(b) employee name;
(c) employee department;
(d) tax code;
(e) National Insurance number;
(f) hours worked;
(g) hourly rate of pay.

System: Car hire
Entity: Car record
Data element/attribute/field:
(a) type of car;
(b) size of car;
(c) number of seats;
(d) engine capacity;
(e) registration number.

System: Credit cards
Entity: Customer credit record
Data element/attribute/field:
(a) credit card holder number;
(b) credit card holder name and address;
(c) credit limit;
(d) minimum payment;
(e) details of purchases;
(f) interest;
(g) remittances.

3.3 Data flow between functions

3.3.1 Arbitrary functional boundaries

Although business activities are functionalised for administrative convenience, for example: stores; production; sales; accounts; data does not recognise these arbitrary boundaries and flows to wherever it serves a useful purpose in the organisation. This requires a detailed analysis of system relationships when systems and procedures are being designed, otherwise systems will not function smoothly — if at all. It must be appreciated that the business as a whole comprises a number of related functions, structured so as to suit the operational needs of the business in pursuit of corporate goals.

3.3.2 Interfunctional data flows

Data produced by one function is usually then used by another as a basis for taking some specific action. Before the manufacture of standard products commences in a factory the marketing function provides sales forecasts to the production planning department which in turn uses the information to establish the quantities of the various products to be produced in specific time periods. The production plans are then drawn up and provide the means for establishing the material and parts required for the production plan, prior to adjustment for current stocks by the stock control department. The purchasing function is then informed of the net requirements for which purchasing schedules must be drawn. The schedules are used for placing forward orders to the relevant suppliers. Sales to customers are notified to the warehouse by the sales office. The warehouse then raises despatch notes and despatches the goods to their stated destination. A copy of the despatch note (unless an integrated computerised order-entry system exists) is sent to the invoicing section of the sales office who raise a sales invoice. A copy of the invoice is sent to the customer and another to the accounts department for recording in the customer's account in the sales ledger. All such transactions are recorded in the books of accounts in the accounting function. Thus the same data is used again and again before a business operation is completed. (*See* Figs. 2.3 and 3.1.)

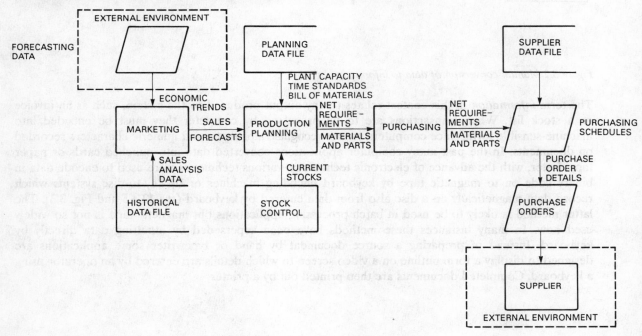

Figure 3.1 Interfunctional data flows: sales forecasting

3.4 Data collection and data capture

3.4.1 Data collection

Data relating to business transactions is generally recorded on source documents by hand using a ball-point pen or pencil, or typed.

Typical source documents used in business are:

(a) clock cards for recording attendance time of employees;
(b) issue notes for recording items issued from the stores to production departments;
(c) sales orders from customers indicating their requirements;
(d) holiday booking form;
(e) meter reading sheets to record gas and electricity consumption;
(f) insurance proposal form;
(g) vouchers for recording details of petty cash transactions;
(h) purchase requisitions indicating items required from suppliers.

The transactions are then processed manually in a clerical system to produce information (*see* Fig. 3.2).

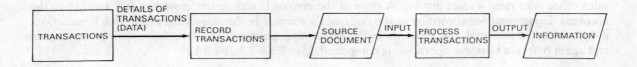

Figure 3.2 Manual conversion of data to information

The term *information* in this context relates to any output produced by the system, such as an invoice or a stock list. When transactions are to be processed by computer they must be encoded into machine-sensible form, since computers cannot recognise alphabetic and numeric characters recorded on documents. In the past many computer applications converted data into punched cards or paper tape. Later, with the advance of electronic technology, various techniques were used to encode data in binary code on to magnetic tape by keyboard encoding machines or by key-to-disc systems which record data magnetically on a disc also from data entered by keyboard (*see* 13.4.5 and Fig. 3.3). The latter method is likely to be used in batch processing applications but magnetic tape is not so widely used now. In many instances these methods have been superseded by inputting data directly by keyboard. Instead of preparing a source document by hand or typewriter some applications are designed to display a form outline on a video screen to which details are entered by an operator using a keyboard. Completed documents are then printed out by a printer.

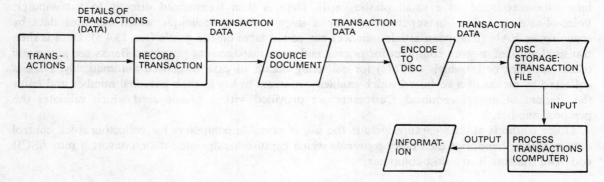

Figure 3.3 Process of data encoding and conversion of data to information

A data collection system is often used for recording and transmitting data from remote locations, such as bank branches or sales or tour operators' offices. This takes place while the customer is present, for example paying a mortgage or withdrawing cash. On-line terminals equipped with a keyboard and printer connected to the central computer by leased transmission lines are usually used for this purpose.

3.4.2 Data capture

The primary objective of applying data capture techniques is to capture data relating to business transactions by the most cost-effective and suitable means in accordance with the nature of business activities. This is achieved by eliminating time-consuming and costly data conversion operations, as outlined above, by using special types of data capture equipment (*see* Fig. 3.4). The clearing banks, for instance, issue cheques to customers printed with magnetic ink characters which are read into the computer by a magnetic ink character reader/sorter after the amount of the cheque has been encoded at the bank branch by a special encoding machine. Some applications print documents in stylised characters for optical character recognition, for example the meter reading sheet produced by electricity boards, which is printed in optical characters specifying the consumer reference number and the previous reading. The meter reader records the units consumed by marks in pre-designated columns. The marks are sensed by an optical mark and character reader and encoded on to magnetic tape for processing. Consumer bills are then printed as 'turnaround' documents, so called because they are returned to the system by the consumer with the remittance. The returned bill is then input for updating the consumer's account.

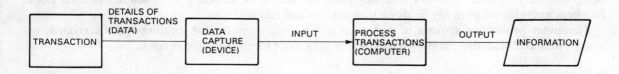

Figure 3.4 Process of data capture and conversion of data to information

In factories the modern method of capturing data is through factory data recorders strategically sited throughout the factory. Data is captured by means of a microprocessor-based terminal which allows data to be input via a keyboard, punched card (*see* 13.4.8) or badge reader (device which reads information encoded on a small plastic card). Data is then transmitted directly to a computer. Point-of-sale operations in supermarkets use a laser scanning technique which captures data by scanning an EAN (European article number) bar coded label on the goods (*see* 13.4.8). Data is then transmitted to an in-store computer for pricing and stock management purposes. Banks use automatic teller machines or terminals (ATMs) for collecting details of cash dispensed automatically. Data is collected by means of a keyboard which enables customers to key in their personal number and enter the amount of money required. Customers are provided with a plastic card which validates the personal number.

Other methods of data capture include the use of portable computers for collecting stock control data in stores: handprint data entry terminals which capture handprinted data, convert it into ASCII code and transmit it to a host computer.

3.4.3 American Standard Code for Information Interchange

The term 'bit' is a contraction of BInary digiT. The term binary stems from 'bi' meaning two, hence is a two-state number system consisting of two digits '0' and '1'. Combinations of 0's and 1's form the basis of the ASCII code — an abbreviation for American Standard Code for Information Interchange, adopted as standard by the American National Standards Institute in 1963. It is widely used on microcomputers and provides the means for transferring data between devices such as from a processor to a printer or terminal to/from a processor. The ASCII code is actually a seven-bit code, thus the number 65 is represented as 1000001, the position of each 1 indicating its binary value. Any book dealing with binary arithmetic will cover this topic in more detail. An alternative code is EBCDIC, an acronym for Extended Binary Coded Decimal Interchange Code, which is used on IBM mainframe computers. The code uses eight binary positions (bits) for each character forming the basis of the eight-bit byte, an alternative term for character. The letter A would be represented by the combination of bits, 11000001. The first four positions are zone bits, the last four numeric. A seven-bit code can provide for 128 different characters whereas an eight-bit code can generate 256 different characters.

3.5 Coding systems

3.5.1 Purpose of coding systems

Code numbers are allocated systematically to specific entries on a planned and coordinated basis in order to provide a unique identity for customers, stocks, expenditure items, suppliers and employees, etc. A code number is a compact means of defining a specific entity as only a few digits are required rather than lengthy descriptions. Descriptions are still required, however, for the purpose of describing items on despatch notes, sales invoices and purchase orders, etc. Such descriptions are complementary to code numbers and they must, of course, be matched by validation checks. Code numbers are referred to as *key* fields on transactions and records.

Computer processing systems in particular utilise code numbers for locating specific records on master files and matching them with transaction data prior to updating the records.

3.5.2 Important features of coding systems

The following summary will serve to indicate the main factors to consider for effective coding systems.

(a) *Uniqueness* — each entity should have a unique unambiguous code number for specific identification.

(b) *Useful purpose* — code numbers in general serve a useful purpose as they assist sorting of transactions which can be done much faster by computer than any other method. It is also much easier to sort by numeric codes than alphabetic descriptions. Code numbers also facilitate the comparison of data items, perhaps for matching purposes, either for updating master files or for comparing actual and budgeted expenditure, etc.

(c) *Compactness* — code numbers require fewer digits or characters than actual descriptions. For example, FASTENER may be abbreviated to FSTNR by eliminating the vowels.

(d) *Meaningful* — although not always possible or desirable, specific parts of a code when relevant should relate to particular facets of the item to which it relates, e.g. size, shape, type, location and specification of component parts held in store.

(e) *Self-checking* — codes should contain self-checking facilities when necessary in the form of check digits for validation purposes (*see* 26.4.6).

(f) *Expansibility* — codes should facilitate expansion by allowing flexibility in the coding structure to allow insertions by leaving gaps between blocks of code sequences.

(g) *Standard size* — all codes of a given type relating to a specific entity should contain the same number of digits to facilitate field checks.

3.5.3 Faceted code

Each position in the code number has a specific meaning, for example if it is required to develop a code for basic raw materials used in manufacturing it may be based on the following structure.

Type of material — 1st digit
1-Steel
2-Copper
3-Brass
Section — 2nd digit
1-Rod
2-Strip
3-Sheet
Size — 3rd digit
1 ⎤
2 ⎥
3 ⎬ Appropriate range of sizes
4 ⎦
Location in stores — 4th digit
1 ⎤
2 ⎥ Appropriate storage
3 ⎥ location
4 ⎦

3.5.4 Serial code

Sequences of code numbers may be allocated to specific types of record to identify specific entities. No information is conveyed by the code number itself. For example, a range of numbers may be allocated for departmental codes, expenditure codes, stock codes, customer account codes, etc.

These code numbers may be applied in the following way.

(a) Departmental code:

Direct:
1 – Press shop
2 – Machine shop
3 – Assembly shop
4 – Finishing shop
5 – Inspection shop

Indirect:
6 – WIP stores
7 – Finished product stores
8 – Consumable stores
9 – Toolroom
10 – Maintenance department

(b) Expenditure codes:

Operating labour:
20 – Tool setters
21 – Labourers
22 – Shop clerks

General operating overheads:
25 – Scrap
26 – Rectification
27 – Waiting time
28 – Shift premium
29 – Small tools
30 – Consumable materials
31 – Lubricants
32 – Works stationery

(c) Combination of codes may be used as follows:
1/29 – Press shop/small tools
9/31 – Toolroom/lubricants
10/20 – Maintenance department/tool setters

Review questions

1   What is data?

2   How is data converted to information?

3   What is the primary objective of data capture techniques?

4   For what reason is data generated by one function found to be useful by another?

5   State the purpose of coding systems and list a number of important features of such systems.

4 Information

4.1 Introduction

Information is the product of processing data. Data is input to a data (information) processing system which after being sorted, computed, merged and compared with other related data produces information. Information is a valuable business resource and plays an increasingly important part in the achievement of business objectives. Information must possess a number of attributes, which are listed in this chapter as are matters relating to quantitative and qualitative information; information related to the level of management; information for planning and control and information flows for decision making.

4.2 Information defined

Information is the lifeblood of any business and is playing an increasingly important part in the day-to-day management of businesses and the decision making process. Information does not simply emerge; flows have to be designed to suit the business need (*see* Figs 4.2–4.4).

Information is obtained after subjecting data to a series of processing operations which convert related groups of meaningless data into a meaningful and coherent form. The generation of information in this way is the purpose of data processing/information systems. Information can be output, for example, in printed form, graphically displayed on a video screen or in the form of graphs on a graph plotter. Printed output often takes the form of *exception reports* (*see* 2.3.3) or, when necessary, of complete listings of the contents of files, e.g. stock files, customer files, insurance files, holiday bookings files or work in process files. Exception reports present only information which requires consideration by management, for example a bad debtors *ageing analysis* or a *stock below re-order level report*.

4.2.1 Information attributes and presentation

Management needs information to achieve defined objectives.
Information must:

(a) enable management to make effective decisions;
(b) be adequate for taking effective control action or for providing valuable details relating to the business environment;
(c) be compatible with the responsibilities of specific managers;
(d) contain an appropriate level of detail for the recipient;
(e) relate to the current situation;
(f) have an acceptable level of integrity;
(g) be compatible with response time needs of systems;

(h) be based on exceptions or variances to accord to the principle of management by exception when appropriate;
- (i) be produced at an optimum cost;
- (j) be easily understandable by the recipient;
- (k) not contain unnecessary redundancy;
- (l) be provided at a suitable frequency;
- (m) be timely;
- (n) be precise;
- (o) be relevant to its purpose.

4.2.2 Nature of information processing

The term *information processing* is more appropriate than the outmoded term data processing as it recognises that it is information which is important to the management processes of business planning, decision making and control. The preparation of reports containing information involves subjecting the basic facts, i.e. the data, to a number of processing operations which typically include: verification (when data has been subjected to data conversion into a *machine-sensible* form), validation, sorting, merging, computing, comparing, updating and printing (*see* Fig. 4.1). (*See* Chapter 15.)

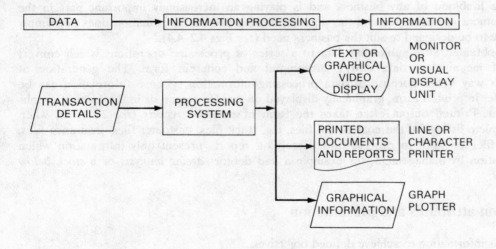

Figure 4.1 Information processing

4.2.3 Quantitative information

This type of information deals with the magnitude of variables: their variability and absolute magnitude expressed in terms of the quantity of various entities. Typical examples are listed below:

(a) variations in the level of income and expenditure;
(b) variations in the level of product costs;
(c) variations from the credit limit allowed to customers;
(d) variations in the level of stocks;
(e) actual quantity produced;
(f) actual quantity sold;
(g) the level of labour turnover;
(h) average queueing time and service time in service functions;
(i) variations in the amount of capital expenditure on projects;
(j) project activity times;
(k) variations in the mix of products and the effect on profit maximisation or cost minimisation.

4.2.4 Qualitative information

This type of information may be defined as that relating to the attributes of an entity in respect of quality factors. Information of this nature is very useful for managerial control and often employs the technique of making comparisons with quality standards and actual achievements as a basis for *management by exception*. Examples of qualitative information are outlined below:

(a) *standard of finish* of a product in respect of paintwork or electro-plating;
(b) variations of *tolerances* of manufactured parts, i.e. deviations from standard dimensions;
(c) variations of *quality* of the ingredients used in the manufacture of foodstuffs which alter taste and texture;
(d) effectiveness of *current methods* of producing information;
(e) quality of information for effective decision making.

4.3 Information and organisations

Individual businesses require information relating to the nature of their operations. A car manufacturer is particularly interested in the extent of competition from overseas manufacturers and to a lesser degree from home-based manufacturers. A tour operator is concerned about purchasing power and its effect on holiday bookings, and the political situation prevailing in the various countries. The following summary will highlight the key facts required by a cross-section of typical businesses to enable them to operate intelligently.

Car manufacturer
(a) Extent of competition from overseas manufacturers.
(b) Technological developments.
(c) Current styling trends.
(d) Success of productivity packages.
(e) Share of market achieved compared with that required.

Tour operator
(a) Status of hotels in various countries and resorts.
(b) Medical facilities and health hazards in various countries.
(c) Political unrest in countries and its likely repercussions on holiday centres.

(d) Expected level of future costs of package holidays in the light of inflation trends and the cost of fuel for aircraft operations.

(e) Availability of holiday accommodation at all resorts at all times.

Stockbroker

(a) Movement of share prices.
(b) State of money market.
(c) Economic climate.
(d) Economic climate in particular industries.

Building society

(a) Clients overdue with mortgage repayments.
(b) Balances on customer investment, share and mortgage accounts.
(c) Likely trend in interest rates and its effect on building society funds.
(d) Trend in house prices.
(e) Government policy relating to mortgage levels.

Students should relate the above to Chapter 9 on database applications and services.

4.4 Information and the level of management

4.4.1 Top management

As a general guide information density and volume vary according to the position of the recipient in the hierarchical management structure. Here is a brief comparison of the different information needs of chairmen and senior managers.

At chairmanship level, information must be very broad in scope, enveloping key factors which pinpoint the economic and financial health of the business. These may include profit comparisons with previous periods to obtain an appreciation of current trends as a basis for taking timely and effective action. The state of the order book is also of extreme importance as it indicates the possible level of future profits or losses, which assists in making strategic decisions.

The trend of cash flows is another important key factor as it indicates the financial health of the business and assists in determining the extent to which lines of credit must be drawn upon, showing whether short-term finance is necessary or whether a share flotation is more appropriate for long-term growth and development.

Current share prices are of great concern to the chairman as they reflect the current financial standing of the business and therefore have a bearing on future share flotations and the value of the business on a *going concern* basis. Share prices also provide an indicator of possible take-over overtures.

The managing director and senior management require similar information but also need details of functional achievements covering the main operating areas of the business. Such information includes details of budgeted and actual income and expenditure, the latter embracing both capital and revenue; progress of contracts, jobs or projects; sales trends; level of production against targets; extent of competition measured by market share; and other information for use in corporate strategic planning and policy determination. Much of this information can be derived from the use of forecasting techniques, spreadsheets and other modelling techniques using micros as part of decision support facilities on an end-user basis. These techniques provide the means for assessing the viability of a number of alternative, mutually exclusive, options as they can assess uncertainty and risk on a defined probability basis. (*See* Chapter 5.)

4.4.2 Functional management

This level of management requires information summaries relating to the departments for which individual managers are responsible. Information should be sufficiently detailed, for example, to allow tactical planning of use of resources in order to achieve specified objectives.

Information is required which relates to current operations as they are taking place, so that appropriate action is taken to control events while those events are in progress. What has happened cannot be remedied for past periods but can, of course, be used as a basis for modifying future actions on a feedforward basis.

Depending upon the nature of the business functional management requires details appertaining to operating expenses, manpower levels both current and projected, plant capacity, spare capacity, amount of capital expenditure incurred on various projects and the level of productivity being attained, the cost per unit of output, the incidence of scrapped production, and so on. Information is often provided on an exception basis in the form of operating statements showing budgeted, actual results and variances for both the current period and for the year to date. Such statements may also include comparative figures for the same period of the previous year to indicate trends.

4.4.3 Operating or departmental management

This level of management requires information of a very detailed nature, relating to specific orders, operations, personnel, materials, parts and costs, etc. because they are essential for pinpointing areas that require immediate action. Accordingly, management needs to know about the efficiency of individuals or of departmental systems so as to take direct positive action. It is not possible to do this on a global basis. Similarly, it is necessary to know cost variances on specific items rather than in total for all costs in order to control them. It is also necessary to know the stock position of each item in the stores to avoid stock-out situations on the one hand and overstocking on the other. In the same context credit control can only be effective by being aware of the account status of individual customers.

4.5 Information for planning and control

4.5.1 Strategic planning information

Business strategy is concerned with how a company proposes to achieve its objectives. The establishment of a suitable strategy is dependent upon information relating to the company's strengths and weaknesses so that future plans can build on major strengths and minimise the effects of weaknesses.

Strategy must also take into account an assessment of risk and constraints to specific courses of action. Strategic decisions have long range consequences, especially when concerned with the development of new products, the building of new factories and warehouses or the extension of existing premises. In these instances information is required on the available or potential market for new products, trend in building costs and development grants available for specific areas of the country, and so on. Information is also required on product life cycles so that plans can be made to *change over* products at the most opportune time and so maintain or increase profits and overall profitability. The degree of competition is always of paramount interest and information relating to market intelligence is essential. In addition, information is required in relation to developments in the economic, technological, financial, sociological and legislative spheres so that strategy can be formulated within the framework of company policies which takes these factors into account.

4.5.2 Tactical and operational planning information

Information for tactical planning is obtained by analysing the strategic plans in great detail in respect of production, sales, expenditure, stocks, purchases, personnel and plant and machinery. The tactical planning activity needs to consider planning in a number of spheres, notably the planning of an effective organisational structure for achieving corporate objectives; product-market development planning; resource development planning; capital expenditure project planning and operational planning. Such plans establish the *tactics* to be employed in pursuit of strategic objectives. They are prepared by functional managers responsible for defined objectives as a means of achieving the overall objectives of the business.

4.5.3 Control Information

Control information emanates from well structured standard, routine systems including quality, budgetary , cost, credit, stock and production control systems. They all incorporate a common feature: *management by exception*. This is because they function on the basis of variances, i.e. deviations from a specified target or standard of performance. This subject has been dealt with fully in Chapter 2.

4.6 Viability of producing more information

4.6.1 Economy of producing more information

There is always a certain doubt whether information available is sufficient for making a specific decision, or whether it is economically justifiable to gather and process more information. It is a matter of assessing whether the quality of the decision will be increased by having more information, and whether the benefits are likely to justify the cost. This is why organisations planning to design and develop computerised systems should conduct feasibility studies (*see* Chapter 24), before any investment is made.

4.6.2 Other factors

It is essential that managers are aware of the availability or *non-availability* of certain classes of information. The importance of such *missing* information must be evaluated so that the manager is in a position to calculate the degree of risk involved in certain courses of action.

It is not possible to make precise decisions on the basis of incomplete information but managers must realise that random influences in the business environment preclude constant availability of up-to-date decision making information. Data must be supplemented with insight gained from past experiences and modified in the light of new circumstances and current trends.

Managers who give careful consideration to these points will be in a sound position to specify their requirements for a computerised management information system. Managers who ignore these basic principles will end up with systems which do not meet their needs.

4.7 Corporate information adviser

Particularly in the larger type of organisation the post of corporate information adviser may well be considered a necessary requirement. The adviser is a specialist in managing the information resources and requirements of the business in the same way that other mangers control the use of resources connected with their activities.

The responsibilities of the post are far-ranging, embracing all aspects of information from that required for initial planning and policy formulation to the provision of information for the tactical control of operations in all functions: sales, production, purchasing, stock control, finance and accounting, research and development, personnel, etc. If a business is developing a database the information adviser may have the title of data administrator.

4.7.1 Coordinating element

An information adviser acts as a catalyst for generating all the information needs of the business and collecting information to produce cohesive reports, fully intelligible by their recipients. The adviser acts in a consultative capacity and conducts discussions with managers throughout the organisation for defining their specific information needs.

After the discussions have been concluded, meetings should be arranged with the data processing manager and organisation and methods manager to outline current and future information requirements. The outcome is the establishment of priorities for the development of specific systems to produce particular information. Such systems may be computer-orientated or clerical-orientated or a combination of both depending upon volumes of data to be processed, response time needs for control and other relevant factors.

When systems are developed and ultimately implemented they should be monitored by the information adviser to ensure they are achieving their defined purpose and operating smoothly and efficiently.

4.8 Information flows in business systems

4.8.1 Information flows in a stock control system

Stock control systems are for the purpose of controlling stocks of products in a warehouse awaiting despatch; stocks of raw materials in a factory awaiting issue to the manufacturing processes; or stocks of component parts in the work-in-progress stores awaiting issue to the assembly line, etc. Fig. 4.2 is a context diagram illustrating the sources of data flows and their destinations within a typical stock control system to be found in most manufacturing businesses. The boxes represent entities and the open rectangle represents the stock file in which all stock records are stored. The direction of the arrow on the relational line indicates the direction of the information flows. The detail on the relational line indicates the nature of each information flow. The diagram indicates that a re-order list is provided by stock control to the purchasing department but it does not show the information flows for making the decision whether to re-order stock items — this aspect is discussed below.

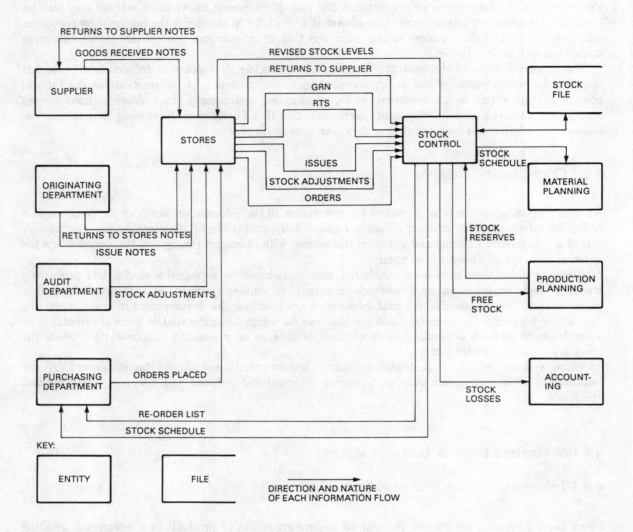

Figure 4.2 Information flows in a stock control system

4.8.2 Information for routine decision making: stock re-ordering

Fig. 4.3 also relates to a stock control system, indicating the entities, data flows and data files of the system. It specifies the information flows which occur in the system for re-ordering items when the quantity in stock has reached a predefined quantity known as the *re-order level*. This is set at a level which is sufficient to satisfy demand or usage during the time which elapses before new supplies are received, known as the *lead time*. The stock controller has overriding authority to modify the re-order level in accordance with changing demand or usage rates to avoid replenishing items when demand is reduced because the quantity in stock is sufficient for the changed situation. Overstocking would otherwise occur. In instances when demand is increased, a shortage would occur if the re-order level were not increased because stock would run out before the new supply was received.

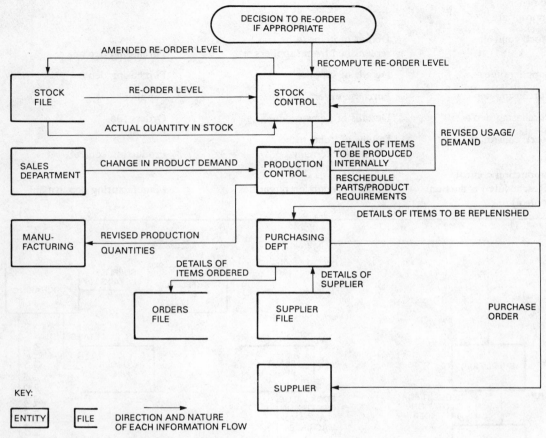

Figure 4.3 Information flows for stock re-ordering

Table 4.1 outlines the entity or data file providing the source of information, the activity taken by an entity to allow for changing circumstances, the information flow between entities or data files and the decision to re-order.

Table 4.1 Stock control system

Source Entity/data file	Information flow	Sink (Destination)
Stock file	Re-order level	Stock controller
	Actual quantity in stock	Stock controller
Sales department parts/products requirements)	Change in product demand	Production control
Production control	Revised usage/demand	Stock controller
Stock controller (Recompute reorder level)	Amended reorder level	Stock level

Table 4.1 continued on p 38

Decision made to
re-order if
appropriate

Stock controller	Details of items to be replenished from suppliers	Purchasing dep't
Suppliers file	Details of supplier	Purchasing dep't
Purchasing dep't	Purchase order	Supplier
Purchasing dep't	Dettals of items ordered	Orders file
Stock controller	Details of items to be produced internally	Production control
Production control (Reschedule Production control)	Revised production quantities	Manufacturing department

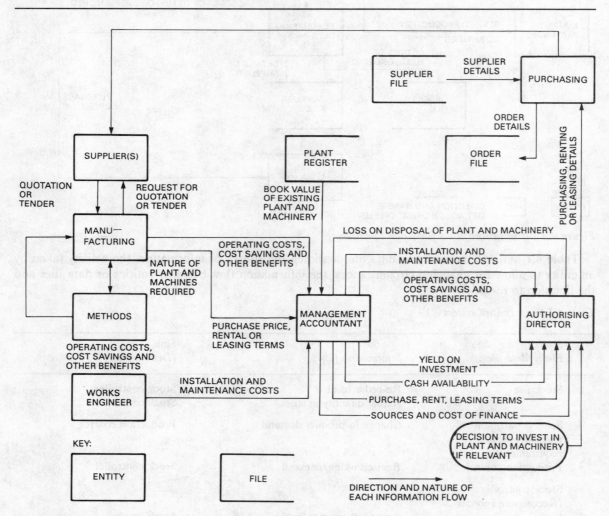

Figure 4.4 Information flows for decision making on whether to invest in plant and machinery

4.8.3 Information flows for decision making: investing in plant and machinery

The procedure for handling investment decisions in respect of plant and machinery follows a set routine, but requires the generation of specific information flows some of which do not currently exist. These relate to the cost of the investment, operating costs, cost savings and other benefits it is hoped will be attained from the investment, installation and maintenance costs and any loss on disposal of existing plant and machinery if being replaced. In some organisations the management accountant is reponsible for collating information from various sources, both internal and external, which is then presented to the authorising director who decides whether or not to sanction the investment. The management accountant discusses with and presents facts to the authorising director relating to the most suitable means of acquisition, whether by outright purchase, rental or by leasing. A deciding factor will be the availability of funds for the investment and/or the sources of finance-lines of credit for such purposes. Table 4.2 outlines the information flows between the various entities concerned with the decision making process (see Fig. 4.4 on p 38).

Table 4.2 Information flows for investing in plant and machinery

Source *Entity/data file*	*Information flow*	Sink *Entity (destination)*
Manufacturing	Nature of plant and machines required	Methods
Decision made relating to the type of plant/machinery required		
Manufacturing	Request for quotation	Supplier(s)
Supplier(s)	Quotation or tender (purchase price, rental or leasing terms)	Manufacturing
Methods	Operating costs, cost savings and other benefits	Manufacturing
Manufacturing	Purchase price, rental or leasing terms	Management accountant
Plant register	Book value of existing plant and machinery	Management accountant
Works engineering	Installation and maintenance costs	Management accountant
Management accountant	Purchase price (capital expenditure), rental or leasing terms	Authorising director
	Cash availability	
	Sources and cost of finance	
	Operating costs, cost savings and other benefits	
	Installation and maintenance costs	
	Loss on disposal of plant and machinery	
	Yield on investment	

Table 4.2 continued on p 40

Decision made to invest in
plant and machinery if relevant

Note: The remaining information flows relate to the procedure for placing an order for purchasing, renting or leasing.

Review questions

1 Define *information*.

2 State the value of information to a business.

3 What is the nature of information processing?

4 Differentiate between quantitative and qualitative information.

5 Businesses require information relating to the nature of their operations. Discuss.

6 Specify the nature of information required for strategic, tactical and operational planning.

7 State the factors to consider regarding the viability of providing more information.

8 What are the responsibilities of a corporate information adviser?

Self-test questions

4.1 Define the difference between the type of information required for strategic planning, tactical planning and business control.

4.2 Outline the nature and purpose of information likely to be used at each of the following levels of a business enterprise:

(a) top management
(b) middle management
(c) supervisory management

4.3 Different types of business require information according to the nature of their operations. Discuss the significance of this statement.

Answers on page 368–70.

5 Management information systems and decision support systems

5.1 Introduction

Management information systems are vehicles for assisting businesses to maintain a state of equilibrium when subjected to buffeting from environmental influences. They provide the intelligence on which to base decisions as well as information for routine administrative and accounting activities such as sales and purchase accounting, payroll, asset records and general ledger. The chapter deals with the principles of decision making initially so that the topics relating to decision support systems become more meaningful. An important computerised decision support system which is gaining momentum is the Executive Information System (EIS), details of which are included in this chapter.

5.2 The nature of management information systems

5.2.1 Information system: CIMA definition

The Chartered Institute of Management Accountants in the booklet *Computing Terminology* defines *information system* (or *management information system*) as follows:

'A computer system or related group of systems which collects and presents management information relating to a business in order to facilitate its control. The term is commonly applied to systems which make use of a database facility for the storage and retrieval of information.'

5.2.2 Characteristics of a management information system

Very often a management information system (MIS) is based on routine data processing systems for the purpose of generating administrative documents, such as payroll and payslips, invoices and statements of account, stock schedules, lists of debtors and creditors, etc. Such systems may be extended to produce various analyses for managerial control and for decision making, particularly on the basis of reports produced on the exception principle. A computerised system is ideal for an MIS as it is capable of an extremely fast response time when geared up for on-line interrogation or enquiry or even real-time control. The objectives of MIS include the provision of information to all levels of management at the most relevant time, at an acceptable level of accuracy and at an economical cost. An essential requirement of an MIS is the provision of *feedback*, i.e. communicating a system's measured outputs to the control system for the purpose of modifying the input to attain a state of homeostasis or system stability (*see* Fig. 5.1).

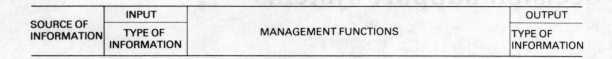

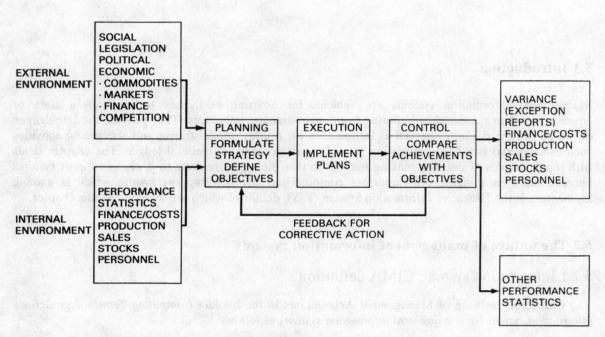

Figure 5.1 Conceptual outline of a management information system

5.2.3 The business operating environment

Business operations take place in a tense national and international arena, an extremely volatile environment largely consisting of random events beyond direct control and in which competition is critical, profit margins are generally narrow and taxation is high. To overcome such formidable obstacles to the accomplishment of business objectives, management is forever needing more 'intelligence' by way of information reports so that it may run the business as effectively as possible and offset such adverse factors. Information, particularly of a strategic nature, is needed to ward off threats on the one hand and to take advantage of favourable events on the other. As a consequence business management realises that to attain the utmost level of effectiveness in production, marketing and distribution, reliable information is a necessity.

Increasingly, managements are recognising that the only way to obtain such information is to invest in information systems. In a competitive environment the business that is quick to react to change will have a distinct advantage over competitors. It is now appreciated that business opportunities are lost through slow communications, lost messages, lengthy searches through antiquated filing systems, and so on. With the advent of information technology 'reaction time' is reduced and this improves the effectiveness of management and staff in pursuit of corporate objectives.

5.3 Decision making

5.3.1 Principles of decision making

Before discussing decision support systems it is useful to know something of the nature of decision making and its underlying principles. In general, the responsibility for making decisions should be as close as possible to the level at which they will be implemented. Tactical decisions (*see* 5.3.2) relating to customer credit are the responsibility of the credit control manager, a decision to re-order stock items is the responsibility of the stock controller and so on. Decisions should be made at the lowest possible managerial level and avoid involving higher level managers in routine decisions, so allowing them more time to plan future activities and solve more complex non-routine problems. The class of decision to be made by specific levels of management should relate to their area of responsibility and be clearly defined. This avoids conflict between managers which could result in decisions not being made at all. Some managers over-delegate, making their subordinates responsible for decisions they should be making. This type of 'buck-passing' arises from their inability to make decisions, and the situation should not be allowed to continue.

5.3.2 Tactical decisions

Tactical decisions are of a routine nature for dealing with current situations as they arise during the course of business operations. The aim is to ensure the business runs smoothly. They are made, for instance, when determining the amount of credit to allow potential customers or the amended amount to allow existing customers in accordance with their credit history. Tactical decisions are also made in stock management — whether or not to re-order an item — and in manufacturing, when deciding on the most suitable method to implement. In such cases it is important to make the right decisions at the right time so as to optimise or improve the current situation. Decisions taken by functional managers are normally operational for the purpose of eliminating an adverse situation or to take advantage of favourable ones.

5.3.3 Strategic decisions

Strategic decisions are of the 'one-off' variety, made by top management as part of its collective responsibility for the continuing prosperity and survival of the business. Correct strategic decisions can create wealth; incorrect ones can lead to insolvency. Such decisions could relate to whether a new factory should be built in a development area, or whether a merger with a major competitor would obtain advantages of economy of scale and the ability to command a greater share of the market, making the business more profitable. Other strategies may include expansion into new markets with existing products or services or expansion of existing markets with new products or services, and so on.

5.4 Decisions by computer

5.4.1 Structured decisions by computer

A computer enables routine decisions to be automated. The rules governing the decision may be defined by algorithms formulated in terms of mathematical relationships, and be built into a computer program which tests whether a certain condition exists and branches to a program routine to deal with it: IF a condition exists THEN do this ELSE do something else. This is the basis on which knowledge based systems (expert systems) are built (*see* Fig. 5.2).

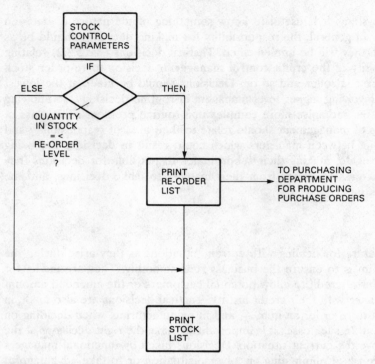

Figure 5.2. Structured decision; stock re-ordering routine

5.4.2 Quantitative problem solving by computer

Before it is possible to make some decisions it is necessary to analyse a problem statistically or mathematically. This requires the application of quantitative techniques including linear programming, queueing theory and critical path method (CPM) for project analysis. Quantitative analysis of this type is often performed by computerised problem solving packages. A widely applied package is the spreadsheet, which incorporates 'What if?' facilities enabling the results of changing the value of specific variables to be obtained, such as the effect on profit if the selling price were increased by £1 a unit or if fixed overheads increased by £5,000 a month. The various results provide the facts on which to select a specific strategy (*see* Chapter 7). Some spreadsheet packages incorporate 'goal seeking' attributes which provide a decision maker with details of what needs to be done to obtain a specified result or goal, rather than the results of a stipulated course of action as provided by What if? facilities.

5.5 Decision support systems

This category of information system is often referred to as an *executive support system*. Facilities enable executives to have the tools to hand for *ad hoc* computing to provide facts for problem solving and for making decisions. The tools include a *query language* for accessing the database; software for extracting data from the files of the mainframe computer for transfer to the user's computer; software for defining new records; a report writer, and *decision support* system including spreadsheets, modelling programs, statistical analysis programs, data manipulation and graphics programs.

All this makes for a more *complete* executive, armed with the means for performing computations and evaluations which hitherto had to be done either by mainframe computer utilising data processing staff, or by slide rule or pocket calculator.

5.5.1 Decision support software

Decision support software, known as Deja Vu, marketed by Intelligent Environments Limited enables information to be structured, analysed and modelled to assist in the decision making process. It provides the framework for breaking down a problem into its constituent elements. Decision modelling evaluates a series of options against a set of criteria in order to determine the choice. Deja Vu enables criteria to be defined by the user and weighted in terms of importance. The user's options are analysed against these criteria and the software then ranks them in terms of best overall fit. In addition, sensitivity or *What if?* analyses can be carried out by changing values and weightings. Results can be examined in summary form to compare and contrast the pros and cons of each side.

Deja Vu makes it easy to store, organise, structure and reference information. Information is stored on pages and each page can be linked and cross-referenced to any number of other pages. In practice the software works like a free-form database, allowing the user to reorganise and modify information without requiring the formality and technicality of conventional data management systems. Access paths make it easy to work with and around information by alphabetical index or by following logical paths around the model. Data entry is straightforward with full text editing and screen scrolling facilities. All the features of the package are easily accessed by means of pull-down menus and function keys.

System features
    (a) The system is available for IBM PC, XT, AT and 100 per cent compatibles;
    (b) runs in a minimum of 256K RAM;
    (c) three levels of help with 120 help screens;
    (d) pull-down menus;
    (e) context dependent prompts.

5.6 Priority decision system

A package known as PDS, which stands for priority decision system, is available from Work Sciences Associates. It is a computer-based support system for solving problems, making judgements and determining policies.

The package is menu driven: a three-part menu is displayed on the screen either to solve a problem, make a policy or put a policy into practice. There is an alternative version with a Lotus-like screen format. PDS is available on IBM PC/XT/AT and compatibles.

5.6.1 Solve a problem

The package can be used by an individual manager or a team and the program will combine the views of members of the team to produce a composite result. It helps decision makers choose between alternatives systematically. To use the package it is first necessary to list the options (up to 20 choices). The personnel who can make the final decision must be named. Only a single name may be necessary but up to 20 can be included. The next stage is to assess how much influence each decision maker is allowed in choosing between the various options. The final stage is to decide the option priorities which means choosing between alternatives. The priorities and the decision maker influences can be determined either by scaling, giving each person or option equal influence, use of intuition, magnitude estimation, or judgement analysis. PDS calculates the individual's valid priorities, pinpoints inconsistencies, states whether he or she has achieved an adequate decision standard or not, produces the overall priorities of the team, and states the degree of agreement or conflict of the team. The whole problem-solving process takes 10–20 minutes from start to finish.

5.6.2 Make a policy

This is similar to the problem routine, but relates to objectives, criteria, or policy matters rather than options or operational problems. The *policy makers* must be named together with the influence they have on the policy — everyone is potentially a policy maker insofar as they think about the issue at all. In choosing a computer, for instance, the criteria could include the type of processor chip which itself is an expression of power in terms of speed of operation; operating system used; extent of the software available to run on the particular operating system; cost of maintenance contract; reliability; upgrading option; cost of hardware and software, etc. PDS elicits the weightings of each criterion or objective for each policy maker. Again, this whole policy-making process takes 10–20 minutes from start to finish.

5.6.3 Policy in practice

When the two previous routines are stored on disc, access is available to the third facility of *policy in practice*. This permits the original option or options, such as the choice of a computer, to be systematically appraised on the basis of the policy criteria. A ranked and weighted list of options is then produced. This process can take 30–60 minutes on complex issues. The PDS system provides a basis for consistent decision making which will provide a greater pay-off than haphazard hunches. In addition it removes inconsistencies in the appraisal of policy matters and resolves conflicts between managers as all points of view are taken into account on every aspect of every issue. It should also save valuable time spent in operational and policy meetings (*see* Fig. 5.3).

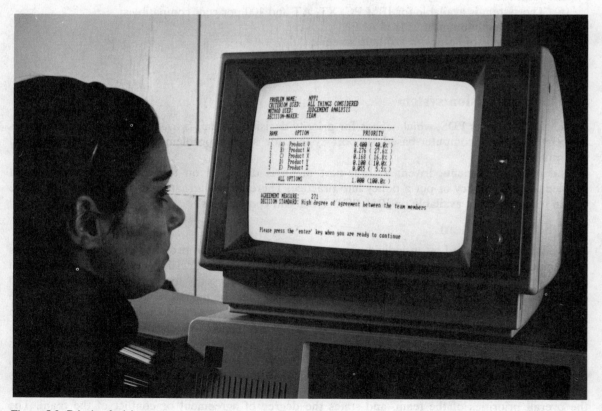

Figure 5.3. Priority decision system

5.7 Executive information systems: decision support systems

5.7.1 Information for decision support

Managing large enterprises is a complex task requiring the use of information as a strategic tool by the entire executive team. Executive information systems (EIS) facilitate this requirement by providing information for decision support in pursuit of the attainment of a competitive advantage. This is achieved by the more effective use of information to determine strategies which will ultimately be expressed by an improved profit figure. Software systems are available which provide facilities for electronic delivery of critical information in the form of reports and charts without the need for executives to learn the technical aspects of computers. An executive does not require keyboard skills to use the EIS because provision is made for using a mouse, a touch screen, or a few keys on the keyboard for performing EIS functions.

5.7.2 Commander Executive Information System

To enable the specific features of an EIS to be described, details of the Commander EIS from Comshare Ltd are outlined. The system has been designed to make strategic information readily available to senior executives while minimising the workload of the information providers who support the executive team. It automates the processes required for the successful implementation of an EIS:

(a) information access;
(b) integration;
(c) analysis;
(d) reporting;
(e) delivery.

5.7.3 Fast access to information: electronic briefing book

The EIS version of the paper-based briefing book is usually implemented as a series of menus. Executives use a mouse to point to the desired report or chart and the information is displayed on the screen in just a few seconds. The displayed reports can be accompanied by colour charts showing important trends. The electronic briefing book can be updated at any time.

5.7.4 Facts in context: exception reporting

Using electronic exception reporting it is possible to identify problem areas sooner and capitalise on successes more effectively. The EIS system provides details of items which vary by more than a specified amount, classed as *significant variances*. Executives can define their own personalised ranges (magnitude of variances) and when a specific report is displayed, variables falling outside the defined range appear in colour as follows:

(a) green — positive variances (favourable): acceptable;
(b) red — negative variances (unfavourable): unacceptable;
(c) yellow — mixed performance.

Corporate standards for good and bad variances can be preset and ranges modified for personal sensitivity. Information may be supplied on business performance not only in traditional profit and loss structures but in ways suitable for managerial control such as by business or operating unit, product group or line, distribution channel, geographical area, customer group or classification and so on. Any one of these views can provide the best perspective where there is a problem or opportunity requiring executive action.

5.7.5 Worldwide information

Effective management of a business requires more than internal information. For strategic decision making up-to-date facts relating to the business's current share price, the trend in competitors' share prices and the latest economic and industrial indicators may be needed. Existing sources for this class of information include the *Wall Street Journal* and the on-line Dow Jones News/Retrieval service. Colourful menus, instead of keyboard commands, make it easy to select and display news and share prices. Strategic decisions can be made based on the latest news about mergers and acquisitions, legal news, industry developments, international situations and so on.

5.7.6 Getting answers: executive problem analysis

Having identified a significant variance an executive needs to view the data from a number of different perspectives. It is not enough to know that an unfavourable profit variance of 5 per cent has occurred at group or consolidated level. Some operating units may have increased profits while others have deviations greater than 5 per cent, and it is important to obtain information on these factors. While an EIS enables executives to ascertain where losses are being made more quickly than the previous reporting system, it is necessary to analyse deeper, not only pinpointing the magnitude of the profit deviations in the different operating areas, but to establish their root cause. Material shortages may be causing a cut-back in production below the level of sales demand or a competitor's pricing policy may be more acceptable to consumers. Analysis may indicate that there are numerous contributory causes, such as customers failing to order a specific product line for a particular reason (analyse the reason) or a reduction in sales in a specific geographical area due perhaps to inferior sales effort by representatives. An EIS can support such multiple levels of investigation. By selecting the highlighted variance on the screen it is possible to obtain more detail of causes, zooming to an explanatory memo which is displayed on the screen. Individual items in a report can be selected like menu choices with higher level report values pointing to lower levels of details. By this means the user gets a feeling of 'zooming' through information taking a closer perspective, in much the same way as a photographer with a zoom lens.

5.7.7 Investigation with Execu-View

Although the general ledger contains a great deal of financial information it is not designed to serve the needs of executives. Deeper investigation requires profitability computing from other strategic perspectives. For this purpose a multidimensional information model designed to support managerial views of financial performance is required. With System W management accounting software, definitions of economic behaviour can be written by specialist financial analysts and applied to raw financial data. For example, in extracting sales and expense data from the general ledger and input to a model for assessing product profitability, allocation rules are used to prorate overheads providing financial data with added strategic perspective. Once an information model is created, the EIS can interface with it to provide executives and financial analysts easy access to the model database. The graphic interface to the information model requires simple application of the touch screen, mouse or a few keys on the keyboard.

The connection between the EIS and the management accounting software opens up unparalleled investigative possibilities. Because the information model can include all the active versions of data, including budget, actual, history and multiple forecasts, every facet of performance may be explored. Unstructured questions can be asked and answers pursued from different directions without advance planning; hunches can be followed to uncover hidden relationships — a boon to analytically orientated executives — providing for success in a number of important managerial areas including:

(a) attainment of required quality standards;
(b) attaining and maintaining a competitive advantage;
(c) achievement of objectives;
(d) accomplishing an increase in productivity;
(e) provision of the right products at the right price;
(f) effective use of human resources;
(g) improved customer service;
(h) selection of effective strategies.

5.7.8 Components of Commander EIS

(a) Commander Executive work station.
(b) Work station manager.
(c) Information integration.
(d) Application packaging.
(e) Execu-View interface to System W DSS.

5.7.9 Commander Executive work station

Executives work entirely within the Commander Executive work station, which runs on standard IBM AT, IBM Personal System/2 and COMPAQ DESKPRO 386. The work station consists of the briefing book, newswire, Execu-View (investigate) and builders' tools. Builders' tools are for use by those who support the executives, the EIS builders. Commander EIS provides easy-to-use tools designed specifically for building and maintaining executive information systems. Features include windows, a 'paint-box'-like interface with pop-up menus and a touch screen interface or a mouse.

5.7.10 Work station manager

The work station manager manages information in the form of reports, charts, memos and programs. It has facilities for automatic communications error checking and retransmission; security for each document; control of information distribution and automatic cataloguing and downloading to the PC.

5.7.11 Information integration

This component has facilities for merging and consolidating data from payroll systems, general ledgers and other data structures. It also has resources to access, extract and interpret data from multiple incompatible sources, including a variety of standard extract file formats and finished report output. It also facilitates access to various databases.

5.7.12 Execu-View interface to System W DSS

This is a multidimensional decision support system which can be used to create the multiple perspectives needed to respond to executives' needs for strategic information. It provides a dynamic and graphic human interface into the System W modelling database, resulting in unparalleled spreadsheet-orientated investigative capability without using commands or syntax. System W modelling features include analytical facilities — multidimensional allocations, simultaneous equation solving, statistical forecasting, reporting and business graphics etc. Up to nine dimensions are supported providing the ability to manage many spreadsheets (*see* Fig. 5.4).

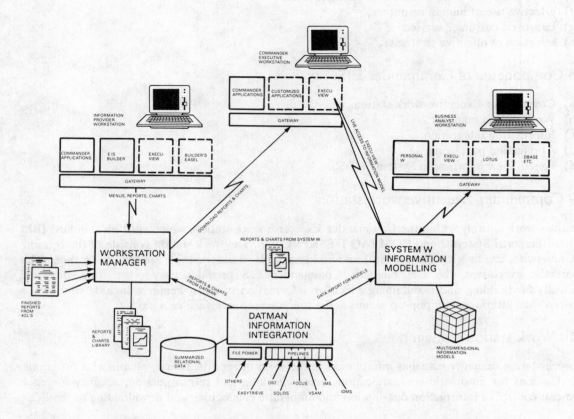

Figure 5.4. Comshare Commander EIS software architecture

5.7.13 Benefits of using an executive information system

(a) Creating an EIS provides the opportunity to identify information most important to the business, which focuses attention on critical operational areas.

(b) After implementing an EIS critical information will become available on demand, reducing the volume of routine information which often requires sifting to detect critical facts requiring managerial attention.

(c) The system provides speedy access to information by hands-on facilities saving valuable time in analysing printouts.

(d) Information is available from computerised data processing system files and databases by the interconnection of mainframe to personal computers used by executives.

(e) Colour graphics are easy to understand and use.

(f) Adjusting and restructuring of screens is straightforward.

5.8 Information retrieval methods

Any manager, accountant or administrator wishes to obtain information from a computerised system in the most expeditious and simplified manner without first having to become a computer expert. The solution to this is to provide information retrieval methods which are easy to use and which do not involve the need to learn commands. To this end various types of information system are taken into account including executive information systems which incorporate multidimensional spreadsheets, stand-alone spreadsheets or those forming part of integrated software packages for obtaining summarised information on the cost of products, current profit and loss accounts, cash flow statements, operating reports, contribution analysis and balance sheets etc.; internal databases incorporating query languages which assist in extracting records with specific attributes; public databases such as Prestel for global economic, financial and other business information; information generated by report modules in accounting packages in respect of lists containing specified details relating to debtors, creditors, stock and personnel. Screen dialogue methods which may be applied include the use of menus to display report options; a mouse and pointer for report selection from a menu; selecting required information by touching the screen of an appropriately designed computer (*see* 5.8.1); the use of a keypad for selecting pages to be displayed on the screen when obtaining information from public databases such as Prestel. The application of query and natural languages is dealt with in Chapter 19.

5.8.1 Use of menus, mouse or touch screen in an executive information system environment

Executive information systems (EIS) (*see* 5.7) provide a solution to the need to obtain summarised information in the form it is required (the user view), when it is required. The EIS is software designed to provide electronic delivery of critical information in the form of reports and charts without the need for executives to learn the technical aspects of computers. Provision is made for using a mouse or touch screen either for performing functions or for pointing to the type of report required. A mouse is used to direct a pointer to the type of report required. With a touch-sensitive screen, it is necessary only to touch with a finger the point on the screen specifying the nature of the summarised information required. It is possible in this way to obtain information stored in multidimensional spreadsheets containing data which may be viewed in many different ways, e.g. information relating to product sales by geographical area, by division and product group, distribution channel, customer group and, at the corporate level, divisional and corporate income, expenditure, profits and losses etc. Any one of these views may provide the best perspective on a problem or opportunity requiring executive action.

5.8.2. Menu selection of reports generated by an accounting package

Sub-menus of various accounting applications provide for the selection of specific summarised information relating to transactions, which can easily be accessed by selecting the required option from those displayed on the screen. A nominal ledger enquiry screen, for instance, provides for displaying account balance details and a reporting screen provides for printing the nominal ledger. (*See* also Chapter 20.)

Review questions

1   What are the primary characteristics of a management information system?

2   What is a structured decision?

3   List the constituent elements of a decision support system.

4   What is the purpose of an executive information system (EIS)?

5   List the benefits of using an EIS.

6   List several information retrieval techniques which allow accountants and other executives to obtain information speedily without the need to be computer experts.

Self-test question

5.1 The primary purpose of collecting and processing data relating to business transactions is to produce information for administration and control. Distinguish between data and information, stating the desirable properties of management information. Also classify these different types of information system.

Answer on page 370–1.

6 Functional subsystems

6.1 Introduction

In this chapter details relating to production, marketing and purchasing subsystems are discussed to provide a more rounded exposition of non-financial subsystems. The term *subsystem* can be interpreted to mean a subsidiary system. In the context of a business organisation viewed as a complete entity, each business system administered by the various functions is a subsystem. Functional subsystems may be grouped into two categories — financial and non-financial. In respect of sales (accounts receivable) and purchases (accounts payable), reference should also be made to Chapter 20 regarding the software for these applications.

6.2 Financial and non-financial systems

Business systems fall into two main categories — financial and non financial. Financial systems include payroll processing; accounts payable and receivable; budgetary, cost, credit, cash flow and capital expenditure control; asset accounting, administration of investment portfolios and hiring and/or leasing of motor vehicles, computers and other assets, etc. Non-financial systems include marketing and selling; stock control and production planning and control; purchasing; building and plant maintenance systems; administrative systems relating to personnel, hotel accommodation, holiday bookings and airline seat reservations.

6.2.1 Functional subsystems

Functional organisation was initiated by F.W. Taylor, one of the management pioneers, well known for his principles of scientific management. With this type of organisation, specialists give direct instructions to personnel on matters relating to work study, personnel, finance and office methods, etc. rather than through a formal chain of command. This leads to confusion as orders from the various specialists tend to conflict with one another. This type of functional organisation is not widely practised because business functions are usually organised on a 'line and staff' basis, more correctly defined as 'line and functional'. This has two distinct elements, the first relating to the 'line' organisation, which specifies executive lines of authority, and the second to the 'staff' organisation, concerned with the functional activities performed by specialists under the control of functional managers. It is important to appreciate that functional managers have line authority, i.e. executive authority over the personnel within their function but not over those in other functions or those in the line functions. Business functions are traditionally organised according to the nature of their activities and are referred to as *functional subsystems*, several of which are discussed below.

6.2.2 Functions in the larger business

Larger businesses tend to organise functions separately often because the volume of work in each of the functions warrants their separation. These factors need to be taken into account when defining the functional requirements of a business. In such instances functions may be separately organised for accounting, manufacturing, personnel, purchasing, production planning and control, and stock control etc.

6.2.3 Functions in the smaller business

Smaller businesses, however, usually group a number of functions together for administrative convenience. Grouping may consist of activities comprising personnel administration, payroll processing, correspondence typing, telephone and postal services; photocopying, telex and facsimile document transmission. This group may be controlled by an executive with the title of office manager. Another executive could be responsible for purchasing, planning and controlling production and stock control.

6.3 Non-financial subsystems

This section provides details of matters relating to the production, purchasing and marketing functions, to give a balanced and rounded view of typical business activities.

6.3.1 Production

The production function is responsible for planning and controlling production to ensure orders or production targets are achieved. It is concerned to ensure that products attain an acceptable level of quality as this is extremely important in a competitive market. The specific products will of course depend upon the nature of the business. The production function is supported by many other secondary functions, including the purchase of raw materials and consumables for use in the manufacturing processes; work study to establish the best working methods; time study to establish standard times for operations; control of work-in-progress; production planning and control; personnel management; material handling for moving work-in-progress to the various operations and/or processes, and so on.

6.3.2 Marketing

This function embraces all those activities concerned with obtaining and retaining customers, and includes market research, sales promotion, selling, distribution and after-sales service. Market research is concerned with collecting, recording and systematically analysing market data for assessing consumer preferences in respect of various domestic or consumable products. This is an invaluable guide to the future strategy of a business; without market intelligence the wrong products or those with an inadequate specification may be manufactured. Sales promotion is directed at selling more products by a variety of publicity campaigns, which may include circulars pushed through letter boxes, direct mailshots, local, national or television advertising and public demonstrations in department stores and local hotels, etc.

6.3.3 Purchasing

This function is performed by the buying office or purchasing department; it is responsible for ensuring that the various raw materials are available when required to implement production schedules; for obtaining consumable supplies such as lubricants, works stationery and other items of a general nature; computer printout stationery; the various forms required by the personnel and accounting functions and so on. The purchasing function is sometimes responsible for the control of items held in the stores until they are needed by the production function. Supplies are often obtained on the basis of the *economic order quantity*, referred to as the EOQ, which minimises total costs, i.e. the sum of the storage costs and ordering costs, which can vary according to the frequency of ordering, the length of time in storage and, of course, the quantity ordered on each occasion.

6.4 Financial subsystems

The financial accounting function is responsible for planning and controlling all financial accounting procedures and the preparation of balance sheets, trading and profit and loss accounts and ensuring that all business transactions are recorded in proper books of account. The function is also responsible, as custodian, for safeguarding the fixed and liquid assets of the business and implementing internal check procedures. Responsibilities also include the control of receipts and payments in respect of the various business transactions undertaken and the maintenance of statutory records relating to payroll (*see* 6.4.1) and VAT on purchase and sales transactions. Aspects of various accounting subsystems are outlined below, each supported by a diagram illustrating the main features of the subsystem, including input of transaction details, elements of storage and the output produced in the form of various documents and lists. The diagrams do not presuppose any specific method of processing — the use of computers is not implied — but portray the features of the subsystems. Computer systems may subsequently be developed using this type of diagram, which provides an overall view of a system, before embarking on detailed analysis.

6.4.1 Payroll

The payroll subsystem of any business is very important since it affects all the personnel of that business. To attain harmonious working relationships throughout the business it is necessary to have an effective payroll system for computing the pay and deductions of all types of personnel, in all functions, including directors, functional and departmental managers, section supervisors, hourly-paid personnel and those remunerated on the basis of payment by results schemes. It is imperative that salaries and wages are computed accurately and on time. (*See* Chapter 20 for other details relating to payroll procedures and the benefits obtained from payroll software packages. *See* also Fig. 6.1.)

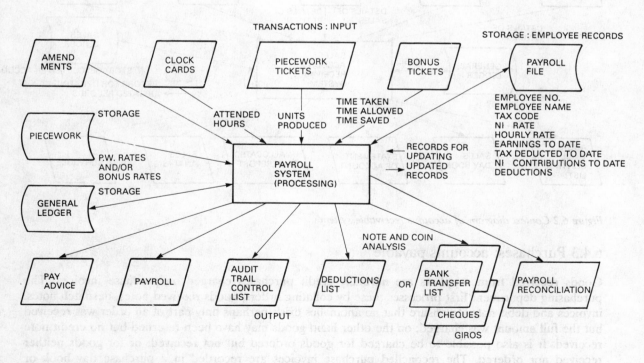

Figure 6.1 Context diagram of a payroll system

6.4.2 Sales: accounts receivable

Goods despatched to customers are usually credit sales recorded on an invoice containing a number of details, including the value of the goods, which is recorded on the customer's account in the sales ledger. The individual invoices are recorded in a sales day book or equivalent. The total value of the sales is credited in the sales account by sales analysis code and debited to a debtor control account in the general ledger. At the end of the trading month statements of account are prepared for each customer. These may show an aged account balance, i.e. how much has been outstanding for one month, two months, and three months or over, for instance. This information is valuable for credit control. The details for each customer are summarised on a *aged balance report*. Balance-forward statements itemise only the invoices or other debits outstanding, whereas open-item statements record all debits and credits and the allocation of remittances so that customers may more easily reconcile the amount outstanding with their own records. Remittances received are debited to the bank account and credited to the debtor control account in the general ledger. A sales analysis is prepared for sales management and an audit trail is produced listing all the transactions for the period. Records are also maintained for the purpose of accounting for VAT. Remittances received but unmatched with sales invoices are recorded on an unallocated cash report. If a remittance cannot be matched to a specific invoice it is normal practice to allocate it to the oldest outstanding transaction (*see* Fig. 6.2).

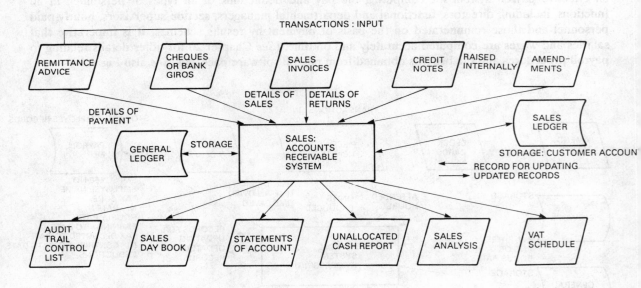

Figure 6.2 Context diagram of accounts receivable system

6.4.3 Purchases: accounts payable

Goods received from suppliers are normally credit purchases charged on purchase invoices. The purchasing department first processes these by collating orders, goods received notes, despatch notes, invoices and debit notes to ensure that no anomalies exist: perhaps only part of an order was received but the full amount was charged; on the other hand goods may have been returned but no credit note received. It is also possible to be charged for goods ordered but not received, or for goods neither received nor ordered. The reconciled purchase invoices are recorded in a purchase day book or equivalent and suppliers' accounts are updated with their value. The total value of purchases is debited to the purchases account by purchase analysis code and credited to the creditor control account in the general ledger. Statements of account are received from suppliers at the month-end and the outstanding balances reconciled with those on the suppliers' accounts. These are then inspected to decide which should be paid and whether in full or in part, and appropriate remittances are then made, accompanied by remittance advice notes, either by giro bank transfer, cheque or the BACS system. The total remittances are credited to the bank account and debited to the creditor control account in the general ledger, which then records the current total amount owing to suppliers. Listings of transactions are produced to provide an audit trail. An analysis of purchases is also produced for internal information requirements and accounting records are maintained in respect of VAT (*see* Fig. 6.3).

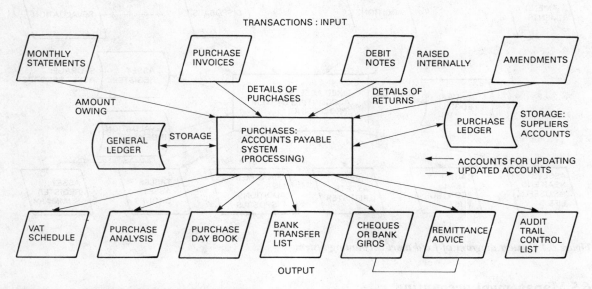

Figure 6.3 Context diagram of accounts payable system

6.4.4 Fixed assets

The original cost of each class of asset purchased is debited to the appropriate asset account in the general ledger. Fixed assets include land, buildings, motor vehicles, plant and machinery. The total amount of depreciation for each class of asset is credited to a depreciation provision account in the general ledger. For each type of asset the total original cost and the depreciation provision to date are recorded on the relevant balance sheet (as at a stated date for the financial year-end) to record the net book value.

Details of each asset are recorded in an asset register. The record serves a dual purpose: it provides general information in respect of each asset, and details of assets for accounting purposes. General information includes the type of asset, its identification number, description, location, supplier, manufacturer, HP rating, floor area occupied (for expense apportionments), date of installation and maintenance history. Additions and disposals are also recorded. Details for accounting purposes include date of purchase, original cost, installation cost, depreciation class, annual amount of depreciation, cumulative depreciation, written down value and the cost of maintenance. The date, cost and depreciation of additions and the amount realised on the disposal of assets would also be recorded.

Assets such as land and buildings are sometimes revalued to allow for current market values. This then portrays the true worth of the business with regard to its asset values on the balance sheet. A revaluation index is used for the purpose. The fixed asset accounting subsystem also provides for reports relating to assets near the end of their useful life and a fixed assets register and summary. A table of asset groups may also be output giving details of the company and department in which the assets are located, depreciation rates, revaluation indexes and general ledger account numbers, etc. (*see* Fig. 6.4).

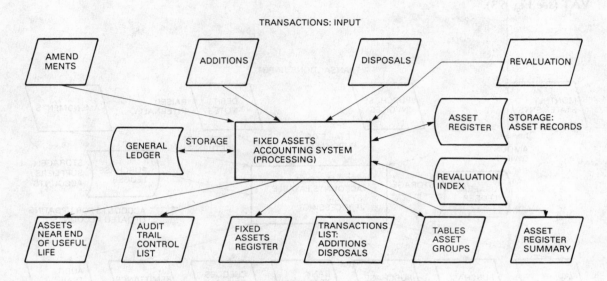

Figure 6.4 Context diagram of fixed asset accounting system

6.5 Management accounting

The management accounting function is responsible for preparing financial control information which can easily be digested by functional and line managers: cash flow statements and projected profit statements and balance sheets; functional and other related budgets; evaluating capital expenditure projects and many different operating statistics and financial ratios to inform management of results for comparison with objectives as a basis for applying corrective action.

6.5.1 Budgetary control

Many control systems are based on the principle of management by exception whereby differences between planned and actual performance are used by management for taking appropriate action. The actual results of business operations are input to a budgetary control system from the accounting subsystems: for example, the value of stocks is obtained from the inventory control subsystem; the cost of wages and salaries is provided by the payroll accounting subsystem; the quantity and value of sales by the sales accounting subsystem; cash flows from the cash accounting or banking subsystem; the value of purchases suitably analysed from the purchase accounting subsystem; depreciation from the fixed asset accounting subsystem via the fixed assets register report, and the value or cost of accruals and prepayments is obtained from journal vouchers, etc.

A budgetary control system compares actual results with budgets and standards, including such financial aspects as the amount of overhead expenditure incurred, analysed by expense code, which is compared with the budgeted allowance for a defined level of performance. The differences between the two factors are computed to obtain what are referred to as *variances*. Other key factors taken into account in a budgetary control system include sales and production achievements compared with budgeted quantities and values, manning levels and efficiency in the use of direct materials. Significant variances are reported to the manager concerned together with other relevant details relating to the results of the same month of the previous year and the year-to-date comparison with the previous year. This provides a basis for assessing the significance of trends as well as the current situation. Managers in charge of budget centres receive this information by means of operating statements, which do not report results which are going according to plan but only factors of significance requiring remedial action to achieve budgeted targets or objectives (*see* Fig. 6.5).

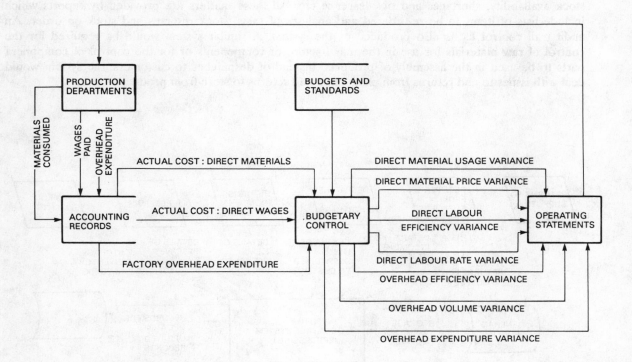

Figure 6.5 Information flows in a budgetry control system

6.5.2 Executive information systems

Modern information retrieval techniques include the personal use by executives of a computer-orientated decision support system known as an executive information system. This type of system allows executives to obtain information relating to budget and actual comparisons according to their specific requirements or views on matters relating to production or sales, and which may be analysed by individual plant or market or on a group basis (see Chapter 5).

6.6 Stock control

The stock control function is responsible for inventory (stock) management, which involves the efficient control of all items held in the stores. Computerised inventory control systems capable of providing a fast response to enquiries and efficient updating of inventory records are often used. These advantages are particularly relevant to such businesses as wholesale food distribution warehouses, which need to avoid building up excessive stocks so as to minimise the amount of capital locked up and consequent interest charges on loans or overdrafts for financing such stocks. On the other hand, if stocks are too low stock-out situations can arise resulting in lost orders. A typical inventory control system relating to consumable goods held for despatch to customers is shown in Fig. 6.6. It portrays a context diagram showing details of a variety of transactions, including receipts from suppliers, despatches to and returns from customers, stock reserves for special orders (which reduce the stock available for lower priority orders), and returns to suppliers of goods surplus to the quantity ordered or which have deteriorated during transportation.

The records in the stock file are updated with all stock movements in order to be aware of current stock availability, shortages and obsolescence etc. All these matters are provided by reports which include lists of items to be re-ordered and analyses of sales, stock reserves and stock on order. An audit trail control list is also produced by the system. A similar system would be required for the control of raw materials for use in the manufacture of components or for the control of component parts to be used in the assembly of products. Instead of despatches to customers, the system would deal with issues to and returns from production and returns to store from production, etc.

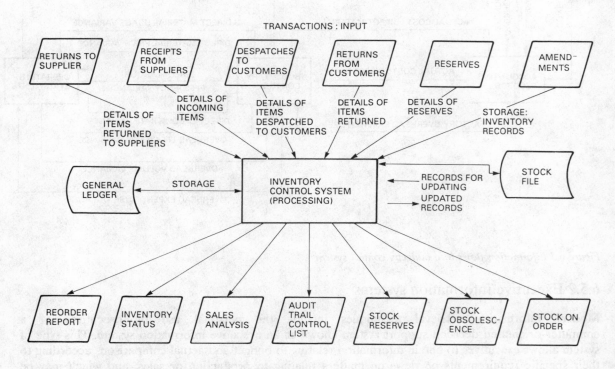

Figure 6.6 Context diagram of inventory control system

Review questions

1 How does the organisation of functions differ between the larger and smaller business?

2 State the purpose of the following non-financial systems:

(a) production;
(b) marketing; *and*
(c) purchasing.

3 List the primary activities of a payroll subsystem.

4 Specify the nature of accounts receivable and accounts payable subsystems.

5 Why is an effective stock control system imperative to the efficiency of a business?

7 Financial modelling 1

7.1 Introduction

This is an introductory chapter for the purpose of providing a background to the use of spreadsheets and their counterpart — the integrated package which combines spreadsheet software with word processing, database and telecommunications. A selection of the spreadsheets currently available and their suppliers is also provided.

7.2 Applications of spreadsheets

Spreadsheet applications are widely used by accountants due to their ease of use, powerful computational facilities and the wide range of applications to which they can be applied.

Integrated packages contain speadsheet modules which allow a user to transfer data from a database or application file to a spreadsheet for analysis purposes. Spreadsheets can both display on a screen and print out numerical data, text and graphs. Report formatting facilities enable the results to be presented in a report. Most spreadsheets let the user create macros — small programs which perform specified operations automatically. Many packages create macros automatically by recording keystrokes when performing commands. Relevant macros can be called in when required for a specific processing task such as printing particular details from a spreadsheet on to a document, a budget statement for instance. More powerful spreadsheets are really financial modelling packages and include facilities for creating a model automatically as the user types in a formula specifying the relationship between variables.

Some packages, Lotus 1-2-3 for instance, have an open architecture which allows other software houses to develop add-ons such as those developed by the 4-5-6 Corporation for adding applications software to the Lotus 1-2-3 spreadsheet.

Two of the most important attributes of spreadsheets are the 'What if?' and 'goal seeking' facilities. What if? facilities provide the results of making changes as a basis for determining decision making strategy (see Chapter 8). Goal seeking is the opposite to 'What if?' in that it states what the value of variables, such as sales, should be to attain a stated level of profit.

A table published by *Accountancy Age* in November 1987 from data collected from a survey conducted by the Chartered Association of Certified Accountants listed a breakdown of modelling activities in order of significance. For UK accountants using PCs the order is:

(a) cash flow forecasts;
(b) budgetary planning;
(c) investment appraisal;
(d) cost/volume/profit analysis;
(e) budgetary control;
(f) financial statement analysis;

(g) consolidations;
(h) foreign currency conversion;
(i) tax planning;
(j) portfolio management.

7.3 Microsoft Excel spreadsheet

This is probably the most powerful spreadsheet for the IBM PC AT, COMPAQ and IBM compatibles. It has a number of interesting features and facilities, some of which are described in order to indicate the characteristics of modern spreadsheets. It has multiple window facilities for linking many spreadsheets together which can then be viewed on the screen simultaneously (*see* Figs. 7.1–7.4). In this way data from different spreadsheets can be compared. This allows the actual results for a department to be compared with budgets for the extraction of variances, for instance. Information can be consolidated from an unlimited number of sources into a single document and charts and data can be displayed concurrently on the screen. Excel generates 44 predesigned charts in seven basic types — area, bar, column, line, pie, scatter and combinations. It has a procedural macro language consisting of 355 functions, and provides for laser and colour printing. The spreadsheet can be used as a database allowing fast searching, sorting and extraction of information. When using Microsoft Windows it allows simultaneous multi-tasking with other applications and provides data links to and from other applications. There is a network version of Microsoft Excel which fully supports all leading network configurations.

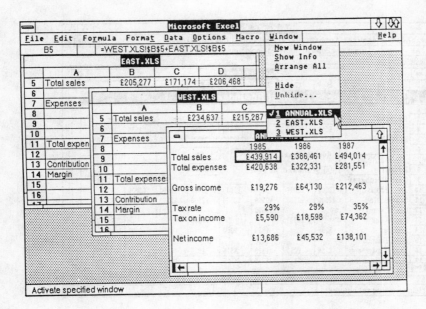

Figure 7.1 Microsoft Excel screen display of a spreadsheet showing multiple windows and drop-down menu. The display is related to Figure 7.2

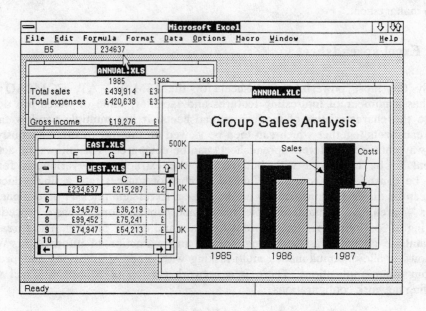

Figure 7.2 Microsoft Excel screen display of a spreadsheet illustrating multiple windows. The display is related to Figure 7.1

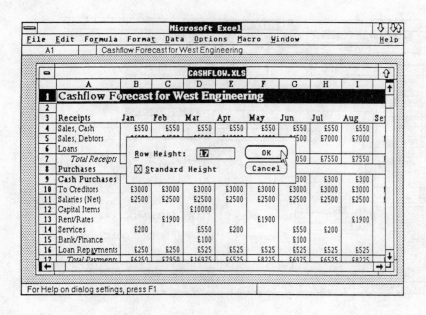

Figure 7.3 Microsoft Excel screen display of a spreadsheet showing a cash flow application with system window. The display is related to Figure 7.4

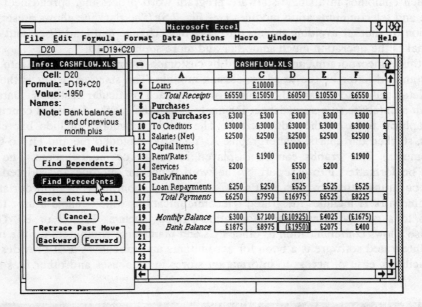

Figure 7.4 Microsoft Excel screen display of a spreadsheet illustrating a cash flow application. System windows are also shown. This display is related to Figure 7.3

7.4 Spreadsheets and suppliers

A selection of the spreadsheets currently available and their suppliers are shown in the following list:

(a) Excel for MS-DOS machines and for the Macintosh (Microsoft Corporation).
(b) Multiplan for MS-DOS machines and the Macintosh (Microsoft Corporation).
(c) SuperCalc 4 for MS-DOS machines (Computer Associates).
(d) Lotus 1-2-3 for MS-DOS machines (Lotus Development Corporation).
(e) Javelin for MS-DOS machines (Ashton-Tate).
(f) Quattro for MS-DOS machines (Borland International).

7.5 Weaknesses of spreadsheets

Spreadsheet models are not subjected to the same degree of documentation, validation and verification as normal information processing applications. The content of cells can be inadvertently corrupted, providing incorrect results and leading to incorrect conclusions.

Spreadsheets do not generally have powerful programming facilities, but this need not be a drawback as many users do not wish to delve into such technicalities.

The size of a spreadsheet model may be restricted by the internal memory capacity.

7.6 General features of integrated packages

The term *integrated package* is used to describe software consisting of several general-purpose applications within one program. A well-known top-selling integrated package is Ashton-Tate's Framework II, which combines in a single software program word processing, spreadsheet including graphics, database and telecommunication modules (*see* Fig. 7.5). The package allows a user to switch from one application to another avoiding the need to save files, change and load discs, and open new files. Integration makes the operation much smoother and more sophisticated.

An example of this is incorporating amounts owed by customers from a customer file into a text file in the form of a standard letter by the word processing module. The standard letter is then printed with the variable data relating to the specific amount owed by each particular customer. Data can also be transferred from a database to a spreadsheet for analysis and the results displayed concurrently in numerical and graphical form on the video screen. The graphics facilities include bar charts, pie charts, line graphs, stacked bar charts, scattergraphs, X–Y charts, exploded pie and Hi-Lo-Close (for share price movements). The graphs can be displayed in colour or monochrome. The text and graphics can then be formatted into a report by the word processor module and printed out. The report may also be transmitted by the user's PC to another computer as appropriate in the circumstances. Framework II includes integrated telecommunications which enable a user to connect through a modem to a variety of external information sources such as Prestel or BT Gold. The telecoms facility also allows communication to other PCs and mainframe computers for the transfer of operational data. Integrated software is a boon for accountants and executives as it provides powerful problem solving facilities, ease of access to information stores in databases and other files as well as report facilities.

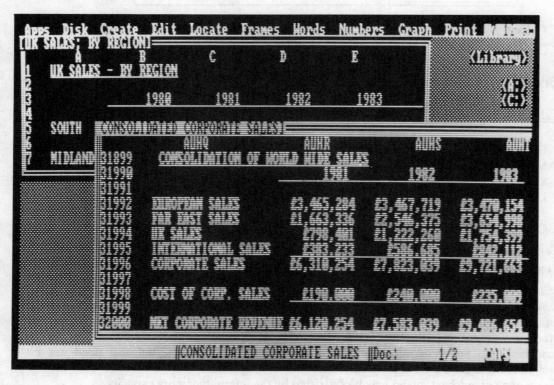

Figure 7.5 Screen display Ashton-Tate Framework II showing a spreadsheet of corporate sales

Prospective users of integrated packages should be aware of the important characteristics to look for, which include the following.

7.6.1 Commands

A fully integrated package incorporates a set of commands which enable the user to use the various applications in a simple manner.

7.6.2 Windows

Windows are a facility which allows the data of several applications to be displayed on the screen simultaneously.

7.6.3 Graphs

This facility allows numerical data in a spreadsheet to be converted into various types of graphs and charts, as indicated above.

7.6.4 Pipelining

After windows have been displayed on the screen, pipelining allows several sets of data, relating to various applications, to be changed simultaneously.

7.6.5 Development software

The provision of software by the manufacturers of integrated packages to other software houses which then proceed to develop modules in order to extend the range of the original product.

7.6.6 Virtual memory

The system automatically uses all internal memory before buffering into disc memory.

7.6.7 Help facilities

These provide guidance on specific aspects of the system operation.

7.6.8 Prompts

These give context-sensitive explanations on choice of commands, parameters, etc. There is a facility for switching off prompts when not required.

7.6.9 Task sequencing

Commands can be stored in a file and used to control the sequence of applications. This is sometimes referred to as a command file.

7.7 Integrated packages available and their applications

7.7.1 Typical packages available

Many packages are currently available provided you have an IBM PC or compatible computer. A selection of these includes:

- (a) Symphony, from Lotus Development;
- (b) Framework, from Ashton-Tate;
- (c) Decision Manager, from Peachtree;
- (d) Open Access, from Software Products International;
- (e) Applework, from Apple;
- (f) Exchange, from Psion;
- (g) Jazz, from Lotus Development;
- (h) Smart, from Innovative Software.

7.7.2 Typical applications and integrated modules

- (a) Strategic planning (spreadsheet and database).
- (b) Report writing (spreadsheet, graphics, database and word processor).
- (c) Project planning (spreadsheet).
- (d) Balance sheet analysis; ratio analysis (database/application files and spreadsheet).
- (e) Marginal costing and break-even analysis (database and spreadsheet).
- (f) Standard letters (word processing and application files/database).
- (g) Plant register (database).
- (h) Budgetary control (database and spreadsheet).

The details in brackets indicate the integrated package modules which may typically be used in the various applications. It is important to appreciate that this is only a guide because what may be done depends on the class of records stored in the database. In relation to strategic planning, the use of the database presupposes that it contains historical operational records which may be used as a basis for establishing future plans. Similarly, the use of a database for balance sheet analysis presupposes that the general ledger is stored in a database or that details can be transferred from an application file — the general ledger in this instance.

Refer to Chapters 8 and 9 for specific examples.

7.8 Advantages and disadvantages of integrated packages

7.8.1 Advantages

- (a) The need to change discs when switching from one application to another is avoided.
- (b) Value for money as they tend to be less expensive than purchasing the applications separately.
- (c) Training is facilitated as packages have a common user interface and fewer commands to understand.
- (d) Increased level of productivity of business activities.
- (e) Job enrichment.

7.8.2 Disadvantages

(a) Require a large internal memory capacity.
(b) Individual modules of an integrated package may have fewer features than equivalent stand-alone software.

7.9 Integrated environment

Some computing systems offer facilities which enable users to configure their own combination of stand-alone applications from individual packages so that they can run on an integrated basis and interchange data under the control of the environment software, such as Windows and OS/2 operating systems. This innovation may result in the demise of or reduce demand for integrated packages.

Review questions

1   Why are spreadsheets widely used by accountants?

2   What is a macro?

3   How are the results of running a spreadsheet presented?

4   What is the purpose of open architecture?

5   Define 'What if?'.

6   Define 'goal seeking'.

7   List the main suppliers of spreadsheets.

8   What are the most popular spreadsheet applications?

9   List the weaknesses of spreadsheets.

10   List the general features of integrated packages embracing work processing, spreadsheets and including graphics, database and telecommunications.

11   What is a window?

8 Financial modelling 2: spreadsheets

8.1 Introduction

This chapter provides a detailed explanation of the nature and operation of spreadsheets, an important aspect of which is that they perform computations very speedily, dispense with the use of analysis paper for recording details of problems and provide information on the results of a particular strategy generated by what are referred to as 'What if?' facilities. The ability of a spreadsheet to recompute data speedily after adjusting variables, such as variable costs, and constants, such as fixed overheads, is significant for accountants. This saves valuable time in recomputing budgets, for instance.

8.2 Nature and purpose of spreadsheets

A spreadsheet is an electronic analysis sheet for solving many different types of problem by computer. It performs computations on data very quickly and recomputes results automatically after data has been amended. Spreadsheets dispense with the use of analysis paper for recording details of problems as data is input by keyboard and then displayed on the video screen. It is important to plan the layout of the spreadsheet in advance to attain a professional appearance, since it will in turn affect the appearance of a printed report containing the results of running the spreadsheet. The details displayed on the screen, such as the value of sales, cost elements and overhead expenses, are referred to as *variables*. Relationships between variables, e.g. 'contribution = sales value – variable costs', are defined by formula.

Spreadsheets are widely used for developing financial models relating to:

(a) marginal costing and break-even analysis;
(b) analysis of profit and loss account and balance sheet for computing financial ratios;
(c) unit cost computations;
(d) analysis of periodic financial results such as the proportion of sales and profit of each product;
(e) monthly profit projections based on specified growth rates and cost levels;
(f) cash flow computations for investment analysis based on net present value for choosing between alternative investments.

A spreadsheet greatly assists the work of accountants, office managers, corporate planners and administrators as it provides a speedy method of obtaining solutions to particular types of problem. Details are located on the screen in predesignated row and column locations. The relationship of each cell needs to be defined within formulas, as will become evident from the spreadsheet applications demonstrated later in the text. It is also possible to perform 'What if?' computations to find out what would happen if sales were increased or decreased by a stated percentage; if variable costs were reduced by a defined amount per unit; and the effect on the break-even point of increasing or decreasing fixed costs or making specific adjustments to the selling price of products.

Software is available consisting of pre-formatted spreadsheets for 31 integrated budgeting schedules, ranging from sales and profit projections and working capital requirements to full profit and loss accounts and balance sheets. The package also provides for 'What if?' requirements. It works with Multiplan, SuperCalc 2 and 3 and Lotus 1-2-3 among others, and runs on IBM, Apricot, Macintosh, Sirius, Amstrad 8256 and most other computers. The package is called Ultraplan and is marketed by Trinity Business Systems of Norwich.

8.3 Operational features of spreadsheets

Different versions of spreadsheets are available from different software houses, each with its own features. It is therefore necessary to consult the specific spreadsheet manual for operating details. All spreadsheets, however, have common facilities for carrying out a whole range of activities, examples of which are:

(a) blank the content of cells to clear unrequired data;
(b) delete or insert a row or column;
(c) clear the current worksheet from the screen;
(d) cancel a command;
(e) entry of text;
(f) entry of values (variables);
(g) entry of variable relationships by formula;
(h) display of formula on the screen;
(i) save worksheet on magnetic disc for future use or amendment;
(j) saved worksheets can be loaded (transferred) into the internal memory from disc for processing;
(k) current values can replace previous values in an original spreadsheet;
(l) reports can be printed out;
(m) rows and columns can be copied to different cells;
(n) worksheets can be displayed one page at a time;
(o) row and column numbers can be deleted and need not be printed;
(p) specified sections of a spreadsheet can be printed by stating the range of cells;
(q) formulas can be replicated when calculations are similar for different cells in which values differ;
(r) text can be formatted, including aligning text or values to right or left in a cell to provide a tidy appearance to a report;
(s) values can be rounded to remove unnecessary decimals;
(t) report formats can be changed regarding the number of lines per page and the width of line in terms of the number of characters;
(u) formulas can be copied into other cells;
(v) the value in cells can be totalled;
(w) values contained in a spreadsheet can be converted into bar, line and pie charts;
(x) built-in functions such as maximum, average, minimum and sum;
(y) the content of cells can be edited.

8.4 Using the spreadsheet

To use a spreadsheet it is first necessary to load the relevant software — the spreadsheet program. The screen then displays a series of rows and columns as shown in Figs 8.3 and 8.4. The top of the screen displays a row of letters which name the columns of the worksheet for columnar references. The initial display of column designations is A–H but the screen can be scrolled (the details moved laterally) to a total of 63 columns, that is, A–Z and AA–BK. A column of numbers is shown down the left of the screen which serve to reference the rows of a worksheet in which details are displayed. Initially rows 1–20 are displayed but up to 254 rows can be displayed by vertical scrolling by means of the cursor control keys. An entry line displays the information as it is entered by the keyboard.

8.5 Entry of data

Data, text, constants and formulas are entered into specific cells. The row and column which contain the active cell are called the *current row* and *column* respectively. The active cell is designated on the screen by the cursor which is shown as a bar. After data is entered the cursor is automatically moved to an adjacent cell. This becomes the new active cell. It is necessary to indicate whether values, text or formulas are being entered into a cell; this will become clear when studying examples later in the text.

8.6 Example 1

The managing director of Industrial Electronics plc requires the financial accountant to provide him at the end of each month with a brief summary containing ratios relating to:

(a) gross profit to sales;
(b) operating profit to sales;
(c) net profit to sales;
(d) return on capital employed;
(e) return on operating assets.

The financial accountant is very interested in using spreadsheets for this type of management reporting. He first obtains a copy of the current balance sheet (*see* Fig. 8.1) and a copy of the profit and loss account (*see* Fig. 8.2). He then prepares a working sheet as shown in Fig. 8.3, which contains relevant data from the profit and loss account and the balance sheet, and defines the relationships between the variables to be used in the computations (*see* rows 22 to 26 in Fig. 8.3). They are analysed as follows:

Row	Formula	Interpretation of formula
22	$+(F4/F3) \times 100$	Cell F4 = gross profit of £200,000 Cell F3 = sales of £500,000 $$\frac{200,000}{500,000} \times 100 = 40\%$$
23	$+(F5/F3) \times 100$	Cell F5 = operating profit of £50,000 Cell F3 = sales of £500,000 $$\frac{50,000}{500,000} \times 100 = 10\%$$
24	$+(F6/F3) \times 100$	Cell F6 = net profit of £45,000 Cell F3 = sales of £500,000 $$\frac{45,000}{500,000} \times 100 = 9\%$$
25	$+(F5/F11) \times 100$	Cell F5 = operating profit of £50,000 Cell F11 = capital employed of £440,000 $$\frac{50,000}{440,000} \times 100 = 11.36\%$$
26	$+(F5/F12) \times 100$	Cell F5 = operating profit of £50,000 Cell F12 = total operating assets of £490,000 (Net assets £440,000 + current liabilities £50,000) $$\frac{50,000}{490,000} \times 100 = 10.20\%$$

The formulas are converted to operating ratios as shown in Fig. 8.4 and printed out. The printout includes column and row references, which should be deleted for neatness of presentation. This is done and the report to be presented to the managing director is shown in Fig. 8.5.

Balance sheet as at 31 December 1988

	£	£	£
Fixed assets			
Land and buildings	250,000		
Plant and machinery	125,000		
Vehicles	25,000		
Total fixed assets			400,000
Current assets			
Work-in-progress	15,000		
Raw material stocks	10,000		
Finished product stocks	25,000		
Debtors	15,000		
Cash at bank	15,000		
Cash in hand	5,000		
Prepayments	5,000		
Total current assets		90,000	
Less: current liabilities			
Corporation tax	10,000		
Creditors	5,000		
Bank loan	20,000		
Proposed ordinary dividend	10,000		
Accrued expenses	5,000		
Total current liabilities		50,000	
Net current assets			40,000
Net assets (capital employed)			440,000
Financed by:			
Share capital and reserves (equity capital)			
300,000 ordinary shares of £1 each		300,000	
Capital reserve		50,000	
Revenue reserve		75,000	
Unappropriated profit		15,000	
Net worth			440,000

Figure 8.1 Balance sheet

Profit and loss account (for the period ending 31 December 1988)

	£	£
Sales	500,000	
Less: cost of sales	300,000	
Gross profit		200,000
Less:		
Selling and distribution	80,000	
Administration	70,000	
		150,000
Operating profit		50,000
Less: interest on overdraft		5,000
Net profit		45,000

Figure 8.2 Profit and loss account

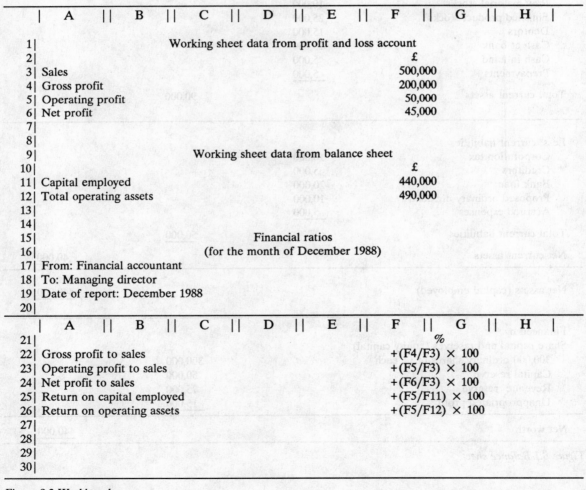

	A		B		C		D		E		F		G		H	
1							Working sheet data from profit and loss account									
2											£					
3	Sales										500,000					
4	Gross profit										200,000					
5	Operating profit										50,000					
6	Net profit										45,000					
7																
8																
9							Working sheet data from balance sheet									
10											£					
11	Capital employed										440,000					
12	Total operating assets										490,000					
13																
14																
15							Financial ratios									
16							(for the month of December 1988)									
17	From: Financial accountant															
18	To: Managing director															
19	Date of report: December 1988															
20																

	A		B		C		D		E		F		G		H	
21											%					
22	Gross profit to sales										+(F4/F3) × 100					
23	Operating profit to sales										+(F5/F3) × 100					
24	Net profit to sales										+(F6/F3) × 100					
25	Return on capital employed										+(F5/F11) × 100					
26	Return on operating assets										+(F5/F12) × 100					
27																
28																
29																
30																

Figure 8.3 Working sheet

	A		B		C		D		E		F		G	
13														
14														
15					Financial ratios									
16					(for the month of December 1988)									
17	From: Financial accountant													
18	To: Managing director													
19	Date of report: December 1988													
20														
21											%			
22	Gross profit to sales										40.00			
23	Operating profit to sales										10.00			
24	Net profit to sales										9.00			
25	Return on capital employed										11.36			
26	Return on operating assets										10.20			
27														
28														
29														
30														

Figure 8.4 Management report including column and row references

---

Financial ratios
(for the month of December 1988)

From: Financial accountant
To: Managing Director
Date of report: December 1988

	%
Gross profit to sales	40.00
Operating profit to sales	10.00
Net profit to sales	9.00
Return on capital employed	11.36
Return on operating assets	10.20

Figure 8.5 Management report excluding column and row references

Review questions

1 Why do spreadsheets dispense with the need to use analysis paper for recording accounting and other data?

2 How are the relationships between variables defined?

3 What is the significance of rows and columns in spreadsheets?

4 List a number of spreadsheet operational features.

5 What are cells and how are they used?

6 List several typical commands for manipulating a spreadsheet.

9 Databases

9.1 Introduction

The topic of databases has been consolidated into one chapter. Database design issues are outlined in Data dictionaries (*see* 9.9) which covers the nature of data and its relationships and dependencies in the database (an important design issue), Organising and processing methods (*see* 9.10) which specifies the various data structures which may be applied and Schemas and sub-schemas (*see* 9.11). Schemas refer to the whole structure of a database, indicating the interrelationships between records, and sub-schemas provide user views which provide access to specific data by particular programs. Device independence (*see* 9.12) portrays the logical and physical concepts of files, and Data independence (*see* 9.13) indicates how data formats are held separately from the programs which use the data.

9.2 Concepts

9.2.1 File of structured data

A database is a file of structured data in the form of records which are accessible to authorised managers and other personnel for administrative purposes and for use in making decisions and controlling business operations (*see* Fig. 9.1). Databases may relate to specific functional requirements such as accounting or may provide for interfunctional information needs. A *query language* facilitates enquiries using English-style words to define commands, and is discussed in Chapter 19.

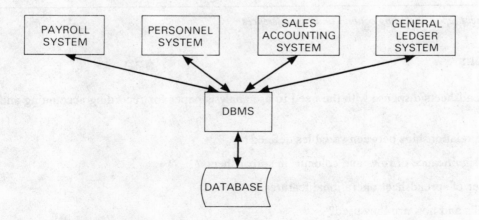

Figure 9.1 Database file structure

9.2.2 Application — specific files

A database eliminates traditional files, which often store the same data in several functional files. This situation duplicates data unnecessarily, creating what is referred to as *redundancy*. One functional file, for instance, stores employee records for use in payroll processing. Each record contains details of individual employees including name, address, employee number, wage rate, department, tax code and NI number etc. Another file used for personnel administration also contains details relating to employees including many already existing on the payroll file. If common data on the several files is not updated concurrently they would be incompatible and likely to create confusion by providing conflicting facts from the different files. This could arise when employees are given a wage award or are transferred to other departments and the changes are not recorded on all relevant files. Data need be input to the database only once since all relevant records are updated, thus providing a greater degree of confidence in the data retrieved by users because of its enhanced integrity or reliability (*see* Figs. 9.1 and 9.2).

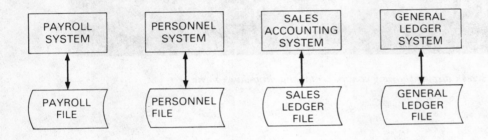

Figure 9.2 Structure of conventional functional files

9.3 Database management systems

A database management system (DBMS) is a set of programs which deal with database management activities, including updating, deleting, adding and amending records. This is accomplished by selecting the required option from a menu displayed on the video screen or by keying in the relevant command from the keyboard. Fig. 9.3 illustrates the screen display showing the control centre of dBASE IV for creating a new file. The DBMS also allows the user to validate, sort, search and print records from the database as well as providing facilities for performing calculations and maintaining a dictionary. Some systems provide for the printing of standard letters and reports and the merging of text with data such as names and addresses. Records can be displayed on the screen and browsed through, making amendments as necessary. Files are reorganised automatically to allow for overflow conditions on disc tracks. Fields may be removed from records and files may be merged or separated according to needs.

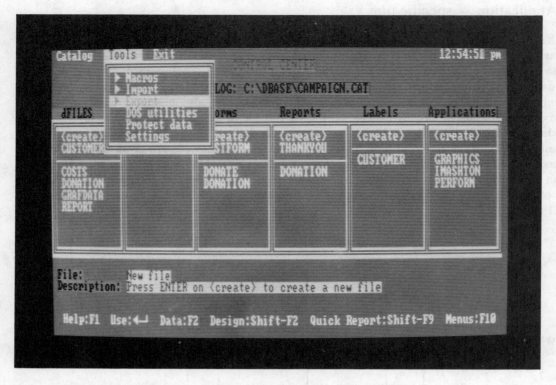

Figure 9.3 dBASE IV screen display showing control centre and drop-down menu

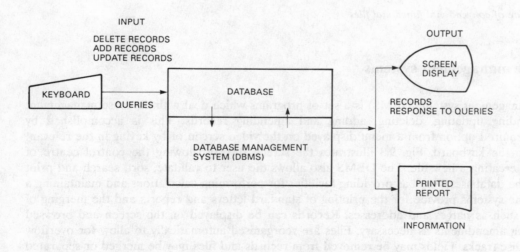

Figure 9.4 Outline of database functions

9.4 Access and security issues

File security is provided for as database systems automatically save files at the end of processing and also make back-up copies of disc files. Elaborate security and privacy checks may require to be incorporated in a database to prevent unauthorised access to the system. Some personnel may be barred from the system as a whole or be given restricted access to specific parts of the database. Some databases require entry of a user name before allowing access and also a password for sensitive or restricted information. Each information owner needs to specify those user names allowed access to that owner's data. A list is also required of other information owners who can view but not alter records in the database. Non-sensitive information may be made available to any user by adding this fact to the user name access list. The DBMS checks a user name with the parts of the database the user requires to access and only if the user name is on the list will access be allowed. Names and/or passwords are not displayed on the video screen when keyed in, so preventing unauthorised users obtaining possession of them.

9.5 Database query systems

A natural English language database query and retrieval system is used for query and *ad hoc* reporting. It provides easy and instant access to information by retrieving the data, computing and presenting the information in a sophisticated columnar display on the video screen. This type of system requires English conversion of the data dictionary describing the database into a lexicon which lists alphabetically all the words and phrases used. The lexicon is used for reference purpose during the processing of natural language queries. This type of query language responds to questions phrased in the following way, for example: 'How many cars of each model did we sell last week compared to target?'

The system will retrieve from the database the target and actual sales for each model and display them on the screen together with the actual and planned sales and percentage deviation from the planned sales for each model.

9.6 Fourth generation languages

Fourth generation languages are designed to assist the manipulation of a database by way of a query language providing facilities for creating, retrieving, updating, appending, deleting or amending data. The query language is an element of the DBMS. When designed to access a database from a terminal keyboard it is classified as an *interactive query language*. Figure 9.5 illustrates a screen display showing the structure of a query in the condition box. In this instance, items costing more than £2,000 require to be retrieved from the database.

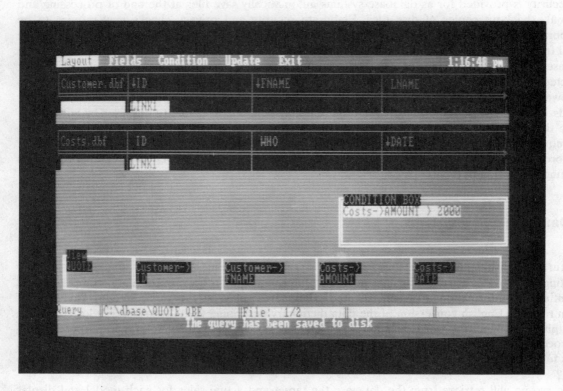

Figure 9.5 dBASE IV screen showing queries

The primary purpose of query languages is to provide non-computer specialists in the various business functions (the *end-users*) with the means to do their own information processing without having to become programming experts. A fourth generation language translates the user's requests into procedural steps to produce the desired output. In this way user views of an application are separated from the mechanics of the system — the end result is important to the user, not how it is accomplished. Fourth generation languages enable personnel changing from clerical to computerised database applications to understand the new working procedures more easily. For example, a database may contain a plant register of machines located in the factory, which includes fields (items of information) for machine type, cost, location, depreciation and book value. If the cost of a particular class of machine is required the query language allows the question to be asked in the following way:

LIST COST, MACHINE, FOR MACHINE = 'PROFILER'

This is interpreted by the database management system as: List the cost of the machine type 'Profiler'. The response provides the record number containing the specific machine and its cost as follows:

00005 8500 PROFILER

This means that the cost of the machine 'Profiler' is £8,500. (*See* also 9.10.3.)

9.7 Searching

A database has *searching facilities* ranging from limited searches on keywords to full text searching. This facility provides the means of extracting from a large volume of data useful facts which could not possibly be found by physical search methods in sufficient time to make a decision. Database commands are becoming increasingly powerful and the application of natural language database query systems is increasing, so greatly assisting users to find the information they are seeking.

9.8 Database applications

Internal private databases may be used for many and varied applications, such as the storage of asset records, which allows acquisitions and disposals to be added to and deleted from the database very easily. The database also facilitates the modification of records when plant and machinery is moved to new locations. Asset schedules may also be printed out for accounting and administrative needs. For instance, it is possible to print a report of assets nearing the end of their useful life as a basis for plant replacement.

Personnel records may be similarly stored and processed which greatly assists their administration as it is an easy matter to add new employees and delete terminations from the database. A personnel database also allows transfers between departments to be speedily recorded and information to be retrieved in respect of employees with specific attributes, such as number of years' service, which will be required for the grant of long-service awards. Order processing systems are simplified as a database can store customer, order and product records which may be cross-referenced for processing purposes. The records in the database may be network, hierarchical or relationally structured, as shown by Figs 9.6, 9.8 and 9.11.

9.9 Data dictionaries

A data dictionary contains details of the data in a database including definitions of each record type, the programs which use the data and its purpose. It may also cover the relationship of data elements, including functional dependencies as well as their format and size, i.e. the minimum, maximum and average number of characters. The dictionary assists in the design of a database and in reducing the level of redundancy to a necessary minimum; it also avoids duplication of data elements and makes for easier identification of *synonyms* (data groups having more than one name) and *homonyms* (one name for several data groups). Details of data structures may also be incorporated in the dictionary outlining the way in which data is grouped.

9.10 Organisation and processing methods

9.10.1 Network structure

This type of database has a complex structure, resembling the logical data relationships existing in the real world of business. It is structured around the concept of a set which is a relationship between two record types, e.g. a customer's order and an order item (*see* Fig. 9.6). An 'owner' of a set, e.g. a customer's order, can have a number of 'members', i.e. order items. A record type may be a member of several sets, an owner of several sets or a member of one set and owner of another.

Sets can be incorporated without members or without owners, for example when new product details are introduced before orders are placed or new employee details are recorded in the database prior to the first pay day. They are known as a memberless sets.

The network defines the route through the database but the user must know what linkages have been established in the database in order to be aware of the basis for data retrieval. Links between records are established through the user of pointers; a customer record can point to several order records which relate to it. Pointers inform the DBMS where the logical record is located. The next record is indicated by a 'next' pointer. Within any occurrence in a set the route to be traversed is to read the 'owner' and then access the 'members' sequentially, eventually returning to the 'owner'. It is not possible to proceed directly from the 'owner' to any specific 'member', but only via all the 'members' consecutively until the required one is reached (*see* Fig. 9.7). This is accomplished by *next* and *prior* pointers. Deletions are achieved by destroying the pointers which access a record. The links between the records on either side of the one deleted are maintained by the DBMS. Records are inserted by the DBMS, which locates the relevant 'set' and enters the record in the most appropriate place. Data integrity is assured by an *integrity check* utility which checks the pointers and links to ensure that sets are closed, for instance.

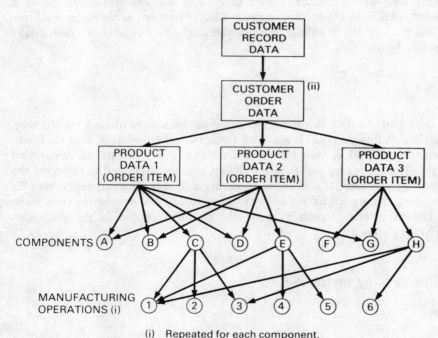

(i) Repeated for each component.
(ii) Repeated for each customer's order.

Figure 9.6 Network structure

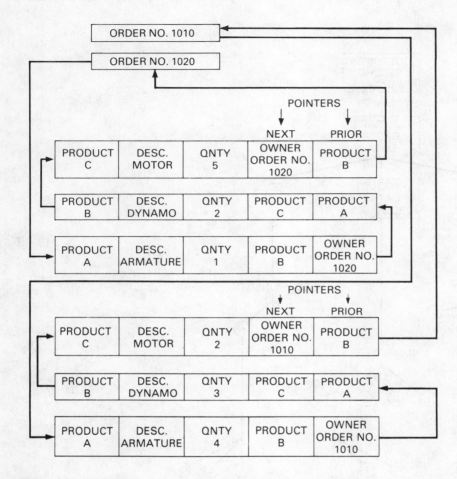

Figure 9.7 Route through network illustrating next and prior pointers

9.10.2 Hierarchical structure

A hierarchical structure takes the form of an inverted tree structure consisting of the main trunk from which stem main branches and which in turn have smaller branches (sub-branches) emanating from them. The structure of the hierarchy determines the record types needed and the amount of redundancy required. In the case of customer's orders, each customer may have several orders consisting of the same product details (the product details would need to be repeated in the database for each order (*see* Fig. 9.8). In addition, the structure outlined in Fig. 9.8 would be required for each customer. The hierarchy defines the route through the database. Access starts at the top and proceeds downwards through the hierarchical structure. Each element may be related to any number of elements at any level below it but only one element above it. One of the problems of this type of structure is that cross-linkages are not catered for. In respect of a sales office, for instance, it would need to know the items ordered by each customer as shown in Figs 9.9 and 9.10. The production control function, on the other hand, needs to know the total quantity of each product ordered from all customers because any order from any customer can consist of any one of the range of products. To obtain this information the whole database would need to be searched. The type of structure required to allow for the production of manufacturing schedules and purchasing requirements is outlined in Fig. 9.8.

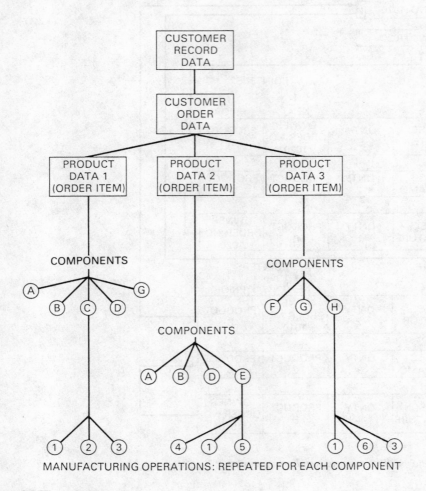

Figure 9.8 Hierarchical structure

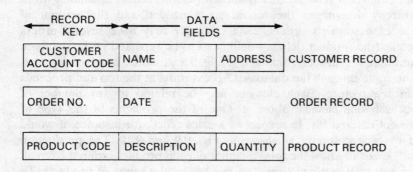

Figure 9.9 Sales order records

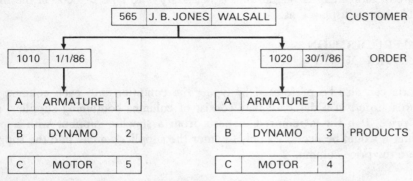

CUSTOMER

ORDER

PRODUCTS

(i)   The product record is repeated for each order from the same customer.

(ii) The complete structure is repeated for each order for every customer.

(iii) This structure summarises the requirements of each order.

Figure 9.10 Sales order hierarchical structure

9.10.3 Relational

A database may be designed on the basis of what are referred to as *relations*, which are two-dimensional tables of data consisting of columns and rows. A 'relation' is also known as an *entity* or *record*. The columns, which must be uniquely identified by a field name, are generally known as data elements or attributes as well as fields. They store data containing values relating to a particular relation which may be a customer, stock item or employee record. Relational data analysis describes a relation by listing its columns. A customer relation contains data categories (columns) called 'Customer number' and 'Customer name' etc. An employee relation contains categories called 'Employee number' and 'Employee name', and so on. Each row in a table contains one record relating to a specific occurrence of an entity, which is referred to as a *tuple*. Thus Atkinson, James, Smith and Brown are all occurrences of the employee entity. This is analogous to records in a file where the file is comparable to a table of relations and the fields are comparable to the columns. Links between tables are maintained by repeated fields.

Figure 9.11 outlines a number of the features of a relational database discussed above. It portrays two relations, 'cars' and 'servicing'. A link may be established between the two relations by the repeating fields 'model' and 'reg(istration) number'. By means of a query language it is possible to access data from the database in respect of the various models in relation to initial cost, servicing cost, date of servicing and the function to which the car is allocated. For example, a query to retrieve information relating to which function a particular model of car is allocated may be phrased as LIST FUNCTION, FOR MODEL = 'SIERRA': the response would be ACCOUNTS SIERRA. A list of the registration numbers of each model can be obtained by phrasing a query as, for instance, LIST REGNO, MODEL. The screen would then display:

E255 REA METRO
B360 BEA CAPRI
D890 CEE SIERRA
C450 DAC CHERRY
A125 JAG ESCORT

Some databases provide the technique of 'query by example' so that the need to learn a formal query language to retrieve data is dispensed with. To enter a query it is necessary to press an 'Enter query' function key and type the selection criteria into the appropriate columns. For example, to obtain a list of cars which cost more than £6,000 all that is necessary is to type > 6000 in the initial cost column. The list would then be displayed as:

CAPRI B360 BEA 6500 PRODUCTION
SIERRA D890 CEE 7500 ACCOUNTS

Multiple selection criteria can also be performed by typing the condition into each column. For example, purchasing records stored in a database may consist of columns containing supplier, part number, description and price. If a list is required of parts from a specific supplier with a price greater than a stated amount it would be necessary only to enter the supplier's name into the supplier column and the amount into the price column.

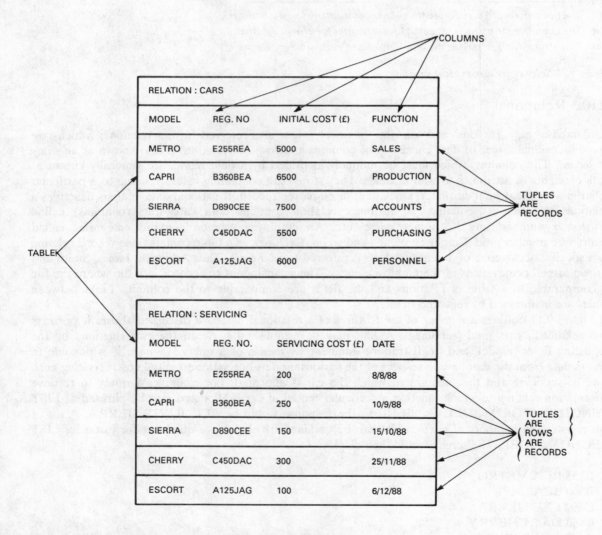

Figure 9.11 Two dimensional relational tables: cars and servicing

9.11 Schemas and sub-schemas

9.11.1 Schemas

A schema refers to the whole structure of a database. It shows the interrelationships between all database records. If a company has developed a company wide database then the schema would represent the data model of the whole organisation. The schema is stored in a computer file and referenced by the database management system (*see* 9.3). Some database management systems hold the schema of the database in the data dictionary (*see* 9.9), others refer to it as being separate from the data dictionary.

9.11.2 Sub-schemas or *user views*

Sub-sets of the schema, known as sub-schemas, provide access to specific data by particular programs. The stock control department, for example, will be denied access to payroll data; the payroll department will have access and authority to update it and the personnel department will have authority to access payroll data but not to update it. The sub-schema concept provides for efficient control of data which facilitates data security. Moreover, in some implementations, the software necessary to compile schemas is not available to application programmers. This is primarily to maintain privacy as the ability to compile schemas provides the means of bypassing privacy checks.

9.12 Device independence (logical and physical concepts)

Individual users of specific applications still define files but the file has become a *logical* rather than a *physical* entity. Users cannot identify their physical functional file as being on a specific physical disc as was the case with separately structured files. This is because the logical data needs of every function are stored in the sub-schemas. Programs and files are not dependent upon the hardware used to hold the various files. If a file is transferred from one disc type to another, necessitating amendments to block length, then this can be accomplished without reprogramming. Logical entities are derived from physical entities by means of database software. (*See* Fig. 9.12.)

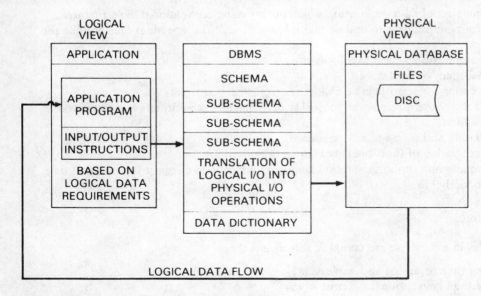

Figure 9.12 Relationship of logical and physical data

9.13 Data independence

Data is stored so as to achieve independence from the programs which use the data. Physical data formats may change without affecting programs as the physical format of the data is held separately (*see* data dictionaries) and not contained in the programs, as it is for conventional processing. Because of this, programmers are not concerned with the size of data items or the way in which a data item is physically stored. It is necessary only to state the records to be accessed and the DBMS presents these. If any fields are changed the only programs that will need to be amended are those that access the specific field. Under DBMS if another field is to be added to a record with data independence, only those programs which actually use the field will need to be recompiled. The operating system refers to a physical file on a specific disc but, because of the facility of data independence, this may be changed without affecting the application software using the data.

It is important to appreciate, however, that if a data structure changes this will affect the relationship between records, and the way a program navigates around the database will require modification. If, for instance, the existing *order-item* record in the database contains the part number, then an on-line enquiry about a specific part number will generate a list of *all* current order-items for that part. However, if the part number is removed from the *order-item* record and located in a *part* record, then this new structure will require access to the *owner* of the part-order set, i.e. the part record, to obtain details of order-items (members) in the part-order set. All existing programs which access order-items via the order-item set will have to be modified so that they can obtain access to the owner of the part-order set and so identify the part being ordered. This process necessitates the insertion into the programs of additional database calls (DML statements). This example indicates the importance of effective data modelling and normalisation to reduce such complex structural changes after implementation.

9.14 Summarising the advantages and disadvantages of a database

9.14.1 Advantages

(a) Reduces the amount of data duplication which occurs using conventional file structures.
(b) Avoids duplicating input data to update multiple functionally independent files holding the same data.
(c) Provides fast and flexible access to information.
(d) Improves consistency of data stored.
(e) Reduces processing for retrospective changes.
(f) Because of all the above advantages the quality of management information is improved thoughout the organisation.
(g) Provides both data and program independence.
(h) Encourages integration of functional areas in an organisation.
(i) Offers useful query and report generation languages which help to offset the cost and time disadvantages mentioned below.

9.14.2 Disadvantages

(a) Data structures in a database are complex, this means they:

    (i) take a long time to design and implement;
    (ii) cost more than conventional systems;
    (iii) require high calibre, experienced and specialised personnel.

In general, however, database solutions can be cost justified when compared with non-database solutions.

9.15 Public databases

Most public databases are accessed via the packet switch stream (PSS) network, which allows users to access distant databases more economically. The hardware and software needed for accessing and retrieving information from a database include a terminal and a modem or acoustic coupler for connecting the terminal to the telephone line. When the number of the host computer is dialled the user is connected to the database. The two data transmission speeds in common use are 300 and 1200 baud. In most cases software is located at the host computer but there are instances when the user will need to obtain software to enable microcomputers to act as terminals. Some database hosts make quite high minimum charges and these should be considered in the context of the level of use to be made of a specific database. In addition, an hourly usage charge, which can be in the region of £30–70, is made, and a charge for each record printed. The cost of telephone calls or British Telecom's PSS charges must also be taken into account. The latter include an initial fee and a quarterly rental for each network user identity, i.e. password into the system. Quarterly usage charges appear on telephone bills based on usage, data volume, call duration and port holding, i.e. an hourly charge for keeping a channel connection open. Finally, there will be the purchase or rental costs of modems or acoustic couplers, the software required and general administration expenses.

Public databases such as Prestel provide valuable business information on matters such as share prices, travel information, the weather, and general information relevant to business: finance, economics, engineering, technology and sciences, etc. Some databases are accessible only by closed user groups, known as CLUGS.

The data in a database is supplied by an *information provider*. A database *host* is the organisation which owns the computer system supporting the database supplied by the information provider for access by *information users* who subscribe to the database (*see* Fig. 9.13). Some databases may be exclusive to one host or available from several.

Information retrieval from databases is facilitated by on-line terminals (*see* Fig. 9.4) from such sources as *The Financial Times*, the Bank of England, the IMF and the UK Treasury. Prestel acts as host to many information providers offering a wide range of information relating to many subjects. New databases are continuously added, details of which are published in the Prestel Directory. It is a source of on-line information but is not an information provider in its own right.

9.16 Prestel

9.16.1 Viewdata

Prestel is a viewdata system operating over telephone lines unlike the BBC Ceefax and IBA Oracle teletext services, which broadcast information in the same way as television programmes. Information is displayed on a television screen for both teletext and viewdata system.

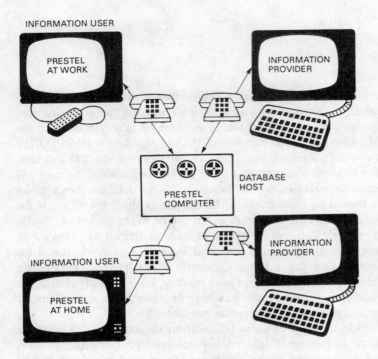

Figure 9.13 Outline of the Prestel viewdata system

9.16.2 Information providers

The information on Prestel is supplied by many independent organisations which rent pages from British Telecom. Some, such as the Consumers Association with its Prestel version of *Which?* and Viewtel 202 with its electronic newspaper, offer information of interest to the general public. Others provide services aimed at particular groups or organisations, e.g. travel agencies.

Many information providers direct their information to the business world as a whole. *The Financial Times*, for example, through its subsidiary Fintel provides a comprehensive range of business news, company information and economic analysis as well as many specialised financial services. *The Economist* concentrates on key statistics for businessmen and an analysis of current events. The Stock Exchange has a direct link from its own computer to provide updates of share prices several times each day. Other organisations providing business information include American Express, the Central Statistical Office, Datastream, Dow Jones, Dun and Bradstreet and the *Wall Street Journal.* There are over 250 tour operators, ferry companies and airlines on Prestel detailing fares, timetables and up-to-date availability, thus saving agents valuable time and money on long telephone calls and improving their service to clients. Most travel information is available to all Prestel users and can be invaluable when planning holidays and business trips.

9.16.3 Interactive system

Prestel is a two-way interactive system enabling the user and Prestel computer to conduct two-way communications, unlike the teletext services which simply transmit information to viewers who are unable to respond interactively. Prestel enables users to send messages to one another on a special computer, and to information providers using *response pages*, which allow the user to order goods, book hotel rooms, reserve theatre seats and perform home banking. Sales representatives away from the office or working at home can transmit their orders directly to the office over telephone lines. Businesses can also set up private information networks on private Prestel, restricting their pages to selected users.

9.16.4 Computer network

The Prestel computer network covers the major population centres. It consists of seven computers, six for subscribers and one for information providers for entering and updating information. The network is star-shaped; each computer stores identical information and amendments are distributed automatically to each computer in the network by high speed links.

9.16.5 Other Prestel services

By means of gateways, private computers can be connected to Prestel sets via Prestel computers. This makes possible such services as Skytrack for airline reservations, Homelink for home banking, Homeview for estate agents and Viewtrade for used cars. Prestel also provides an education service for schools and private Prestel for closed user groups.

9.16.6 CitiService

Prestel CitiService (*see* Fig. 9.14) provides up-to-the-minute information from the world's financial centres for investment advisers, commodity traders and financial decision makers. Stock market and commodity prices, foreign exchange and interest rates, unit trust prices and business and financial news and analysis are continuously updated. The service is a joint venture between Prestel and ICV Information Systems. The latest development is a London Stock Exchange prices service, which provides a continuous update facility. An interactive system known as Tax Manager enables tax computations to be performed at home on the TV screen. This service costs £2.50 for each use. Other personal financial planning services envisaged include pensions management and an annuities package.

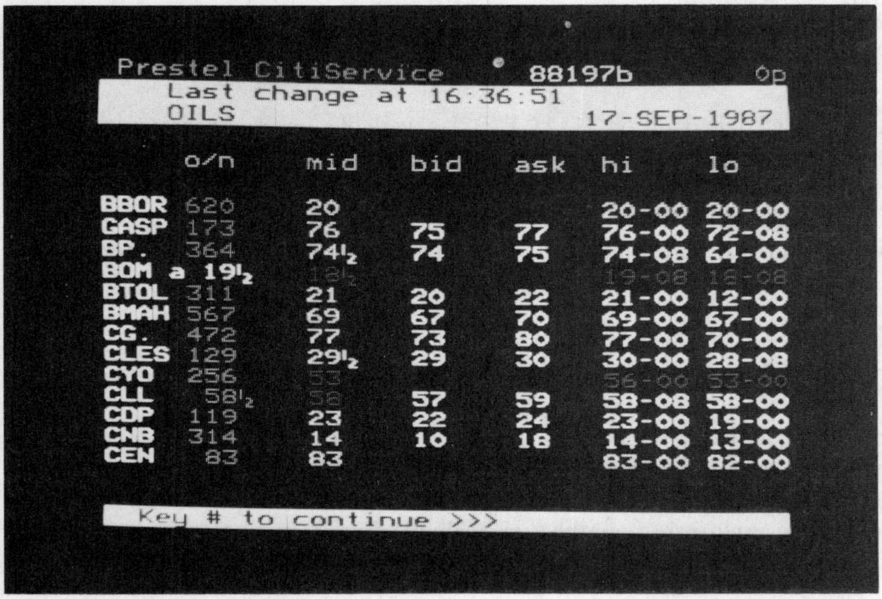

Figure 9.14 Prestel screen, city information

9.17 Full-text services

Full-text services now provide complete documents instead of abstracts. Datasolve's World Reporter provides the full text of the *Guardian*, *Washington Post* and *The Economist*. A full-text service for lawyers is provided by Lexis, consisting of a file of legal cases relevant to the UK, USA and France. The database can be searched in a variety of ways to obtain information in respect of precedents and so on.

9.18 Accounting databases

Accounting databases being developed by the English ICA include one containing the complete financial statements of the top 1,000 public companies and building societies. It also includes statements of standard accounting practice and accounting recommendations, international accounting standards, auditing guidelines, exposure drafts and so on. Further developments include a database containing regulatory material produced by the Stock Exchange, the Bank of England, the Council of Lloyd's and other major regulatory authorities in connection with accounting or reporting requirements and the like.

An extremely useful ICA publication is *Accountants Digest 166: On-line Information Retrieval Systems — A Guide for Accountants*.

9.19 British Standards Institution public database

The British Standards Institution has a public database which embraces all current British standards. The database is stored on an external host computer directly accessed by means of a telephone line and a terminal. It provides instant responses to questions and operates interactively on matters such as newly introduced standards, amendments to standards, revisions and specifications.

9.20 Official Airline Guide Electronic Edition

The Official Airline Guide Electronic Edition (OAGEE) is available on Telecom Gold. It is a fare-based, unbiased airline flight-information system available 24 hours each day. It contains schedules of both direct and connecting services of over 750 airlines worldwide, and details of 350,000 North American fares updated daily, 60,000 international fares updated weekly, fare price comparisons and departure and arrival times. Other details include airline and flight number, journey time, aircraft type, meal service and the number of stops.

9.21 International databases

Databases are not restricted to national boundaries. In the USA and many European countries, including West Germany, Switzerland, Denmark and Luxembourg, many contain information of international interest. To gain access, subscribers need only dial the specific telephone number of the database. Some databases may be exclusive to one host or available from several. Some services allow the user to take screen dumps of the information directly, others send copies for a stated fee.

Review questions

1   What is a database?

2   Outline the nature of database functions.

3   What is a database management system (DBMS)?

4   What back-up facilities are provided by databases?

5   What is a password and what purpose does it serve?

6   What is a database query system?

7   What is the objective of fourth generation languages?

8   Outline the features of two database applications.

9   What details are stored in a data dictionary?

10   Specify three types of database structure.

11   What are schemas and sub-schemas?

12   Summarise the advantages and disadvantages of a database.

13   What is the value of a public database such as Prestel?

14   Who are information providers?

10 Expert systems

10.1 Introduction

Expert systems, or knowledge-based systems, are increasingly being applied in business and will undoubtedly become a predominant feature of information systems and form part of normal computerised accounting systems in the near future. This is due to their value in providing expert knowledge to non-experts. A user of an expert system sits at a PC (microcomputer) and by means of a keyboard asks the system questions. The system responds by displaying answers on the video screen under the control of software for the particular branch of knowledge, for example the procedure for granting loans to employees or perhaps VAT regulations. This chapter deals with some of the technical aspects of expert systems indicating the underlying concepts and how they function (*see* Fig. 10.1).

10.2 Features of expert systems

10.2.1 Expert systems are knowledge-based systems

Expert systems belong to the branch of information technology know as knowledge-based systems (KBS), which themselves form part of that branch of knowledge relating to artificial intelligence. They may be defined as computerised systems which simulate human knowledge by making deductions from given facts using the rules of logical inference. Boolean algebra is used to define the logic of a problem based on two possible values — true and false — represented by the binary values 1 for true (yes) and 0 for false (no). This will become clear later in the text. Expert systems may be used on a stand-alone basis or be embedded into routine accounting applications. An expert system consists of three primary elements:

(a) an *inference engine* which acts as a rule interpreter;
(b) a *knowledge base* which stores the specialised knowledge of human experts in the form of rules;
(c) a *database* containing facts relating to the status of a system of a particular subject (*see* Fig. 10.1).

Inferencing is the process of reaching a solution or decision by reasoning. An inference engine functions in combination with the knowledge base, and is a program that directs the search for knowledge and determines the sources required for input: responses to questions from users, databases or spreadsheets to infer a conclusion to a problem. The knowledge base stores knowledge of a specific subject in the form of rules consisting of facts and relationships (*see* 10.1). The inference engine questions the user and interprets the rules of relationship. It matches rules in the knowledge base with the information in the database. As each rule is examined and fired the resulting actions may amend the content of the database which changes the status of the problem. The inference engine can communicate with the existing corporate database, programs or files in the process of seeking its goal.

The initial conditions of the problem to be solved are stored in the database from which the starting point of the search process is derived. It may ask questions of the user, to which answers are typed in, or display options in a menu from which the user can select the one required. In effect the database is part of the working memory storing information relating to the current status of the problem being solved which may be altered by the inferencing process as stated above. Initially, known facts are stored in the database and new facts are added as they are generated by the inference process.

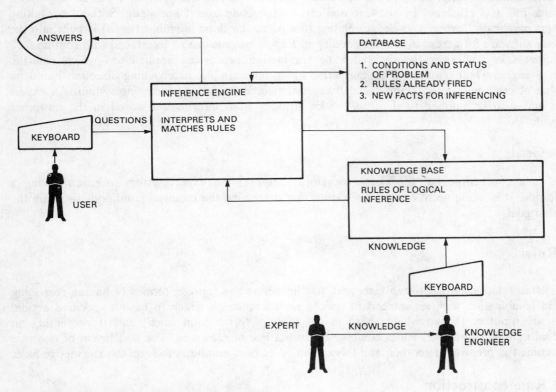

Figure 10.1 Elements of a knowledge-based system

10.2.2 Collecting knowledge

The development of expert systems requires a high degree of coordination between researchers, sometimes referred to as *knowledge engineers*, and experts on a defined subject, known as *domain experts*. The experts are interviewed by researchers to assess ways of collecting and transferring their knowledge into knowledge-based computerised systems. This requires an evaluation of how experts analyse a problem. Structuring the volume of details collected from the experts is a major problem as there are many cause and effect relationships, one leading to another in what at times appears a never-ending uncoordinated stream. Some interviewers attempt to remedy the lack of structure by carefully planning the questions to be asked during interviews to avoid possible omission of important facts, but knowledge does not flow from the mind of the expert in such a structured form. During interviews it is practical to record facts on a tape recorder for future analysis. This limits the amount of written detail required, so saving time and minimising any problems of hurried notes later proving illegible.

10.2.3 Applications

Everyone in an organisation can be provided with expert knowledge, obtained from experts, by sitting at the keyboard of a small business computer using the expert system for the particular subject about which knowledge is required. The system asks the user questions as a means of obtaining information on which to base an answer by the process of inferencing from inbuilt rules. Expert systems can be designed to provide details of company procedural and policy matters such as granting credit to customers, handling customers' orders, computing corporation tax, and granting loans to employees. This aids business efficiency by allowing non-experts to obtain expert knowledge without consulting an expert personally. Expert knowledge relating to a particular domain (subject area) is built into the computer software for access by anyone needing it. Expert systems can be interfaced with routine data processing tasks performed by the batch or transaction processing applications which call the inference engine when required. This may arise when, for example, determining discount, based on the value of customers' orders and the delivery distance, in an order processing system. An expert system may also be applied to determine sales strategy from information stored in the customer history file.

10.2.4 Goals

A goal is a conclusion that the system developer requires the expert system to reach during a consultation. It is made up of one or more rules that determine the required conditions to attain the stipulated goal.

10.3 Rules

Rules define relationships between facts and may be defined as representations of human reasoning which in combination with an antecedent specify an inference on which to base a specified action. Details are input to the knowledge base in the form of 'production rules', each representing an individual item of knowledge. Rules combine to form a line of reasoning. The conclusion of one rule may become the premise of another, and this collection of rules combines to form the knowledge base.

10.3.1 Rule construction

Each production rule consist of two parts:

(a) the left-hand side contains an IF clause consisting of a premise or condition;
(b) the right-hand side contains a THEN clause consisting of a conclusion, action or consequence.

If the premises in a rule are true or the condition is met, the right-hand part is also true. The rule is then 'triggered'. When the right-hand side of the rule is implemented it is said to be *fired*. This process consists of taking a specified action when specific situations are true on the basis that: IF A is true AND B is true THEN do a stated action

Production rules are useful for representing all types of knowledge for attaining goals (*see* 10.2.4). Every rule has one IF clause and one THEN clause. A clause is similar to a sentence with a subject, a verb and an object that states some fact. Most commercial systems apply the IF–THEN format. Such rules can be defined applying the technique of structured English as demonstrated in the following examples.

Example 1
Rule contains an IF and THEN clause:
   IF the quantity in stock is equal to the reorder level THEN place an order to replenish supplies.

Example 2
Rule contains an IF, THEN, ELSE clause:
   IF the order quantity is greater than 1,000 THEN provide a discount of 5 per cent ELSE provide a discount of 2 per cent.

Example 3
Rule contains an IF, AND, THEN clause:
   IF the volume of production is less than 50,000 units AND the production cost per unit is greater than £5 THEN do not pay bonus.

Example 4
Rule contains an IF, OR, THEN clause:
   IF the volume of production is greater than 50,000 units OR the production cost per unit is less than £5 THEN pay a bonus of 6 per cent.

10.3.2 Rule amendments

Rules may be amended if they prove to be ambiguous or inaccurate. The integrity of the knowledge base depends upon the accuracy of the knowledge it contains and the degree to which it relates to current circumstances. Some business systems frequently modify the control parameters in order to cope with changing circumstances such as the level of demand for items supplied from warehouse stock, the credit limit and credit period given to customers, or amendments to the value of goods sold to customers as a basis for applying variable discount rates based on sales value.

10.4 Help, why and how facilities

An expert system provides a help facility to provide the user with assistance on questions, goals and rules to establish an understanding of the nature of the system. The 'why' facility explains why a question is being asked, the 'how' facility how a particular conclusion was arrived at. A user may not understand or even agree with an answer provided by an expert system and, in such instances, will want to know how the system arrived at its conclusion. The system may do this by displaying the rules which formed the basis of the conclusion and the sequence in which they were dealt with from details stored in the database. In this way the user can assess the line of reasoning by going through the rules sequentially, assessing the logic inferences at each stage of assessment (*see* Fig. 10.1). Some systems incorporate explanatory statements in the rule which may be studied by the user. This is an important facility because it provides confidence in the system, which is essential for making important decisions based on the conclusions provided.

10.5 Adaptive learning

Knowledge-based systems learn from their own experience because, during the course of processing, the inference engine makes conclusions which generate new knowledge. Newly generated knowledge is stored in the database, which can create a new rule to be applied to future use. Learning in this context may be defined as the process of teaching the system new knowledge by the addition of new rules or the amendment of existing rules.

10.6 Dealing with uncertainty

10.6.1 Imprecise facts or unknown facts

Knowledge-based systems are able to deal with incomplete or uncertain details relating to a problem. When the system displays a question on the screen the user may not have a precise answer or any answer at all. Knowledge-based systems are designed to deal with this situation and will provide a solution even though an input is missing or ambiguous. In such instances they may qualify the answer given based on the available facts. This situation can sometimes be catered for by including rules which apply when information is not known and trigger a specific action. Business decisions are often made in the absence of complete facts so a knowledge-based system in such instances emulates the real-world situation. Normal programs are structured on an algorithmic basis whereby instructions consist of a series of IF–THEN–ELSE statements as previously illustrated.

10.6.2 Certainty factors

The degree of certainty of a condition occurring is determined by the domain knowledge expert who may assess it from experience, published statistics such as the probability of male smokers dying from cancer below the age of 60, or the number of days in a year that it rained or snowed and so on. In other instances the degree of certainty may be assessed by pure guesstimating. Certainty or confidence factors are used with the IF and THEN elements of a rule. The degree of certainty may be based on a scale of 0 to 1 where 0 represents no certainty at all, i.e. 100 per cent uncertainty, and 1 represents 100 per cent certainty. Other intermediate degrees of certainty can be established from the scale. The inference engine decides if a specific rule is to be fired on the basis of its evaluation of the confidence factor, which may require to be above a predefined value.

10.7 Fuzzy logic

Fuzzy logic may be applied when attempting, say, to define high or low production volume. What is a high volume and what is a low volume? This depends upon the normal achievements of the business: low volume of a large business may equal high volume of a small business, for instance. Volume must be specific to particular situations and a range of values must be given to which high volume applies. 'Low volume' must be given a different range of values. The derived values must be accompanied by a relevant probability factor. In such instances a 0 possibility means that volume is not in the range given but a possibility of 1 implies that volume is within the range of values.

Fuzzy logic is a means of dealing with unreliable or perhaps imprecise data of this nature. The method attempts to allocate a value between 0 and 1 to imprecisely defined attributes. An assigned value between 0 and 1 signifies some degree of possibility that an attribute is within a given range. This approach facilitates the reasoning process but is not so widely used as confidence factors.

10.8 *Modus operandi*

10.8.1 Backward and forward chaining

A knowledge-based system can work in either of two ways: by working backwards through supporting evidence to establish the truth of a previously selected conclusion by applying backward chaining, or by forward chaining which commences with appraising the evidence as a basis for selecting a goal. Declarative languages such as Prolog and Lisp are used to describe the relationships between data.

10.9 Development tools

10.9.1 Software for building knowledge-based systems

Software for building knowledge-based systems is available from software houses specialising in this branch of artificial intelligence. This type of software is known as a *shell, generator* or *builder*. A shell provides a basic framework in which data, rules or knowledge can be input and processed. A shell does not contain a knowledge base but provides facilities for its creation for specific subject areas. Some packages allow rules to be typed in as notes or full sentences and do not require syntax, a rule language or compilation. A dictionary can be used to copy and select rules. Full-text and graphic screens can be used to illustrate answers, advice or questions. Logical operators can be used in any combination at any level of the structure. Some software has a menu interface and facilities for linking with other software for mathematical computations or to a natural language processor, for instance. Some software provides for an alphabetical listing of all the rules in the system together with each piece of evidence and text, with cross-references. The evidence behind any conclusion is explained as is the reasoning behind any question, which allows the user to explore or navigate the entire logic of the system.

10.9.2. Languages

The most popular languages for developing knowledge-based systems are Lisp and Prolog, both designed for artificial intelligence applications. Systems have been developed using many different languages, including BASIC, Fortran, C, Forth and Pascal. Assembly language is also used which reduces the amount of code required compared with the high level languages mentioned above.

Expert programmers may elect to develop knowledge-based systems using these languages but it is often preferable to use expert system shells as discussed above.

Review questions

1   What is an expert system (knowledge-based system (KBS))?

2   Specify the elemental structure of an expert system.

3   What is a knowledge engineer?

4   What applications may beneficially use an expert system for the solution of problems?

5   What is a goal in the context of a KBS?

6 What is the significance of rules in a KBS?

7 What is fuzzy logic?

Self-test question

10.1 What is an expert system? State its purpose and its elemental structure.

Answers on pages 371–72.

11 Office automation

11.1 Introduction

Office automation is in fact a synonym for information technology. The topic is considered to be of paramount importance, being the catalyst for all other topics in this section and has accordingly been dealt with as the main topic leading to other related topics falling under the office automation umbrella.

On the question of implementing office automation, management needs to adopt an overall corporate integrative strategy taking into account all functional considerations regarding its information technology (IT) requirements. IT should be viewed globally, not in a fragmented manner with functional aspects dealt with in isolation. It is necessary to coordinate functional activities to achieve corporate harmony and overall effectiveness. This means doing the right things, in the right way, at the right time and this cannot be better achieved than by the correct blend of office automation particularly in the use of networks which physically link functions for data interchange. In the past, large computers were installed for high volume data processing tasks operating as stand-alone centralised systems. A computer must no longer be viewed merely as a high powered number cruncher but as the central node of a communications command centre serving the needs of the whole business by a corporate database. Businesses now tend to be 'information organisations' shunting information around the business in order to maintain its equilibrium in pursuit of profitable opportunities to maintain or increase corporate profitability. Nowadays PCs can be linked to the telephone network for transmitting data to other PCs; the telephone can also be connected to national or international telex and fax services and to on-line financial information services, providing the basis of a fully integrated office system. It is imperative that businesses recognise this situation because improved information flows are an essential requirement to the road to success.

11.2 Convergence of electronic technology

Information technology is an all-embracing term incorporating office automation, which is the process of applying electronic technology for increasing the level of productivity in the performance of administrative activities and in the provision of information to all parts of the business. Information technology may therefore be considered to be the harnessing of electronic technology in its various forms to improve the operations and profitability of the business as a whole. The term 'convergence' is often used to describe the merging of electronic technology including the application of PCs for electronic processing and storage of information; the application of spreadsheets and business modelling packages to assist office managers, production managers, stock controllers and accountants in solving business problems and as aids to making effective decisions; word processing for preparing standard reports and other correspondence efficiently and at high speed; electronic mail for transmitting messages from one office or site to another, without the use of paper, by means of a local area network (LAN) or wide area network connecting the personal computers of the various users to one another; and the use of databases for the effective storage, processing and retrieval of data in a form suitable for the purpose to which it is to be applied. (*See* Figs. 11.1 and 11.2.)

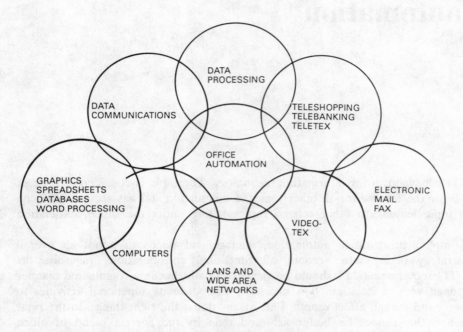

Figure 11.1 Convergence of electronic technology

Figure 11.2 Electronic office

11.3 On-line information systems

Office automation also incorporates on-line information systems such as British Telecom's Prestel or private internal viewdata systems such as ICL's Bulletin. These are interactive systems which enable users to book hotel accommodation or order goods at a supermarket by means of a keypad. Office automation also includes distributed processing, whereby the various operating units of a business are equipped with their own computing facilities which are connected to other operating units by a network. This arrangement allows the interchange of information between different parts of an organisation while sharing central resources such as a database supported by a mainframe computer, high capacity storage devices and high speed printing facilities (*see* 16.10). The technology also includes the use of message switching and digital PABX facilitating both voice and data transmission as well as electronic printing equipment.

11.4 Historical aspects of office automation

The philosophy of the electronic office was first adopted in 1947 by J. Lyons, the British catering company, when the viability of applying computers to office activities was discussed. As a result of these deliberations not only did the company apply computers to its office routines and procedures but it built its own computer for the task. The computer was known as 'LEO', an acronym for Lyons Electronic Office, which became operational in 1951. Businesses must respond to change to remain economically viable, or even survive, in the highly competitive business arena. Electronic technology enables business activities to be conducted in the most efficient manner, reducing the time for information to flow to the various parts of an organisation, often by providing computing power wherever it is most needed in the organisation. Businesses are very vulnerable to competition, and the use of up-to-date machines, equipment, methods and techniques is one factor enabling them to ward off threats from that quarter. Information technology comes to the fore in allowing business operations to be conducted using the most up-to-date methods to suit the circumstances.

11.5 Automation

11.5.1 Automation and information technology

It is not possible to discuss the subject of information technology without considering the nature of automation. The term *automation* is often used to describe the mechanisation of industrial operations and processes, i.e. machines are used to a greater extent than people. The same principles apply to office activities and machines are being used more and more to reduce the ratio of administrative costs to manufacturing costs as well as to improve the level of efficiency. Automation increases the level of productivity by achieving greater outputs of high quality at a lower cost than was possible using outmoded methods and techniques. This enables individual businesses to be more competitive, particularly overseas, which is essential for the country to attain a healthy balance of payments with the rest of the trading world. Unfortunately, overseas businesses have the same competitive outlook. The ability to produce the same or a greater quantity of goods with fewer people can lead to a high level of redundancy, a very important social problem which is extremely difficult to eliminate.

11.5.2 Feedback control process

Strictly speaking, an automated process must be able to modify its behaviour when deviations from standard performance are detected by inbuilt control mechanisms. The deviations are determined by comparing results with predefined parameters which form the basis of the feedback control process for modifying the state of the system. The system inputs are adjusted according to the magnitude of the deviations (*see* 2.4.2).

11.5.3 Automatic operation by internally stored program

Computers used in administrative functions operate automatically under the control of an internally stored program. A specific application can modify its behaviour by branching to different parts of the program in accordance with the results obtained from tests conducted at various stages of processing. This may apply in a stock control system when it is necessary to branch to a part of the program for printing details of items to be replenished after the quantity in stock has been compared with a predefined re-order level.

11.6 Evolution of information technology

The way in which accounting transactions are recorded and the production of management information have undergone evolutionary changes in the past 50 years. Early office mechanisation included mechanical keyboard accounting machines for posting details of, for example, the payroll, or of transactions to the sales ledger, or the purchase ledger and to the nominal ledger. This speeded up the recording process and enabled several administrative tasks to be carried out simultaneously.

Comptometers were also used for high-speed calculations and, in the hands of a competent operator, were very efficient in their day. Other developments included crank-driven calculators and adding/listing machines for obtaining control totals and listing items posted to ledgers. Addressing machines assisted the handling of mail — addresses were embossed on metal plates (an early form of data storage) and fed into the machine automatically from a feed hopper — and postal franking machines were introduced.

Larger businesses later installed punched card equipment in place of mechanical accounting machines for increased speed, and flexibility of accounting routines. Data could now be captured (stored) on punched cards and was then processed by various means — sorters for sorting data; collators for merging master files and transaction files in the form of packs of cards; multiplying punches for computational requirements, and so on. The equipment was 'programmed' externally by plug boards: wires were located in different holes to specify data fields to which computational and/or printing operations could be applied. This was referred to as *automatic data processing* (ADP).

The first generation of computers replaced the earlier punched card installations. They were extremely large, often filling a room with the various cabinets and devices that made up the system — the processor, control unit, memory unit, device controllers for controlling the function of tape decks and disc drives, and printers. Early installations used card readers for input of data and card punches to obtain output in the form of carried forward master files for subsequent use in a later processing cycle. The cards were used initially to familiarise staff with the new equipment. Programs were stored internally and direct, speedy access to instructions via the control unit was possible. The first generation lasted until the mid–late 1950s. The computers were constructed of large wired panels, thermionic valves (known as vacuum tubes) and condensers.

The second generation were based on solid-state (i.e. no mechanical moving parts) technology, consisting of printed circuits (which replaced wired panels), transistors and diodes (replacing thermionic valves and condensers).

Third generation computers were introduced around 1964 and were based on *microminiaturisation* technology, employing mico-integrated circuits. This technology greatly decreased the physical size of computers and enhanced their processing power and flexibility immensely. They had higher capacity internal memories, were capable of processing several programs concurrently (multiprogramming) and possessed data transmission capabilities.

Fourth generation computers (mid-1970s) introduced a new concept of standard systems network architecture allowing networks of computers to be upgraded without altering programs. The 1970s also saw the introduction of microcomputers based on silicon-chip technology: thousands of transistors and diodes were etched on a single silicon chip no more than five millimetres square. Retail terminals, databases, word processors, electronic mail and local area networks emerged from the new silicon-chip technology.

Fifth generation computers will be highly complex knowledge-based systems with built-in artificial intelligence, using languages such as Prolog and Lisp, which feature enhanced symbol manipulating and logic programming facilities. They will be capable of being addressed in natural language. Instead of instructions being obeyed in a sequential manner they will be executed when relevant data is available for processing, input from a comunications network channelling instructions to instruction queues related to individual processors. The computer executes the instructions irrespective of where they are located in the program. It is said that data flow computer architecture will provide the means for handling as many as five hundred processors allowing the execution of up to one billion instructions per second. Fifth generation computers will also provide for pattern recognition and speech synthesis, the latter providing facilities for the preparation of business documents directly from the input of human speech. They will also be capable of automatic foreign language translation from one language to another, thus increasing the effectiveness of international computer communications.

Such machines will be in effect KIPs, i.e. Knowledge Information Processing systems, and are likely to have a memory capacity of one billion bytes and a data transfer speed of 1.5 billion bytes per second.

11.7 Technological life cycle

The pattern which technological change tends to follow is known as the technological *life cycle*. This pattern was in the past as relevant to machines employed in the factory as it is now to equipment used in the office. It follows these stages:

(a) introductory phase;
(b) growth phase;
(c) maturity or stability phase;
(d) decline or decay phase.

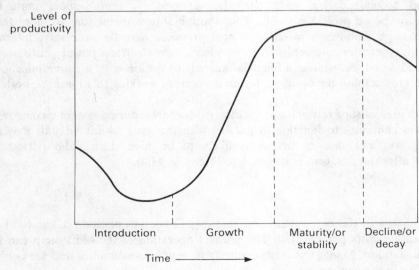

Figure 11.3 Productivity related to stages of technological life cycle

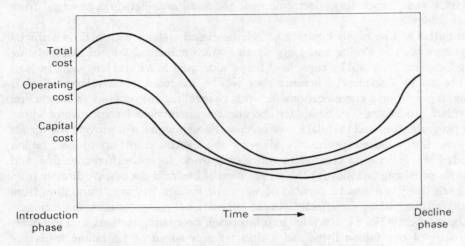

Figure 11.4 Cost curve in relation to stages of technological life cycle

Figures 11.3 and 11.4 illustrate the effects on productivity and the cost of the implementation of technology during its life cycle.

11.7.1 Introductory phase

The introduction of new technology requires capital expenditure which varies according to the nature and extent of envisaged changes. A mainframe computer supporting local area networks can cost many thousands of pounds and for extensive proposals such expenditure needs to be sanctioned by senior executives as part of the formal capital project proposal procedure. In addition to initial investment, operating and accommodation costs must be assessed — every aspect must be cost-efficient to ensure the proposed project is viable. Thus the initial investment runs to more than cost of equipment. For a large mainframe installation new premises may be necessary; internal services must be rearranged; typewriters are replaced by terminals; new electrical power sources and power points are added, and so on. As well as a financial analysis to decide cost, a *communications analysis* is usually conducted to establish the optimum layout in terms of working relationships, both of personnel and equipment.

Almost certainly, some degree of staff retraining is necessary. Moreover, during system changeover, assuming the present system continues to function in parallel with the new, additional staff may be required. Thus, operating cost per unit of output is likely to be high during the period of implementation but will fall after the changeover is completed (*see* Fig. 11.4).

11.7.2 Growth phase

As staff become more familiar with the new system and gain experience in operating it, the level of productivity rises and operating costs per unit fall. The parallel operation of the old system can be discontinued and costs will stabilise. Management, too, adjusts to new responsibilities and seeks cost and time saving opportunities in the new system.

11.7.3 Maturity or stability phase

After the new system has become fully operational it will reach its peak performance level — staff settle into a new work routine and become more confident, and the company as a whole adjusts to a new work environment, a faster rate of administrative turnaround and an overall improvement in terms of efficiency and output. Productivity and operating costs stabilise at the optimum performance level.

11.7.4 Decline or decay phase

Due to the rate at which new technology advances, systems are superseded, machines become worn and so performance declines. As (new) equipment ages, its value depreciates and maintenance charges, unless set at a fixed cost, are no longer economical. Productivity falls due to machine down-time and, as rival companies adopt newer technologies, competition increases.

11.7.5 Managing the life cycle

An important part of the management of IT is to anticipate the life cycle of technology and so minimise system delays, increases in operating costs and low levels of performance. Management must remain aware of new developments and predict the right moment for change.

11.8 Office automation and its effect on business

11.8.1 Changing nature of employment

Change is inseparable from progress and there has always been a need to modify business systems so that they accord to changing circumstances within the business environment. Change varies in degree and complexity: it can be the simplification of tasks to improve efficiency (e.g. on factory production lines), the installation of machines for efficient handling of increasing work loads, or it may arise from the need to incorporate new legislation, as when PAYE routines were introduced. Change of methods always involves some restructuring of the organisation so that it is compatible with the altering nature of business operations; reallocation of management responsibilities and retraining, transfer or even redundancy of personnel are inevitable.

11.8.2 Staff reorganisation

The personnel function is responsible for the human resources of an organisation and on the implementation of new technology must reassess staffing needs, not only in administration, but in the business as a whole. It is important, for example, that management research all retraining options and so avoid redundancies wherever possible. Without the full cooperation of personnel the introduction of technology can be a difficult task — staff are suspicious of changes which may reduce the workforce, they lose trust in the management and the work environment is badly affected. Change is more likely to succeed with the support and confidence of employees and therefore management staff/relations must be maintained throughout organisational upheaval and job changes or redundancies must be discussed with staff representatives from the outset.

The changing nature of employment must be provided for by suitable internal or external training, to help staff adjust to new tasks, routines and responsibilities. Redeployment is always preferable to staff cuts, but redundancy is often unavoidable if changes are to be economically viable. Careful personnel management can soften the blow — by keeping staff informed, explaining the necessity of competing in a developing business environment, by careful selection of workers to be made redundant and by encouraging participation in retraining programmes.

The sections which follow outline the personnel decisions open to management.

11.8.3 Analysing personnel needs

The first step to restructuring the staff system is to assess exactly how many people with which skills will be needed to run the business efficiently and cost effectively. When switching from manual or mechanical systems to sophisticated electronic systems there will be a fundamental change: manpower is replaced by machine power and one employee is able to perform a number of tasks.

An analysis of staff will give an indication of who to retrain and how. It is essential to know which jobs will be 'deskilled' when detailed routines for performing a task are built into computer software. On the basis of the analysis, new job specifications can be prepared and salary scales recompiled for the new grades.

11.8.4 Staffing and motivation

Changes in the staff structure must, as we have seen, be negotiated by management and staff representatives. Effective staffing involves the appointment of the most suitable personnel to new posts and retraining them to attain the highest possible level of efficiency.

The introduction of new technology will be greeted differently by different sections of personnel: younger staff may be willing to accept the new ways and means of working in a hi-tech environment; older members of staff may be reluctant and suspicious of change. Management must motivate employees, stressing the long-term advantages of using technology to keep up with competition and pointing out that training will increase individual skills and is therefore an added benefit for employees. Explaining technology and the changes it incurs and encouraging staff participation from an early stage will increase employee cooperation once equipment is installed. Through tactful explanation, it may be possible to persuade older personnel to take voluntary early retirement, or to transfer staff displaced by the new technology to sections of the business which are unaffected by these changes and likely to remain so for the foreseeable future.

11.8.5 Overcoming resistance to change

As has been stated, personnel will not readily be responsive to change: those approaching retirement age may be quite content to continue with current business practices; the less qualified worry about redundancy. Opposition to change can lead to the following problems:

(a) overmanning;
(b) inefficiency;
(c) low productivity;
(d) failure to meet objectives;
(e) out-of-date methods, procedures and systems creating high processing costs;
(f) failure to compete in the business environment.

Management can encourage acceptance by inviting personnel to attend informal technology meetings or participate in technology committees. In-house education and training programmes prior to implementation may also assist in overcoming resistance to change, particularly if personnel can see for themselves that their own area of work or their own work skills will benefit from the envisaged changes.

Other ways of encouraging staff to accept technological change are summarised below.

(a) Inform personnel affected by pending changes of the reason for such changes.

(b) Enlist the cooperation of personnel by explaining any possible benefits of changing systems.

(c) Discuss objections to change and if practicable, compromise with staff suggestions.

(d) Allow staff to participate in the development of systems and routines, implementing their practical ideas when appropriate.

(e) Provide examples of similar changes occuring in other companies and outline the effects on the staff structure.

(f) Attempt to overcome prejudices, real or imaginary, and attempt to dispel rumours at the outset by adequate communication.

(g) Look carefully and sympathetically through personnel files or distribute a staff questionnaire to research skills which employees are not putting to use in their current positions. Restructure staff in accordance with their preferences and capabilities as well as their past experience.

11.9 Managing information technology

11.9.1 Management agreement

An initial step towards implementing change is to justify to senior management both the expense and the company upheaval which it will incur. It is essential that managers encourage and support new directions in corporate policy; their cooperation will be a major motivating factor for the personnel they direct.

One of the problems of obtaining management agreement to proposed technological change is the fact that most benefits, although they increase the efficiency of the administration as a whole, are of an 'intangible' nature and cannot be immediately and directly linked to increased profit. Management, quite rightly, likes to be sure that a quick and certain return of investment is possible before any outlay of capital. Unfortunately it is not always possible to evaluate implementation of technology in terms of profit, but benefits in terms of cash flow are obvious. For example, if more statements of account can be produced in a shorter time by computer, then cash flow should be forthcoming sooner, and so costs incurred on short-term overdrafts or loans do not arise. Moreover, automatic stock control systems can give immediate assessments of stock levels, and so unnecessary investment in surplus stock and, to some extent, stock obsolescence are avoided.

11.9.2 Management of innovation

Managers are agents of change which means they must be capable of dealing with innovation to achieve optimum productivity in offices. As well as looking for areas of change *within* the organisation, managers must look *outwards*, assessing competition and changes in market trends, and identifying the correct moment for and degree of technological change necessary to compete in an increasingly automated business environment. A management which has carefully researched its administrative needs, the current available technology and its future objectives will be able to pinpoint the degree and rate of implementation of technology needed to improve its administrative system and cope with increased demand.

11.9.3 Elements of management

The advent of new technology does not affect the basic elements of management which apply regardless of methodology or technology. The primary role of a manager is to *manage* resources, i.e. manpower, money, machines and materials. A manager is responsible for planning, organising, controlling, staffing, directing, coordinating, motivating, delegating, problem solving and decision making. These basic responsibilities are not affected by the type of business, but apply equally to banks, insurance companies, factories, warehouses, travel agencies or hotels.

11.9.4 Planning

The implementation of new technology needs to be planned within the framework of an organisation; it must be an integral part of corporate objectives rather than a series of uncoordinated departmental projects. The purpose of installing technology is to increase overall productivity by eliminating existing organisational, systems and communication weaknesses and the problems they cause. Replacement of outmoded practices and outworn, outdated equipment results in the strengthening of business operations and techniques so that new challenges can be met and increased productivity and efficiency can be achieved.

Careful planning is the key to successful changeover to an advanced administrative system. Requirements in terms of internal and external communication, computational needs, word processing, electronic filing and electronic mail, etc. must be assessed systematically and accurately. The best way is to consult a systems specialist, whether internally or externally, before drawing up detailed plans. Specialist advice at an early stage prevents unnecessary purchase of unsuitable equipment and time wasted following up impracticable ideas.

11.9.5 Organising, coordinating and controlling

This may involve merging what were previously separate activities or functions because of the integrative nature of some electronic devices and processes. This will necessitate the restructuring of departments, sections and tasks, and the reallocation of managerial responsibilities. All changes must be monitored after they have been implemented to ensure they attain specified objectives, which may relate to speed of response to customer enquiries or the provision of information at a specified time.

11.10 New dimensions of management

Management is, as we have seen, largely concerned with planning, controlling and decision making, all of which require timely and accurate information. Any improvement in information flow or response time will lead to an improvement in managerial performance. In some companies, IT is the domain of management: managers are increasingly turning to personal microcomputers to access information quickly and directly. Executives too are being provided with teleconferencing facilities — cutting down on time spent travelling to or participating in meetings. In manufacturing and design, computer aided systems are increasingly common and an awareness of their capabilities is essential to innovative management.

11.10.1 Home-based executives

The modern tendency is for executives such as management accountants, chief buyers, cost controllers, sales managers or stock controllers to work at home. This involves setting up a portable terminal or computer with an acoustic coupler for connecting the equipment to a public telephone line (necessitating a telephone handset and connection point), and a monitor or domestic television set. These electronic office facilities are connected to a remote mainframe computer and database by the telephone link. Alternatively a portable computer may be used with a built-in standard interface for use with a printer (*see* Fig. 11.5).

Connection to the mainframe is achieved by simply dialling its number, as on a normal telephone call. When connected, the executive keys in a password to gain access to files. The computer is programmed to recognise each executive's password and identify the files he or she has authority to access.

A more sophisticated home-based electronic office may be equipped with a work station which has an electronic hand-operated device known as a *mouse* (*see* below) and a jack plug for connecting the work station to the telephone line to link up with the remote mainframe computer.

The home-based work station can be linked to a local area network consisting of work stations, microcomputers and word processors as well as a mainframe.

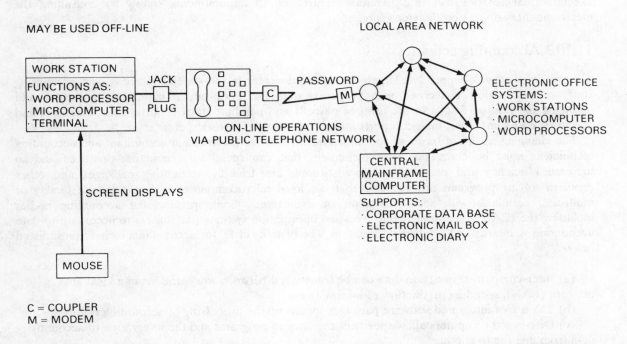

Figure 11.5 Linking up with the world from the home-based electronic office using a work station and telephone

The network supports electronic mail, electronic diary and file access via the database. The database allows data to be retrieved in respect of the master and/or functional budgets; cash flow projections; projected profit statements and balance sheets; stock lists; contract cost schedules; outstanding orders; premiums due for renewal; holiday packages due for payment and many other files according to the nature of the business and the responsibilities of the executive.

If desired the work station can be used in an *off-line* mode, i.e. not connected to a larger computer, and used for various tasks including computations, word processing, message retrieval from electronic mailboxes when using electronic mail facilities and for the development of personal programs.

All functions can be controlled by the hand-operated *mouse*. This is an electronic device used for moving the cursor around on the screen of a monitor. It indicates the current working position on the screen when entering data. Some portable computers and work stations are provided with *icons*, which are small symbols representing various office functions such as in-tray, out-tray, calculator, printer, file copying, file deletion, and so on. In this instance the mouse is used to point to the desired icon. If, for instance, the mouse is pointed at the file icon this will generate file handling facilities.

11.10.2 Office services

Office services include secretarial, typing, filing, reprographic, postal, telex, telephone, facsimile and other communication services. Electronic facilities used for these purposes include word processing, communication facilities in the form of electronic mail and digital PABX systems and the use of databases in relation to filing and data retrieval systems, etc.

Technological advances in these areas improve administrative efficiency, eliminating unnecessary delays in communicating to different parts of the organisation and dealing with routine desk work, filing and correspondence. A useful example is the electronic diary which records the times arranged for meetings by one executive and automatically transfers the information to the diaries of other executives. Secretaries can thus maintain control of all appointments simply by consulting the electronic diary display on the video screen.

11.10.3 Accounting activities

The role of the book-keeper has largely disappeared except in the smaller business, and accounting staff are now mainly concerned with preparing data for input into a mainframe computer and analysing the printed results in the form of payrolls and payslips; stock reports; lists of debtors and creditors; cost summaries; budget reports and labour turnover statistics, etc.

The changing nature of business operations means that the professional accountant and accounting technicians must be conversant with technology that can speed up accounting practices and so increase efficiency and productivity. Sophisticated, user-friendly accounting packages and other problem solving programs are available that use local microcomputers as a stand-alone facility or multi-user terminals with access to minis or mainframes. Some professional accounting bodies including the ICAEW are implementing on-line information systems (databases) to access up-to-date accounting standards and taxation information. The benefits of IT for accountants include those listed below.

(a) Inter-company transaction data can be transferred between work stations in a local area network (LAN), speeding up the flow of information.

(b) The use of integrated software packages speeds up the processing of accounting routines.

(c) Disc-based computers allow speedy changeover of programs and the integration of accounting data from one file to another.

(d) Text from word processing files can be combined with data from data files which improves efficiency.

(e) Data can be speedily converted into graphical form for achieving greater clarity in the interpretation of operating results, such as sales and expenditure trends.

(f) Access to a database for information to be incorporated into reports, such as budgeted expenses for the current operating period and for the year-to-date.

(g) Automatic printout of reports from information collected and stored on disc.

(h) High speed printout of schedules relating to stocks, debtors and creditors, assets, depreciation, etc.

(i) The use of spreadsheets aids budgeting and profit projections.

11.10.4 Artificial intelligence

Artificial intelligence (AI) is an important factor in manufacturing processes, particularly developments in automated flow lines implemented for the mass production of motor cars and other complex products. Artificial intelligence is the application of machines which are programmed to perform specific tasks automatically and are capable of modifying their behaviour according to changing environmental conditions. Computers apply 'logic' when testing for conditions: the program branches to a section designed to deal with specific conditions and so takes the appropriate actions when these arise. This furnishes computers with automatic 'decision-making' attributes. This includes 'expert systems', dealt with in more detail in Chapter 10.

11.10.5 Computer-aided manufacture

Computer-aided manufacture (CAM) is used in a number of ways: production planning and control; preparation and modification of shop and machine loading schedules; computation of stock levels and purchase commitments; and so on.

A business may also employ a computer for the numerical control of machine tools, such as borers, lathes, etc. A special program determines the sequence of operations and executes them automatically with a high degree of accuracy. The computer then transmits signals generated by the program to an activator which effects the appropriate machine movements and changes tool stations as required.

A computer can also be used to monitor the flow of production. The computer receives signals relating to the state of the system — its input, and output — which are then compared with control parameters. Any variances are used as the basis for applying corrective action. The necessary adjustments are generated by signals to an activator or effector to open or close valves and so increase or decrease the rate of flow, or to adjust the temperature level, etc.

Robots are mechanical devices with inbuilt artificial intelligence which can assist the manufacturing processes of material handling, paint spraying and welding by performing them automatically in accordance with predetermined programs. This is a feature of modern car manufacturing plants.

11.10.6 Computer-aided design

Computer-aided design (CAD) enables product outlines or building plans to be drawn and modified on a video screen using applications software. The image on the screen can be rotated to obtain a three-dimensional perspective. Designs can be stored on disc and recalled when required. Similarly, standard shapes can be stored and retrieved for incorporation with other designs when necessary. The technique is widely used in engineering and design environments, particularly in the design of cars and aircraft. Similar techniques are applied to the development of business systems using CASE tools, i.e. computer-aided systems engineering.

11.11 Summary of typical benefits arising from the implementation of office automation

(a) Increased level of office productivity, due to handling higher volumes of data with fewer personnel.

(b) Improved quality of decisions as a result of accurate, objective, wide-ranging and timely information.

(c) Integration of diverse activities, either by multi-tasking or multi-user facilities using integrated software packages and computers of suitable capabilities.

(d) Problem solving improved by decision support systems.

(e) Improved communication by the use of local or wide area networks.

(f) Information more easily accessible by means of databases and on-line information systems.

(g) On-line processing improves overall efficiency.

(h) Improved organisational control because of electronic mail and other electronic facilities.

(i) Increased customer satisfaction as a result of expedient and efficient administration.

Review questions

1 What is office automation?

2 What is the purpose of applying electronic technology to business activities?

3   What are the stages of the technological life cycle

4   Why is it necessary to reorganise staff with the inception of office automation?

5   What actions may be taken to overcome resistance to change?

6   Office automation or electronic technology creates new dimensions of management. What form do they take?

7   Define the abbreviations: IT; AI; CAM; CAD.

8   Summarise the benefits of office automation.

Self-test questions

11.1 Describe the facilities provided by office automation.

11.2 What steps can be taken within an organisation in order to encourage the acceptance of technological change?

Answers on page 372–3.

12 Computer types and configurations

12.1 Introduction

This chapter provides an outline of some of the technicalities of computers so that a better understanding of their features and characteristics will be attained. It is important to be aware of some of the terms used such as PCs, bytes, megabytes, gigabytes, internal memory, add-on memory modules and migration path, etc. Of particular significance is the need to know the nature of the computer system and its configuration for different types and sizes of business.

12.2 Types of computer

The distinction between micro, mini and mainframe computers was quite well defined in the past but is now becoming increasingly indistinct. Minicomputers are tending to rival all but the largest mainframe computers in power while PCs (microcomputers) are becoming increasingly more powerful. PCs are very effective for processing accounting and other administrative data for the smaller business, being well supported by accounting, spreadsheet, word processing and other software.

Minis and micros do not need those specially controlled environment conditions (voltage, temperature, dust and humidity) which are essential for the effective operation of mainframe computers. These are, however, less critical with modern mainframes as they have smaller electronic components which do not generate so much heat, and the fixed disc drives are sealed units which prevent dust settling on the disc surfaces.

12.3 Mainframe computers

A mainframe computer is the largest type of computer used for business and accounting applications. Large businesses usually require large computers for the efficient processing of large volumes of accounting and other types of data. Mainframes are usually sited at the head office of large organisations, or in town halls for municipal accounting and administrative applications. Mainframes require to be operated by expert DP professionals because of the complexity in the use of commands to the operating system, etc. (*See* Figs. 12.1 and 12.2.)

They can be used as stand-alone computer systems or for supporting a large network of terminals facilitated by its telecommunications, distributed data processing and systems network architecture (SNA) capabilities. Input is usually by keyboard, including remote terminal keyboards, for on-line processing applications but transaction files for batch processing may be encoded on discs by key-to-disc equipment. A powerful operating system provides for multiprogramming allowing the interfacing of multiple VDUs, industrial, retail and financial terminals both locally and remotely. Printer output is by means of various models of printer, including laser printers, and graph plotters for graphical output. Modems are required for communication-orientated configurations for linking terminals to the computer via a multiplexor. (*See* Chapter 14; *see* also Fig. 12.2.)

Backing storage consists of banks of disc drives each with a capacity in the region of 100+ MB or, in some instances, nearing a gigabyte (1,000 million). The discs may be fixed or exchangeable but would need to be fixed for on-line operations from remote locations to allow for demand processing needs.

Mainframes support a large database for servicing the needs of major operations such as order processing, airline reservations, banking, etc. They also facilitate report generation, on-line program development and applications relating to accounting and information processing.

The various manufacturers of mainframes, such as ICL, IBM and NCR, use different architectures, usually on a modular basis incorporating independent subsystems. This makes it possible to increase computing power by migrating to a more powerful processor in the range. The capacity of internal memory can also be increased by add-on memory modules. The structure of a mainframe is very complex with specialised microprocessors supporting the main 32-bit processor. A memory interface provides the logical connection between memory array chips and the address translation chip. Mainframes are constructed on very large scale integration (VLSI) technology, which enables the circuits to be on a single chip the size of a 5p piece. Computers based on VLSI technology are smaller, cost less and, as they generate less heat and their lower power consumption makes them less liable to blow integrated circuits (ICs), they tend to be more reliable. The internal memory capacity is in the region of 20 MB (20 million bytes or 20 megabytes) of RAM. Its addressing capabilities are very high and it functions on the basis of internal and external virtual memory. Virtual memory is a storage management technique which enables the limited internal storage capacity to be enhanced by disc backing storage which stores software which is segregated into pages. Only those pages required for immediate processing are called into internal memory. The pages previously stored in memory are overwritten by the latest segments (pages) of software required for processing.

Figure 12.1 IBM 3090 mainframe computer

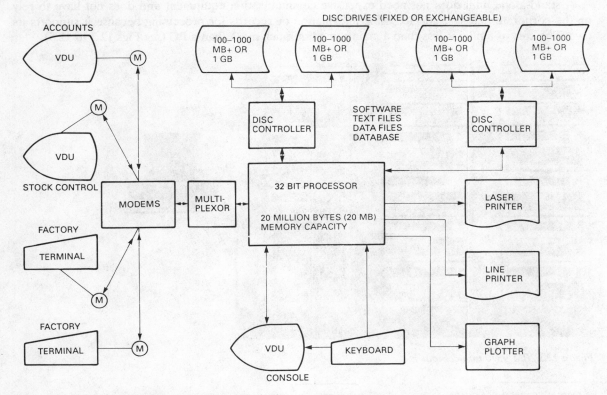

Figure 12.2 General mainframe computer configuration outlining modular construction and terminal support

12.4 Minicomputers

In many cases the minicomputer fills the gap between the larger PC and the smaller mainframe. Minis are produced by a number of manufacturers including DEC (Digital Equipment Corporation), Hewlett Packard, IBM, ICL and GEC. They tend to be used by medium sized organisations which cannot currently justify a mainframe. Applications processed on a mini include accounting routines, databases and other management information systems. They are also used for numerical control of machine tools in the factory and for monitoring various types of processes. When the capacity of a mini is exceeded it is often necessary to switch to a mainframe to attain a more powerful processing capability and larger internal memory. Like a mainframe, specialist DP staff are required to operate a mini, because of its complexity compared to a PC. When management considers the implementation of distributed processing, a strategy which provides computing power where it is most useful in a dispersed organisation, a minicomputer is often implemented in the various locations. Typically it is used for local accounting routines, payroll, stock control and order processing. It may be connected to other minis in a network for data interchange or for gaining access to information, such as budgets, in a corporate database (*see* Fig. 12.3). On the other hand it may function as a stand-alone system with its own database.

Transaction data is usually input by keyboard and output by a printer. The processor is based on 32-bit technology with a memory capacity in the region of 6–16 MB. The processor has a built-in Winchester hard disc drive with a capacity between 80–320 MB which may be supplemented by an integral tape spooler for backing up files (taking copies). In addition, backing storage may be further complemented by exchangeable and floppy disc drives.

A stand-alone mini does not need expensive communication equipment and does not have to rely on the corporate database for accessing information or records for processing because it supports its own. The cost of a mini is less than a mainframe but much more than a PC (*see* Figs 12.3 to 12.5).

Figure 12.3 IBM 9370 minicomputer

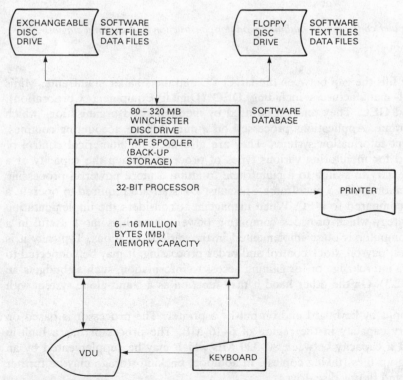

Figure 12.4 General configuration of a stand-alone minicomputer

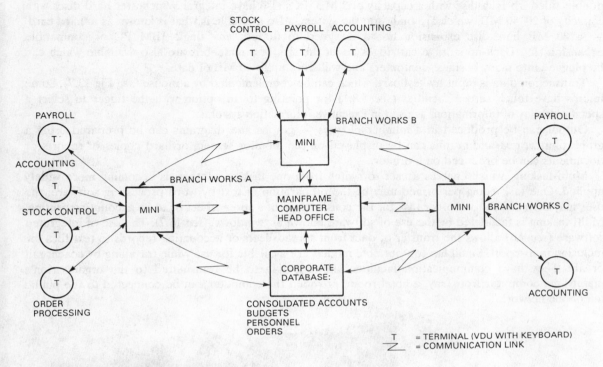

STOCK CONTROL   PAYROLL   ACCOUNTING

T   T   T

BRANCH WORKS B

MINI

PAYROLL

T

ACCOUNTING

T

STOCK CONTROL

T

ORDER PROCESSING

T

BRANCH WORKS A

MINI

MAINFRAME COMPUTER HEAD OFFICE

CORPORATE DATABASE:

CONSOLIDATED ACCOUNTS
BUDGETS
PERSONNEL
ORDERS

BRANCH WORKS C

MINI

PAYROLL

T

ACCOUNTING

T

T = TERMINAL (VDU WITH KEYBOARD)
∑ = COMMUNICATION LINK

Figure 12.5 Minicomputer network configuration

12.5 Microcomputers: personal computers

Manufacturers of microcomputers for business use include IBM (the IBM PC), Apple (Apple Macintosh), Amstrad and Compaq, who market a range of models. Micros are normally stand-alone machines operated by end-users for their own particular processing needs such as payroll, stock control and general accounting routines (*see* Figs. 12.6 and 12.7). They are also widely used by accountants for problem solving using spreadsheets. They can, however, be linked into a network consisting of mainframes, minis and other micros for the purpose of interchanging data between operating units and accessing a corporate database (*see* Fig. 12.5). They can also be connected to facsimile systems which transmit and receive images, drawings and diagrams, and telex systems which transmit and receive textual messages. They may also share the resources of high speed printers and high capacity disc storage. They are smaller than minis and much simpler to operate — the non-professional can become quite proficient in a short space of time. Micros have brought offices and accounting practice into the twentieth century while also providing a greater degree of job enrichment to the user (*see* Figs 12.6 to 12.8).

The internal memory capacity of a micro is typically 512 KB (512,000 bytes) but this can be increased to six megabytes (six million bytes) or even higher as some computers allow a memory upgrade to 8 MB on the main circuit board (the motherboard). Magnetic discs can be simulated on electronic circuits (chips) which allows programs to be permanently stored in a computer. This provides the means to increase internal memory capacity and saves time by obviating the need to transfer programs to the internal memory from the disc storage where they are normally stored.

Floppy discs, either 3.5 or 5.25 inches in diameter, are normally used for backing storage. A 3.5-inch disc may have a capacity of 720 KB but the new IBM PS/2 computer incorporates a double-sided 3.5-inch disc with a capacity of 2 MB. PCs also have integral Winchester hard discs with capacity of 20–40 MB, which are built into the system. Also available is what is known as a 'hard card' — a 20 MB hard-disc expansion board designed to fit into any single IBM PC or compatible expansion slot. Back-up storage cartridges about the size of a matchbox are also available which can be plugged into many business computers and will store up to 40 MB of data.

Transaction data is input by keyboard which can be complemented by a mouse (*see* Fig 12.7). Some micros have touch screen facilities (*see* 5.8.1) for pointing to an option with the finger to select a specific display of information, as used in executive information systems.

Output can be produced in a number of ways — graphs and diagrams can be prepared using a graph plotter; text and graphs can be displayed on the monitor screen, or hard copies of reports or documents can be produced on a printer.

Multi-tasking, which enables a user to switch from one task to another, is becoming more widely applied. One task being performed may be the preparation of text by word processing software; the user may then switch to another task for the construction of a spreadsheet or to an accounting routine. Multi-tasking is facilitated by the use of software known as 'windows' (*see* 16.7). The use of integrated software (*see* 7.6) allows the transfer of data from spreadsheets or accounting records to text files for inclusion in a report. Small lap-top portable models are available for use while travelling by coach, rail or air. They have communication facilities allowing data to be transmitted to the organisation's mainframe computer from, say, a hotel room, provided the computer can be connected to the public telephone network.

Figure 12.6 IBM System/2 minicomputer

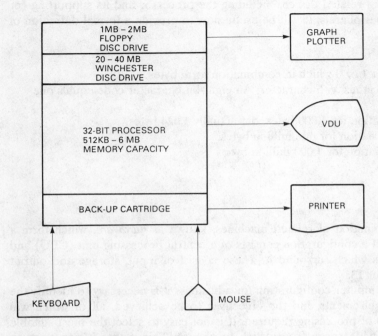

Figure 12.7 Stand-alone microcomputer (PC) configuration

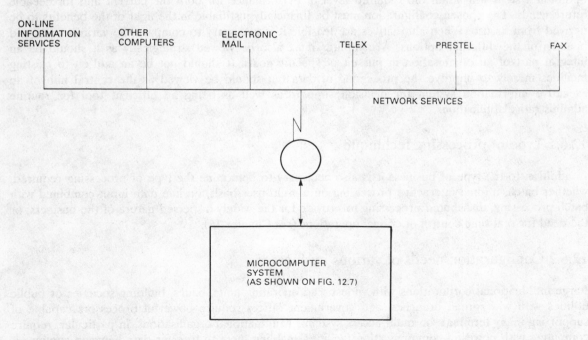

Figure 12.8 Microcomputer and interlinking network services

We have just discussed the major differences between mainframes, minis and micros — also called PCs, remember. The text and diagrams show that the different types of computer do not consist of just one machine but a combination of related devices including the processor and its supporting (or surrounding) devices — also called peripherals. It will be useful now to provide a formal definition of the term configuration.

Remember also the following terms:

(a) Bit — short for BInary digiT, a 1 or 0 which in combination form bytes.

(b) Byte — a term which is synonymous with character. An eight-bit character code equals one byte.

(c) Kilobyte — or KB, an abbreviation for 1,000 bytes, but actually 1,024 bytes.

(d) Megabyte — or MB, an abbreviation for one million bytes.

(e) Gigabyte — or GB, an abbreviation for 1,000 million bytes.

12.6 Computer configurations

A computer configuration is a combination of related machines, known as *hardware*, which form a complete computer system. In general a configuration consists of a central processing unit (CPU) and its peripherals, which are the devices which surround it. These consist of input, storage and output devices which are discussed in Chapter 13.

Before it is possible to specify a computer configuration for a business it is necessary to identify the type of business, its information requirements and the objectives to be achieved, all of which will provide a basis for assessing the type of processing required. It is not easy to select the most suitable computer configuration, due to the wide range from which to choose. This makes it necessary to analyse the way in which a business functions internally — inter-functional relationships — and the manner in which it interacts with the external environment including suppliers and customers. The optimum system will attain the required level of performance for both the current and foreseeable future needs. The chosen configuration must be financially justifiable in the light of the benefits to be derived from its use. When alternatives are feasible it is necessary to compare the various costs and benefits of the different options. A computer must also be viewed strategically as it should be an integral part of an organisation in pursuit of specific goals. It should not be an add-on to existing facilities merely to improve the processing of data but should be viewed as the central hub of an executive information system for decision support as well as being an efficient tool for routine administrative applications.

12.6.1 Type of processing technique

In addition to the type of business it is also necessary to determine the type of processing required, whether batch, on-line interactive processing on a multi-user basis, on-line data input combined with batch processing, distributed processing to provide for the widely dispersed nature of the business, or the need for real-time control of critical operations (*see* Chapter 16).

12.6.2 Configuration needs of various businesses

Large multinational corporations with widespread operating units, banks, building societies or public utilities with widespread branches, and government offices require powerful processors capable of supporting many terminals on multi-access systems. Multinational organisations, in particular, require computers with powerful communication facilities enabling them to transfer data between computers in different parts of the world at high speed. Distance is no object in the modern technological world in which business operates especially with the extensive coverage of the globe by satellite communications.

Banks require specialised data collection equipment for automated cash dispensing facilities as well as magnetic ink cheque encoders for recording the amount on each cheque presented. Magnetic ink reader/sorters are also required for reading (sensing) the transaction details printed along the bottom edge of cheques. Public utilities and local authorities require optical character reading devices for sensing transaction data on consumer bills. These are examples of turnaround documents. Supermarkets require retail terminal-orientated computer systems at check-out points for laser scanners automatically to list and price items purchased by scanning bar coded labels attached to the items. (*See* Fig. 12.9.) Factory-based operations require computer systems for capturing data relating to works orders and material movements by strategically located factory terminals throughout the factory.

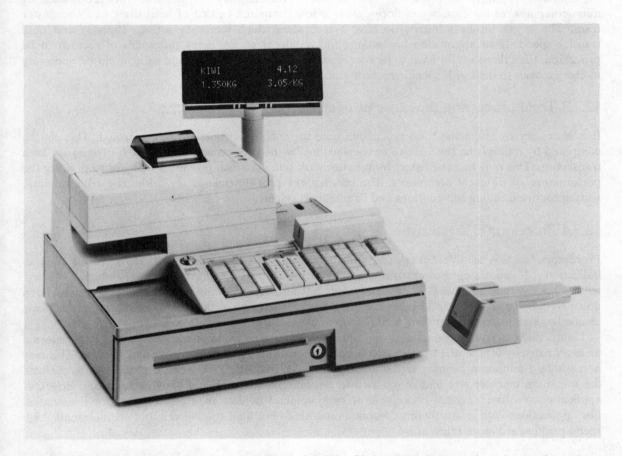

Figure 12.9 Retail terminal components include: cashdrawer, 50 key keypad, magnetic stripe reader, printer, alphanumeric display and hand held bar code register

12.7 Selecting a computer

When selecting a computer, the following points should be considered.

12.7.1 Volume of transactions

The number of transactions to be processed is an important factor to consider as it leads to an assessment of the type of input device required and the nature of the processing techniques to be established. Relatively low volumes can be handled by a business microcomputer using keyboard data entry. This is a very slow method of data input, however, and larger volumes may necessitate the use of a small, medium or large mainframe using a key-to-disc method of data collection and validation. This then enables data to be transferred into the computer at high speed from magnetic disc.

12.7.2 Volume and length of records

Files containing many thousands of records of average length in terms of characters (bytes) will require a large computer system with high backing storage capacity and high speed data transfer capabilities. Applications consisting of 500–1,000 records may be suitable for processing by microcomputer, as the capacity of floppy discs is low compared to that of hard discs, i.e. Winchester discs. The larger business micros do have Winchesters which increases storage capacity and data transfer speed. If an application has a large file requirement, i.e. many thousands of records to be processed, then these would have to be recorded on several floppy discs and so it would be necessary to change discs to deal with specific records stored on them.

12.7.3 Total processing time: use of benchmarks

It is necessary to assess the total processing time for each application to be processed. This can be computed by multiplying the volume of transactions by the processing time for each process on each transaction. This may be established from benchmark timings which provide a basis for appraising the performance of different computers. The benchmarks provide timings for arithmetic computations, sorting routines, calling sub-routines and handling arrays, etc.

12.7.4 Processor characteristics

Processors function at different speeds, and the size of the storage unit — 8, 16, or 32-bit — is an indication of processing power, the more powerful processors having greater internal storage addressing capabilities. (An 8-bit processor only has an address bus of sixteen channels which allows up to 64 KB, i.e. 2^{16} or 65,536 bytes capacity, whereas a 16-bit processor often has twenty address channels which provide addressing facilities up to 2^{20} or 1,048,576 or one megabyte.)

If integrated accounting packages and spreadsheets are to be implemented then a large internal memory capacity is essential to store the large number of instructions the programs contain. This may necessitate a minimum memory size of 256 KB or even 512 KB. The package specifications indicate the minimum memory size and other hardware requirements, such as floppy or hard disc drives. If applications require frequent processing of large volumes of data then a fast processor is essential. For applications with relatively few computational needs but high volume printout requirements, high speed printers are more relevant.

12.7.5 Operating system

The operating system adopted by a specific computer model should be carefully evaluated: industry standard models have a vast amount of application packages already available, whereas the less widely adopted operating systems have less software. The cost of non-standard software is likely to be higher as the development costs are spread over a smaller number of potential users. It is also necessary to consider if operating systems have multi-task or multi-user facilities as this may be an important factor in the choice of system. (*See* Chapter 16).

12.7.6 Relative costs of hardware and software

In the early days hardware was very expensive but costs are falling as advances are made in electronic technology. However, while hardware costs are falling the labour intensive task of producing software is not.

Some manufacturers provide bundled software, i.e. the costs of software are included in the quoted cost of the system. This means it is essential to assess the total cost of any proposed computer system covering both hardware and software, particularly when software packages are to be paid for separately. Only then can true comparative costs be formulated.

12.8 Methods of selection

12.8.1 Assess strengths and weaknesses

Relative strengths and weaknesses of specific models must be assessed before a shortlist can be drawn up. Specifications of selected models should be compared against the facilities required. For example, if a business has a large number of geographically dispersed offices, warehouses or factories then the number of communication channels a computer can control is of major importance.

12.8.2 Points rating

A points rating method of selection may be adopted whereby selected attributes are listed and points awarded from a maximum of ten for each attribute in the context of its utility to the business for its prospective applications. A points league table may take the form outlined below.

(a) Processor:
    (i) number of communication channels;
    (ii) 8, 16 or 32-bit processor;
    (iii) memory capacity;
    (iv) number of peripheral ports for plug-in devices, e.g. serial or parallel centronic ports for printers, terminals and other devices;
    (v) speed.
(b) Operating system installed – industry standard or otherwise.
(c) Software:
    (i) bundled or unbundled;
    (ii) availability of suitable software for potential applications.
(d) Total purchase, lease or rental costs.
(e) Degree of manufacturer's support:
    (i) installation support;
    (ii) software support;
    (iii) staff training services provided.
(f) Cost of maintenance agreement.
(g) Programming languages supported.
(h) Backing storage capacity.
(i) Multi-user/multi-tasking capability.
(j) Speed of printer.
(k) Other options, i.e. COM compatibility.

12.9 Dealing with manufacturers and suppliers

12.9.1 Invitation to manufacturers to tender

Obviously, when the system under consideration is in the multi-million pound bracket the capital expenditure required for the investment in hardware and software cannot be taken lightly. In such situations it is normal procedure to invite a number of reputable manufacturers to tender for the contract.

The initital specification of requirements submitted to selected manufacturers would typically include:

(a) details of the systems to be computerised;
(b) volumes of data to be processed;
(c) communication requirements;
(d) number of terminals/work stations required;
(e) multiprogramming considerations;
(f) standby needs;
(g) priorities;
(h) real-time or on-line processing needs;
(i) content of reports required, their distribution and frequency of production;
(j) maintenance contract considerations.

12.9.2 System documentation

Flowcharts, organisation charts, document layouts and details of business operations should also be provided to manufacturers as subsequent proposals are based on this information and the details are discussed by manufacturers' sales representatives, systems staff and executives of the business. Discussions should cover all possible solutions to the needs of the business. Management should discuss all proposals with systems staff who will subsequently recommend a specific course of action.

12.9.3 Proposals

Manufacturers' proposals will include a great deal of data relating to the nature and extent of hardware requirements, software support, the level of staff training to be provided and the extent of systems support and equipment maintenance. Detailed cost schedules relating to the various facets of hardware and software and the overall purchase cost will be provided. It is important to consider the alternative financing methods available, including purchasing, leasing or rental before arriving at a final decision.

12.10 Changing computers

It is sometimes necessary for a company to change its mainframe computer to that of a second manufacturer. A company contemplating a changeover should appreciate that no compatibility will exist between the two models. There will be differences in architecture, i.e. the design philosophy on which the computers are based, in operating systems and assembly codes.

Transfer of a large batch system will entail program recoding as the different operating systems will have different implementations of the high level language in use. Even if this is COBOL which, of course, is a common language for use on any mainframe, there will still be a need to recompile programs into the *native* code of the particular computer.

The problems which are likely to occur include:

(a) disruption during the changeover period;
(b) the need to maintain the current system until the new system has proved to be satisfactory;
(c) prolonged system testing and comparison of the results of the two systems to detect errors;
(d) high overheads for running two systems in parallel;
(e) staffing problems due to excessive overtime;
(f) need to input transaction data twice – to each of the systems separately;
(g) need to reformat disc files;
(h) need to prepare new master files;
(i) time and cost of recompiling programs;
(j) need to prepare accommodation for the new system or arrange temporary space.

Review questions

1   Outline the main features of a mainframe computer.

2   Indicate how a minicomputer differs from both a mainframe and a microcomputer.

3   What is a computer configuration?

4   Why is it necessary to assess the computer configuration requirements of particular types and sizes of business?

5   List several important points which must be taken into account when selecting a computer.

6   Indicate the stages and methods required to select a computer.

7   What problems are likely to arise when a business changes its computer to another model?

Self-test questions

12.1 Describe the essential characteristics and differences between the three main types of computer.

12.2 Before implementing a computer it is essential to collect information relating to alternative models to assess which one is most suitable for the needs of the business. What information would you collect and what activities would you undertake before selecting a computer?

Answers on pages 373–4.

13 Input, output and storage devices and techniques

13.1 Introduction

It becomes increasingly difficult to separate input from output devices because a monitor screen used on terminals and PCs display input from the keyboard, messages generated by the operating system and prompts from applications software, while also displaying the output derived from processing operations.

Disc storage devices use a magnetic disc as a storage medium which is an input, storage and output device. The output from one system may be recorded on disc and stored until required for input for further processing on a related system.

This chapter provides details relating to the keyboard, which is a widely used device for the direct input of data in modern multi-user systems and terminal operations including telex systems. The term WIMP, an acronym for Windows, Icons, Mouse and Pointers, should be remembered as it is likely to occur frequently in examinations, if not as a direct question, as an element of a general question which should include WIMP in the answer. This may apply to selection of files from drop-down menus using the pointer in combination with a mouse or when switching between jobs in multi-tasking operations. They are not strictly input devices but techniques which avoid the extensive use of a keyboard.

This eleminates the need for inexperienced personnel having to learn keyboard skills and operating system commands because the pointer, in combination with icons, takes their place. This is dealt with in more detail later in the chapter.

The chapter also ranges over general input, storage and output techniques, some of which depend on specific operations such as those related to handing cheques in a bank or documents printed in optical characters which are used by water boards and local authorities for billing purposes.

13.2 Direct input devices: keyboard

13.2.1 Keyboard characteristics

The keyboard is one of the most widely used devices for inputting data into a computer for processing. A keyboard connects a user to a computer, effectively allowing the user to drive the computer in the same way that a steering wheel allows a driver to drive a car. The user can determine what the computer is to do by selecting programs and/or files by commands entered through the keyboard. Data is then input for preparing text files or for building spreadsheets. Although the design of keyboards varies they all have keys for the entry of alphabetic, numeric and special characters. Some have a separate numeric keypad for the high speed entry of large volumes of numeric data, and function keys to be used in conjunction with specific software packages. Keyboards have other function keys, including:

(a) ESCape key, to escape from a specific routine.

(b) Control key, for use in conjunction with defined character keys to perform a specific function, such as Ctrl-R to display details one screen backwards, Ctrl-C to display details one screen forwards and Ctrl-U to move cursor to end of line. Cursor control keys control the movement of the cursor (electronic indicator which indicates the current working position when entering data or the position of the cursor on the screen for location purposes). For example, Ctrl-E = cursor up; Ctrl-X = cursor down, etc.

(c) Caps lock key for switching from upper to lower case characters.

(d) Edit keys. When in edit mode, preparing text with a word processor, a number of keys may be used for specific needs, e.g. HOME positions the cursor at the extreme left of the screen on the current line. In other instances depressing the HOME key locates the cursor at the top left corner of the screen. *Insert* allows a character to be inserted, and *Delete* to be deleted, at the position indicated by the cursor (to delete, it should be in the character position after the one to be deleted).

13.2.2 Form displays and input by keyboard

Many applications are designed to display on the video screen the layout of a form, which is completed by an operator entering data into the appropriate boxes (fields) by keyboard. The user reading from a transaction document keys in data in the sequence of the fields displayed on the screen. When data entry is completed the relevant document is printed out. *See* Chapter 29 for further details.

13.3 Direct input techniques and devices: windows, icons, mouse and pointers

What follows does not relate strictly to input devices but to techniques for inputting commands to the computer by means of a keyboard and monitor screen. The exception is the mouse, a specific tangible hardware device which can be held in the hand. Windows, icons and pointers are electronic techniques built into the software and are intangible so far as the user is concerned. They are used to display and select files, applications and specific routines, and avoid unnecessary use of the keyboard to input what the inexperienced computer user may see to be technical commands.

13.3.1 Windows

A *window* acts as a viewing area of the computer's memory. In multi-tasking operations software may be used which opens a window for a particular application. Several tasks can be viewed on the screen simultaneously, avoiding the need to exit from one program to access another. The window may be closed when switching to a different task while the original task is being executed. Spreadsheet programs have facilities for displaying sections of a large spreadsheet, perhaps the top and bottom sections, simultaneously.

13.3.2 Icons

An *icon* is a pictorial representation of a physical object or activity depicted by means of a stylised symbol. It is a very useful technique for selecting specific requirements and is used in conjunction with a cursor or pointer. An icon is selected by moving the pointer to the relevant symbol be cursor control keys or a mouse if one is in use. If a file icon is selected a list of files or programs on a particular disc will be displayed on a drop-down menu. The name of the required text file or program is then selected by moving the cursor to point to the one required. Icons and pointers eliminate the need to use complex commands and so enable the non-expert to use a computer with comparative ease. Icons also display office desktop functions, including in and out baskets, calculator, printer, file folders, diary and disc symbols. Selection of a diary icon loads a diary program, a disc icon causes a series of other icons to be displayed for file copying or formatting, and so on.

13.3.3 Mouse (and pointer)

A *mouse* is a hand-held electronic device used instead of a keyboard. It has one or more switches on its upper surface, and ballbearings on the lower to allow it to be moved around the screen by traversing it in the required direction over the surface of a desk or graphics tablet. A pointer (or cursor) on the screen moves in synchronisation with the mouse. For selecting specific options the pointer is directed to, and located at, the one required on a drop-down menu. The switch on the upper surface of the mouse is then depressed to make the selection. The mouse is used in this way to select files, programs or options in particular routines, such as screen painting, which selects the background and foreground when displaying graphs and charts on the screen. A mouse may be used in conjunction with drop-down menus and icons.

13.3.4 Pointer

A *pointer* is another name for a cursor. It is an electronic indicator, a moving bright bar on the surface of a screen, which indicates the next position for entering characters. A pointer also signals the current cell in a spreadsheet. On occasions a winking cursor is used as a prompt for drawing attention to a specific section of the screen. In the absence of a mouse, cursor control keys on the keyboard can be used to control its movement. Many business applications display a menu for selecting alternative options of a specific application, or specific applications such as payroll, accounts payable or accounts receivable. One method of selection is to locate the cursor adjacent to the required option and depress the enter or return key on the keyboard.

13.4 Other input devices and techniques

13.4.1 Light pen

This device is dealt with in Chapter 17, to which reference should be made for further details.

13.4.2 Touch screen

A touch-activated screen allows a user to select a menu item on a screen with a finger instead of using a pointer and mouse. The positions touched are recorded by the computer as coded signals.

13.4.3 Kimball tags

These are small tags with holes punched into them which contain data such as the price and part number of an article to be sold in a retail outlet. Once an item is sold the tag is removed and input to a device which produces paper tape for processing by a paper tape reader. This is a reasonably efficient and inexpensive method of capturing data concerning retail sales and is still popular in the retail clothing trade.

13.4.4 Magnetic tape and disc encoders

These devices were the forerunners of key-to-disc and key-to-diskette input systems (see below). Data was first entered via a keyboard and encoded on to a magnetic disc or tape which was then loaded on to a disc or tape drive attached to the central processing unit. Later models incorporate a central processing unit which is used for carrying out data validation (*see* Fig. 13.1) while data is being keyed. Discs are used for backing storage because of their direct access facilities for retrieving and correcting data. Hence the development of key-to-disc and key-to-diskette.

13.4.5 Key-to-disc

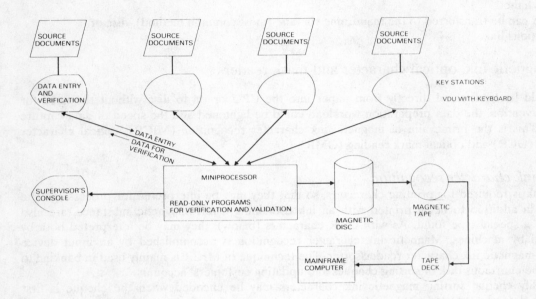

Figure 13.1 Key to disc

Students familiar with visual display units (*see* 13.4.7) may wonder why data is not entered into a VDU which is linked on-line to the mainframe's central processing unit, so that it can be processed immediately. The reason is that if the application does not require immediate processing and large volumes of data are to be input, as for example in a payroll system, manual input methods would unnecessarily tie up the mainframe's central processing unit. The data capture process may also take longer, since the mainframe is dealing simultaneously with other applications and so cannot respond to the speed of the keyboard operator. One solution for dealing with non-critical high volume data input is to prepare the data *off-line* to the mainframe computer so it can be processed by the mainframe in batch mode outside normal office hours (*see* 12.3). Key-to-disc is a mini or microcomputer dedicated to off-line data capture (*see* Fig. 13.1)

Configuration of key-to-disc
A typical configuration is as follows:

(a) 3 to 40 key stations (usually VDUs);
(b) supervisor's terminal (used to monitor progress);
(c) CPU;
(d) disc unit(s) of a capacity of 10 + megabytes;
(e) tape unit.

Features of key-to-disc

(a) Validation rules can be programmed.

(b) Data can be recalled and amended.

(c) Key-to-disc improves data control in terms of accuracy, correction, security and progress monitoring.

(d) The main disadvantage of key-to-disc equipment is downtime. If the CPU is down then all key stations are halted.

(e) Data can be transferred to the mainframe via tape (most common method), disc or communications link.

13.4.6 Magnetic ink, optical character and mark readers

If data could be transferred directly from paper into the CPU or on to disc without the need for human intervention, the data preparation workload could be lightened and the speed of data capture increased. This is the prime aim of magnetic ink character recognition (MICR), optical character recognition (OCR) and optical mark reading (OMR).

Magnetic ink character recognition

Magnetic ink is required for printing characters, so that they may be interpreted for processing. The characters, in addition to being printed with an ink containing a ferromagnetic substance, are also designed in a special type fount. As with OCR characters (below), they may be interpreted both by humans and by machines. Magnetic ink character recognition is accomplished by an input device known as a magnetic ink character reader/sorter. The technique of MICR is mainly used in banking to cope with the enormous task of sorting cheques and updating customers' accounts.

To simplify cheque sorting magnetic ink characters may be encoded when the cheque is first printed. The data pre-encoded would include:

(a) serial number of the cheque;

(b) bank branch number;

(c) customer's account number.

When a cheque is presented to a bank by a customer, the bank encodes the amount of the cheque. The encoding is carried out by a machine known as a MICR cheque encoder which has a manually operated keyboard. Alternatively, this may be performed by an encoding machine connected to a keyboard listing machine. When cheque details are recorded on a summary sheet the data is simultaneously encoded on the cheque by the encoder.

Optical character recognition

Optical characters are designed in a special type fount capable of being interpreted both by man and machine.

There are two basic OCR founts in use, both of which are approved by the International Standards Organisation:

OCR-A (*see* Fig. 13.2)
OCR-B (*see* Fig. 13.3)

Special ink is not required for printing OCR characters.

Optical characters are sensed by an input device, an optical character reader, which transfers data to the processor.

```
ABCDEFGHIJKLM
NOPQRSTUVWXYZ
 0123456789
•ᒣ:╡=+/$*″&|
 '-{}%?♪ᒿᒣᒣ
 ÜÑÄØÖÆ£¥
```

Figure 13.2 Optical characters, OCR–A

```
ABCDEFGH abcdefgh
IJKLMNOP ijklmnop
QRSTUVWX qrstuvwx
YZ*+,-./ yz m åøæ
01234567 £$:;<%>?
89       [@!#&,]
   (=) ¨´`^ ~
ÄÖßÑïïÆØ  ↑≤≥×÷°¤
```

Figure 13.3 Optical characters, OCR–B

The printing of characters on documents for optical reading is not as complex as printing magnetic ink characters, mainly because the fount is less intricate and the use of special ink is unnecessary. It is still necessary, however, to print the characters with a high degree of precision.

Encoding of characters may be performed in the following ways:

(a) *hand printing*, in accordance with specified rules for the formation of characters;

(b) by *typewriter* equipped with OCR fount characters;

(c) *automatically*, by the line printer fitted with a print barrel embossed with OCR fount characters;

(d) by cash registers, adding and accounting machines *equipped with OCR fount characters*.

Optical mark reading

This method of collecting data utilises pre-printed source documents such as employee clock cards and meter reading sheets as used by gas and electricity boards. It is a very speedy method of collecting data but care must be taken to ensure that marks are recorded, usually by hand, in the correct column otherwise invalid data will be processed causing error correction problems at a later date.

The documents are designed with predesignated column values and a mark is recorded in the appropriate column to indicate the number of hours worked on a specific job by an employee, etc. or to record the units consumed as indicated on a gas or electricity meter (*see* Fig 13.4).

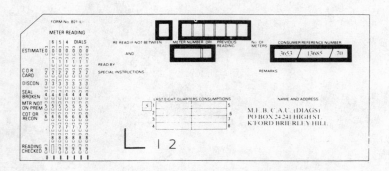

Figure 13.4 Meter reading sheet: OMR and OCR: off-peak supply

As an example, the Midlands Electricity Board produces meter reading sheets by computer which contain details printed in optical characters. The meter sheets are used by meter readers who record meter readings (electricity consumed by customers) by marks in pre-designated meter reading columns. The details are then transferred to magnetic tape by optical mark and optical character reading.

The magnetic tape file is then used to produce consumer bills with stubs. These are sent to the consumer who detaches the stub and returns it with the remittance. The stub is then read by an optical character reader and transferred to magnetic tape to provide a file of cash receipts. The cash receipts are then recorded against the consumer record to provide an updated file of consumer details on magnetic tape. Both the meter sheet and the bill stub are turnaround documents as they are initially produced by the computer as an output and subsequently become the basis of input to the computer for further processing. The computer has actually produced its own input data at an earlier output stage.

13.4.7 Terminals

First and foremost, terminals are devices for transmitting and/or receiving data over a communication channel.

Terminals may either be special purpose or general purpose, depending upon the operating environment. Examples of special purpose terminals are bank cashpoints; point-of-sale cash tills; and clocking-on terminals for recording hours worked.

Conversational or *interactive* processing means the user of the terminal and the computer to which it is linked have a dialogue, usually of a question and answer nature.

Terminals are used in many and varied environments, e.g. a portable terminal can be used in the home or hotel room, or anywhere there is a telephone extension for connecting the terminal to a computer, for such purposes as: time sharing or teleshopping via the videotex system such as Prestel Viewdata facility; for airline seat reservations; for booking hotel accommodation or theatre tickets; for the booking of holidays by tour operators; and for gas and electricity board consumer enquiry systems.

It has already been indicated that the primary purpose of a terminal is the transmitting and/or receiving of data but a brief summary, prior to further study, of the different forms this may take should be beneficial.

(a) Transmission of data from one location to another or between computers in a local area network environment for text, data or electronic mail processing purposes.

(b) Access to a computer for the time sharing facilities either for program development, problem solving or file processing.

(c) Random enquiry facilities for credit status enquiries, product availability, account status or hotel or airline seat availability.

(d) Real-time control of manufacturing processes and airline seat reservations.

(e) Point-of-sale data capture in supermarkets.

(f) Access to cash outside banking hours by means of cashpoint terminals.

(g) Processing business operations such as:
    (i) on-line order entry;
    (ii) on-line stock control;
    (iii) on-line payroll processing.

(h) Collection of data relating to works orders.

(i) Transmission of handwritten data and signatures by handprint data entry terminal.

(j) Console unit for controlling computer operations.

Visual display unit

The VDU, which is often referred to as a video unit or video terminal, is a general purpose terminal which can be used for a wide range of business applications. In appearance a VDU is like a television set with a keyboard or even like a microcomputer.

The screen is a cathode ray tube (CRT) which displays images such as graphs, diagrams and text. If a copy of the screen image is required it can be accomplished by copying the screen display to a printer connected to the VDU. A light pen may be used in conjunction with the VDU for graphical applications.

Data is displayed on the screen from incoming signals or direct from the keyboard as everything that is keyed in is displayed. The screen can be cleared by a function key without destroying the contents of the memory. Data can be corrected (edited) on the screen before transmitting it to another terminal or computer. Windows or split screens are available for displaying several different elements simultaneously; different document images for instance.

A cursor, a moving bright spot on the surface of the screen, indicates the next position for entering characters. Sometimes, a winking cursor is used as a prompt for drawing attention to a specific section of the screen. Data is usually buffered allowing it to be transmitted in blocks of characters, instead of individual characters; this effectively increases the speed of transmission.

Other features which VDUs possess include character sets switchable to other languages such as Spanish, German, French and English. Some models have screens which can be tilted and swivelled to suit the ergonomic needs of individuals. In addition they have switchable emulation facilities which allow one model to act as a different model. Various character resolutions are also available including characters made up of a number of bits in a matrix, among which are 8×10, 7×10 and 14×10. (*See* Fig. 13.5.)

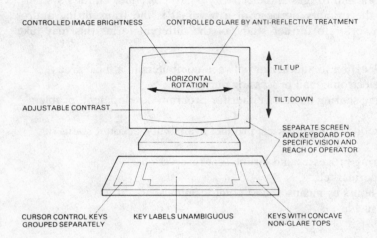

CONTROLLED IMAGE BRIGHTNESS   CONTROLLED GLARE BY ANTI-REFLECTIVE TREATMENT

HORIZONTAL ROTATION

TILT UP

TILT DOWN

ADJUSTABLE CONTRAST

SEPARATE SCREEN AND KEYBOARD FOR SPECIFIC VISION AND REACH OF OPERATOR

CURSOR CONTROL KEYS GROUPED SEPARATELY   KEY LABELS UNAMBIGUOUS   KEYS WITH CONCAVE NON-GLARE TOPS

Figure 13.5 Features of a workstation

Intelligent terminals

Terminals with inbuilt processing capabilities are referred to as *intelligent* terminals, as they can perform tasks such as validating data before it is transmitted to a main computer. This relieves the main computer from the task allowing it to concentrate on high speed *number crunching* activities. The use of intelligent terminals generates a higher level of processing productivity. Intelligent terminals can be programmed to perform computing tasks which means that they are computers which can be used on a stand-alone basis or as part of a distributed network. Note that to operate stand-alone, a backing storage device is needed to gain access to software and files. Microcomputers are often used as intelligent terminals. Unintelligent terminals do not have built-in computing logic, only data transmission facilities.

13.4.8 Special purpose terminals

Factory terminal

A typical set up would be a microprocessor-based terminal which allows data to be input via a keyboard, with a 10-column badge and 80-column punched card. A large, clear display for input instructions, error messages and replies to enquiries is ideal for factory use.

The prime types of data recorded include the completion of specific tasks, the movement of materials and components and attendance of personnel. Authorised personnel can retrieve up-to-date file information via the display. Typical enquiries include job status, next job details, component location or stock availability.

Variable information is entered via a 12-key numeric keyboard or a 42-key alphanumeric keyboard. The keyboards are pressure sensitive. To simplify data entry, fixed information such as personnel or part numbers can be read in via a plastic badge.

The terminal has a card reader to accept standard or plastic 80-column punched cards. The terminal can hold up to 10 basic transaction programs which, together with guidance instructions, can be easily specified and amended by the user's own staff.

Initial program loading is done either directly through the system control unit or via a card reader. A user identity check can be included in any program. The terminals can be located up to 7.6 wire km (4.7 miles) from the processor but this can be extended by a modern booster. The transmission speed can be up to 4800 *baud* or bits per second (*see* Fig. 13.6).

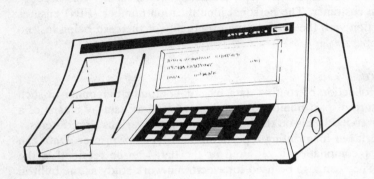

Figure 13.6 ICL 9603 factory terminal

Article numbering and checkout scanning

Article numbering is done through a European Article Number (EAN) bar code (*see* Fig. 13.8) which is a series of bars and spaces of varying width to a predetermined structure and standard. A bar code is the machine-sensible version of a product's article number which is unique to each size, colour and pack of every item.

Checkout scanning involves the scanning of the bar code on items sold by a low-intensity laser scanner and other electronic scanning devices such as light pens or slot scanners. These devices are sometimes referred to as bar code readers. The advantage to shoppers is a more efficient checkout service, with itemised till receipts identifying each item and its price, fewer items out of stock and possibly lower prices as a result of more efficient management of the supermarket.

9 780273 022077

Figure 13.7 Example of a bar code

Auto teller terminals

These terminals are for automating payments to bank customers and data collection. Many bank branches have facilities for providing customers with a cash withdrawal service outside normal banking hours. The availability of the service is determined by each bank. Each customer is provided with a plastic card which is placed in a special cash dispensing and recording machine (the auto teller terminal, installed through the wall of the bank. The customer keys in the personal number previously provided on the numeric keyboard of the terminal and enters the amount of money required on the same keyboard. The data is entered by the depression of a data entry key. The cash required is dispensed automatically (auto teller). The customer then removes the cash and the card from the terminal.

The transactions are recorded on the customer's statement, indicating which facility was used. A weekly withdrawal limit is given to each customer. The personal identification number (PIN) ensures security because this is used in conjunction with the card. In the eventuality of the card being lost no one can use it without the personal number.

Portable computer for data capture

Portable data capture is used for the collection of routine data by non-computer personnel in such environments as the stores for the capture of part numbers, quantities and other data by means of a bar code reading wand, which reads bar coded labels on the bins containing the various stored items.

These portable machines can be interfaced for printing reports on most types of printer. Data can be transmitted to a central database for compilation if required or the data can be retained in the internal memory until the next period. They can also be used for electronic work study as the built-in calendar clock facilitates accurate timing of individual operations.

Handprint data entry terminal

This can be a local or remote terminal which enables handprinted data to be captured at the time of writing and the data is validated simultaneously. The device converts the handprinted alphanumeric characters into ASCII computer code (*see* 3.4.3) and transmits this code to any host computer via a standard interface.

It comprises a pressure sensitive writing surface, an inbuilt microprocessor and an integral 40-character line display. Data and signatures are written using an ordinary ballpoint pen or pencil on documents designed by the user to suit their specific applications. This method of data capture may be used for entering customer order details, retail point of sale recording, payroll and file amendments, etc.

Available options allow the data to be transmitted or validated immediately it is written or stored and transmitted in blocks.

Speech synthesis

The recognition of speech is achieved using allophones, the basic speed sounds, by storing a digitised pattern in the form of a reference matrix. This is a pattern of signals unique for each vocabulary word; any English word can be constructed and spoken by this means. Words are recognised by a matching technique and the speech pattern of several speakers can be stored simultaneously. Having obtained a matrix pattern of the words the computer performs a search routine for the nearest match. When this is located it compares the bit count relationship with the memory pattern. The chosen word is then displayed. If a satisfactory match is not achieved it is necessary to repeat the word spoken.

It is possible to incorporate speech in BASIC programs to be run on microcomputers so that spoken words can be integrated in the normal program to be generated as output for games and other applications. Speech synthesisers have built-in amplifier, volume control and speaker.

Analogue (digital) input

This type of input is applicable to process and machine control, data logging, patient monitoring systems and laboratory projects, etc. A sensor collects details relating to the status of the system being controlled in the form of analogue signals which are converted to digital signals by a digitiser. Analogue data is represented in a continuous form as contrasted with digital data which is in discrete form, i.e. finite values. Analogue data is represented by physical variables such as voltage, resistance, temperature, pressure and rate of flow. As variations in these variables take place they are input to the digitiser which is continuously scanned by the computer.

13.5 Output devices

The most appropriate output device will depend on the requirements, availability and cost of equipment. The main output devices are character, line and page printers; visual display units (VDUs); and computer output on microfilm/fiche (COM).

13.5.1 Character printers

Character printers print one character at a time in the same way as a typewriter, but also have facilities for bi-directional printing, i.e. printing from left to right and right to left.

The dot matrix printer

This prints characters via a print head consisting of a matrix of pins which form the shape of the characters. The typical printing speed is in the region of 120/150 characters per second (cps), largely due to the bi-directional printing facility. The printer is designed to print *on the fly*, i.e. while in motion, with the print-head moving bi-directionally at a uniform horizontal velocity.

These printers are comparatively low priced and have the capability to print graphics. However, they are not suitable for producing letter quality print, although manufacturers are continually making improvements and some do claim a *near letter quality* (NLQ).

Daisy wheel printers

Daisy wheel printers have a set of characters embossed on the tips of individual stalks which radiate from the central hub of the wheel, thus resembling a daisy. The wheel rotates until the selected character is positioned in front of a hammer which strikes the tip of the stalk against a carbon ribbon and so produces an image of the character. The daisy wheel printer is slower than the dot matrix mainly because the daisy wheel is momentarily stationary during positioning. The daisy wheel prints at a typical speed of 40/50 cps and cannot print graphics but the print quality is superior to that of the dot matrix printer.

Thermal printers

This type of printer uses thermal electrosensitive paper which has a thin coating of aluminium over a black or blue inked surface. By passing an electrical current through a needle on to the paper, a spark is formed which removes a small area of aluminium and so exposes the black or blue undersurface in the shape of specific characters.

The main advantages are that thermal printers are silent (non-impact) and hence are suitable for use in office environments, and that they have graphic capabilities. The major disadvantage is the cost of the special thermal paper required.

Ink jet printers

These are non-impact printers with graphics capabilities and some have a colour printing option. One type of ink jet printer has a selection of ink wells which it can link to its printing head. The print head comprises a fine nozzle through which the ink is ejected. One disadvantage of non-impact printers is that they cannot print multiple copies; impact printers can do so using carbon paper.

13.5.2 Line and page printers

Line printers

Line printers are so called because they appear to print a complete line at a time. Typical speeds range with the age, manufacture and complexity of the model from 200 to 3,000 lines per minute (lpm) but costs are much higher than for character printers. They are appropriate for high volume printing from mini and mainframe computers. There are two main types: barrel and chain printers.

Barrel (or drum) printer. This has character sets embossed around a barrel. When a line is to be printed the barrel rotates so that all the As are printed followed by the Bs and so on. There are a series of hammers corresponding to each print position so that, for example, all As in a line of print can be printed at the same time.

Chain printer. A chain printer has characters embossed on a chain which rotates so that every character passes the print position. A hammer prints the required character.

Laser printer

Laser printers are usually referred to as page printers because they appear to print a page at a time. Laser printers are currently being used with microcomputers in the field of desktop publishing. A laser beam fires the image to be printed on to a drum which becomes electrically charged with the image. A toner is then applied which is attracted to the laser treated parts of the drum only and this passes the image through a heat fixing plate, transferring it on to paper. The drum is then wiped clean before it starts its next cycle. Laser printers produce very high quality print at high speeds and can print graphics. Complete forms such as invoices, customer statements or payroll slips can be printed and so pre-printed stationery is no longer necessary. Initially laser printers were very expensive costing in the region of £20,000 to £100,000 but they are now available at prices of around £1,400 upwards. Bear in mind that there are cheaper models which can be used with microcomputer configurations, but these are much slower and so do not classify as page printers.

13.5.3 A summary of the features of printers

As stated above, printers are sometimes categorised as *impact*, for example dot matrix and barrel printers, and *non-impact* (silent), for example thermal and laser printers.

The following list summarises the main points to consider when selecting a printer.

(a) speed;
(b) column width, e.g. 80 or 136 characters;
(c) tractor or friction feed;
(d) colour printing;
(e) parallel or serial interface as appropriate for microcomputer;
(f) graphics capabilities;
(g) bi-directional printing;
(h) condensed and double-width printing;
(i) alternative character sets;
(j) plain or thermal paper;
(k) cut sheets or continuous stationery;

(l) singly or multi-part sets;
(m) varying character pitches;
(n) price;
(o) quality of print.

Most of the above points relate to character printers suitable for micromputers or for attachment to VDU terminals. The main considerations for line printers, which are more appropriate for minis and mainframes, are speed, price, quality and perhaps graphics, which indicates the need for a laser printer.

13.5.4 Visual display units

These can function as both input (*see* 13.4.7) and output devices. When the VDU is functioning as an input device the screen displays the data being entered at the keyboard for reference by the user to verify what is being typed. As an output devide the VDU displays information *already* held within the computer, for example current stock availability; customer balances; airline seat availability, etc. Screen output is a key feature of real-time systems where immediate access to current information is required. It is worth noting that in some on-line systems printers are attached to the VDU so that a hard copy printout of the screen can be produced if required. Graphics can be displayed on VDU screens so they can be used for displaying business graphics, for example bar charts showing current and previous years' profits.

13.5.5 Computer output on microfilm

Microfilm in its simplest form is most commonly used in local libraries but has other computer applications. When it was first introduced the film was produced simply by photographing paper documents. With the advent of computer technology the obvious development was to remove the need for printing a hard copy and produce the microfilm directly from a device on-line to the computer, or from an off-line device capable of reading disc or tape backing store. This became known as computer output on microfilm (COM).

Hardware and software requirements
A typical COM system is minicomputer controlled and produces alphanumeric or graphical output on imaged, cut and processed dry silver microfiche. This is done directly by means of a COM recorder connected to the host processor, or via COM formatted magnetic tapes for off-line mode. Disc drives are used for storage of parameters and job details. Software provides facilities for drawing and outputting forms. Reduction ratios are typically $24\times$, $42\times$ and $48\times$. Images can be stored either on film or 105mm microfiche. The COM system adds an index to each image for reference and retrieval purposes. Microfiche is more popular than roll film as images are more easily accessed by simply moving the microfiche under the viewer to the desired image. This facilitates the location of component parts for a particular unit so that it can be located in the stores of a spares organisation, for instance. Related images can be stored on the same microfiche. Fiche are more easily stored than rolls of film and fiche readers are less expensive than roll film readers, are capable of a much higher quality of image reproduction and are also less complex.

Information retrieval
Information stored as images on film or microfiche can be accessed for retrieval purposes by a microfilm or fiche *viewer*. If a hard copy is required this is done by a *demand* printer.

Advantages:

(a) space – the ratio of the amount of information that can be stored on microfiche to the amount that is recorded on paper ranges from 1:50 to 1:500;

(b) durability;

(c) cost – microfilm is cheaper than paper and because of its compact nature distribution costs are lower;

(d) speed: output can be produced up to 20 times faster than when using a line printer. Note that laser printers alter this ratio significantly.

(e) searching for information – retrieval by microfilm is far more efficient than by documented listings.

Disadvantages:

(a) information access – information cannot be accessed without using a reader;

(b) updating information – frequent updating is not practical as the microfiche or roll of film has to be reproduced. Microfilm is most suited to large volumes of static, for example historic, information. Oudated ledger information which has to be kept for seven years for record purposes is ideally suited to microfilm.

13.6 Backing storage

Computers have an internal memory for storing data and programs during processing which is known as random access memory or RAM. It is a volatile type of memory and any data or instructions stored in memory locations are lost when the computer is switched off. Even though internal memory capacity is quite extensive on larger computers it is insufficient to store all the applications software and files required by a business, which is why backing storage is necessary. Files and programs are held on magnetic discs until required when they are transferred to the internal memory to be used in processing a particular application such as payroll, stock control or sales accounting. Disc files are the counterpart of filing cabinets in a clerical system. A clerical system stores related sets of documents in folders or filing trays which themselves are stored in filing cabinets. The files are retrieved from filing cabinets and relevant documents or accounting records (ledger cards) from folders or filing trays when required for reference or updating. The same purpose is served by computer backing storage, which is a mass storage facility. In a computer system records, the counterpart of documents or ledger cards, are retrieved from specific files, the equivalent of folders or filing trays, from a specific disc, the counterpart of a particular filing cabinet.

13.6.1 Discs

Discs are direct access devices. Files can be organised which enables records to be accessed directly without reading through all the records preceding the one required. It is worth noting that the ability to access records directly is dependent on both the backing storage device and the type of file organisation. It is possible to organise files on disc which do not allow direct access to records on that file. The different types of file organisation which facilitate direct access will be discussed later. (*See* Fig. 13.8.)

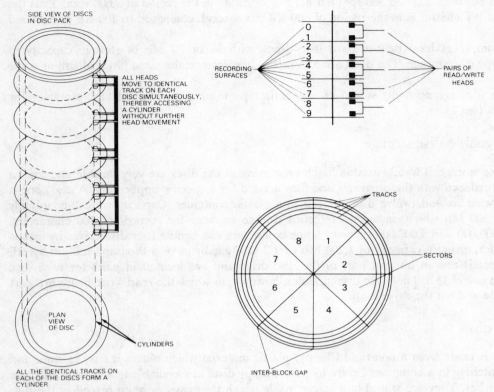

SIDE VIEW OF DISCS
IN DISC PACK

ALL HEADS MOVE TO IDENTICAL TRACK ON EACH DISC SIMULTANEOUSLY, THEREBY ACCESSING A CYLINDER WITHOUT FURTHER HEAD MOVEMENT

RECORDING SURFACES

PAIRS OF READ/WRITE HEADS

PLAN VIEW OF DISC

CYLINDERS

ALL THE IDENTICAL TRACKS ON EACH OF THE DISCS FORM A CYLINDER

TRACKS

SECTORS

INTER-BLOCK GAP

Figure 13.8 General terminology relating to hard discs

13.6.2 Hard discs

Winchester and exchangeable disc packs are *hard discs* as they are made from a rigid light alloy coated on both sides with a layer of magnetisable oxide. The discs rotate at very high speed on the drive and access to records is made as the disc rotates. Data is stored on the disc surfaces along concentric tracks. These tracks are divided into sectors. A track index locates specific records directly without having to search the file (as with magnetic tape). Data on the the discs is stored in binary code and is written to the disc from data stored in the processor's internal memory. Similarly, data is read from the disc and transferred to the processor's memory for reference or processing purposes. Read/write heads do not come in contact with the disc surface but float above it on a cushion of air. Because of this Winchester discs do not wear as easily as floppy discs and are therefore suitable for frequent usage.

A disc cartridge is another type of hard disc used on some minicomputer systems. Some computer systems use very large capacity fixed discs for storing large volumes of frequently used data. Such discs are sealed within the disc drive and unlike exchangeable disc storage (EDS) cannot be interchanged (*see* Chapters 21 and 25).

13.6.3 Winchester discs

Winchester discs are used to complement floppy discs or, in some models of microcomputer, to replace them. They have a much greater storage capacity, typically 5, 10 and 20 MB (megabytes); floppies have in the region of 250 K–1 MB. A Winchester disc is rigid and is sealed in a case. It rotates at a much faster speed than a floppy and so data is transferred much faster: floppy discs typically rotate at between 200 and 360 rpm but hard discs rotate in the region of 3,600 rpm. Thus the access speed of a Winchester is in the region of 800 KB per second, compared to 100 KB per second for floppy discs.

Some microcomputers have built-in hard disc drives with 10 or 20 Mb of storage capacity to complement floppy disc storage. The discs are 5.25 inches in diameter, the same physical size as some floppy discs.

Copies of the files are normally stored on magnetic tape using a high speed tape streamer for back-up purposes (*see* 13.8).

13.6.4 Exchangeable disc storage

Exchangeable disc storage is widely used in batch processing as the discs are very flexible and can be exchanged in accordance with the programs and files needed for a specific application. A *disc pack* is made up of between six and twelve discs, stored in a plastic container. Capacity varies accordingly between 60 and 300 Mb which, in terms of record storage capacity for records of 100 characters, stores between 600,000 and 3,000,000 records. Some computers can handle four disc drives by means of a disc controller, giving a capacity of 1,200 Mb or 1.2 Gb (gigabytes or a thousand million bytes). The read/write heads are an integral part of the disc drive and are located in pairs for each disc surface, as shown in Fig 13.8. There are disc modules, however, in which the read/write heads are part of the disc module and not the drive itself.

13.6.5 Floppy discs

This type of disc is made from a non-rigid (floppy) plastic material which makes it easy to store and suitable for despatching to a computer centre by post. Floppy discs are available in a number of sizes: 3.5, 5.25 and 8 inches. They are stored in a sleeve inside which they revolve when placed in the disc drive. Different versions of floppy discs are available, including pre-formatted or unformatted; single side/single density; single side/double side/double density; single side/quad density; and double side/quad density. The higher the recording density the higher the quality of disc required.

13.6.6 Formatting discs

A new disc must be formatted by a special program before information or programs can be written to it. The program places identifying data on to the tracks for reference by the Disc Operating System (DOS). Formatting is done by either of two techniques according to the particular model of computer. Some adopt 'soft sectoring' whereby the sectors on a disc are identified by coded signals recorded on the disc tracks. The technique of 'hard sectoring' identifies sectors on a disc by means of holes punched through the disc around the central hole marking the beginning of each sector.

In some instances discs are formatted by inserting a blank disc into the drive and selecting the 'disc' icon and the 'format disc' icon which is automatically displayed on the monitor screen. The operating system then performs the formatting routine. In others, formatting is accomplished, after inserting a blank disc into the disc drive, by typing in the command 'Format'. It is then necessary to indicate whether it is a single or double-sided disc, which is done on some machines by locating the cursor on the screen over the prompt 'Single or double-sided disc'. Formatting is then performed automatically after locating the cursor over SELECT TO START and pressing the ENTER key.

The number of tracks on disc surfaces varies; typically 35, 40, 48, 80 and 160 tracks. The number of sides, i.e. single or double sided, and the density of recording (how close together the bits are recorded) are factors which determine the disc's storage capacity. Capacities vary from 250 Kb for a single-sided, single-density disc of 40 tracks, to 1 Mb for a double-sided, double-density disc of 80 tracks.

The read/write heads on floppy disc drives come into contact with the disc surface and this causes them to wear. They are thus unsuitable for high frequency use. Although a double-sided disc can store more data than a single-sided disc in the same physical space (discs are the same size), the drive requires two read/write heads, making double-sided discs more expensive.

13.6.7 Fixed discs

Large computer systems have banks of fixed discs which allow current records to be constantly on-line, thereby improving processing productivity: it is unnecessary to change files when processing different applications. Some fixed disc storage units for large computer systems consist of two drives, each with a capacity in the region of 1,260 Mb, a total of 2,520 Mb or 2.52 Gb. The data transfer speed is typically 3 MB/s (megabytes per second) with an average access time of 16 ms (microseconds).

13.6.8 Optical discs

Optical data discs are rotating storage devices which use lasers to read and write data to and from disc. They are read-only devices but erasable systems are expected to become available in the near future. Information is held on a metallic layer that is sandwiched in a protective transparent envelope made from glass or plastic. Information is stored on the disc by a laser beam which burns a hole in the metallic layer or raises a small blister. Information is read by a beam bounced off each hole or blister on to a light-sensitive device which interprets or reads the beam's angle of refraction. The use of this technique is expected to expand greatly in the future mainly because of its vast storage capacity.

Here is an example of the storage capacity of optical discs. If a filing cabinet in an office contains in the region of 10,000 A4 documents of 2,000 characters (bytes) each, then this is equivalent to 20,000,000 bytes. An optical disc of one gigabyte capacity, i.e. 1,000,000,000 bytes, has the capability of storing 500,000 of such A4 pages. This would require 2,000 floppy discs, each of 500,000 bytes capacity; fifty 20-Mb Winchester discs or fifty reels of magnetic tape of 20Mb capacity. Moreover Winchester discs are fixed, which can be a rather expensive hardware requirement if vast amounts of data need to be stored and accessed, as each disc requires its own drive.

Optical disc devices are expensive but the costs must be related to the amount of data they are capable of storing. From a security point of view, data on an optical disc cannot be erased accidentally as may happen with other discs.

13.7 Tape decks

Magnetic tape is not so widely used for the storage of records on computer systems as in the past, being largely superseded by disc storage of one type or another as discussed above. Tape streamers are, however, used for back-up purposes as discussed below.

13.8 Tape streamers

Tape streamers are tape drives used in asssociation with micro and minicomputers for back-up purposes. When files are updated on a Winchester hard disc, for instance, they are copied to a tape streamer at very high speed. This avoids the cost of using expensive hard discs for back-up purposes and eliminates the need to handle many floppy discs, due to their relatively low capacity compared with hard discs, for this purpose.

Review questions

1   What are the primary characteristics of a keyboard?

2   What is the purpose of a keyboard?

3   Explain the term WIMP.

4   What is a window?

5   What is an icon?

6   What is a mouse?

7   What is a pointer?

8   What is a light pen?

9   What is a touch screen?

10   What are Kimball tags?

11   What is the purpose of a key-to-disc system?

12   What is the meaning of:
(a) MICR;
(b) OCR;
(c) OMR?

13   Outline the purpose and nature of terminals.

14   What is a VDU?

15   What is the purpose of bar code scanning?

16   What type of discs are in general use?

17   What is formatting?

18   What is a tape streamer?

19   Distinguish between the following: dot matrix, daisy wheel, thermal, ink jet, line, page and laser printers.

14 Data communications systems

14.1 Introduction

Data communication is the transmission of data from a sender to a receiver over some kind of electrical transmission system in coded form. The counterpart of data communication is voice communication between one person and another by means of the public telephone network or by an internal private automatic branch exchange (PABX). Data communication between businesses is increasing mainly as a result of the use of networks which link together computers at one location — office to office or person to person — by local area networks. Linking geographically dispersed computers — company to company — is accomplished by wide area networks which allow the high speed, accurate interchange of data. This chapter deals with many of the ramifications of modern data communications, including an outline of the devices and systems required such as modems, cluster controllers, terminals, multiplexors, front end processors and the various network topologies. The importance of digital communication in attaining higher transmission speeds than analogue signals is noted. The value to business operations of satellite communication, which replaces the use of surface lines, is also indicated. Value-added data services (VADs), which embrace added services to telecommunication networks, are gaining momentum. Such services include electronic mail, facsimile document transmission (fax), telex, teletex, electronic data interchange (EDI), electronic funds transfer at point of sale (EFTPOS) and teleconferencing.

14.2 Data communications systems

A number of communication devices and terms to be discussed in this section are listed below, to highlight them as an aid to the memory:

(a) acoustic coupler;
(b) modem;
(c) cluster controller;
(d) communication line;
(e) terminals;
(f) analogue signals;
(g) digital signals;
(h) multiplexor;
(i) front end processor.

These terms will be discussed in the context of an on-line computer-orientated data communication system. On-line refers here to terminals which are connected to, and controlled by, a computer which may be located in another part of the country. The connection is by means of the public telephone system (or private leased lines), used to transmit data instead of voice transmissions. A communication system requires a *modem* at either end of each communication line. Sometimes an *acoustic coupler* is used at the user terminal instead of a modem but it serves the same purpose (*see* 14.1). A modem is a device which serves a dual purpose because it performs both as a *mo*dulator and *dem*odulator, hence modem. It is used for converting digital signals transmitted by terminals into analogue signals for their transmission by telephone line. When the signals are received from the terminal at the computer end of the line, another modem acts as a demodulator and converts the analogue signals back to digital signals for input to the computer — which of course is a digital not an analogue computer (*see* Fig. 14.2). Several terminals in one location may be controlled by a cluster controller which connects each of them to a modem on a shared line basis. The communication lines at the receiving end may be connected to a *multiplexor* or *front end processor* (a device which handles communications from terminals to the computer). A multiplexor is a device which receives signals from terminals via communication lines which transmit at a relatively slow speed. The multiplexor accommodates a number of channels or lines on a single high speed line connected to the computer. This enables the computer to receive signals at a higher speed because the multiplexor combines the signals from the various terminals (*see* Fig. 14.3). Various types of software are required for on-line systems to function, including a powerful operating system to allow for time sharing, communications software supporting the operation of the front end processor, and applications software.

The function of a front end processor in a system with a large number of remote terminals is to support the operations of a mainframe computer. It performs functions which the mainframe would otherwise have to do including code conversions, editing, validation, terminal recognition and controlling the communication lines. The front end processor takes over these functions to let the mainframe concentrate on normal processing tasks instead of spending valuable time acting as a data transmission manager. (*See* Figs 14.1−14.3.)

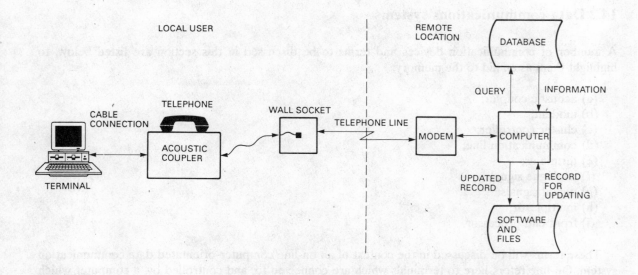

Figure 14.1 Terminal with acoustic coupler

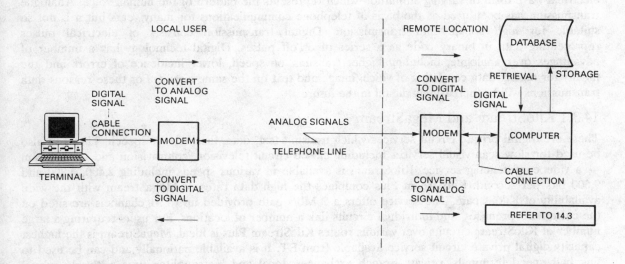

Figure 14.2 Communications illustrating digital to analogue and analogue to digital conversion

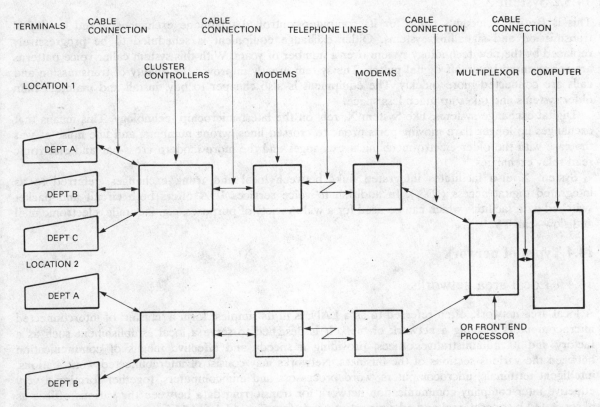

Figure 14.3 Communication system illustrating the use of cluster controllers, modems and multiplexor

14.3 Digital transmission

The term *analogue* has been mentioned previously. In the context of data transmission it is an electrical wave form of varying amplitude which represents the pattern of the human voice. Analogue transmission has been used as the basis of telephone communications for many years but it is not so suitable for high speed data transmission. Digital transmission consists of electrical pulses representing data in binary code as a series of on/off pulses. Digital technology has a number of advantages over analogue, including higher transmission speed, lower incidence of errors and the facility for mixing data consisting of voice, image and text on the same circuit. For these reasons data transmissions will be increasingly digital in the future.

14.3.1 KiloStream and MegaStream

These are digital private circuit services which transmit text, data, facsimile or speech. They can also be used for slow scan visual services including closed circuit television, confravision and videostream — a videoconferencing service. KiloStream is available in various speeds including 2,400, 4,800 and 9,600 bits per second. KiloStream Plus combines the high data rates of MegaStream with the wide availability of KiloStream. The service offers a 2 Mb/s path provided up to 31 channels are sited on the customers' premises, and individual circuits link a number of locations. For users requiring a large number of KiloStream circuits over various routes KiloStream Plus is ideal. MegaStream is the highest capacity digital private circuit service available from BT. It is available nationally and can be used to link high-speed terminals, private branch exchanges, local and metropolitan area networks, visual services and mainframes; voice and data can be mixed. MegaStream is ideal for corporate networks.

14.3.2 System X

This is British Telecom's name for its computer-controlled telephone exchanges linked by digital transmission and signalling systems. Older exchange equipment is scheduled to be progressively replaced by the new technology system over a number of years. With this system caller voice patterns are represented by on/off digital pulses. The system greatly improves the quality of transmission and calls are connected more quickly. The equipment is also cheaper to buy, install and maintain than older systems and takes up much less space.

Digital exchange systems, like System X, rely on the latest microchip technology. This means that exchanges no longer have moving parts prone to crossed lines, wrong numbers, and line noise as was the case with the older electro-mechanical exchanges and the more modern cross-bar and electronic read relay exchanges.

System X also facilitates integrated links between local and trunk exchanges, referred to as integrated digital access (IDA). In addition to voice services IDA offers both circuit and packet switched data facilities which can be used for a wide variety of purposes, e.g. facsimile, electronic mail and slow-scan TV.

14.4 Types of network

14.4.1 Local area networks

A local area network, often referred to as a LAN, is in its simplest form a 'cluster' of interconnected microcomputers forming a network or 'net'. It is designed to serve a local establishment such as a factory and its administrative offices, providing a speedy and effective means of communication between the various sections of the business. Networks may consist of interconnected work stations, intelligent terminals, microcomputers, word processors and minicomputers, together forming a very effective inter-company communication network for transferring data between the various offices as necessitated by operational and administrative needs (*see* Figs. 14.4 and 14.5).

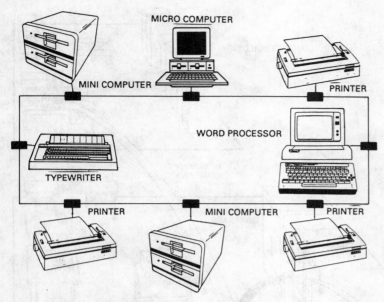

Figure 14.4 Local area network (LAN)

Networks have different topologies, protocols and methods of data transmission. The type of cable used may be twisted-pair, coaxial or fibre-optic.

Two-way communication is possible between the various computers in the network for transferring data or messages electronically, i.e. electronic mail. The speed of transmission varies between one and twelve million bits per second, much faster than the speed of telephone lines. Modems can link LANs to British Telecom's telephone system and to gateways to other networks, thus providing facilities for teleshopping, airline seat reservations, to viewdata and other on-line information systems.

A variety of facilities is required to enable networks to function, including a communication server which connects users to a variety of communication devices by telephone lines. Shared facilities include a print server providing each network user with high speed printing facilities and a file server which facilitates the storage of documents, programs and data files on high capacity hard disc. A database may form part of the network and can be accessed by any authorised user.

LANs can be either broadband or baseband. The former have a number of channels multiplexed together, one of which serves as a high speed data channel, the others being available for purposes such as video. Their bandwidth is greater than a voice-grade line, which makes them faster but more expensive than baseband, which provides only for data transmission in one direction at a time. It uses lower cost cable than broadband because of the lower bandwidth required for a single channel.

14.4.2 Wide area networks

Whereas a local area network serves the requirements of an organisation for interdepartmental communications, a wide area network serves a wide geographic area, embracing a whole country or even the world. A wide area network usually takes the form of a packet switching network. However, a system known as integrated services digital network (ISDN), a single network able to carry and switch a wide variety of telecommunications services, is expected to evolve from an integrated digital network (IDN), a telephone network in which digital transmission systems are fully integrated with digital switching systems. Such systems are likely to incorporate most of the telecom services embracing speech and data transmission including electronic mail, facsimile document transmission, videotex such as Prestel, interactive videotex (on-line shopping), electronic funds transfer, inter-computer data transmission by packet switching and so on (*see* Fig. 14.5).

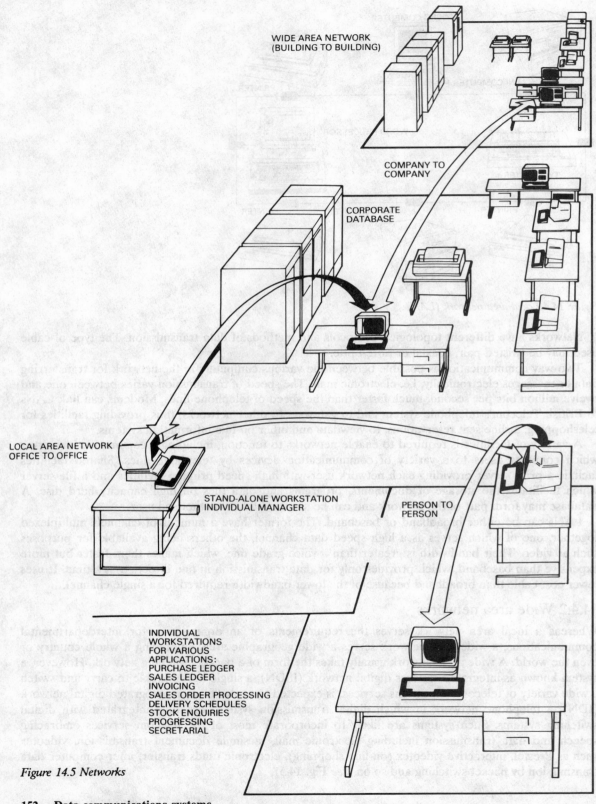

WIDE AREA NETWORK
(BUILDING TO BUILDING)

COMPANY TO
COMPANY

CORPORATE
DATABASE

LOCAL AREA NETWORK
OFFICE TO OFFICE

STAND-ALONE WORKSTATION
INDIVIDUAL MANAGER

PERSON TO
PERSON

INDIVIDUAL
WORKSTATIONS
FOR VARIOUS
APPLICATIONS:
PURCHASE LEDGER
SALES LEDGER
INVOICING
SALES ORDER PROCESSING
DELIVERY SCHEDULES
STOCK ENQUIRIES
PROGRESSING
SECRETARIAL

Figure 14.5 Networks

14.5 Network topology: ring, star and bus networks

There are three primary types of topology: *ring*, *star* and *bus* networks. Each of these will be explained in detail.

14.5.1 Ring network

This type of network is formed by a continuous ring of nodes, i.e. devices, each linked to the next (*see* Fig. 14.6). The devices may be a work station, terminal or microcomputer, each having a unique address for identification purposes. Messages are passed from one node to the next until the one to which the message is addressed is reached. Labelled packets or units of data constantly revolve around the loop or ring. The labelled packets have data written to and read from them continuously. As the packets could be carrying data from any micro to any other it is necessary for each micro constantly to check them as they pass through its node. In addition, in order to ensure that the signals sent from the transmitting machine have been correctly received by the specified micro, the transmitting micro checks the packet again as it passes through the network. Various techniques may be applied to basic ring networks to prevent system degradation as a result of faults on any terminal in the network. Dual ring systems have two complete circuits around the ring: one is the main circuit, the other provides fail-safe standby facilities. If the main circuit fails in any part of the ring the standby circuit is automatically switched in to maintain continuity of the ring. Braiding systems have three circuits around the ring, two of which are available in each direction from each terminal. The third circuit provides additional standby facilities in the event of a failure on any part of the ring. Ring networks are commonly used in the UK mainly as a consequence of the development of the *Cambridge Ring* at Cambridge University.

A ring network developed by IBM is known as the *token ring local area network*. The token ring works by sending free tokens around the ring. A user wishing to transmit data round the network has to wait until a free token arrives before being able to do so. IBM considers this to be the future foundation of office automation. The system is flexible as it is possible to increase the speed of transmission and incorporate additional users or new equipment at any location on the network pathway. The network can support up to 260 terminals. Signal boosters are necessary for dispersed networks requiring a number of kilometres of cable. Speeds of 16 mbs (16 million bits per second) are possible, which is a vast increase compared to the current four million bits per second. That is not all, however, as tests are under way on prototype systems using fibre-optic cables (replacing twisted pair copper cables) which it is expected will attain speeds of 100 mbs. IBM provides software for connecting a token ring network to PC Net, a lower performance network. It is also possible to connect mainframe computers on a token ring LAN either directly using a specially programmed PC or a Series 1 minicomputer. Links are also facilitated via other gateways. Because data is in labelled packets the network can carry traffic using IBM's systems network architecture protocols and the internationally accepted open systems interconnection (OSI) protocols.

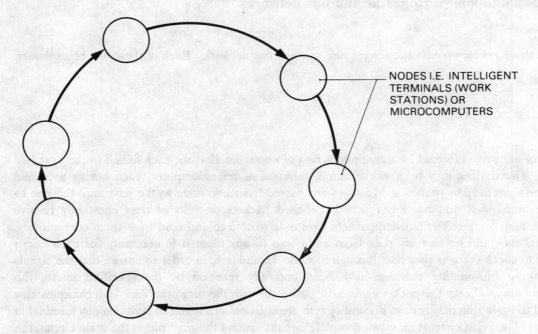

NODES I.E. INTELLIGENT
TERMINALS (WORK
STATIONS) OR
MICROCOMPUTERS

Figure 14.6 A ring network

14.5.2 Star network

A typical star network has a central network controller or file server, usually a microcomputer controlling a disc drive, to which all nodes are connected (*see* Fig. 14.7). The network transmits data to specific nodes in accordance with the destination address.

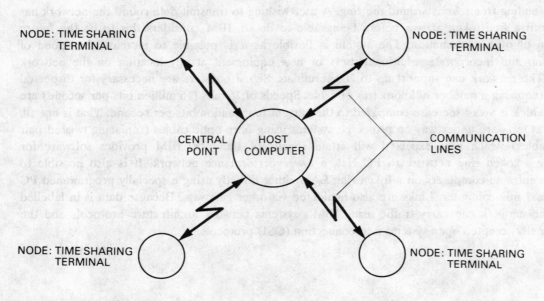

NODE: TIME SHARING
TERMINAL

NODE: TIME SHARING
TERMINAL

CENTRAL
POINT

HOST
COMPUTER

COMMUNICATION
LINES

NODE: TIME SHARING
TERMINAL

NODE: TIME SHARING
TERMINAL

Figure 14.7 A star network

This type of network is used in time sharing systems whereby the central controller is a host computer to which all terminals are connected via modems (or acoustic couplers), multiplexors and telephone lines. If the central controller, whether a file server or central time sharing computer, breaks down the network ceases to function.

14.5.3 Bus network

A *bus* may be defined as a communication line or channel to which are connected the various work stations, word processors or microcomputers by means of cable taps. Any device can easily be removed or added to the network as required. Each device or node has a specific address and messages are routed to all nodes until the one to which the communication is addressed is reached. If one or several devices fail the network continues to function (*see* Fig. 14.8).

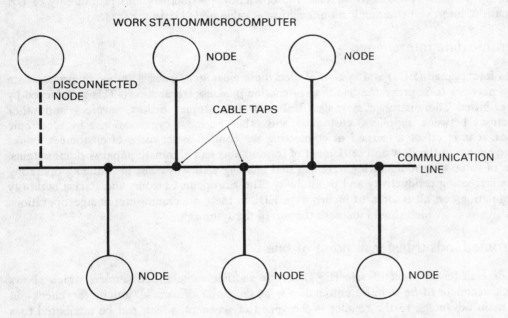

Figure 14.8 A bus network

An example of a bus network is Ethernet, which uses a system known as CSMA/CD, an abbreviation for *carrier sense multiple access with collision detect*. With this system terminals listen to the carrier wave to detect if any other terminals are transmitting data. All terminals on the network can do this at any time because of the multiple access nature of the system. If two terminals listen simultaneously and both detect that no transmissions are occurring then both transmit data concurrently. Consequently both transmission signals collide. Both terminals detect this situation by the collision detect facilities and both wait a random period of time before retransmitting the data.

14.5.4 Close-coupled networks

This type of network is also known as a multi-processor system. Each terminal has it own processor for local processing needs. Communication takes place on a bus (electronic board) which has a file-serving processor alongside the application processors each of which is able to share any other's memory. The communication distances are very short which enables transmission speeds to be achieved in the region of one million characters per second — much faster than local area networks using coaxial or twisted-pair cables. The central processor does not poll each user's processor for detecting data to be transmitted but is *demand* activated or *interrupt driven*. The protocol to handle data transmissions is less complex than that required for LANs and the complex protocols to deal with data collision and for ensuring the integrity of data are dispensed with.

14.6 Value added data networks

Value added data networks (VADs or VANs) provide additional services to telecommunication networks by third party vendors under government licence. To qualify for a VAD licence an operator must interconnect services, such as 'store and forward' message services, viewdata and electronic mail, to enhance the value of existing telecommunication networks, usually the public telephone network. The underlying purpose of VADs is to increase the efficiency, productivity and profitability of UK business by means of improved communication facilities — value added data services.

14.6.1 Electronic data interchange

Electronic data interchange (EDI) is a system of electronic messaging using a public or private data communication network to improve the handling of routine business transactions. This is achieved by replacing paper-based administrative systems (dealing with customer orders, invoices and other similar transactions between suppliers, customers and other business organisations) by electronic communications. It is in effect a method of connecting the computer networks of customers, banks and suppliers to speed up the flow and settlement of transactions and eliminate paperwork mountains. EDI should be of value to manufacturing, retailing and banking as it will assist in reducing operating costs as well as increasing productivity and profitability. The European Customs and Excise authority is imposing regulations on all traders to incorporate EDI in their document-interchange operations within the next five years, which should increase the use of the system.

14.6.2 Electronic funds transfer at point of sale

Electronic funds transfer at point of sale (EFTPOS) is another value-added service, which allows customers' bank accounts to be debited automatically at the point of sale — usually the check-out terminal. The main advantage to the retailer is the speed of payment, which can be attributed to a reduction in the handling of cash. Payment by cheque also leads to delay while the cheque is made out and authenticated. Some check-outs have a system which allows credit cards to be 'wiped' through a reader terminal. The credit-card company authorises the payment and updates the user's account. The retailer obtains the benefit of the transaction being authorised for payment before the sale is finalised.

14.6.3 Facsimile document transmission

Facsimile document transmission (fax) is an electronic mail service which transmits copies of documents electronically to worldwide locations. It has been described as an on-line photocopying facility. It uses a public electronic carrier — the telephone — to make the initial connection with the recipient. The operator dials the recipient's number, waits for the signal and then feeds in the page(s) of text, diagram or document to be transmitted. The fax system scans each page but instead of making a copy on site, like a photocopier, it transmits a facsimile of the original by means of the public telephone network or private leased line to its required destination, which can be an adjacent office or an overseas country. Standard telephone charges apply when transmitting. The line can be used to discuss the document by pressing a 'talk' button.

There are four groups of machine available, which use the telephone to make the connection. Groups 1 and 2 are manually operated and slow: group 1 machines take four to six minutes to transmit a single A4 sheet of paper; group 2 takes about three minutes. Group 3 machines are automatic and are based on digital technology capable of transmitting a page in 20-35 seconds. Group 4 works on a store and forward basis (*see* 14.13). It can process an A4 page in four or five seconds, and incorporates a telex networking facility. The service is gaining momentum — approximately 200,000 machines installed in the UK. Some machines can transmit at 9,600 bps (bits per second).

14.6.4 Telex

The telex system has been in existence for many years. In 1932 the service had just 14 London subscribers; there are now some 60,000 UK users and over two million in 200 overseas countries. Telex is a public switched network service separate from the telephone network. It is a development of the electro-mechanical teleprinter and is still the largest international electronic mail network and a primary element of an office automation system. Mechanical systems are being superseded by electronically stored program control systems with computerised exchanges providing message switching for efficient handling of transmissions. It can be linked through message switches or telex-management systems with other equipment such as VDUs, printers, electronic typewriters and PCs and allows text to be downloaded from word processors. The telex service transmits text from one subscriber to another, providing the sender with an exact copy of what was transmitted. Each telex machine is connected to others through the telex network. Text is transmitted using a five-bit code. The same message can be sent to a number of users by specifying the relevent subscribers' numbers. Earlier systems were very noisy but modern versions are compact, quiet and have facilities to edit, store and forward messages. In effect they have the same kind of functions as word processors and may be defined as text processing machines. Facilities are also provided for automatic retry to avoid wasting time attempting to establish contact on busy lines. Telex transmission speed is 50 bits per second, equivalent to 70 to 100 words a minute. It is important to note that telex is the only electronic mail service legally recognised because it provides printed documents.

BT has launched a new service called Text Direct, which allows users to send and receive national and international telex messages from existing PCs in their own offices. Some BT machines have password protection, large memories, VDU screen, text editing and prompt facilities which guide users through each stage including the preparation of documents, editing and sending.

14.6.5 Teletex

Teletex, not to be confused with telex, was introduced in the UK in 1984. It is the international text communication service, embracing a set of internationally agreed standards which ensure the interworking of terminals, including electronic typewriters, word processors and suitably equipped PCs, from any manufacturer on a number of different networks. Basically, the system operates via a microprocessor which stores and moves messages and, if so required, the system can be used as a word processing unit. It offers speeds up to thirty times faster than telex and uses a standard eight-bit computer code. Teletex provides upper- and lower-case characters whereas telex systems have only upper case. It transmits, receives and reproduces text documents including business letters, messages and data, which can be transmitted between otherwise incompatible terminals at speeds of approximately 20 seconds a page. The cost of transmitting 20 pages of text in the UK is said to be in the region of 10p. Teletex uses the public telephone network rather than the telex network and the cost of transmission is lower especially when text is transmitted on the PSDN network rather than the PSS. Teletex faces competition, however, from the greatly improved telex service and the electronic mailbox network.

14.6.6 Electronic mail

Electronic mail is the fastest-growing of the value added data networks and is an important element of office automation, with over 100,000 users in the UK in late 1988, which number is said to be doubling each year. Electronic mail is a technique for distributing mail electronically and can function solely between one computer terminal and another but is normally incorporated in local area networks or may be provided by a public service such as MicroLink, which uses the British Telecom Gold network and mailing facilities. Telecom Gold provides access to European and US mailboxes. Electronic mail uses a central switching centre which is responsible for renting mailboxes to subscribers and acting as the public telephone network link. In addition, Digital PABX telephone exchanges, which form a catalyst for the electronic office as a whole, provide access to local area networks, mainframe computers, terminals, word processors, telexes, microcomputers, electronic printing equipment and electronic mail stations.

Creating and receiving messages

When a message is created on the sender's system it is addressed to a remote mailbox and is transmitted by means of a modem and telephone line to the mailbox service operator and forwarded to the receiver, who enters a personalised code via the keyboard on his or her terminal, which allows messages to be read on a video screen.

Types of user

There are two main types of user of electronic mail — the closed user group (CLUG) or the open user mailbox. A CLUG is suitable for a large organisation with a need to restrict information to specific users. The open user mailbox is not restricted in any way and allows users to contact all other users in a manner similar to the public telephone system. This type of system could prove to be very useful to a business with a need to maintain a close contact with its customers and suppliers, for instance.

Advantages of electronic mail

Electronic mail has a number of advantages over normal postal services, principally its speed of transmission which far outpaces postal delivery times. In fact the only delay in receiving a message is when a recipient is out of the office. With the normal postal service important mail may be lost or delayed, with drastic consequences to the business — perhaps losing important orders. Advantages over the normal telephone system include the fact that a person does not have to be present (or have an answering machine available) at the time a message is transmitted. Electronic mail resolves the type of problem that arises when an accountant wishes to discuss a budgeting query with the marketing manager but finds the telephone is continuously engaged — often causing a great deal of frustration and delays in completing the budget.

Messages can be transmitted to any location provided the terminal or microcomputer can be connected to the telephone system. Electronic mail is not suitable for all business communications or document handling needs, however, such as documents requiring an authorising signature, long texts or photographs.

14.7 Telecom Gold

This electronic system provides a number of facilities such as an electronic diary, word processing, a range of compilers for different languages and electronic mail. The system is used by thousands of people using either the telephone with 300 or 1,200 bps modems or via the PSS. The system has six

PRIME computers on the Dialcom network, numbered from 79 to 84. Others include System 88 in Hong Kong, 15 in Germany and 11 in Singapore. The system is worldwide.

It is necessary for a subscriber to *log in* to the system by entering the relevant user-ID, which consists of three letters identifying the user group followed by three digits identifying the group member. A password is also required, which is not displayed for security purposes. If the user-ID and password are accepted the user is allowed access to the system.

Each user of the system is allocated a *mailbox*, which is a segment of the computer's internal memory that stores messages. Each mailbox is labelled by the user's ID. The input of the command 'MAIL' connects the user to the electronic mail system. The computer then expects the user to enter either 'SEND', 'READ' or 'SCAN'. When SEND is entered the computer requires the user to state the ID's of the recipients of the message to be sent. The READ command allows the user to read the whole of a message, but SCAN lists only the sender of the message, the time, date, and a single line describing the message content. If no messages are stored for a user, the response to a READ or SCAN command is the message 'No mail at present'.

Messages can be sent to a number of people without being physically reproduced. This would allow all nodes in a local area network to receive the same message if it was relevant for them to do so.

A reply can also be attached to a message for automatic transmission back to the sender of the original message.

14.8 Prestel's electronic mail service

This service, known as Mailbox, can be accessed by 96 per cent of Britain's telephone users on a local call basis. Each Prestel client has a message mailbox which is the electronic equivalent of a pigeonhole in which letters are placed in a normal postal service. The service maintains an alphabetical directory of clients which is updated every week. Bulletin board hosts and personal advertising sections quote a Mailbox number as the means of establishing contact.

The way in which Mailbox functions is to call up Prestel in the usual way, select a message page from the mailbox index, enter the recipient's mailbox number and any message. The page is then transmitted and stored in the addressee's mailbox. Addressees are informed of messages awaiting them the next time they contact Prestel. Any number of messages can be stored in the mailbox for any length of time. The system provides for a wide selection of page designs including memo layouts, standard message layouts, etc.

14.9 Mailpost

Mailpost is a facility on the Telecom Gold mail system providing a service consisting of a combination of old and new technologies. The text of a letter and the address of the recipient are transmitted by electronic mail to Mailpost's mailbox on Telecom Gold. The letter is then typed on to paper by the Mailpost staff who post it in the normal way. At the time the service was launched in early 1986, a typical letter sent to a UK addressee cost in the region of £1. There is also a once-only registration fee of £135, which includes the provision of a Telecom Gold mailbox. The system is run by New Technology Systems, which operates its own Telecom Gold user group. A complementary service is also provided to enable the non-electronic mail addressee to reply to the communication by telephoning a Mailbox number and dictating a message to Mailbox staff, who then forward it electronically to the initial sender's Telecom Gold mailbox.

14.10 Telecom Datel services

Telecom considers data transmission facilities of such importance to commercial, business and industrial undertakings as to merit the provision of a separate group of communications services known as *Datel services*. Datel is a word derived from (Da)ta (tel)ecommunications. It is important to appreciate that it is necessary to obtain permission from Telecom to connect any communications equipment to Telecom services.

Datel services are summarised in Table 14.1.

Table 14.1 Datel services at a glance

Service	Signal path	Transmission speed – bits per second	Operating mode	Remarks
Datel 200	Public Telephone Network	300	Asynchronous	300 bit/s may not always be attainable with older equipment
	Private Circuit	300	Asynchronous	
Datel 600	Public Telephone Network	600	Asynchronous	Speeds of up to 1200 bit/s are also possible
	Private Circuit	1200	Asynchronous	4-wire private circuits are required for duplex working
Datel 1200 Duplex	Public Telephone Network	1200	Synchronous or Asynchronous	
Datel 2412	Public Telephone Network	2400	Synchronous	Over some connections it may be necessary to switch to 1200 bit/s
	Private Circuit	2400	Synchronous	A 4-wire private circuit is required
Datel 4800	Public Telephone Network	4800/2400	Synchronous	Over some connections it may be necessary to switch to 2400 bit/s
	Private Circuit	4800/2400	Synchronous	A 4-wire private circuit is required
Datel 4832	Private Circuit	4800/3200	Synchronous	A 4-wire private circuit is required
	Public Telephone Network (Standby)	4800/3200	Synchronous	PSTN only operation is not available
Datel 9600	Private Circuit	9600/7200/4800	Synchronous	A 4-wire private circuit is required
	Public Telephone Network	9600/7200/4800	Synchronous	
Datel 48K	Wideband Circuit	40.8k 48k 50k	Synchronous	

(Courtesy British Telecom)

14.11 Satellite communications

14.11.1 Initial concepts

The primary object of satellite communications is to provide an efficient worldwide communication system affording simultaneous transmission/reception of all forms of communications including telephone, radio, television, data and facsimile. A communications satellite launched into the right orbit and placed at the right height circles the world at the same speed as the earth revolves on its axis, and is thus permanently located over the same spot on the equator. This is known as 'geostationary' orbit and allows 'earth stations' to be continuously pointed at the same point in the sky.

The early communication satellites such as Telstar were not geostationary. Earth stations could locate them above the horizon for only 20 or 30 minutes at a time, and had to traverse speedily to track the satellites.

The world's first communications satellite service was provided by 'Early Bird', which was launched and placed in geostationary orbit over the Atlantic Ocean in June 1965. Satellites then became operational over the Pacific and Indian Oceans to give complete global communications coverage.

14.11.2 Advantages of satellites

Satellite communications provide distinct advantages over ground-based radio transmission, which suffers from a number of problems such as interference between different transmissions, and atmospheric disturbances which distort signals.

The problems are overcome to some extent by the use of satellites because the aerial (antenna) beam covers only a limited area of the earth's surface. Also, the altitude of the satellite is such that radio waves are not affected to any great extent by topography of the terrain. Compared to cable communications satellites tend to be more flexible and less expensive. The power of satellite transmissions is to be increased so that the size of earth station aerials can be decreased. This may allow the future use of aerials in the home to receive satellite television transmissions in competition with cable television.

14.12 Packet switching

Packet switching is a technique whereby the terminal or computer in a data transmission system collects data into a block which is allocated an address. The block is sent to the local packet switching exchange which transmits it to its destination exchange. The communication lines between exchanges are only engaged when a packet is being transmitted. During lapses in transmission, lines are available to other users. If data is transmitted by the normal telephone network a charge is incurred for the length of time the line is used, even for the time when no data is being transmitted. Packet switching is designed to eliminate this. In the UK this applies where telephone calls or data transmissions on public switched telephone lines are charged on a time used basis.

14.13 Store and forward

The term relates to the temporary storage of a message in a computer system for subsequent transmission to its destination at a later time. Store and forward techniques allow for routing over networks which are not always accessible. This necessitates one or more computer controlled exchanges or nodes which are able to store messages and release them for onward transmission when a transmission path becomes available. Messages for different time zones can be *stored and forwarded* to the destination during normal daytime by this means.

14.14 Data communication terms

14.14.1 Serial transmission

Each bit (binary digit) in a character code is transmitted separately and sequentially. The least significant bit is transmitted first, e.g. 0100011. Transmission speed is expressed in bits per second (bps).

14.14.2 Parallel transmission

All the bits in a character code are transmitted simultaneously, e.g.

```
0 ⌉
1 |
0 |
0 ⎬
0 |
1 |
1 ⌋
```

Although it appears that seven bits (signals) are transmitted simultaneously this is not so because in practice combined codes are used to limit the number of signals to be transmitted concurrently. The speed of transmission is expressed in characters per second (cps).

14.14.3 On-line transmission

Communication lines are connected directly to the computer either by a multiplexor or an interface unit which scans the line frequently to detect those ready to send or receive data. When a line is ready to transmit the scanning ceases and the channel number of the line is signalled to the processor. If the processor is available the transmission commences.

14.14.4 Off-line transmission

In this type of transmission the communication lines are not connected directly to the computer. Remote job entry systems are used to transmit data, which is collected on an off-line disc drive prior to processing and later input to the computer by an on-line disc drive.

14.14.5 Asynchronous transmission

Each character is preceded by pulses in the form of stop/start signals which initiate the receiving mechanism for the transmission of a character. The start bit triggers a timing mechanism in the receiving terminal which counts the succeeding bits of the character as a series of fixed time intervals. The stop signal resets the receiver ready for the next character. This mode of transmission is used in slow-speed devices like teleprinters which may use start/stop signals between blocks of characters instead of between individual characters.

14.14.6 Synchronous transmission

The synchronisation of transmitting and receiving terminals is maintained by clocks which keep the devices in step with each other. Synchronisation is assured at the beginning of the transmission by means of special synchronisation characters which align the clocks at each terminal. Synchronous transmission is used for high-speed digital transmission.

14.14.7 Fibre-optic transmission lines

Fibre-optic transmission lines are replacing coaxial and twisted pair cables in local area networks. Fibre optics are transparent glass strands, each as fine as a human hair, capable of dealing with more than 1,000 telephone conversations simultaneously. The advantages of fibre optics are high transmission speed and being unaffected by electrical interference, which should decrease the error rate in data transmission.

Review questions

1   What is the nature of data transmission?

2   What is a modem?

3   What is a multiplexor?

4   What is a front end processor?

5   What is digital transmission and what advantages does it provide compared with analogue transmission?

6   What is a local area network (LAN)?

7   What is a wide area network?

8   Distinguish between ring, star and bus networks.

9   Define close-coupled and value added data networks (VADs).

10   Explain the terms EDI, EFTPOS and fax.

11   Distinguish between telex and teletex.

12   Indicate the features and purpose of electronic mail.

13   Define the following:

   (a) satellite communications;
   (b) packet switching;
   (c) store and forward;
   (d) on-line and off-line transmission;
   (e) asynchronous and synchronous transmission.

14   What are the features of fibre-optic transmission lines?

Self-test questions

14.1 Define the following terms:

    (a) digital PABX;
    (b) packet switching; *and*
    (c) teletex.

14.2 Local area networks (LANs) can be structured in three different ways, have three main types of carrier and allow expensive resources such as disc drives and laser printers to be used on a shared basis. Discuss these features of LANs.

Answers on page 375–6.

15 Data processing

15.1 Introduction

It is important to be aware that a difference of emphasis, if not of meaning, exists between the terms *data processing* and *information processing*. The nature of the end product is a deciding factor as to whether a system is an information or a data processing system. If the output is for management control and decision making it may be categorised as an information processing system, particularly if it is an executive information system as outlined in Chapter 5, because this type of system is for the purpose of restructuring information which has already been processed and is held in storage for different analyses and emphases, which are achieved by multi-dimensionality. This means that data (or should it be information?) is stored in multi-layered spreadsheets permitting information to be analysed in different ways by geographical location, product or service, market and other organisational viewpoints. If the primary purpose of processing data is for routine administrative and accounting tasks such as payroll, sales and purchase accounting, stock control, etc., it is a data processing system. Such systems fall short of being information systems due to the nature of their end product. Some applications do, however, go a stage further and analyse payroll data for costing and budgetary control purposes, sales analysis is also tucked on to sales accounting routines to provide information for sales management, and stock control systems often produce stock lists for stock management as well as stock re-order lists. When systems incorporate automatic decision making based on exception reporting, where facts are restricted to those of significance requiring some managerial action, the system is tending towards information processing. Such reports have the advantage of optimising management's time by notifying them only of matters which command their attention in order to maintain the stability of system performance.

A computerised system is ideal for supporting an information system because of its ability to respond speedily to enquiries by on-line or real-time systems (*see* 16.3). The objectives of such systems include the provision of information to all levels of management at the most relevant time, at an acceptable level of accuracy and at an economical cost.

15.2 Data processing

The discussion below relates to all those fundamental data processing operations which convert uncorrelated facts about business transactions into a meaningful form suitable for their designated administrative and/or accounting purpose. In other words, we are discussing fundamental data processing. The process of conversion has a counterpart in the processing of raw materials in a factory manufacturing finished products such as cars, washing machines or television sets. The raw materials are the equivalent of unprocessed transaction data and the processing operations are the conversion processes. Although data is processed by clerks in many small businesses, others apply small but powerful computers to their accounting routines (*see* 15.3.5 and Fig. 5.6). Computerised systems incorporate rules, conditions and actions into a set of instructions known as a program. This is equivalent to the clerk's instructions in a procedure manual. Programs (software) are stored internally in the processor's memory and are executed automatically, one instruction at a time, under the control of the operating system. Computers function at a high speed because the instructions for processing data are instantly accessible. Computers, particularly those in batch processing environments, can process large volumes of data at extremely high speed, enabling payrolls and ledgers to be updated faster than by any other means. This attribute often achieves staff savings and usually has a pay-off in improved administrative systems and the earlier availability of documents and schedules such as statements of account which may help to speed up cash flows from customers. Many businesses have similar applications, such as payroll and stock control, which can be processed by standard routines often in the form of application packages for the various systems. The different applications are modules providing details of the various transactions to the general ledger, also referred to as the nominal ledger, from which final accounts and balance sheet are prepared. This is shown in Fig. 15.1.

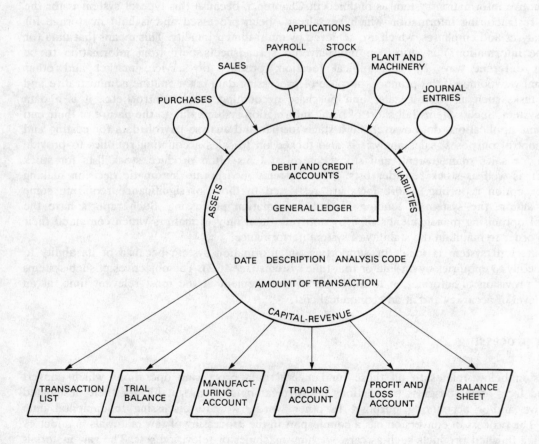

Figure 15.1 The general ledger is the centre of the accounting system

15.3 Typical processing operations

Although written in the vernacular of computers, many of the operations discussed below are also relevant to manual clerical operations even though carried out by different techniques and methods. Figure 15.2 will assist you in understanding the relationship between the various operations. The primary operations shown in Fig. 15.2 are common to most applications to a greater or lesser extent, due to the necessity to verify and validate data, sort it into a relevant order, compute the value of transactions, update records and print documents and accounting summaries. It must be appreciated that processed results — the output produced by the data processing system — can be only as accurate as the initial transaction data. The next important factor is to be aware that in batch processing applications the output from one process is often the input to the next, following a logical sequence. For example, it is not possible to update a serial file, where records are physically stored on a serial access media such as magnetic tape, before they have been sorted. Equally, it is not possible to update a file until the value of transactions has been computed. Similarly, until all items relating to a specific record have been processed it is not possible to compare the actual state of a system with a control parameter on which to base a decision according to the facts disclosed by the comparison. Chapter 27 provides a detailed discussion of flowcharts, which are constructed from standard symbols which are fully explained.

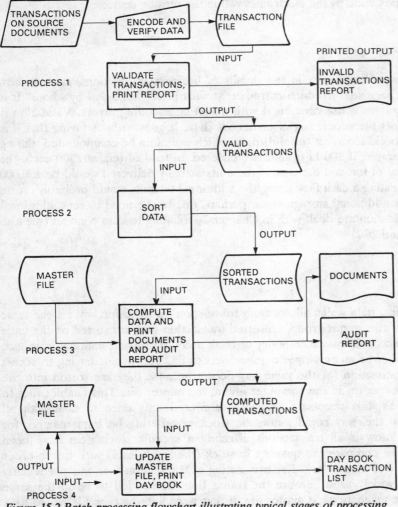

Figure 15.2 Batch processing flowchart illustrating typical stages of processing

15.3.1 Verification

Verification is an activity generally applicable to batch processing applications when it is necessary to encode details from source documents to a magnetic medium such as magnetic disc. Encoding errors occur when the operator presses the incorrect character key. A second operator verifies the coding by keying in the data a second time on the encoding machine. The second operator is unlikely to interpret the same character incorrectly or to press the same, wrong key; this would be too coincidental. The encoding machine signals when two key depressions differ enabling the position to be checked and any necessary corrections made. Do not forget that the activity is concerned with verifying the accuracy with which data has been encoded, not whether the data on the document is correct. That is checked by the validation routine. The verification of data before it is processed is essential to avoid erroneous data entering the system. Remember the term GIGO (garbage in, garbage out). Encoding is necessary in many applications since computers cannot recognise handwritten details but require input in a form they can interpret, i.e. binary code. In some specialised applications characters can be recognised without conversion, such as electricity bills printed in optical characters or the magnetic ink characters on bank cheques. These methods of representing characters are automatically converted into binary code by the electronics within the sensing devices.

15.3.2 Validation

This operation detects initial recording errors in the details of business transactions, such as how many units, of which item, have been sold to which customer, at what price, when and by whom? It is important to note that this operation is *not* concerned with detecting encoding errors. Validation is extremely important as it prevents the processing of erroneous data. It goes without saying that it is pointless, even dangerous, to process incorrect (invalid) data, which can often be compounded during computational activities. For example, if 100 hi-fi units are ordered, instead of ten, at £300 each, the magnitude of the error is a factor of ten and the cost of the units actually delivered would be £30,000 instead of £3,000. Apart from creating a cash flow crisis, the additional 90 units would probably create storage problems and may incur additional storage costs, perhaps due to the need to rent additional premises. Further aspects of validation are dealt with in Chapter 26, relating to data controls (*see* also 16.2.3 and Figs. 15.2, 16.2, 26.1 and 26.2).

15.3.3 Sorting

Sorting is the process of assembling data which allows every transaction for the same key, i.e. the same customer or employee, to form a contiguous group. Unsorted transaction files are sorted on the basis of a key field, which may be an account, insurance policy or bank account number, national insurance number, catalogue or stock number or an employee number, and so on. This avoids having to access the same record each time a transaction for the same key occurs because they are sorted into the same sequence as records in a ledger or, in the computer idiom, the master file. This enables files to be processed more effectively as it is necessary to access a record only once to deal with all transactions affecting it. Only in this way could automatic stock re-ordering be implemented, for example, as it is necessary to know if all transactions affecting a specific stock item have been processed before the program can compare the quantity in stock (the stock level) with the re-order level (the reference input or control parameter). The pre-sorting of transaction files was particularly important when tape files were widely used because the transaction file needed to be in the same serial order as the records on the magnetic tape master file. If they were not, the tape file would have to be wound forwards and backwards until the required record was under the read/write heads on the tape deck — not a practical proposition. Even though disc files are capable of being directly addressed to access a specific record it is still useful to pre-sort transactions.

15.3.4 Computational and logical operations

Calculating is concerned with computing the product and/or quotient of related values (or variables as they are called), for example computing – for invoicing and sales accounting – the gross value of sales, i.e. the product of the quantity sold multiplied by the price per unit, less any discount allowed to the customer; this generates the net value to which VAT is added to obtain the invoice value. Similarly, payroll computations require gross wages to be computed for each employee based on the calculation of hours worked multiplied by the hourly rate, or the quantity produced by the rate per piece, from which are subtracted tax and other deductions to produce the net pay.

Application software such as spreadsheets has a number of built-in mathematical functions, including:

(a) obtaining a sum of a series of values;

(b) obtaining the minimum or maximum value of an array of values;

(c) computing the square root of a value;

(d) exponential notation;

(e) defining an absolute value;

(f) computing the net present value of a series of cash flows;

(g) trigonometrical functions;

(h) raising a value to a power.

In addition, logical operators are provided which include AND, OR, NOT; is equal to; is not equal to; is less than; is less than or equal to; is greater than; is greater than or equal to, etc. These functions allow variables to be compared for automatic decision making (*see* 15.3.5 and Fig. 15.6).

Comparing is a very important operation in data processing as the outcome of comparing different items of data implies the course of action which should be taken to control an activity, e.g. an unfavourable variance between budgeted expenses and actual expenditure indicates that managerial action is required to remove the cause of the variance. A typical operating statement showing overhead variances is illustrated in Fig. 15.3. Customer credit is controlled on an on-line enquiry system by comparing both the period and amount of credit allowed with the status of the customer's account. The procedure is shown in Fig. 15.4. The operator receives an order from the customer but before it is accepted checks the customer's credit status by entering the customer code. The customer's account details are then retrieved from the customer file and displayed on the video screen. If the credit is satisfactory the order details are recorded on an orders file for batch processing or further on-line processing; if unsatisfactory the customer is informed accordingly. The matter may then be taken further by the credit controller, who should be aware of the customer's account status from previous *aged balance reports* produced as a routine task by a sales ledger application (*see* Fig. 15.5).

Expense Code	Description	Current Month			Year to Date		
		Budget (£)	Actual (£)	Variance (£)	Budget (£)	Actual (£)	Variance (£)
	OPERATING LABOUR: WAGES						
	Assistant Foreman	143	150	7 (A)			
	Setters	115	125	10 (A)			
	Labourers	77	85	8 (A)			
	Shop Clerks	91	100	9 (A)			
	Sub-total	426	460	34 (A)			
	GENERAL OPERATING OVERHEADS:						
	Scrap	6	60	54 (A)			
	Rectification	6	50	44 (A)			
	Overtime Premium	3	10	7 (A)			
	Shift Premium	—	—	—			
	Holiday Pay	184	190	6 (A)			
	Make-up Allowance	6	5	1 (F)			
	National Insurance	67	70	3 (A)			
	Graduated Pension	12	15	3 (A)			
	Electricity (metered)	46	60	14 (A)			
	Waiting Time	6	40	34 (A)			
	Sub-total	336	500	164 (A)			
	CONSUMABLE SUPPLIES:						
	Small Tools	12	90	78 (A)			
	Lubricants	12	20	8 (A)			
	Consumable Materials	46	70	24 (A)			
	Works Stationery	6	10	4 (A)			
	Sub-total	76	190	114 (A)			
	TOTAL OVERHEADS CONTROLLABLE BY FOREMAN	838	1,150	312 (A)			
	EQUIPMENT COSTS:						
	Depreciation of Machines and Equipment	135	135	—			
	Maintenance Contracts	—	—	—			
	Spare Parts	23	115	92 (A)			
	Leasing Charges	—	—	—			
	Sub-total	158	250	92 (A)			
	TOTAL DEPARTMENTAL OVERHEADS—DIRECT	996	1,400	404 (A)			
	SERVICE DEPARTMENTS AND GENERAL FACTORY OVERHEAD ALLOCATION AND APPORTIONMENT	1,994	2,100	106 (A)			
	TOTAL DEPARTMENTAL OVERHEAD	2,990	3,500	510 (A)			

Month: January 19..   Department: Press Shop

Figure 15.3 Operating statement

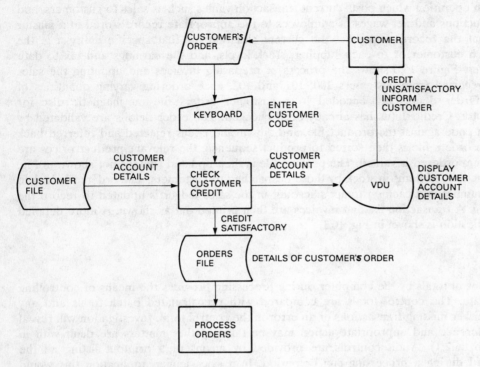

Figure 15.4 On-line customer credit check

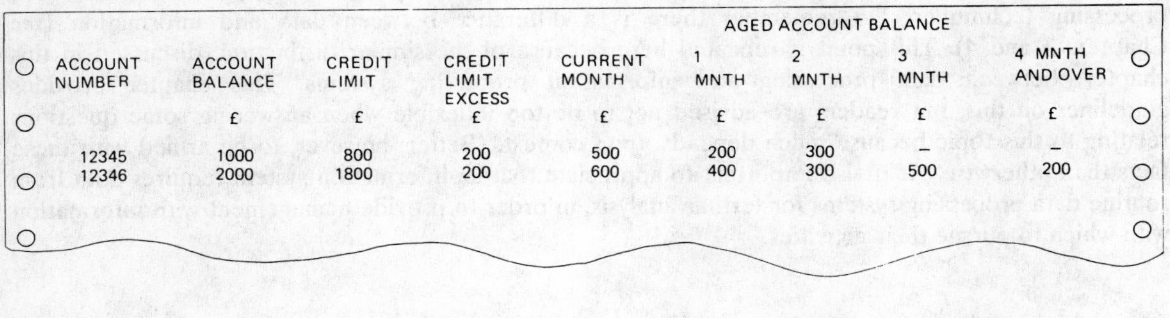

ACCOUNT NUMBER	ACCOUNT BALANCE	CREDIT LIMIT	CREDIT LIMIT EXCESS	CURRENT MONTH	AGED ACCOUNT BALANCE			
					1 MNTH	2 MNTH	3 MNTH	4 MNTH AND OVER
	£	£	£	£	£	£	£	£
12345	1000	800	200	500	200	300	–	–
12346	2000	1800	200	600	400	300	500	200

Figure 15.5 Credit limit excess and aged balance report, age analysis

15.3.5 Updating

Updating records is an operation which posts current transaction values such as sales to customers, and gross wages, tax deductions and net wages of employees to the appropriate record stored in a master file. This ensures that the records represent the current situation for that specific entity, e.g. the amount owed by each customer or to each supplier, stock levels, and the earnings and tax to date situation of employees. Figure 15.6 shows the process of preparing invoices and updating the sales ledger. Orders are received from customers 100, 101 and 102, each ordering varying quantities of different products. Order details are encoded to a customer orders file on magnetic disc for processing by computer. Credit status has already been checked. The order details are validated by checking the product code against the product file, and any invalid codes rejected and referred back to the customer. The orders file is then sorted to product sequence, the relevant product prices are retrieved and each item ordered is valued. The product file is then updated (details not shown in Fig. 15.6), reducing the quantity of items in stock by those despatched to customers. The orders file is then sorted to customer number and each customer's account in the sales ledger is updated to record the current amount owing. A transaction list and invoices are then printed out as shown. A more detailed flowchart of this application is shown in Fig. 16.1.

15.3.6. Controlling

The generation of control totals by the computer during processing provides the means of controlling the throughput of data. The control totals are compared with precalculated batch totals and any difference indicates either missing transactions or an error in the control total. Investigation will reveal the cause of the difference and appropriate action may be taken. Other matters are dealt with in Chapter 26 (*see* also 16.2.1). Audit controls are provided by means of a printout listing all the transactions processed during a processing run or period. In a sales ledger application this would include a list of all invoices, credit notes, remittances and journal adjustments. Some accounting packages facilitate the work of an auditor by printing out a system checklist indicating balances on the sales ledger and the corresponding balance in the debtor control account in the nominal ledger. The printout may also specify the number of the last invoice or credit note, and similar details relating to the payroll and purchase ledger. Copies of source documents can also be stored for future reference.

Audit packages allow selected records to be printed from master files so that they can be subjected to further scrutiny to determine if all transaction details affecting the record are shown. By this means it is also possible to examine control parameters to ensure they accord with current needs. This applies to stock control levels in a stock control system and credit limits in a sales ledger system.

Note: Further aspects of data processing are discussed in Chapter 16 dealing with the various processing techniques. Do remember there is a difference between data and information (*see* Chapters 3 and 4). This point is repeated here because of the similar distinction, discussed in this chapter, between data processing and information processing systems. This chapter provides guidelines on this, but readers are advised not to be too inflexible when answering some questions relating to this topic because much depends upon context. (Better, however, to be armed with these facts than otherwise.) It is also important to appreciate that an information system requires data from routine data processing systems for further analysis, in order to provide management with information with which to pursue their activities.

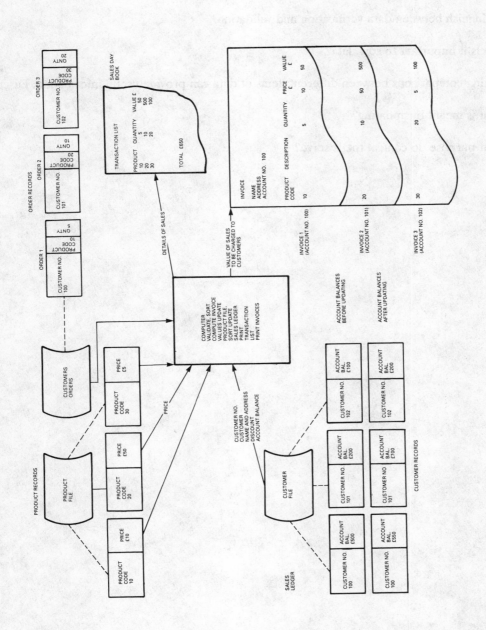

Figure 15.6 Invoice preparation and sales ledger updating routine

Review Questions

1   Outline the nature of data processing.

2   List typical data processing operations.

3   Distinguish between data verification and validation.

4   Why is it important to sort data?

5   Making comparisons between different items of data can provide useful information. Discuss.

6   What is meant by updating?

7   What purpose do control totals serve?

16 Processing techniques and configuration requirements

16.1 Introduction

This chapter has a wide range, covering batch processing (entry of data, processing characteristics, validation of data, correction of errors, back-up facilities and the type of configuration required) and on-line processing. Discussion of the latter covers the same details as batch processing and also the different types of on-line processing: interactive (transaction) processing, real-time systems, multi-user and multi-tasking systems; on-line order processing; point-of-sale systems and distributed processing.

This chapter is crucial to an understanding of why data is processed in various ways which, of course, depends on a number of factors such as volumes of data to be processed, the nature of the business activity — whether routine or critical — and the nature and size of the business. The features of the various techniques are illustrated by system flowcharts providing a visual impact. Flowcharts are discussed in Chapter 27, to which reference should be made for further details. *See* also Chapter 15 for a detailed exposition of data processing.

16.2 Batch processing

16.2.1 Entry of data

Batch processing handles batches of transactions automatically through a sequence of processing runs at predefined frequencies. Processing frequency is inherent in some applications — a weekly factory payroll is naturally processed weekly. What of invoices? The frequency will depend on the volume of invoices to be produced: large volumes may need processing daily to keep down the backlog; weekly processing may well be suitable for smaller volumes.

Each batch is identified by a batch number which is recorded on a *batch control slip*. The slip also contains control information, including the number of items in the batch and any other control totals such as a hash total made up of transaction references. These controls enable missing items to be located, since the control total generated by the computer will disagree with that on the control slip. All transactions are processed together as a batch through each separate stage of processing (known as a 'run'), which are usually validate, sort, compute, update and output (*see* Figs. 16.1 and 16.2). This mode of processing distinguishes it from on-line processing (to be discussed below).

16.2.2 Processing characteristics

Batch processing is an economical method for processing large volumes of routine data relating to various business applications, including stock control, general ledger, order processing, invoicing and payroll. After data has been processed the master files relevant to the various applications are updated to show the current status of supplier, customer, stock (product) or employee records. Master files are usually stored on magnetic disc but in the past some applications used either magnetic tape or disc storage according to the needs of the system, which normally depended on its characteristics. For example, it was considered economical to store high activity files on magnetic tape as it was less expensive than discs. A high activity file is one which requires a high proportion of records to be accessed and updated with current transactions each time the application is run: a payroll file is a good example — each record must be processed each pay period. On the other hand, a stock control system requires direct access storage facilities in those instances when only a small proportion of the records on the file are affected by transactions. This situation avoids having to access records, whether there are any transactions affecting them or not. Records on magnetic tape are stored serially along the length of tape and it is not possible to process a record until it is reached and is located under the read/write heads of the tape drive. In general more efficient file processing can be achieved by using disc instead of tape files as records can be accessed and updated much faster. For this reason most batch processing applications use disc files to store master files. Users located at sites remote from the central computer complex can transmit data via a terminal, which data is collected on disc for subsequent batch processing.

16.2.3 Validation: detection of errors

Data is validated for the purpose of detecting errors such as incorrect reference numbers, e.g. stock numbers or account codes, or incorrect values or quantities, which are detected by means of range and limit checks built into validation programs (see Fig. 16.2).

16.2.4 Correction of errors

Errors are printed out on an invalid transactions report, which defines the nature of the error. This is done by the data validation program. Obvious errors are corrected by the data control section in consultation with the originator. In most instances error reports are delivered to the department originating the respective batch for correction, which will then be delayed until the next batches are processed. Amendments will then need to be made to batch control totals. Subsequently corrections must be encoded and fed into the system and processed through the system as new transaction data (see Fig. 16.2).

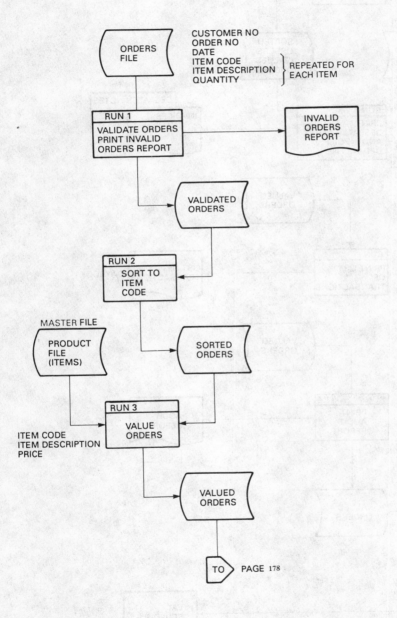

ORDERS
FILE

CUSTOMER NO
ORDER NO
DATE
ITEM CODE
ITEM DESCRIPTION } REPEATED FOR
QUANTITY   EACH ITEM

RUN 1

VALIDATE ORDERS
PRINT INVALID
ORDERS REPORT

INVALID
ORDERS
REPORT

VALIDATED
ORDERS

RUN 2

SORT TO
ITEM
CODE

MASTER FILE

PRODUCT
FILE
(ITEMS)

SORTED
ORDERS

RUN 3

VALUE
ORDERS

ITEM CODE
ITEM DESCRIPTION
PRICE

VALUED
ORDERS

TO PAGE 178

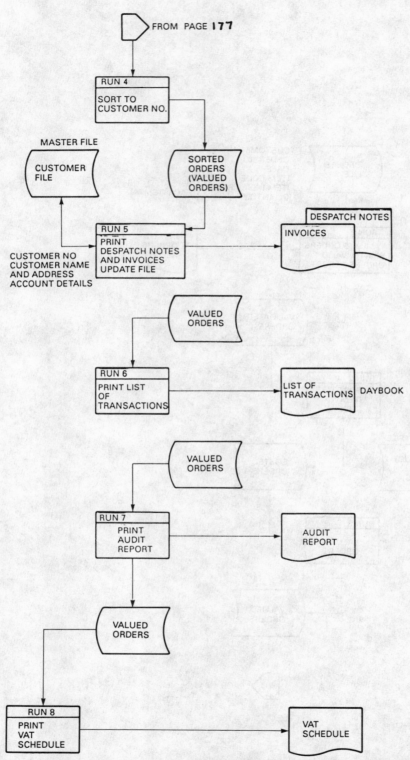

FROM PAGE **177**

RUN 4

SORT TO
CUSTOMER NO.

MASTER FILE

CUSTOMER
FILE

SORTED
ORDERS
(VALUED
ORDERS)

RUN 5

PRINT
DESPATCH NOTES
AND INVOICES
UPDATE FILE

CUSTOMER NO
CUSTOMER NAME
AND ADDRESS
ACCOUNT DETAILS

DESPATCH NOTES

INVOICES

VALUED
ORDERS

RUN 6

PRINT LIST
OF
TRANSACTIONS

LIST OF
TRANSACTIONS   DAYBOOK

VALUED
ORDERS

RUN 7

PRINT
AUDIT
REPORT

AUDIT
REPORT

VALUED
ORDERS

RUN 8

PRINT
VAT
SCHEDULE

VAT
SCHEDULE

Figure 16.1 Batch processing flowchart illustrating the preparation of invoices and updating the customer file

178 Processing techniques and configuration requirements

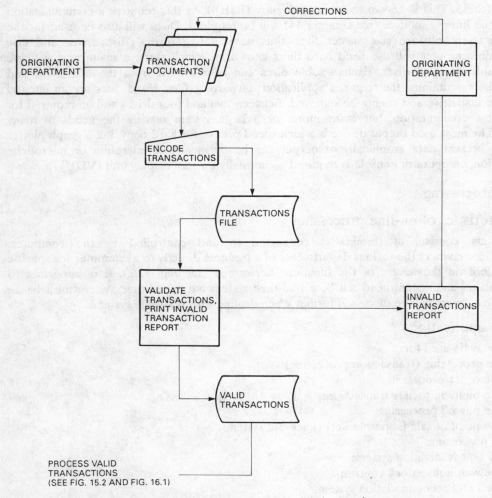

Figure 16.2 Batch processing flowchart illustrating data validation routine

16.2.5 Back-up facilities

Back-up facilities (file security) for master files are normally achieved by making a copy of the file either to another disc or to a tape streamer — a device, usually used on minicomputers, which allows high speed copying of files while avoiding the use of expensive hard discs. Back-up facilities for transactions can be achieved by retaining the original file and/or making a copy of the file, which may be supported by producing printed records of the transactions.

16.2.6 Configuration

A fairly powerful mainframe or minicomputer is required with a large internal memory capacity capable of controlling terminal operations with multi-tasking and multi-user capabilities. The specific input devices used relate to the nature of the business, as previously discussed, but for general requirements details of transactions can be collected by a key-to-disc system which produces a transaction file from which data is input for processing. In other instances data may be transmitted by terminal from remote locations and collected on a disc which stores the transactions for subsequent processing in batches. (This is known as *remote job entry* (RJE).) As this requires a communication link over telephone lines, a modem (*see* Chapter 14) will be required. Discs will also be used for the storage of application software and master files, thus necessitating several disc drives and disc controllers. A minicomputer will use fixed hard discs known as Winchesters; a mainframe will use either exchangeable or fixed discs. Exchangeable discs can be removed from the disc drive and replaced with others containing the required application software or files. Fixed discs are an integral component of the disc drive and cannot be removed. Between two and four drives will be required for a small mainframe configuration, but many more for a large system serving the needs of many operating units. The most used output device is a high speed printer for hard copy, but a graph plotter may be used to present data graphically or output can be by means of microfilm or microfiche (COM). In addition, an operator console is required — normally a visual display unit (VDU).

16.3 On-line processing

16.3.1 Characteristics of on-line processing

An on-line system consists of terminal(s) connected to and controlled by the computer. Communication lines connect the various departments of a business directly to a computer for specific purposes dependent on the nature of the functions performed (*see* Fig. 12.2). It is important to appreciate that an on-line system need not be a real-time system but a real-time system must be an on-line system. This aspect will be discussed further when dealing with real-time systems.

16.3.2 On-line applications

On-line systems may be used for:
- (a) Interactive processing (transaction processing):
    - (i) on-line order processing;
    - (ii) on-line building society transactions;
    - (iii) on-line payroll processing;
    - (iv) on-line point of sale (supermarket) check-out systems.
- (b) Real-time processing:
    - (i) airline seat reservation system;
    - (ii) on-line warehouse stock control;
    - (iii) on-line hotel accommodation system;
    - (iv) on-line banking.
- (c) Random enquiries:
    - (i) on-line credit enquiries;
    - (ii) on-line product availability enquiries;
    - (iii) on-line account enquiries;
    - (iv) on-line package holiday availability enquiries.

16.4 Interactive processing

16.4.1 Processing characteristics

Interactive processing handles transactions individually in what is referred to as *conversational mode* processing, unlike batch processing which deals with them in batches. The software prompts the user indicating the needs of the application, which may specify the data required for processing, ask if it is a debit or a credit or if there are any more transactions for the item currently being processed, to which the user responds interactively. The system may then ask if there are any more transactions and the user responds accordingly. At the end of the posting run back-up copies of master files are produced for security purposes (*see* below). See 16.2.3 relating to data validation and *see* Chapter 30 relating to dialogue design. Interactive processing can be done on a stand-alone basis by a single user or on a multi-user basis, which allows each user to enter and process data according to his or her specific needs (*see* 16.6). This type of processing technique receives and processes data at random time intervals. If transactions are dealt with as events occur and the files are updated with the details immediately, it is a real-time system (*see* below). Transactions need not be processed as they occur; for example, despatches to customers can be input the following day for the production of invoices. Transactions are still dealt with on an individual basis, however, and this is the key factor distinguishing this type of processing from batch processing (*see* Fig. 16.3).

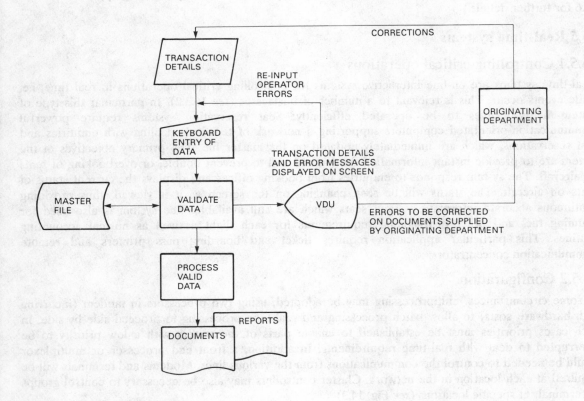

Figure 16.3 On-line processing flowchart

16.4.2 Back-up facilities

Prompts from the software inform the user when to load discs for obtaining a back-up copy of a master file at the end of the posting routine. As most transactions are recorded on a source document the retention of the documents provides a back-up file which may be used for reconstituting the master file in the event of its corruption or loss. For audit control and back-up requirements the transactions currently dealt with may be printed out to provide the details necessary for security purposes.

16.4.3 Configuration

Interactive processing may be carried out either on a stand-alone basis using a single PC or by a multi-user system. In both situations data will be input by keyboard. Data communication equipment will be required if the interactive system has geographically dispersed terminals. (*See* Chapter 14.) The type and size of processor required will depend on whether a stand-alone PC or multi-user system is used. In the latter instance a mainframe or mini with a large internal memory capable of handling the relevant number of terminals would be required. Backing storage for a PC may be a combination of a 3.5-inch floppy disc storing approximately 720 KB and a Winchester of 20 MB capacity. The mainframe or mini would be supported by a number of Winchester disc units of, for example, 60 Mb. Disc controllers would also be required. The PC will be equipped with a dot matrix or daisy wheel printer. Each location on a multi-user system may require local printers for printing documents and schedules. In addition, a high speed printer would be required at the mainframe or minicomputer installation to produce documents and reports from batch processing applications. (*See* 16.6 for further details.)

16.5 Real-time systems

16.5.1 Controlling critical operations

Real-time systems are on-line interactive systems for controlling critical operations in real time, i.e. while events occur. This is relevant to a number of businesses (*see* 16.3.2). In particular this type of system helps airlines to be operated efficiently. Seat reservation systems require powerful communication-orientated computers supporting a network of terminals dealing with enquiries and seat reservations, which are immediately updated on the master file. The primary objectives of the system are to provide instant information on demand and to prevent double, or overbooking of seats on aircraft. The system responds to enquiries from booking offices and displays the current status of seats on aircraft. The status will be seen changing on the screen as it is viewed, thus providing continuous accurate information about seats which are still available. The system is also used for planning fuel and other provisioning requirements for each flight as well as normal accounting routines. This particular application requires ticket and boarding pass printers and remote communication concentrators.

16.5.2 Configuration

In some circumstances multiprocessing may be adopted, using two processors in tandem (incurring high hardware costs) to allow batch processing and real-time processing to proceed side by side. In such cases priorities must be established to enable parts of the system with a low priority to be interrupted to deal with real-time requirements. In addition, a front end processor or multiplexor would be needed to control the communications from the various lines. Modems and terminals will be required at each location in the network. Cluster controllers may also be necessary to control groups of terminals at specific locations (*see* Fig. 14.3).

16.5.3 Back-up facilities

It is imperative that a critical real-time system has adequate back-up facilities. In a multiprocessing system the processor assigned to batch processing is programmed to switch immediately to the real-time operation in the event of a malfunction in the real-time processor. This is a fail-safe routine to protect the integrity of the data and to avoid the system going down, which would be chaotic in a critical, widely dispersed operation such as airline seat reservation. Restart procedures are an inherent part of the system and restart and audit data is 'dumped' (copied) to disc every two or three minutes. In the event of a malfunction the system can be restarted from the details last dumped.

16.5.4 Software

Highly sophisticated software will be required to control the real-time operation, including interrupt facilities as appropriate, with provision for controlling background tasks such as the processing of routine applications in batch mode. The software takes the form of a powerful operating system. Communications software will also be required to handle enquiries from the various terminals.

16.6 Multi-user applications

16.6.1 Characteristics

A modern method of information processing allows a number of users consisting of various people in different departments to process their own particular requirements, whether computing wages and payroll processing, preparing invoices and updating the sales ledger or updating the stock file. Such operations are known as on-line because each of the users is connected to the computer by a terminal (*on-line*) which is under the control of the processor. The nature of the processing is referred to as a *multi-user* application. The terminals replace the key-to-disc system used for batch processing. This type of operation requires terminal controllers for controlling the operations of groups of terminals. In addition, if terminals are located remotely, modems, multiplexors and *maybe* front end processors will be required as well as private leased communication lines.

Terminals are both input and output devices, but in addition local printers may be required at each dispersed office for printing documents and summaries. A printer would also be required at the mainframe installation as well as a console to enable the computer operator to monitor the system.

Backing storage consists of banks of fixed disc drives, each allocated to the various applications, and disc controllers for controlling groups of disc drives.

A powerful processor is required to support the multi-user environment as it must be capable of polling the lines to allocate time slots to each terminal. It also requires a large memory capacity for storing the various user programs as well as the high overhead required for storing the operating system. The term *overhead* refers to the area of the internal memory of the computer which is inaccessible to the user. It is in effect unproductive memory, in the sense that it cannot be used for storing data or records.

16.6.2 Recording, locking and unlocking

Multi-user systems require a protection feature for preventing system crashes as a result of several users processing the same file simultaneously. Record locking and unlocking facilities are also required to prevent a record being accessed by a user at the time it is being updated by another user. The first user of a record is allocated complete control to update the record and other users are denied access until the record is updated.

File locking is similar to record locking but control is applied at file level. Record locking is more desirable since file locking prevents other users accessing any records on the file during update. Note that record and file locking techniques can be used on local area networks.

16.7 Multi-tasking

Multi-tasking is a technique which facilitates the running of two or more tasks concurrently on microcomputers. In mainframe environments multi-tasking is referred to as *multi-programming*, but in both instances the technique allows high speed switching between different tasks while allowing access to multiple sources of information as with integrated packages. This means that information can be obtained from different spreadsheets for integration with text files, functional files, graphics and databases, etc. Each task has its own window on the screen, which acts as a viewing area of the computer's memory (*see* 13.3.1).

A mouse is used to select the files required from drop-down menus. Windows can be closed when switching to different tasks while the original task is being executed. Windows can be displayed on the screen at any desired location and the size of a window can be adjusted. Multi-tasking provides facilities for the transfer of information from one application to another with high speed switching between them by means of special operating systems such as Microsoft Windows, OS/2 for the IBM PCs and MultiFinder for the Apple Macintosh (*see* Fig. 16.4).

The operating system needs to know details of the different programs before they can be executed; for instance, it needs to know how much RAM is required, the resources required (such as disc drives and printers) and how the program writes to the screen, etc. For this purpose each program requires what may be called a program information file which defines the various parameters. To write one's own Windows-compatible applications, a programmer's toolkit is required to aid the construction of pull-down menus, dialogue boxes, mouse support and application icons.

Figure 16.4 Screen displaying windows in a multi-tasking environment

16.8 On-line order processing systems

On-line order processing systems are quite prevalent and a number of factors need to be considered regarding the type of computer and devices required to support the system. One essential factor is to know how many terminals/work stations will be required which, to some extent, is dependent upon the location of the terminals: for example, if they are located within the same general area as the computer special communication lines will be required for linking them together. If the distance is within, say, 4,000 feet, then internal lines can be used but if the terminals are geographically dispersed, perhaps in branch sales offices, then leased private telephone lines will be necessary in order to obtain exclusive use of them whenever they are needed. If the public telephone lines are used then delays will occur due to lines being engaged when required. This tends to negate the purpose of the system which is aimed at increasing administrative efficiency and avoiding bottlenecks in the processing of orders, eliminating shortages and reducing delivery delays. If more than one terminal is envisaged then a multi-access computer which can effectively control the number of terminals on-line is needed. The computer's memory capacity must be quite substantial to deal with multi-user operations as it needs to store sophisticated software by way of the operating system as well as the application programs. Large capacity magnetic disc storage devices may be required to take advantage of direct access capability, as an on-line order entry system must have direct access to records. For example, before an order is accepted it is necessary to access the customer's record on the customer file to check the credit status, and the product records on the product file to assess the availability of each item ordered, i.e. the stock status. The customer can then be informed of the delivery situation. Modems and multiplexors may be required for remote terminals, and perhaps cluster controllers to control groups of terminals. A line printer is necessary for printing picking lists, invoices, shortage lists, despatch documentation and various statistical reports. The speed of the printer required depends on the volume of orders to be processed daily.

16.9 Point-of-sale systems

The term *point-of-sale* is used to describe the technique used for capturing transaction data as sales occur in supermarkets and department stores. Data is captured (recorded) using special laser scanners at check-out points. A scanner senses data printed in the form of a bar code on the label of the product. The bar code used in Europe is the European Article Numbering (EAN) code. The light and dark lines of the code are converted into a number by the scanner which is sent to the in-store minicomputer. The computer looks up the number in its memory to identify the product and transmits the price of the item to the check-out terminal. The price is displayed and the price and description of the commodity are printed on to the customer's receipt, together with the total amount, the value of cash received (unless a cheque or credit card is used) and the amount of change to be given. Other details are also printed including the date and check-out number, etc.

A system has been developed which uses speech synthesised microchips which generate verbalised prices for customers. The digitised sounds are stored in a semiconductor store and released on instructions from a bar code reader.

The equipment required to operate a point-of-sale system, depending upon its exact configuration, includes retail terminals at each check-out point which can function as free standing sales registers equipped with a laser bar code scanner; keyboard and VDU which can be used as a back-up system in the event of a malfunction with the bar code scanner; an in-store minicomputer supporting the terminals at the various check-out points in the store; a printer for printing customer receipts and, if the system is linked to an electronic funds transfer sytem, a data communication link to the various banks' computers for credit check enquiries and the transfer of funds. The minicomputer acts as a system controller and may be linked to a central mainframe at head office.

This type of system reduces the time customers spend queueing at check-out points and provides itemised till receipts to give customers a visible check on the price of the goods.

The efficiency of stock management is increased through this system, enabling the level of stocks to be reduced, saving both funds and storage space. The overall efficiency of store administration is enhanced as management is provided with frequent up-to-date information, which has a bearing on the profitability of the business (*see* Fig. 16.5).

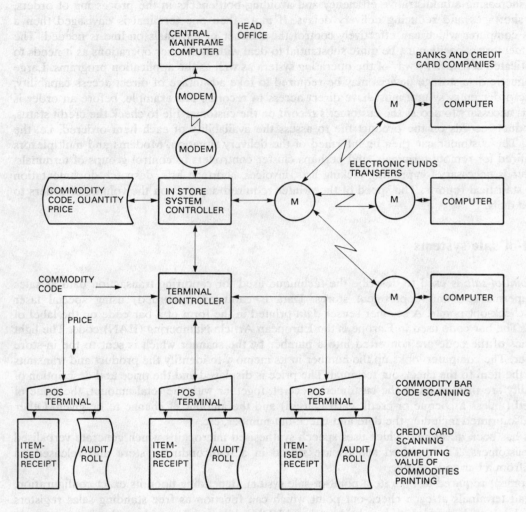

Figure 16.5 Flowchart illustrating a retail Point-of-sale configuration

16.10 Distributed processing

Distributed processing must not be confused with decentralised processing, even though decentralisation is a feature of distributed processing. Prior to the advent of the computer, different companies in a group may well have used their own data processing installation, i.e. decentralised facility. The centralisation of data processing was the trend of the 1960s, but the tendency of the 1970s and 1980s has been a reversal of this situation, largely due to the development of work stations, mini and microcomputers. These cost much less than mainframes, which makes it a viable proposition to install them in departments and branches on a distributed processing basis. This is the philosophy of providing computer power where it is most needed, instead of concentrating all processing in a single centralised computer system. Systems architecture is a design philosophy whereby small computers in dispersed operating units may be connected by a communications network to one another and also to a large, centrally located mainframe. The mainframe may support a large database, which would allow information of a strategic nature to be retrieved on demand for corporate planning. This would be a distributed processing network (*see* Fig. 16.6).

Simplicity of gaining access to a computer by relevant operating personnel at all levels of an organisation is not an easy matter to accomplish even within a single unit business organisation equipped with terminals. This problem is accentuated when there are many dispersed units within the organisation, many of which may be interdependent, e.g. marketing and manufacturing functions, as all units must be fully aware of the operational status of one another's sphere of operations.

It becomes even more of a problem when a business is a multinational organisation with widely dispersed subsidiaries. With the implementation of distributed processing systems, this is not so much of a problem because it is of no consequence whether the small computers are located in the same building as a mainframe computer or whether they are situated the other side of the ocean. Distributed processing allows a business to select the level of processing autonomy in respect of depots, factories, warehouses or sales offices.

Distributed processing also includes the use, on a decentralised basis, of intelligent terminals, i.e. terminals with processing capabilities which may be used on a local basis for off-line operation or for on-line operations linked to a host computer. The choice of terminal may be selected according to local needs and may include badge readers and data collection terminals in factory departments, tag readers and point-of-sale terminals in retail sales outlets, visual display units (VDUs) for offices; VDUs and/or printers for warehouses and video units in the sales department for on-line entry of order details (*see* Fig. 16.6).

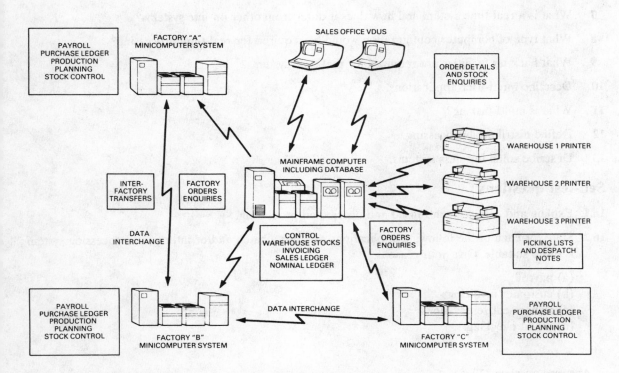

Figure 16.6 Outline of characteristics of a distributed processing network

16.11 Small business systems

In smaller businesses staff are increasingly using small business computers for accounting routines using software packages specially designed for this purpose. Previously, accounting and other administrative systems were processed by manual methods, perhaps with the aid of add-listing machines and small desktop calculators. Some businesses recognised the value of using computers and did the next best thing by employing the services of a computer bureau. When the technological breakthrough occured with the advent of the silicon chip, small business computers quickly came on the scene, many with more computing power than their big brothers, the mainframes of a decade ago. Software houses and computer manufacturers have developed small business applications software for small business computers, which has caused many to apply them to their own accounting routines because it is within their financial capability to do so. (*See* Chapter 20 and 23.3.)

Review questions

1   Describe batch processing.

2   What type of computer configuration is required for batch processing?

3   Describe on-line processing, saying how it differs from batch processing.

4   List several on-line applications.

5   What is meant by interactive processing?

6   The type of computer configuration required for interactive processing depends on a number of factors. Discuss.

7   What is a real-time system and how does it differ from other on-line systems?

8   What type of computer configuration would be required for real-time processing?

9   What back-up facilities are required for real-time systems?

10   Describe multi-user applications.

11   What is multi-tasking?

12   Define distributed processing.

13   Describe small business systems.

Self-test questions

16.1   Explain and contrast centralised and distributed processing.

16.2   State for each of the following applications whether a batch and/or interactive processing system is more suitable. Give your reasons.

(a) payroll;
(b) customer invoicing;
(c) airline seat reservations;
(d) credit checking.

Answers on page 377–8.

17 Image processing

17.1 Introduction

Image processing is a very widely applied technique in modern business. It is concerned with the conversion of images to digital signals for processing and storage purposes and reconverting them to their original form, or in an amended form having been reduced or enlarged and/or combined with other images, as in desktop publishing. The original image may be a photograph, a graph such as a pie or bar chart, a drawing or whatever. Digitisation converts images to binary digits (1s and 0s) to form a two-dimensional array of data which can be stored and processed by computer. Each element of the two-dimensional array is called a *picture element* (*pixel*), which is the smallest element in an image display. The shape of an image on a screen is determined by the pattern of the pixels which are activated. The quality of the image displayed depends on the number of pixels on the screen — the higher the number the higher the resolution. High resolution graphics provide the sharp and clear image essential for the production of graphical output. The AppleColor High Resolution RGB monitor, for instance, has a 640×480 pixel resolution, which provides professional quality text and graphics in both colour and grey scales. Other monitors have much higher pixel resolutions, $1{,}024 \times 768$ for instance. It is possible to zoom in on an image displayed on the screen to view the individual pixels from which it is constructed, which enables detailed amendments to be made to the image.

17.2 Graphics

Graphics is the term used to describe the processing, display and printing of images in the form of graphs, charts, company logos, pictures, maps and diagrams. Special software, known as a *graphics package*, is required for painting and drawing images on a video screen. Graphics software is incorporated into spreadsheet and desktop publishing packages as well as being available on a stand-alone basis. Graphical images, whatever form they take, can be printed using a laser or matrix printer to obtain a hard copy as well as being displayed on the video screen (*see* Fig. 17.1).

17.2.1 Painting and erasing

Boxes and circles displayed on the screen can be filled with colour or patterns automatically. In addition, different colours, shades and patterns can be painted freehand by specifying the thickness and shape of the paintbrush. A spray-can may be used instead of a paintbrush to give a spray or air-brush effect. Images can also be erased, using the electronic eraser as one would a normal everyday eraser, removing everything with which it makes contact.

17.2.2 Text

Text can be integrated with graphical images, a bar or pie chart for instance, for the purpose of indicating the subject displayed — say the value of sales, which may be captioned 'sales value'. In addition, the proportion of sales of each product or sales line may also be incorporated. The month, day, week or period number to which the data displayed on the graph relates may be defined by 'time labels' as shown in Fig. 17.2. Variable labels may also be displayed specifying the product, employee, customer or other variable name to which the graphical illustration relates, also illustrated by Fig. 17.2. Graphics packages provide a range of text founts from which to choose and the size of characters can be altered.

Figure 17.1 The Apple Macintosh II running business graphics software

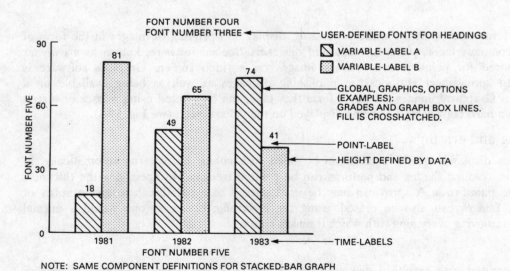

Figure 17.2 Bar graph

17.2.3 Drawing lines and shapes

Freehand images are often constructed by tracing their shape using a mouse in 'pencil' mode. By this means straight, vertical or horizontal lines, rectangles, circles and ellipses can be drawn on the screen and can be edited to stretch a line or make a circle into a different shape. The thickness and type of line can also be varied.

17.2.4 Special effects

It is possible by means of special effects tools to rotate images, reverse colours, scale images horizontally or vertically, or stretch or compress their shape along either axis.

17.2.5 Summary of graphical input techniques and devices

    (a) Video screen.
    (b) Graphics tablet.
    (c) Mouse.
    (d) Graphics stylus.
    (e) Light pen.
    (f) Electronic scanning machines (*see* Fig. 17.4).
    (g) Video camera digitisers.

A *graphics tablet*, or *digitising tablet*, is constructed of a sensitive semi-conducting material which can trace the movement of a stylus forming graphical shapes. The shapes are converted into digital signals which are input directly into the computer. A mouse may be used as an alternative to a graphics stylus. A *light pen* in combination with a video screen can be used to display or modify images on the screen. This is achieved by passing the light pen, an electronic device in the form of a photo-diode, across the surface of the screen to trace the outline of the image to be displayed. The computer detects the location of the pen on the screen surface by counting the number of vertical and horizontal synchronisation pulses. *Electronic scanning machines* convert photographs and other images from documents and drawings into electronic form for desk top publishing (DTP) (*see* Fig. 17.3 and 17.4). There are also digitisers, for use with video cameras, which convert images to electronic form.

17.2.6 Summary of graphical output techniques and devices

    (a) Graphics printer.
    (b) Video screen.
    (c) Graph plotter.
    (d) Interactive video.

Graphical images can be printed out as well as being displayed on the video screen. For this purpose a printer with good printing definition is required, for example the Apple Image Writer LQ, a 27-pin impact dot matrix printer which prints up to 216 dots per inch Letter Quality. (LQ). The device known as a graph plotter plots two-dimensional images by means of moving pens over the surface of a sheet of paper. The location of the pens is determined by coded signals providing the coordinates for forming the shape of the image from the computer.

17.3 Interactive video

The heart of an interactive video system is an optical video disc capable of storing more than 50,000 high quality colour images per side. The video disc is computer controlled and any image can be located instantly and stills, motion pictures or a combination of both can be displayed on a video screen. The displayed images can include text or graphics from the computer's memory. This provides the nucleus of a visual information system which may be used in many ways — for demonstrating how expert systems or databases function by interacting with a computer; the display of product details to potential customers; for providing learning programs in offices such as accounting routines and for other branches of industrial training such as the safety requirements for handling machines, etc. Many types of audio-visual material can be recorded on the disc including film, videotape, photostills, microfilm, printed text and computer printouts.

17.4 Facsimile document transmission

Facsimile document transmission (fax) is an electronic mail service which transmits copies of documents electronically to worldwide locations. Fax may be defined as image processing because it electronically scans the image to be transmitted. (*See* 14.6.3 for further details of this topic.)

17.5 Desktop publishing

This subject is not specifically stated in the syllabus but is included because it is a current state of the art technique and because of its close relationship to graphics and text processing. Desktop publishing (DTP) is becoming widely used due to its relative simplicity compared with the skill and experience required for traditional publishing. It is increasing the productivity of businesses because they are able speedily to produce documents internally while also reducing printing costs. Special DTP software allows a PC (personal computer) to be used as a publishing and design tool, facilitating the production of top quality publications.

17.5.1 Features of desktop publishing

The main features of DTP relate to composing pages consisting of a mixture of text and graphics to produce camera-ready artwork without typesetting (*see* Figs. 17.3 and 17.4). A graphics block can be inserted into a text block and the text will automatically flow around the graphics block whatever its shape. Text can be entered by keyboard or be imported from a text file produced by a word processing package or may be obtained from electronic scanning. The video screen acts as an electronic pasteboard complete with screen ruler, column guides and other design aids. Pull-down menus are used for selecting options and a mouse is used for the selection and manipulation of text, graphics and menu options. DTP packages have built-in word processing and graphics functions with text editing facilities for deleting, cutting, pasting, inserting or creating new text. DTP packages differ from word processing packages in that they can integrate graphics and text. The graphics may be generated by the DTP package itself or imported from a graphics package or spreadsheet package with graphics facilities. The graphics of the DTP package incorporate aids for drawing lines, boxes and circles but are not so powerful as stand-alone graphics packages. Graphics imported from stand-alone packages can move graphic blocks to different locations and then scale, crop or trim them to enable them to be positioned in the most suitable location on the page being composed. It is usually necessary to integrate separate word processing and graphics packages with the DTP package, as shown in Fig. 17.3

Pages can be viewed in actual or reduced size or be enlarged to obtain an overview before printing. Some packages have facilities for aligning details on a page by means of a grid consisting of vertical and horizontal lines. Vertical and horizontal guidelines are also provided by some packages, which allows spacing and position to be changed. Grids and guidelines have a 'snap-to' facility which neatly aligns text and graphics blocks automatically with the gridlines and guidelines to avoid an untidy dog-leg appearance. Blocks of text can be linked, a necessary requirement when text continues from the bottom of one column to the top of another and then to another on a different page. This facility allows text to flow from one column to the other automatically, in the specified sequence, when text is deleted or added. Pages larger than the physical capabilities of the printer can be obtained by overlapping normal size printed pages by a process known as 'tiling', which generates the larger size document or diagram required. Other facilities include spelling checks, automatic hyphenation, kerning — which closes up spaces between characters to improve the appearance of the text — line spacing options, and the ability to print white characters on a black background ideal for highlighting headings. Some packages permit thumbnails, or miniature pages, providing up to 64 miniature pages on one sheet to give an overview of a publication's layout before it is published.

DTP provides on-screen near-'What you see is what you get' (WYSIWYG) display of founts, type sizes and layout so that it is possible to know what the final product will look like before it is printed.

17.5.2 Development of desktop publishing

DTP became possible as a result of the development of high quality, inexpensive laser printers; the increasing power and reduced cost of PCs together with higher capacity internal memory and backing storage; the development of interfaces allowing the import of graphics and text from other packages, and the adoption of page description languages (*see* below).

A combination of hardware and software is required for desktop publishing, which is illustrated by Figs. 17.3–17.4 and summarised below.

17.5.3 Summary of requirements for desktop publishing

Hardware
   (a) *Microcomputer* with keyboard (usually an Apple Macintosh, IBM PC or compatible with a hard disc). Inputting text and graphics by keyboard or transfers from other packages.
   (b) *High resolution monitor* (monochrome or colour).
   (c) *Mouse* — moves the cursor around the screen more quickly than cursor control keys.
   (d) *Scanner* for conversion of images into electronic form for display on screen
   (e) *Laser printer* (minimum resolution of 300 dpi (dots per inch) for high quality printed output of documents and graphs, etc.
   (f) *Dot matrix printer* (instead of a laser printer) for lower quality printed output.

Software
   (a) *Word processor* for compiling and editing text files.
   (b) *Graphics* package/*spreadsheet* package/*integrated* package for more powerful graphics functions.
   (c) *DTP package* for the primary desktop publishing functions.
   (d) *Page-layout software*, typically with PostScript drivers.
   (e) *Scanning/digitising drivers* for the capture of half-tones and other images.
   (f) *Interface software*. If an IBM PC is used, a user interface is required, typically GEM or Microsoft Windows which provide the essential Apple Macintosh environment.

17.5.4 Applications of desktop publishing

DTP applications are many and varied and include the publication of many business forms such as invoices, purchase orders, memos and technical documents; letter heads; labels for addresses or file reference; bulletins for office notice boards; advertising pamphlets, price lists, leaflets, brochures, sales catalogues and mailing lists; office layouts, diagrams and organisation charts; in-house magazines and business cards; management reports and so on. The list is as varied as the work produced by outside printers.

17.5.5 Languages

PostScript is a programming language used by many DTP systems which enables programs to be written by users to specify the details of the page to be printed. It is a page-description language (PDL) which avoids having to build up a page piece by piece, consuming large amounts of memory while doing so. Without PostScript the software can output to only one device but software with PostScript drivers can output to any PostScript device. The application program generates the PDL code, which is translated by the PDL interpreter in the output device generating the page image.

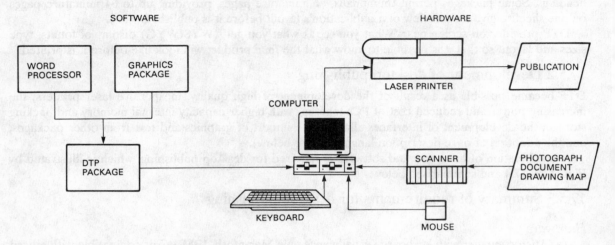

Figure 17.3 A desktop publishing system

Figure 17.4 A scanner

Review questions

1   Define the term graphics.

2   Text and graphics can be integrated. Discuss.

3   Summarise the various graphical input techniques and devices which may be applied.

4   Summarise the various graphical output techniques and devices.

5   What is interactive video?

6   Specify the purpose and characteristics of desktop publishing (DTP).

18 Text processing

5. What is interactive video?

18.1 Introduction

Text processing (or word processing) deals with words (text) and is usually referred to as *word processing*. If an examination question refers to *text processing*, it is probably referring to word processing. It is important, however, to be aware that the term text processing tends to be used when discussing desktop publishing (*see* 17.5). Word processing is a widely applied application on microcomputers because it greatly improves the productivity of the typing and correspondence activities of a business. Time and effort are reduced by the application of more efficient methods in preparing and correcting standard letters and documents. Word processing has no significant advantage over a typewriter for preparing one-off letters, however, since the primary benefits are obtained when frequently processing large quantities of standard letters, forms and documents. The features of different packages vary in the ways in which menus are displayed for the selection of options (*see* Fig. 18.5) and in which routines are performed. It is therefore essential to study and work to the manual for the specific package being used.

18.2 Primary processes

The primary processes include the initial preparation of letters and documents, which are then edited either to correct errors or to modify the layout of the text. The final drafts of standard letters or documents are stored on disc until subsequently retrieved for amendment or to print additional copies. Text can be modified or rearranged with little effort and as many copies as required printed automatically. Text can be printed in various type founts, such as enlarged or condensed mode, or may be right justified, as illustrated in Figs. 18.1 to 18.4. It is also possible to insert, delete, move and copy text − including the rearrangement of sentences and paragraphs, etc.

18.3 Range of facilities

Different packages provide a range of facilities some of which are not directly related to general word processing operations. Framework II marketed by Ashton-Tate, for instance, is a software package which combines word processing with spreadsheet, database, graphics, telecommunications and mailmerge. The word processing module includes a spelling checker, mailmerge and outlining. Figure 18.5 illustrates a screen display for the selection of options when preparing a letter or document. It provides for the selection of specific requirements including the width of the left margin expressed as a number of column positions; the number of lines to be printed on a page; line spacing requirements, single or double, for instance; the line width expressed as the number of characters to be printed per line and the type of print fount, condensed for instance. Also displayed are options for headers and footers (*see* 18.4).

The following text is printed in enlarged mode

A technique referred to as
mailmerge'is widely used in
combination with word processing
applications because it allows a
list of names and addresses
to be combined with standard
letters which produces a
`personalised` original ribbon
print letter for each
addressee.Standard letter
are used for circulating specific
details to customers, price lists
for instance;or requests for
quotations sent to suppliers,etc.
Labels can also be addressed for
the despatch of circulars.

Figure 18.1

The following text is printed in condensed mode

A technique referred to as `mailmerge` is widely used in

combination with word processing applications because it allows a

list of names and addresses to be combined with standard letters

which   produces a `personalised` original ribbon print letter

for each addressee.Standard letters are used for circulating

specific details to customers, price lists for instance; or

requests for quotations sent to suppliers,etc.Labels can also be

addressed for the despatch of circulars.

Figure 18.2

```
The following text is right justified
```

```
Word      processing     is     a     widely     applied     application     on
microcomputers   because    it    improves    the    word    processing
activities of a business by saving time and effort as a result of
applying  more  efficient  methods  for  preparing  and  correcting
letters and documents.
```

Figure 18.3

```
The following text is not right justified
```

```
Word processing is a widely applied  application on
microcomputers because it improves the word  processing
activities of a business by saving time and effort as a result of
applying more efficient methods for preparing and correcting
letters and documents.
```

Figure 18.4

18.4 Headers and footers

A *header* is standard text printed at the top of every page. A *footer* is standard text at the bottom of the page. They are usually applied when preparing lengthy documents or chapters of a book and contain details such as page number, date and document title. Headers and footers can be selected directly from the menu displayed on the screen or may be embedded (included in the document) prior to preparing a particular document.

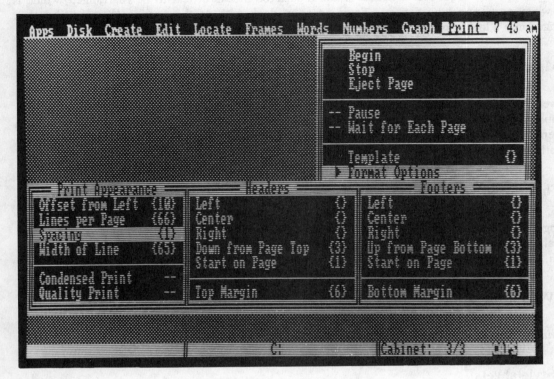

Figure 18.5 Screen display of formatting options FRAMEWORK II

18.5 Mailmerge

A technique referred to as *mailmerge* is widely used in conjunction with word processing applications because it provides facilities for combining names and addresses with standard letters to produce a 'personalised', original ribbon print, letter for each addressee. Standard letters are used when circulating certain information to selected addressees, for example price lists to customers or requests for quotations to suppliers. Some packages provide conditional merge facilities making it possible to select from a database addresses for a particular area to be circulated. Labels can also be printed with addresses for the despatch of circulars.

18.6 Spelling checkers

This facility provides an automatic check on the spelling of words by means of an inbuilt dictionary and any errors are advised accordingly. This avoids errors in external correspondence — which can create a poor company image. You can even add your own words to some dictionaries, which is useful when dealing with those subjects, such as accounting, which have a specific terminology.

18.7 Outlining

Outlining allows the sequence of headings and associated blocks of text to be rearranged, which is useful when preparing long reports. Topics can be dealt with as they spring to mind and then rearranged into a logical order. The headings are automatically renumbered.

18.8 Macros

The several commands required to achieve a specified task when using a word processing package can be combined by a series of keystrokes relating to control and function keys. The contents of the macro can then be repeated automatically by pressing a couple of keys. This saves time when using frequently applied routines which require a large string of commands.

18.9 Thesaurus

Selecting the right word can be very important when dealing with correspondence and, especially, for technical writers or authors. A *thesaurus* instantly displays a list of alternatives when a specific word is typed in. It is then possible to select an alternative to replace the original word.

18.10 Windowing

Windowing allows many documents to be displayed on the screen and processed simultaneously.

18.11 Style sheets

Style sheets provide facilities for specifying the structure of different documents to obtain a uniform appearance. The layout of the document — including margins, line spacing, type founts, etc. — is specified and saved on disc. The required style can then be called by a single command rather than having to deal with the formatting commands separately.

18.12 Other facilities of word processing packages

(a) Page preview facilities.
(b) Support a range of printers.
(c) Newspaper-style columns on the screen.
(d) Maths facilities for adding, subtracting, multiplying, dividing and percentages.
(e) Background working, allowing the preparation of one document while printing another.
(f) Zoom facilities for viewing a full page in miniature.
(g) Automatic page numbering.
(h) Search facilities to locate a specific word in a long document.
(i) Glossary, allowing the use of abbreviations for long words or sections of text which recur. When the abbreviation is typed in, the full word or text is inserted by the software.
(j) Sorting facilities for sorting lines and paragraphs alphabetically for producing columns or tables.
(k) Indexing facilities.

18.13 Examples of word processing packages

Special software is required for word processing. Many packages are available, a number of which are listed below:

(a) SuperWriter for MS-DOS machines — used on Apricot computers: SORCIM/IUS, a division of Computer Associates International, Inc.

(b) Microsoft Word — for the Macintosh: Microsoft Corporation.

(c) WordPerfect for MS-DOS machines — for the IBM PC: WordPerfect Corporation.

(d) Multimate Advantage II for MS-DOS machines — for the IBM PC market.

(e) Wordstar 2000 (upgraded version of Wordstar) for MS-DOS machines: MicroPro International Corporation.

(f) Lotus Manuscript: Lotus Development Corporation.

(g) Displaywrite.

(h) Sage PC Write: Sagesoft.

(i) Turbo Reflex and Sidekick: Borland International (UK) Ltd.

18.14 Operation features of SuperWriter

The following relates to the SuperWriter package for use on MS-DOS machines. The details are not exhaustive and do not attempt to cover all the finer attributes of the package. They are presented to provide a practical outline of the nature of a specific package.

18.14.1 Operating instructions

The routine for setting up the computer for running the SuperWriter software is as shown below.

(a) Switch on the computer, monitor and the printer.

(b) Load the applications disc containing the software.

(c) Select SuperWriter icon, or:
   (i) exit to DOS and type alongside the prompt A >, SW, i.e. A > SW;
   (ii) press ENTER key.

(d) Main menu is displayed with the cursor located at the EDIT option.

(e) Create a document by first pressing the ENTER key.

(f) Prompt on screen displays: TYPE NAME OF DOCUMENT.

(g) Directory: if the document name is not present the message is displayed DO YOU WANT TO CREATE A NEW DOCUMENT? (Y/N). Type Y for YES, press ENTER.

(h) Type author name, press ENTER.

(i) Screen goes blank with cursor in HOME position, i.e. top left corner.

(j) Enter embedded *headers* and *footers* and embedded print formatting commands (*see* 18.4).

(k) Type letter, document, form or other text.

(l) Correct mistakes — see *control keys* and *codes* below (*see* 18.14.4).

(m) Press ESC key — the screen then displays a series of options including: C D F G I M N R S X Z CR / TAB ESC ?

Details of these options may be obtained from the manual but two are described in (n) and (o) below.

(n) Press S key to SAVE the letter or document on disc or Z to ZAP it (clear it) from the workspace.

(o) Screen changes with the cursor located at SAVE DOCUMENT on the sub-menu when S is typed.

(p)Press ENTER key.

(q)Document recorded on disc for future reference.

(r)Screen changes to MAIN MENU for further editing, printing or document creation.

(s)Press ENTER key.

(t)Screen displays TYPE NAME OF DOCUMENT.

(u)Type name of document to be editied or select option to PRINT as the case may be.

(v)Screen displays READING (name of document).

(w)Display of document on the screen.

(x)Repeat routine from stage (g).

18.14.2 Menus

The program functions on the basis of *menus*, the first of which is the *main menu*, which lists six options:

    (a) EDIT document
    (b) QUIT SuperWriter
    (c) PRINT a document
    (d) CHECK spelling
    (e) DISK directory
    (f) UTILITIES

Some of these options display other sub-menus, the structure of which is:

    (a) *Top line:* name of document being worked on.

    (b) *Status area:* size and other details of the document, including the number of words, characters, lines and pages.

    (c) *Menu area*: screen title, e.g. print menu and list the options available.

    (d) *Cursor location*: the screen is displayed with the cursor at the first option.

    (e) *Prompt line*: this is at the bottom of the screen and specifies actions, e.g. space bar = move the cursor, CR = select, ESC = cancel, ? = answer key.

Notes:

    (a) Press ESC key which causes the previous screen, from which the menu was selected, to be redisplayed.

    (b) Press the ? key and the answer screen will display the purpose of each option. This is a HELP facility.

    (c) CR = ENTER key.

18.14.3 Control codes for use with the edit screen

    (a) CTRL-A: cursor moves back a word. Locates cursor on first letter of next leftmost word.

    (b) CTRL-B: cursor located above text to be moved. The cursor is moved down to the end of the document.

    (c) CTRL-C: cursor located above text to be moved. Screen moves forward by 22 lines.

    (d) CTRL-D: cursor moved to the right or, alternatively, the *right* arrow may be used.

    (e) CTRL-E: cursor moved upwards or, alternatively, the *up* arrow may be used.

    (f) CTRL-F: cursor moves right to next word. Cursor located on first letter of next rightmost word.

    (g) CTRL-G: deletes character on the right of cursor.

    (h) CTRL-N: deletes all or remainder of a line of characters.

    (i) CTRL-O: changes mode — provides four options of entering characters into a document: typeover, auto insert, insert and page insertion.

(j) CTRL-P: displays formatting features on the screen.
(k) CTRL-R: screen moves backwards by 22 lines.
(l) CTRL-S: cursor left or left arrow.
(m) CTRL-T: cursor moves to beginning of document.
(u) CTRL-U: cursor moves right to end of line.
(o) CTRL-W: screen moves down line by line.
(p) CTRL-Y: delete a word.
(q) CTRL-Z: screen moves forward line by line.

Review questions

1   What are the nature and purpose of word processing (sometimes referred to as text processing)?

2   What range of facilities is provided by word processing software?

3   What are headers and footers?

4   What is mailmerge?

5   How does a spelling checker check spelling?

6   What is outlining?

7   What are macros?

8   What is a thesaurus?

9   What is the purpose of style sheets?

10 List the general facilities offered by word processing packages.

11 List the names of eleven packages currently available.

12 Many packages functions on the basis of menus. Discuss.

19 Programming and programming languages

19.1 Introduction

Programming is specifically defined later in the text. At this juncture it is important to appreciate that users of microcomputers — accountants, executives and office staff generally — are not programmers and often have no programming knowledge. However, this does not prevent them from operating the computer. The reason for this is that the programming for a specific task has already been carried out, and is available as a package from specific distributors. Some accountants and executives with a flair for computing have trained themselves in the art of programming so that they are able to write and run their own programs for specific needs where a package does not exist. Fourth generation languages provide non-specialists with the means for processing information without the need for programming expertise. Programming is largely the province of the professional programmer, often employed in the data processing department of a company engaged in writing and testing programs for internal use. Other programmers work for software houses (more about this in Chapter 20) writing software packages for applications common to many organisations.

19.2 Programming

Programming is an activity which consists of preparing (writing) sets of instructions (a program) for performing specific operations (processing) on data (input) to produce a specified document or report (output). Programs in effect inform the computer of the procedural steps required to attain a specific result, in the same way that a procedure manual informs a clerk of the steps required to achieve a given result. Programming is done using a specific programming language, which is usually different from the language of the computer, i.e. machine code. The programming language is translated into machine code by software utility programs (*see* Chapter 21).

19.3 Computer programs

19.3.1 Instructions

Each operation performed by a computer (on transaction data relating to a specific application) is in accordance with a pre-defined instruction. All instructions are stored internally in memory.

Each instruction defines a basic operation to be performed, identifies the address of the data to be processed, the location of the data affected by the operation and the input or output device to be used. The complete set of instructions necessary to process a job is known as a *program*.

Instructions are of five basic types as follows.

(a) *Arithmetic/logic*. Add, subtract, multiply, divide, shift, round-off, collate and compare, etc.

(b) *Data transfer*. Read input, write output, read a character, read a word, read a block of data, print a line, transfer data to different locations in the memory, etc.

(c) *Conditional branch or jump*. The presence of specific conditions in the data being processed is established by a comparison of data factors or the testing of a counter which causes the computer to branch or jump to the next appropriate instruction.

(d) *Unconditional branch or jump and loop*. When it is necessary to execute an instruction which is not the next in sequence in the internal memory, this is achieved by an instruction known as an unconditional branch or jump. This provides the means of creating a loop in the program for executing a common sequence of instructions repeatedly on different units of data. A loop is terminated by a conditional branch after effecting a test.

(e) *Counter*. A counter is a memory location (unit of storage) used for the purpose of storing a control parameter for automatically controlling a processing sequence. A counter may be set with a specific number which is decremented by '1' after each event being controlled. The counter may then be tested to detect whether it reads '0', for instance. If a '0' is detected then a conditional branch is executed to a specific set of instructions. If the counter does not read '0' then a conditional branch is executed to a different set of instructions, perhaps to execute a further loop in the program.

19.3.2 Stages of program preparation

A lot depends on the nature of the processing technique and computer configuration to be used. A different approach will be necessary for programming a system to run on a batch processing configuration from one to run on an interactive basis on a microcomputer. The stages outlined below apply in general:

(a) Define the nature of the problem by studying the system specification which contains details of the program specification.

(b) Decide on the type of language to use; assembly code (low-level language) or high-level language, which in the case of a mainframe computer may be COBOL, and in the case of a microcomputer BASIC.

(c) Determine sub-routine requirements, print format and layout, whether data is to be input via the keyboard of the console or microcomputer or within the program and the checks and controls to be incorporated etc.

(d) Prepare decision tables and program flowcharts as appropriate to the complexity of the problem.

(e) Determine programming strategy relating to the approach to developing programs, whether to adopt monolithic, modular or structured programming.

(f) Specify breakpoints.

(g) Code each statement (instruction) of the program in the relevant programming language. This stage produces the *source* program.

(h) If a microcomputer is being programmed the statements may be input via the keyboard. They will then be interpreted directly into machine code. For a batch processing configuration the *source* program together with the assembler or compiler are then input to the processor for conversion into a machine code *object* program.

The process of assembling or compiling records the *object* program on either magnetic tape or disc and prints out details of the source program including errors at the same time — this is known as a program listing. The programmer checks the list for errors and corrects them accordingly.

(i) The program is tested using test data as defined in the program specification. Any errors are noted and corrected.

(j) The program is stored on a suitable backing storage media for future use. For a mainframe computer this would be a Winchester magnetic disc, for a microcomputer either a floppy disc or Winchester disc.

19.3.3 Breakpoint

A programmer must determine the point in a program where it is necessary to insert a breakpoint when applicable. This is the point where a program is interrupted for a specific reason, perhaps for the operator to input a parameter or to change the type of stationery on the printer. For interactive processing by microcomputer it may be defined as the point in the program where a message is displayed on the screen asking the user to enter specific data to allow processing to continue.

19.4 Program specification

A program specification is a formal directive from the system designer to the programmer defining the requirements of a program to attain the purpose and objectives of a specific system. The specification is an important element of system documentation and provides an interface between the system design and programming. The specification identifies the program(s) and the name of the analyst(s) who designed the system. The logical requirements of the system are indicated in great detail specifying the validation checks to be incorporated; the type of processing required — batch or on-line (transaction) processing, multi-tasking or multi-user, centralised or distributed and so on; the name of the files to be updated and how often, the organisation of the files and the file media to be used — fixed or exchangeable discs, for instance. It also specifies the data to be input for processing, the content and layout of reports and documents and auditing requirements.

The specification should also indicate that programming methodology and documentation should accord to programming standards (*see* 19.5 and 19.6). The specification should provide information relating to priority interrupts, when operating in a multiprogramming environment, recognising that specific jobs have a higher priority for the use of input and output devices than others. These factors are defined in the job control language. The processing procedures for dealing with abnormal situations such as error conditions and when to abort a program must also be included; error detection and correction procedures; utility programs to be employed; library sub-routines to be incorporated and the use to be made of open and closed sub-routines; dump and restart procedures, etc. It is imperative that back-up requirements are implemented to ensure files can be reconstituted in the event of loss or corruption.

19.5 Program documentation

After programs have been prepared all the relevant documentation is held in the systems folder or manual which is referred to as a *systems specification*. The documentation includes low-level flowcharts indicating the broad characteristics of the system; decision tables outlining the logic of the system regarding the nature of the conditions to be provided for and the actions required to deal with them when they arise; program coding sheets of the source program prepared by the programmer together with the subsequent source program listing obtained from the compilation (or assembly) run; operating instructions for running the program specifying breakpoints in the program and stationery changeover needs, etc.

In addition, the documentation contains input, output and file formats; data structure charts; charts consisting of sections relating to input, processing and output. The processing section describes the processes necessary to convert inputs to outputs; program flowcharts are also included which illustrate interactions between data and the various processing operations.

19.6 Programming standards

If programs are produced within the framework of data processing standards this will aid the continuity of program development in the event of programmers leaving the company. New programmers will be in a position to assess the documentation as far as it has been developed and continue from that point on the basis of laid down standards relating to the construction of flowcharts, decision tables and coding, etc. Accordingly, they will attain an acceptable level of productivity and expertise much sooner than otherwise would be possible.

Standards have been developed by the National Computing Centre (NCC); the British Standards Institution (BSI); IBM and other major computer manufacturers; the International Organisation for Standardisation (ISO), the American National Standards Institute, Inc. (ANSI) and the European Computer Manufacturers' Association (ECMA). The BSI represents the UK in international organisations concerned with the preparation of international standards. Standards have been established for flowchart symbols and computer languages. The standards relate to file organisation methods, checkpoint/restart routines, job control programs, routines for label writing and checking on file media. Standardisation also includes the use of standard coding sheets and modular programming.

19.7 Approach to program design

19.7.1 Top-down approach to program design

It now tends to be standard practice to adopt a *top-down* approach to program design, which requires a specific objective to be defined for a program. This is then analysed into subsidiary functions in increasing levels of detail. Each module should ideally consist of 50–100 instructions, which simplifies the detection of errors and program testing.

19.7.2 Functional decomposition

This is a method for segregating a monolithic program into specific modules. The approach is to partition a list of program activities into separate functions on the basis of the frequency of processing, the type of input and output and processing activities.

A basic functional decomposition applicable to many programs would comprise the following elements.

    (a) *Program set-up:*
        (i)   open files;
        (ii) define registers;
        (iii) define constants;
        (iv) define work areas;
        (v)   define variables;
        (vi) data input.
    (b) *Inner loop:*
        (i)   input data;
        (ii) compute;
        (iii) update files;
        (iv) print/display output.
    (c) *Program termination:*
        (i)   print control totals;
        (ii) close files.

Larger programs would subdivide the inner loop which converts a single level structure into a tree structure or a modular hierarchy.

19.7.3 Data-driven design

This is an alternative method for segregating a monolithic program into specific modules. This approach is based on the philosophy that the structure of a program should be determined by the structure of the data which it processes. The approach consists of a number of stages as follows.

(a) *Data stage*. This requires the preparation of a data structure diagram for each set of data to be processed.

(b) *Program stage*. The separate data structure diagrams are combined into a single program structure diagram based on the details indicated above in respect of program set-up, inner loop and program termination.

(c) *Operation stage*. The operations required to produce the output are defined and listed and each operation is structured in the program according to the logical requirements.

19.8 Program generators

19.8.1 System C

Program generators are software packages which allow non-computer specialists to develop their own application programs. An example is marketed by Systems C Ltd. The package may well be used to develop traditional business applications such as payroll, accounts, invoicing and stock control. It can also be applied to the development of programs for applications where ready-made programs are unavailable (*see* Fig. 19.1). This type of package can also be usefully employed by experienced programmers as the Sycero programs are structured and documented in a manner which facilitates linking with other programs. By means of prompts and menus new records or files can be incorporated.

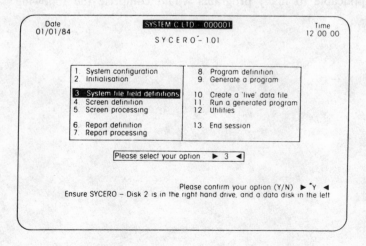

Figure 19.1 Program generator screen (Courtesy System C Ltd.)

19.8.2 Building a program in seven steps

Using Sycero as an example of program builders or generators, the process of program building is very straightforward and can be accomplished in seven steps.

(a) *Plan the system*. Define the elements of the system you want to create, the types of data to be input, the screen layouts for required displays and the number of files needed.

Determine how the program is to handle the information.

(b) *Specify the system*. With the micro running proceed to select items from the main menu. By following the prompts proceed to define the types of files required and what items of information they will contain.

The menu offers the following options (*see* Fig. 19.1):

   1 system configuration;
   2 initialisation;
   3 system-file-field definitions;
   4 screen definition;
   5 screen processing;
   6 report definition;
   7 report processing;
   8 program definition;
   9 generate a program;
  10 create a 'live' data file;
  11 run a generated program;
  12 utilities;
  13 end session.

(c) *Draw the screens*. Having specified where and how data is to be stored it is necessary to specify how the data is to be entered and displayed on the screen of the computer.

On each screen type in descriptions of the items to be entered and the exact position on the screen where the item is to be displayed. Graphic facilities can be used to sketch in lines and boxes giving the system a professional finish.

(d) *Check the data*. With the screens built it is prudent to incorporate a validation/verification procedure to detect when data has been entered incorrectly. Prompts indicate what needs to be input at any point, such as stock number, and also advise on the range of figures acceptable. Error messages can be displayed.

(e) *Define the program*. Define the program to operate on the data. There are certain standard operations which will almost always need to be carried out. Each system will require a file maintenance program to enter, amend and delete information. An enquiry program allows instant on-screen access to all data in any chosen form. Posting programs handle the logic of recording all transactions against a single item and updating files.

(f) *Produce the printout*. The system is now built and it is necessary to specify the printed output requirements, i.e. the *report definition* or the formatting.

The system provides facilities for defining where on a printed page columns are to appear, how they will look, what their headers will be like, and so on. Column totals can be generated, each page can be numbered and printouts can be stamped with the date and time.

(g) *Generate*. The Sycero software requires to know the name of the program. It then translates the data defined and specified into a computer program. The code produced is very lucid and structured.

19.8.3 Michael Jackson structured programming

Software known as Program Development Facility (PDF) provides for program development using structured programming methodology. It dispenses with the traditional program methodology of preparing detailed program flowcharts followed by program coding. The PDF technique uses interactive graphics to develop structure diagrams known as *hierarchy* charts which replace traditional program flowcharts. The structure diagrams are stored on disc and facilities are provided to modify them as necessary. The screen may be considered to be a window through which a diagram is viewed. A simple command generates pseudo-code (JSP structure text) and source code ready for compilation or preprocessing.

19.9 General aspects of programming

19.9.1 Monolithic programming

The National Computing Centre publication *Program Design Methods* states that the term 'monolithic programming' relates to the largely undisciplined and non-formalised approach to the development of computer programs in which the programmer is allowed a completely free rein. Programs produced in this way reflect the programmer's own experience and personal interpretations.

19.9.2 Modular programming

This approach to programming adopts the technique of developing suites of related programs. The overall program is divided into modules, each of which is developed separately but on a coordinated basis. This enables the complete suite of programs to be prepared by a team of programmers if appropriate and programs become available more quickly as a result. It is also easier to debug programs and maintain them when they are constructed in this way. Modules include those for housekeeping, input, processing, output and the closing of files.

19.9.3 Portability of languages

Digital Research Inc. develops languages which allow the user to design applications programs, which can then be applied to various processors and operating systems allowing full portability from 8-bit to 16-bit or 32-bit environments: from microcomputer to mini or mainframe. Programming productivity has been enhanced by Digital Research as it provides the most important commercial programming languages in sophisticated compiler implementations which are portable. Some aspects of these programs are outlined in what follows.

19.9.4 Procedural vs descriptive languages

Programming languages may be classified into two different categories: procedural and descriptive. Most are procedural because they are used to write a series of instructions for carrying out a sequence of processes to convert inputs to outputs. The instructions are executed in sequence unless directed to branch to a sub-routine to deal with a particular condition arising in the procedure. The procedure is repeated by the process of looping as long as data exists for processing. Procedural languages include BASIC, Fortran, Pascal, C and Lisp, and are solution-orientated. A non-procedural language is a declarative language: instead of defining a sequence of instructions the programmer provides facts and relationships about a problem. (*See* Prolog in 19.12 below.)

19.10 Low-level language – machine code and assembly code

At one time, in the early days of computers, all computer programs were written in machine code, i.e. an instruction (operation) code specific to a particular manufacturer's computer. Programs of instructions had to be written in a form that the computer could interpret and execute and accordingly this type of programming was classified as *machine-orientated* as the instructions were in a form required by the computer but not in a form to assist the programmer to solve the problems under consideration, i.e. not *problem-orientated*.

To overcome these difficulties and to avoid the laborious task of writing programs in machine code, each computer manufacturer devised his own assembly code or assembly language. The advantage of an assembly language is that it enables a program to be written much more easily, at the same time allowing the same degree of flexibility that was available when writing programs in machine code. This means that programs can be prepared much more quickly than is possible with machine code, without the sacrifice of machine-running time when processing a job, which is not so with the high-level languages to be discussed later.

An assembly language enables program instructions to be written in mnemonic or symbolic code, that is in pseudo-code (a language which is not machine code). Programs written in this type of language are known as *source* programs and they have to be translated into a machine code program by a programming aid (software) known as an *assembler*. After assembling, the object program is input each time the job to which it relates is to be processed. The process of writing instructions in mnemonic or symbolic code is known as *autocoding*.

Instead of writing 5 for *add* and possibly 10 for *compare*, the programmer writes ADD and COM in accordance with the symbolic code for a particular computer. Also, instead of specifying actual storage addresses (internal memory locations) symbolic addresses are indicated in each instruction, i.e. OLDBAL, which is the symbolic address for *old balance*.

An instruction in assembly language, for a single-address type computer, would take the form:

LDX 1 OLDBAL

This instruction means *load the item of data named OLDBAL to accumulator 1*. The assembler automatically assigns a core store location to OLDBAL, which is indicated in the object program.

Assembly languages are still rather complex, and generally the number of instructions which have to be written are still the same as for machine code programming unless *macro-coding* is used. Such a language is also biased towards the machine rather than the problem.

19.11 Third generation languages – high level languages

High-level languages, normally designated as third generation languages, are not so efficient with regard to machine running time as those written in an assembly language. The reason for this is that a language such as COBOL or BASIC produces generalised sets of instructions from high-level statements which are required in more detail at the machine code compilation stage.

Third generation languages (3GLs) include COBOL, Fortran, BASIC and C. These languages are designed to assist the programmer by enabling programs to be written in a high level language, which is converted into machine code by a compiler which translates a complete sub-routine from one high level 3GL statement.

A high level language is any problem-orientated programming language which allows instructions to be written in a form with which the user is conversant, such as the use of mathematical equations for a mathematician and plain English-style statements for business applications, as distinct from machine-orientated languages which relate to a specific machine rather than the type of problem to be solved. Examples of high level languages are outlined below.

(a) *Algol.* Algol is an acronym for *ALGO*rithmic *L*anguage which is a high level problem-orientated language for mathematical and scientific applications using algorithms. The language defines algorithms as a series of statements and declarations in the form of algebraic formulae and English words. Each operation is represented as a statement and each unit of data is known as a variable and assigned a name by the programmer. An instruction or assignment statement of the form: b: = a + c + 5.0; effectively adds 5.0 to the numbers in the locations a and c and places the answer in location b. The statement consists of the name of a variable followed by : =, followed by any arithmetic expression whose answer is put into the left-hand side variable.

(b) BASIC. A programming language widely used for time sharing applications and for programming mini- and microcomputers. It is a high level language relatively simple to learn by non-computer specialists. The term BASIC is an acronym for *B*eginners *A*ll Purpose *S*ymbolic *I*nstruction *C*ode. (*See* 19.16.1, 19.16.2 and Figs. 19.3 and 19.4.)

(c) CBASIC *Compiler.* This is the Digital Research Inc. industry standard commercial dialect of BASIC suitable for the business environment. CBASIC Compiler is a direct enhancement of CBASIC that is five to ten times faster in execution than most versions of BASIC. It is possible to write, test and combine separate modules for creating complete programs applying the modular, top-down approach. It includes facilities for graphics, expanded file processing techniques, supports multi-user operating systems and is compatible with CP/M Graphics.

(d) *Other versions of* BASIC. Microsoft BASIC which is very widely used; XBASIC which is a British engineering and mathematics-orientated version with matrix-handling and XTal BASIC another British version which has a choice of screen or line-based editors. Then there is BBC BASIC which is of a structured nature.

(e) COBOL. This is an acronym for *CO*mmon *B*usiness *O*riented *L*anguage. It is a high level programming language designed to assist the task of programmers by enabling them to write programs in a more simple form than is possible with assembly code. The language is largely used for mainframe computer applications. It is problem-orientated rather than machine-orientated as it is designed to assist the solving of business problems for such applications as stock control, payroll, sales and purchase ledger accounting.

COBOL consists of four divisions, these are:

  (i) identification division;
  (ii) environment division;
  (iii) data division;
  (iv) procedure division.

(f) CIS COBOL. This version of the language is that of Micro Focus Ltd. The CIS stands for *C*ompact *I*nteractive and *S*tandard. It is a complete system for compiling, testing, debugging and executing standard COBOL programs. It has become the most widely favoured version of the ANSI 1974 COBOL language. It can be used for running existing mainframe and minicomputer programs on a microcomputer. A micro can also be used to develop COBOL software for larger computers.

(g) *Level II* COBOL. This version of the language is also attributable to Micro Focus Ltd. It provides the full facilities of mainframe COBOL on 8-bit or 16-bit microcomputers allowing the user to develop mainframe programs with the interactive facilities of a microcomputer. It allows portability of software between mainframe and microcomputers. Employs dynamic paging to allow implementation of programs greater than 64 KB on 8-bit microcomputers. Provides for interactive screen handling.

(h) *Pascal.* This is a high level programming language which is highly structured, enabling programs to be written more efficiently without the problems of writing long programs using monolithic structure.

It executes programs quickly, much faster than interpretative languages like BASIC, but it is more complex and time consuming to learn initially. When preparing a program Pascal words are typed in bold face. Modules consist of separate procedures each of which is an element of the main program. The main program *calls* the procedures in the order they are to be executed.

(i) *Pascal/MT+*. This is a version of Pascal by Digital Research Inc. It provides speed and accuracy for developing microcomputer programs. It is a direct-compiling dialect of the full ISO standard Pascal — greatly enhanced and extended to maximise the inherent versatility and portability of the language. Pascal/MT+ Native code compiler executes much faster than traditional p-code Pascal compilers.

(j) PL/1. A powerful all-purpose language which rivals Fortran for scientific applications and COBOL for commercial applications. Digital Research Inc. has developed a version of the language for implementation on microcomputers. It is based on the ANSI Standard Subset G. It is easily transported from micro to mini to mainframe or from mainframe to mini to micro.

(k) C. An advanced programming language built for coding power and speed of execution with a minimum of constraints. It allows skilled software developers to take full advantage of the inherent structure of the computer. C is ideal for applications which must achieve a high level of performance and for systems level programming.

(l) LOGO. A structured programming language which is becoming popular in the field of education as it is designed to allow very young children, in the four or five years' age group, to program a computer. LOGO takes the form of a *turtle,* i.e. a mechanical device or a triangle of light on the screen of a computer. Both forms provide the means for drawing lines either on a sheet of paper or on the screen.

(m) *Fortran*. An acronym for *FOR*mula *TRAN*slation. It is a high level language for scientific and mathematical use. The language was introduced by IBM in 1957 but has since developed into different forms. It has been replaced to some extent by BASIC and other high-level languages.

(n) *Lisp*. One of the oldest higher level languages which was designed to process data in the form of lists, hence its name *LIS*t Processing. Instead of using statements and commands the language uses procedures or functions to operate on the data. The data consists of words called *atoms* which can be numbers or symbolic names for some object, place or event. The atoms are grouped together to form lists which are then manipulated to achieve the desired purpose. A procedure is an operation that is applied to the atoms and lists. The basic operation of Lisp is read the procedure, evaluate and print the result. This cycle is repeated on each procedure until the required processing occurs.

(o) *Coral*. A high level programming language for real-time applications developed by the Royal Radar Establishment at Malvern, England.

(p) *Forth*. A high level programming language designed for small computers having the advantage of requiring a small amount of memory and being independent of a specific machine.

(q) *Prolog*. This is a declarative, problem-orientated language used for developing knowledge-based systems. It is non-procedural because it does not define a sequence of instructions as with procedural languages. It acts upon facts and relationships relating to a problem from which new facts are inferred which are used to solve the problem. (*See* Chapter 10.)

Table 19.1 Major differences between high and low level languages

Low level language	High level language
(a) Known as *assembly symbolic or mnemonic code* — operation codes are defined as mnemonics, e.g. LDA for load accumulator; operands are allocated labels or symbolic addresses, e.g. REC or ISS for receipts and issues.	(a) Uses expressions with which the user is conversant when problem solving without the aid of a computer. Various languages allow the use of normal scientific and mathematical notation in respect of Algol and Fortran, for instance. On the other hand COBOL allows the use of English-style statements for business applications. Operation codes are referred to, depending upon the language, as *keywords* such as LOAD, LIST and PRINT in the case of BASIC. Operands, known as variables in BASIC, are allocated identifying letters and sometimes a number such as A or A1 to represent specific operands. COBOL, as an example, allocates a name to operands such as RECIN for receipts into store and ISSIN for issues from store.
(b) Machine-orientated as the language is specific to a particular manufacturer's computer	(b) Problem-orientated as high level languages are not *machine specific*.
(c) Object programs are *assembled* by software known as an *assembler*.	(c) Object programs are compiled by software known as a *compiler* or firmware known as an *interpreter* depending upon the type of computer as mainframes normally compile and micros interpret.
(d) The translation from program code to object program in machine code is normally on a one for one basis where one machine code instruction is generated for each assembly code instruction.	(d) Translation from high level language to object program in machine code is normally on the basis of many for one, i.e. many machine code instructions are generated for each high level statement.

Table 19.2 Advantages and disadvantages of high and low level languages

Low level language	High level language
Advantages	*Disadvantages*
(a) Runs faster because it is machine specific (the features of a particular machine have been taken into account within the structure of the language).	(a) Runs slower due to the generality of the statements and the fact that they are portable between different machines providing a suitable compiler is available. Such languages are machine independent.
(b) Requires fewer instructions to accomplish the same result.	(b) Requires more storage overhead as programs require more instructions, due to their generality, to accomplish the same result.

Disadvantages	Advantages
(a) Programs take longer to code because of the more complex nature of the language.	(a) Programs can be written more quickly, in general, as the coding is easier to learn. Applications become operational much sooner.
(b) Lack of portability of programs between computers of different makes.	(b) Portability between computers of different types (*see* Disadvantages (a)).
(c) Languages take longer to learn.	(c) Languages easier to learn.
(d) Programmers have to learn new languages when moving to installations using different machines with different low level languages.	(d) Programmers can move to different installations using high level languages without having to learn new languages.

19.12 Fourth generation languages

A fourth generation language (4GL) is a computer-based language in which the programmer, or user, specifies *what* is to be done and not *how* to do it. *What* is to be done is written in a ultra-high level English-like language. Fourth generation languages are designed to assist the manipulation of a database by way of a *query language* providing facilities for creating, retrieving, updating, appending, deleting or amending data. The query language is an element of the database management system. When the query language is designed to access a database from a terminal keyboard it is classified as an *interactive query language*. The primary purpose of query languages is to provide non-computer specialists in the various business functions, the end-users, with the means to do their own information processing without having to become programming experts. A fourth generation language translates the user's requests into procedural steps to produce the desired output. In this way user views of an application are separated from the mechanics of the system making it transparent – the end result is important to the user, not how it is accomplished. Fourth generation languages assist personnel when changing from clerical to computerised database applications as it enables them to understand the new working procedures more easily.

Fourth generation languages include:

(a) database query languages (*see* Chapter 9);
(b) spreadsheets (*see* Chapters 7 and 8);
(c) screen painters (*see* 19.3 and Chapter 22);
(d) application generators (*see* 19.14);
(e) report generators (*see* Chapter 22).

19.12.1 Natural language in accounting applications

Software houses are responding to the requirements of users to make their products easier to work with. Accounting software is being developed which enables the computer to recognise commands input in a natural language, so simplifying their use. The natural language facility lets users omit all the usual steps of choosing options from menus and filling in boxes on the screen – the computer performs these tasks. Commands are entered as normal sentences; for example, it is possible to type in 'enquire account 33011' and the system identifies the verb 'enquire' as a command, the item name as 'account' and the item reference as '33011'. The sentence can be structured in different ways provided the item reference follows the item name. Words can be abbreviated to three letters for speed of entry and commands can be repeated by pressing the full stop key. Additional and unnecessary words in sentences can confuse the system and it dislikes words between the item name and item reference: the sentence 'enquire account code 33011' would cause it to start searching under 'code' rather than '33011'.

If the user is uncertain what needs to be input it is possible to proceed word by word and the system will prompt for the information required; for example, if the user enters 'enquire' it will prompt 'enter account' and so on. After the sentence is typed the system will display its interpretation in full for the user to accept or abandon. Such systems may have a number of preset commands and users can teach the system others as required. It is possible to view a dictionary of available commands at any time by pressing the question mark key.

To teach the system new commands the user types in 'learn' plus a name for the command and the system is ready to increase its repertoire. Once in the learn mode the user can go through the usual menu-driven, box-filling methods of performing a function to teach the system the correct sequence of actions. Wherever the operator must make a choice the system will stop and prompt for input with a question. Inexperienced users can be prompted all the way through a natural language entry. The experienced user can input all the necessary parts of the command in a single abbreviated sentence.

The system can be used in batch mode to automate voluminous tasks carried out at the end of the day or month. It can also be taught to go through an entire process for batch jobs such as printing reports. The computer can be left to do this work unattended provided the risk of a printer running out of paper or a malfunction is accepted. This is an approach towards artificial intelligence as it allows experts to teach the system how to handle difficult parts of a task, leaving junior staff to fill in extra details in response to set prompts. Context-sensitive help screens also help the user on the action to take at any stage.

19.12.2 Natural language processing: technical aspects

You may dispense with reading this section if you do not wish to know some of the technical aspects of natural language processing dealing with grammar, syntax, semantics and lexicon, etc. The information provides the underlying concepts of natural language processing, which come within the sphere of artificial intelligence as they are knowledge-based systems allowing users to communicate with a computer in their natural, ethnic language.

Its purpose is to simplify the use of computers for non-specialists, so avoiding the need to learn operating system commands and computer languages. An interface is provided to simplify the use of software such as databases and knowledge-based systems.

Natural language messages are translated into the language of a specific computer by software known as a *compiler*. To understand a natural language enquiry a computer must have built-in knowledge to analyse and interpret the details input by the user. Before action can be taken in response to the input the computer must have a built-in understanding of grammar, syntax, semantics and the definition of words:

(a) *grammar* provides the rules for constructing sentences;
(b) *syntax* refers to the way in which words are assembled for the construction of phrases and sentences;
(c) *semantics* provides the means for analysing the meaning of words.

All the words and phrases of a language are organised into a *lexicon* — a dictionary listing all words alphabetically. Search and pattern matching techniques are used for processing the inputs. The computer responds by generating a natural language output, which is achieved by built-in sentences, phrases and paragraphs. Applying the *key word search technique*, the natural language processor program searches through a sentence for key words which have been input. Key words are then subjected to pattern matching by comparing them with words and phrases stored in the key word directory within the program. When a match occurs a built-in response is generated. It will be necessary to consider synonyms to allow for the different uses of specific words; for example, items sold to customers may be known as products, items or goods.

The use of key word pattern matching is restricted because of the problem of dealing with the variations in language expression. A superior and more widely applied technique designed to remove this problem is the analysis of the syntax and semantics of the details which have been input. This technique enables the meaning of an input to be more precisely defined. A problem still exists, however, because of the large number of words having a variety of interpretations and the various ways in which they can be structured into sentences.

19.13 Applications generators

SQL Forms, marketed by Oracle Corporation UK Ltd, is a fourth generation tool that facilitates the development of form-based applications quickly and easily. It is an interactive applications generator using pop-up menus, windows and screen painting to help users design, build and modify form-based applications that can maintain and query a database. Instead of programming an application, it is developed by making menu choices allowing non-technical users to develop their own systems easily. It combines instructions with information from Oracle's data dictionary to generate an application. Form-based applications are developed very quickly with minimal effort and the software automatically handles all routine form operations – insert, update, delete and query – without requiring the user to write a line of programming code. Full-screen data entry is facilitated which ensures user specifications are met.

SQL Forms' non-procedural approach allows the speedy prototyping of applications. The facility is used by first developing a prototype form. Prototyping provides users with the opportunity to refine an application as it is built. As the design is improved the changes are specified and SQL Forms incorporates them automatically. In this way design improvements are concentrated upon and codes do not need to be rewritten. It is possible to incorporate a user's own programs into SQL Forms' open architecture. When the design works satisfactorily the application is complete because the user's prototype *is* the application. Because SQL Forms software and the Oracle database are non-procedural, applications and data structures are easy to change. This enables the user to prototype applications effectively. With SQL Forms, instead of describing a system to users by means of detailed specification documents, the tool itself actually shows how the system works. After trying fully operational prototypes users can suggest improvements in function and layout. New application requirements are inevitable but changes are, as we have seen, easily implemented with this system whereas traditional development methods take much longer.

19.14 Program flowcharts

19.14.1 Flowchart

Program flowcharts, sometimes referred to as computer procedure flowcharts, are often prepared as a preliminary to program coding to assist in determining the logical aspects of a problem and the correct sequence of statements required. Program flowcharts also show input operations, setting of counters, testing of counters, loops and branching, etc. (*see* Fig. 19.3–19.5).

19.14.2 Flowchart symbols

By convention there exist a number of standardised symbols used for the drafting of flowcharts of all types. The symbols used for program flowcharts distinguish between an operation, i.e. a basic processing step, and a test including logical tests for establishing whether certain conditions exist in the data to be processed which determine the conditional branching requirements of a program. (*see* Fig. 19.2).

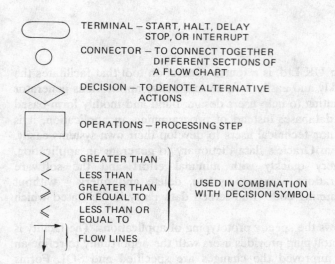

TERMINAL — START, HALT, DELAY
STOP, OR INTERRUPT

CONNECTOR — TO CONNECT TOGETHER
DIFFERENT SECTIONS OF
A FLOW CHART

DECISION — TO DENOTE ALTERNATIVE
ACTIONS

OPERATIONS — PROCESSING STEP

GREATER THAN

LESS THAN

GREATER THAN
OR EQUAL TO

LESS THAN OR
EQUAL TO

USED IN COMBINATION
WITH DECISION SYMBOL

FLOW LINES

Figure 19.2 Program flowchart symbols

19.15 Demonstration

Customers' orders are processed for despatch, invoicing and updating the accounts in the sales ledger. The treatment of this problem is simplified for ease of comprehension but the initial requirement is to define the logic of the problem. The preparation of a program flowchart is recommended before attempting to code a complex problem. In some cases a decision table should be prepared to aid the construction of a program flowchart before coding takes place. The numeric variables inherent in the application must then be identified and allocated variable names, which are often abbreviated to a single character as indicated below — these are the values to be used in computations. String variables must also be defined — these are combinations of alphabetic and numeric characters (strings) for specifying item reference numbers, for instance, such as the code number of an item ordered by a customer in this example. The program must be able to deal with each item on an order by computing its value and printing on a list the order number, item code, quantity, price and value. This routine continues until no more items exist, which stage concludes the processing routine for one order. The program then branches to a statement to print the total value of the order.

When a test indicates that the item code is '5555' it shows that all items on a specific order have been processed. The code '5555' is selected because it is outside the range of item codes, i.e. a non-item code. The process is repeated until the last order is processed, which is determined by testing if the order number = '9999'. This causes the program to branch to a statement which concludes processing by printing a total value of all orders. The order number '9999' is selected for the same reason as item code '5555'. The routine is illustrated in Fig. 19.3 which portrays a flowchart showing the logic involved in the programming problem.

(a) *String variables:*

    A$ = Order number

    B$ = Item code

(b) *Numeric variables:*

    A = Quantity of each item ordered

    B = Price of each item ordered

    C = This is a register for showing the value of each item which is the product of A and B (A*B)

    D = This is a register for accumulating the total value of the order

    E = This is a register for accumulating the total value of all orders

The registers must be set to zero: after each item has been computed, ready for the next item; after each order in readiness for processing the next order; and at the completion of processing all orders.

19.16.1 Unstructured BASIC program

The following program is based on a version of the unstructured BASIC programming language. The program is designed to process transactions interactively on a PC (*see* Fig. 19.3).

```
 10 D = 0
 20 E = 0
 30 INPUT 'ORDER NUMBER'; A$
 40 IF A$ = '9999' THEN 220
 50 INPUT 'ITEM CODE'; B$
 60 IF B$ = '5555' THEN 190
 70 INPUT 'QUANTITY'; A
 80 INPUT 'PRICE'; B
 90 C = A*B
100 D = D+C
110 E = E+D
120 PRINT 'ORDER NUMBER'; A$;
130 PRINT 'ITEM CODE'; B$;
140 PRINT 'QUANTITY'; A;
150 PRINT 'PRICE'; B;
160 PRINT 'VALUE OF ITEM'; C
170 C = 0
180 GOTO 30
190 PRINT 'TOTAL VALUE OF ORDER'; D
200 D = 0
210 GOTO 30
220 PRINT 'TOTAL VALUE OF ALL ORDERS'; E
230 E = 0
240 END
```

It is said that unstructured BASIC is cumbersome and confusing because it tends to have too many GOTO and IF–THEN statements directing control to different segments of the program. This situation is resolved by the application of structured programming, which is outlined below.

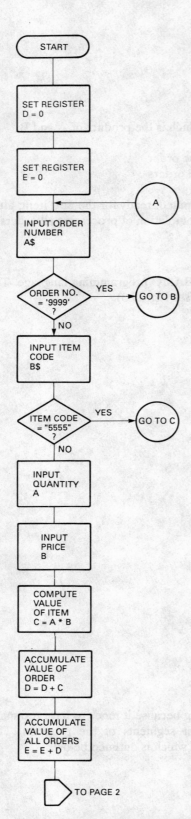

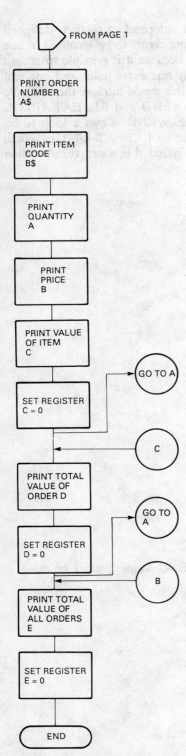

Figure 19.3 Program flowchart illustrating interactive processing

19.16.2 Structured programming

Structured programming techniques develop a program as a series of independent sections designed to perform only one specified task. This approach enables programming errors to be localised to one section of the overall program and also assists program maintenance because it is possible to amend one section without affecting any other. Each section must have only one entry point and one exit point and there should be no jumps to statements in other sections as this would infringe the principle of entry and exit points. Structured programming includes WHILE–WEND and REPEAT–UNTIL expressions which perform a series of statements in a loop. WHILE–WEND allows a loop to be executed as long as a logical expression is true. This is the opposite to REPEAT–UNTIL, which continues while the condition is untrue. These expressions will now be included in a structured version of BASIC based on the same problem outlined above. (*See* Fig. 19.4.)

```
D = 0
E = 0
WHILE not end of orders file D0
   INPUT order number (A$)
      IF order number (A$) = '9999' THEN
         PRINT 'Total value of all orders'; E
         E (Total value of all orders) = 0 ELSE
            WHILE not last item on order D0
               REPEAT
                  INPUT 'Item code'; B$
                  INPUT 'Quantity'; A
                  INPUT 'Price'; B
                  C (Value) = A*B
                  D (Total value of order) = D + C
                  E (Total value of all orders) = E + D
                  PRINT 'Order number'; A$
                  PRINT 'Item code'; B$
                  PRINT 'Quantity'; A
                  PRINT 'Price'; B
                  PRINT 'Value of item'; C
                  C (Value of item) = 0
               UNTIL Item code = '5555' THEN
                  PRINT 'Total value of order'; D
                  D (Total value of order) = 0
            WEND
               END WHILE
```

The same problem can be specified applying nested WHILE–WEND loops instead of using a combination of WHILE–WEND and REPEAT–UNTIL expressions.

```
D = 0
E = 0
WHILE not end of orders file D0
   INPUT order number (A$)
      IF order number (A$) = '9999' THEN
         PRINT 'Total value of all orders'; E
         E (Total value of all orders) = 0 ELSE
            WHILE not last item on order D0
               INPUT item code (B$)
               IF item code = '5555' THEN
                  PRINT 'Total value of order'; D
                  D (Total value of order) = 0 ELSE
```

INPUT 'Quantity'; A
INPUT 'Price'; B
C (Value) = A*B
D (Total value of order) = D + C
E (Total value of all orders) = E + D
PRINT 'Order number'; A$
PRINT 'Item code'; B$
PRINT 'Quantity'; A
PRINT 'Price'; B
PRINT 'Value of item'; C
C (Value of item) = 0
WEND
WEND

TO PAGE 224

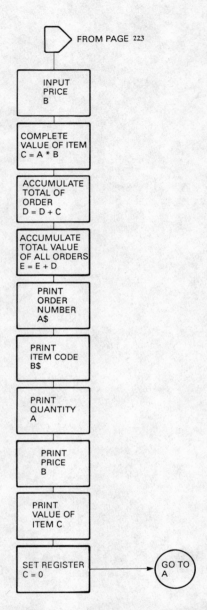

FROM PAGE 223

INPUT
PRICE
B

COMPLETE
VALUE OF ITEM
C = A * B

ACCUMULATE
TOTAL OF
ORDER
D = D + C

ACCUMULATE
TOTAL VALUE
OF ALL ORDERS
E = E + D

PRINT
ORDER
NUMBER
A$

PRINT
ITEM CODE
B$

PRINT
QUANTITY
A

PRINT
PRICE
B

PRINT
VALUE OF
ITEM C

SET REGISTER
C = 0

GO TO
A

Figure 19.4 Program flowchart illustrating interactive transaction processing of customer's orders

19.16 Program flowcharting exercise

This is a question set by the Chartered Association of Certified Accountants. The solution necessitates testing for the end of a record and the end of a file; computing and accumulating values. It relates to batch processing.

Data from a batch of customers' orders is held on magnetic tape and, for each customer, consists of: (i) customer account number; (ii) quantity of each product ordered; (iii) price per unit of product. Where a customer orders more than one product, quantity and price are repeated for each item until all his requirements have been included. The end of customer marker is '0' and the end of file marker is '-1'. You are required to draft a program flowchart to print out:

(a) the value of each separate product sale on each order;
(b) the total amount to be charged to each customer;
(c) the total value of the entire batch of orders.

Solution: Fig. 19.5 provides the solution to this question.

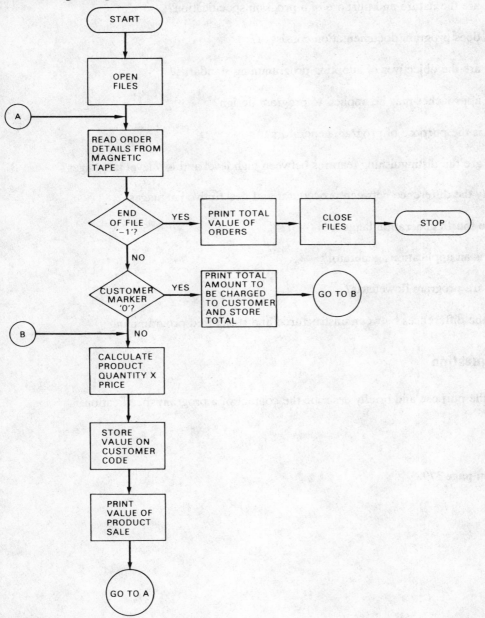

Figure 19.5 Solution to program flowcharting exercise

Review questions

1 What are the nature and purpose of programming?

2 List the stages of program preparation.

3 What is a breakpoint?

4 What are the nature and purpose of a program specification?

5 What does program documentation consist of?

6 What are the objectives of adopting programming standards?

7 What approaches may be applied to program design?

8 What is the purpose of program generators?

9 What are the distinguishing features between high level and low level languages?

10 Specify the difference between procedural and descriptive languages.

11 Define fourth generation languages (4GLs).

12 What is an applications generator?

13 What are program flowcharts?

14 State the differences between unstructured and structured programming

Self-test question

19.1 State the purpose and briefly describe the content of a program specification.

Answer on page 379.

20 Applications software

20.1 Introduction

The term *software* relates to all the different types of program used on computer systems, complementing the hardware, i.e. the processor and its peripherals, without which it is inanimate and is unable to function. To become operational a computer must have software, known as an operating system, resident within its memory. This is *control software*, which is the subject of Chapter 21. This chapter is concerned with the software which is required for processing specific business applications including payroll, stock control, invoicing, sales ledger, integrated order processing and integrated accounting, etc. Software relating to specific requirements has already been discussed in the chapters listed below, to which reference should be made to obtain a complete picture of the nature of software.

(a) Chapter 5: decision support systems;
(b) Chapters 7 and 8: spreadsheets and integrated packages;
(c) Chapter 9: databases;
(d) Chapter 10: expert systems;
(e) Chapter 17: image processing, including graphics and desktop publishing;
(f) Chapter 18: text (word) processing.

Software is written by programmers, who may be employed by a business in the data processing or systems department to prepare programs for internal system requirements in conjunction with systems analysts. Alternatively, programs referred to as *applications packages* are written by programmers employed by software houses or computer manufacturers.

20.2 Package defined

Packages are pre-written computer programs which are widely used for common applications in order to avoid unnecessary duplication of similar programs by many users. It is a means of rationalising programming effort but this does not imply that the same type of package is not available from more than one source. They are sometimes provided to suit the needs of different models of computer and sometimes in competition. The need to shop around is no less than with competing sources of supply of other commodities and products.

A package consists of a suite of programs, sometimes on the same storage media, for the different routines required to achieve the purpose of the specific application. It consists of documentation in the form of a program/systems manual, containing details of how to set up the program and run it on the computer. The package also includes the relevant media on which the program is stored. This is usually disc.

20.3 Package compatibility

Whether a package is suitable for a particular model of computer depends upon a number of factors. Packages for a specific make of computer are designed to run on the model with a defined memory capacity, and will not therefore run on machines with less than the specified memory capacity. Compatibility also depends on the operating system being used, e.g. MS-DOS or PC-DOS, UNIX or XENIX in respect of small business computers. Standard operating systems have a wide range of packages available which can run on any machine using that particular operating system, regardless of the make of machine.

When manufacturers of the larger mainframe computers launch a new model they normally provide for a migration path from one machine to another by making software compatible for the older model and the later model.

20.4 *International Directory of Software*

This is a publication by Computing Publications Ltd, which assists the selection of software packages. The products contained in the directory include Accounting, Administration and Banking, Communications, CAD/CAM, Data Management, Development Aids, Distribution, Insurance, Microprocessor Systems, Modelling and Statistics, Production and Utilities.

20.5 Source of packages

Packages are available from a number of sources depending upon the type of computer. Programs for microcomputers, for instance, are available from mail order sources as advertised in computer magazines; or over the counter from retail shops and stores. Packages are also available from dealers in microcomputers, who provide hardware and software, and directly from the computer manufacturer in some instances.

Software for the larger computer, i.e. mainframes, is available from a number of sources including the manufacturer of the hardware who also develops the software, from specialist organisations known as software houses, and from private organisations who have developed programs for their own use which they make available to other users for an appropriate fee. Packages are also available from a number of computer bureaux which have expanded their activities.

20.6 Cost of software

Sometimes a minimum of software is supplied free of charge when the hardware is purchased; this is referred to as being *bundled* and would include the operating system, utilities and applications software. Other software has to be purchased as required on an 'unbundled' basis; it is charged separately.

Microcomputer manufacturers often have a sales promotion policy of providing extensive software with the machine at no extra cost, in order to generate sales of the hardware. This depends on the economic circumstances which prevail at the time and whether a new model is to be launched or new software is becoming available, etc.

20.7 Vertical market applications software

Applications software is dedicated to specific industries and types of business. Vertical software is particularly important for the operations of the smaller business. Such businesses include distribution, manufacturing, marketing, retailing, farming, construction, solicitors, estate agents, insurance brokers and motor dealers, local government, travel agents and tour operators and so on.

20.7.1 Accountancy practices

Many suppliers provide facilities for accounting practices allowing them to computerise the preparation and production of accounts for clients. Some of the facilities required include time and fee recording, foreign currency accounting, work-in-progress scheduling, and the normal range of accounting routines including nominal ledger, fixed asset accounting, profit and loss account and balance sheet, VAT schedule and the production of an audit trail. Apart from the accounting software a database is ideally suited to the storage and retrieval of client information. Word processing software would also benefit the preparation and storage of standard letters, which may be used in conjunction with mailmerge software for selective mail shots.

20.7.2 Estate agents

Estate agents need to prepare and store details of many properties coming on to the market, and delete them when the property is sold. A database can be used for this purpose and for maintaining records of clients' property requirements. The searching facilities of a database would greatly increase the productivity and efficiency of this primary task.

Software is available from many suppliers to allow estate agencies to computerise their operations, and provides for the needs of specialist agencies dealing with, for example, commercial, shop and residential properties. Packages should ideally have facilities for producing property advertisements, computing commission on property sales, mortgage services, accounting, valuations and auctions. Electronic diary facilities could be used to advantage for maintaining a record of viewing appointments and other critical time-based activities. Estate agents need to be aware of their exact needs to ensure the selected package(s) covers these requirements.

20.7.3 Solicitors

Packages for the legal profession cover conveyancing, litigation support, wills and deeds registers, archiving, time recording, debt collection and trust accounting. Routine accounting procedures are also catered for, including bank reconciliation and cheque writing. The profession also benefits from word processing software due to the numerous types of standard letters to be processed.

20.7.4 Stockbrokers

The advent of information technology and de-regulation of the financial services industry have emphasised the fact that efficiency is the keynote to success, and the only effective way to achieve this and obtain a competitive advantage is to computerise operations. Apart from routine accounting applications stockbrokers can apply to advantage computers for accessing current share prices from various databases. Packages should offer modules for share dealings and settlements, etc.

20.7.5 Insurance brokers

Packages for this type of business should provide modules for motor vehicle, fire and accident, property and holiday insurance cover, etc. Administrative routines which should be provided for include policy documentation and administration, billing, enquiries, claims administration and provision for processing renewals including instalment plans.

20.8 Accounting packages

Efficient accounting systems are imperative for any business and accounting packages designed to achieve these are available from many sources. Accounting packages can provide valuable information on business performance at the time it is wanted, and provide inbuilt checking facilities to prevent costly errors during computations and when posting transactions to ledgers. Accounting routines to be performed at different frequencies — daily, weekly, monthly and annually — are catered for by appropriate packages and formal reports are usually produced at the month-end.

20.8.1 Checklist for accounting packages

(a) What computer and operating system is the software designed for?

(b) Is the package for single or multi-user environments? Can single user software be upgraded to multi-user?

(c) Can the package be integrated with software from other suppliers?

(d) What memory capacity is required?

(e) What security facilities does it possess, i.e. access control via passwords and automatic back-up facilities for file security?

(f) What is the purchase cost?

(g) What are the terms for multiple copies for internal use at different sites?

(h) Is software maintenance provided and at what cost?

(i) Does the software have a reliable history of use in similar types of business?

(j) Does the package contain the latest leading edge technology?

(k) Could the package be adapted to meet specific internal requirements and at what cost?

20.8.2 Understanding accounting packages

Accounting packages automate accounting routines, providing increased productivity and accuracy of processing, faster reporting and the facility for updating master files on a transaction basis as they occur. Many packages use a *mouse* to point to the *icon* of the application, to 'open' and to point to and select the data represented on the screen. *Pull-down menus* are used to select and control the functions performed by the package.

The first major consideration before attempting to run any accounting package is to study the manual and set up the system accordingly. The section relating to the nominal ledger (*see* 20.9) provides information on how this is done. The decision when to change the system over from manual to computer must be made. Usually this is best done at the beginning of a financial year, as balances need to be brought forward in respect of debtors, creditors and fixed assets, etc. New accounts are also opened for sales and expenses at this time. If the system is changed over during a financial year any comparisons with previous years require the figures from the previous system to be added to those produced by the computer — a very tedious process. A year-end date, once established, must be used consistently. Accounting packages are generally user-friendly, guiding the user through each processing stage by means of prompts. Some packages are designed to run on a single user basis but others are designed as multi-user or multi-user/multi-company systems. Some packages provide for account enquiries during data entry activities and the screen displays relevant account details and a printout is provided if required.

20.8.3 The nature of integrated accounting packages

An integrated accounting package is a suite of interrelated programs, often in modular form. Each module is designed to run on its own or as part of the package. Integrated accounting packages streamline the accounting routines by allowing the transfer of common information or data relating to business transaction from one application module to another either directly or through a batch file. Typically this relates to the transfer of transaction details from sales and purchasing modules to the nominal ledger. Integrated packages usually include modules covering the following applications:

- (a) sales, purchase and nominal ledger;
- (b) invoicing;
- (c) stock control;
- (d) payroll and costing;
- (e) data analysis.

Chart of accounts
All accounting systems *must* have a well-structured and effective coding system. Coding structures are specified in a *chart of accounts*, which lists expense, customer, supplier, nominal ledger and departmental (cost centre) codes which facilitate data transfers and postings between ledgers. Customers and suppliers are typically allocated a six-digit code, i.e. a code consisting of six alphanumeric characters, A12345 for instance. Nominal ledger accounts may be structured on the basis of a three- or four-digit nominal code followed by a two-digit department code, A10001 for instance, of which the nominal ledger code is A100 and the departmental code is 01 (up to 99). Some systems have pre-set account names and numbers which are common to many smaller businesses. Some packages allow for unsuitable codes to be deleted and additions incorporated using a nominal ledger maintenance program.

Program back-up
When initially setting up a system it is imperative to take copies of the master programs by copying them to other discs. This is a safeguard against the risk of damage to the discs as a result of a malfunction or a disc being corrupted by inadvertent overwriting. Program discs can be very expensive to replace.

File back-up
Prior to becoming operational copies of the converted master files, sales, purchase, fixed assets, stock, payroll and cost ledgers should be taken as a security measure against loss or corruption.

Defining parameters
A specific application must be tailored to suit the needs of a specific business, requiring parameters to be redefined such as those indicated in Figure 20.3. Initially the parameters are defined as a standard set based on typical business characteristics.

Audit trail
For purposes of generating an audit trail most packages print out details of transactions, including the value and number of invoices; value and number of credits; cash transactions, amendments, deletions, additions and schedules of updated ledger accounts including the sales ledger and purchase ledger, etc.

File security: completion of processing

Typical packages also provide for the creation of back-up files for file security as part of the end of posting routine. Prompts inform the user when to load the discs for copying purposes.

Reports

Most packages provide for a variety of reports, details of which can be stored on a predefined spooling file which allows print runs to be accomplished as one task at a suitable time after the period-end processing is completed.

20.9 Nominal ledger packages

The nominal ledger package described below is based on information supplied by Apple Accounting (UK) Ltd, and the operational details are relevant to the Apple Macintosh with a minimum of 512 KB of memory and a hard disc.

The nominal ledger collects details relating to a business's financial transactions. It is structured to classify transactions according to their nature, i.e. sales, purchases and expenses — including wages, salaries, establishment charges, and administrative, selling and distribution expenses — and to compute gross and net profit for the profit and loss account. Details of fixed and current assets including plant and machinery acquisitions, disposals and depreciation; liabilities including creditors, VAT and corporation tax; and the various types of capital account are recorded in a balance sheet, which shows the financial standing of the business as at a defined date. Nominal ledgers can be integrated with sales and purchase ledger packages and the sales invoicing and stock control packages or be used independently. A coding system is used to identify different types of record and to facilitate the analysis of income and expenditure enabling reports to be produced from several points of view.

20.9.1 Setting up a nominal ledger

When a nominal ledger is being set up for the first time the program discs have to be established. The 'file' option is then selected from the menu bar by clicking the mouse, causing a screen to be displayed which prompts for the name of the company to be entered. A disc is then selected for storing the data files, which can be labelled by clicking the mouse on 'save'. A company name icon will now be displayed at the bottom of the screen whenever the file is opened. The 'Data entry' choice on the menu bar is then accessible (see Fig. 20.1). When the mouse is clicked at 'Data entry' on the menu bar it is then moved to 'configuration' and clicked which causes a screen for configuring the nominal ledger to be displayed. The information entered into this window is used to map out or reserve internal memory for the nominal ledger data files. The screen for nominal ledger configuration is shown in Fig. 20.2, which displays the number of ledger account records that will require to be stored and the average number of transactions to be maintained on file for each nominal ledger account. This will vary according both to the nature of the business and whether open-item or balance forward accounts are to be implemented. The number of standing orders to be provided for comes next. The screen finally displays the storage space required and available.

20.9.2 Parameters

It is then necessary to select parameters from the 'data entry' menu. The nominal ledger parameter screen is shown in Fig. 20.3, which illustrates the details to be input, including:

(a) Company name and address — up to five lines are allowed.

(b) Number of periods per year — if accounts are prepared by calendar months the number of periods is 12. If every four weeks, the number of periods is 13.

(c) Last month of financial year — this is the calendar month or period number of your year-end. If the year-end is December it is necessary to enter 12; if March, enter 3.

(d) Current NL period/month number — this is the month or period the system is to commence being processed by computer. If the financial year runs from April to March, month 1 is April.

(e) Accounting years — these are used as headings on financial reports which are updated by the system.

(f) Ledger code breakdown — refer to Fig. 20.5. If only a simple 1 level code is required, ranging from 0 to 999, i.e. three digits, then 3 is entered in the first box followed by 0 and 0.

(g) Master password — any password required is entered in the appropriate box on the screen. When used it enables the user to gain access to all functions of the particular company. If not required, OMIT is entered and no password will be requested.

The setting up of parameters continues and includes details of VAT type and tax code and the code ranges allocated to sales/income, purchase/expenditure, fixed assets, current assets, current liabilities and capital. Mandatory account codes relating to bank accounts, petty cash and tax accounts are also entered (*see* Figs. 20.4 and 20.5).

20.9.3 Data entry and other routines

All data input to the system is accessed through the data entry menu (*see* Figs. 20.6 and 20.7). Input from other systems is accomplished by reading in transaction files created by other applications. The screen confirms the company name the data belongs to; the source of the information, the purchase or sales ledger for instance; the date of the day book which created the file and the nominal ledger period for which the data is intended. Provision is made to add or amend account details by an 'add/amend ledger account' screen as shown in Fig. 20.7. 'End of day' routines are also incorporated which print day books listing all the transactions input since the last 'close day' was run. 'End of period' routines provide for the printing of reports such as general accounts, trading statement, balance sheet, analysis report and tax summary. 'End of year' routines are mainly concerned with transferring balance sheet balances into the new year's accounts by a journal transfer. The NL system also provides for enquiries, which can be accessed by selecting 'Reports' on the menu bar and then selecting 'Enquiry'. Reports may be selected at any time for such requirements as a transaction list, account details, account balances, trial balance, standing order list, budget listing, ledger code description, systems parameters report, general accounts chart and analysis report.

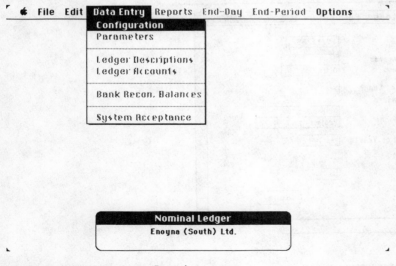

Figure 20.1 Nominal ledger: configuration

```
═▢════════════ Nominal Ledger Configuration ════════════

    Ledger Account Records                    200

    Average Transactions per Account           10

    Standing Order Records                     50

    Storage Space required            674K Bytes

    Storage Space available          1745K Bytes


                                        ┌──────────┐
                                        │   Done   │
                                        └──────────┘

            Enoyna (South) Ltd.
```

Figure 20.2 Nominal ledger: configuration

```
═▢═════════════ Nominal Ledger Parameters ═════════════

    System Date                      19/11/85

    Passwords – Nominal Ledger Access    OMIT
              – New Account Access       OMIT

    Balance Forward A/Cs at Period End ?   Yes
    User Defined field Descriptions
       – Ledger A/C field             Authorised
       – Transaction field            Project

    Reversing Journals – Monthly or Yearly  Yearly

    Is this Nominal Ledger to be
    consolidated with other
    Nominal Ledgers ?                   No

                                        ┌──────────┐
                                        │   Done   │
                                        └──────────┘
```

Figure 20.3 Nominal ledger: parameter screen

234   Applications software

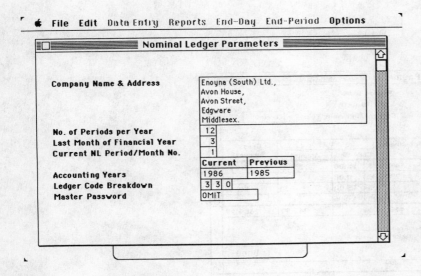

Figure 20.4 Nominal ledger: parameters screen

Nominal Ledger Parameters

Ledger Account Code Ranges

-Code Range Breakdown Level [1]

	From	To
– Sales/Income	000	100
– Purchase/Expenditure	101	200
– Fixed Assets	201	300
– Current Assets	301	400
– Current Liabilities	401	500
– Capital	501	999

Figure 20.5 Nominal ledger: parameters, accounts and codes

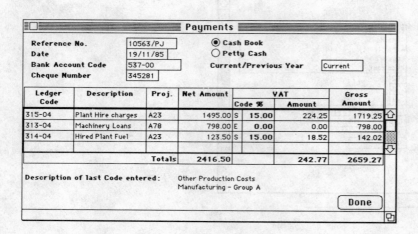

Figure 20.6 Nominal ledger payments screen

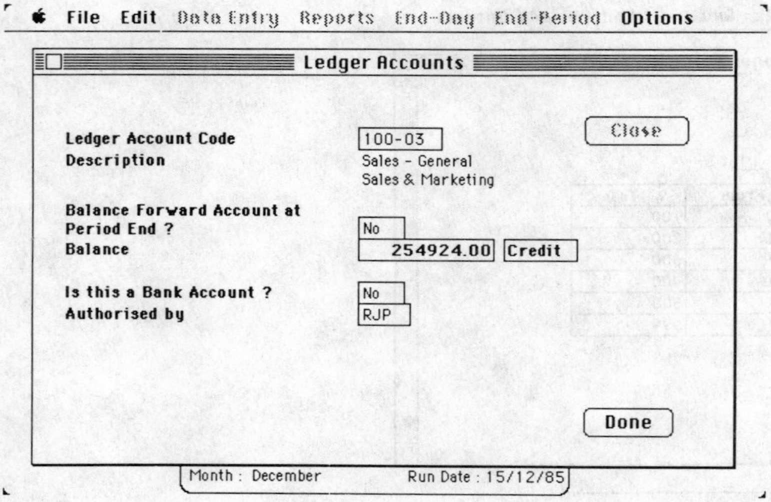

```
▢▤▤▤▤▤▤▤▤▤▤▤  Ledger Accounts  ▤▤▤▤▤▤▤▤▤▤▤▤

        Ledger Account Code           100-03              ( Close )
        Description                   Sales - General
                                      Sales & Marketing

        Balance Forward Account at
        Period End ?                  No
        Balance                          254924.00  Credit

        Is this a Bank Account ?      No
        Authorised by                 RJP




                                                          ( Done )

        Month : December          Run Date : 15/12/85
```

Figure 20.7 Nominal ledger account screen

20.10 The sales and purchase ledger

Of necessity the following details are restricted to those which provide an overall appreciation of the features of sales and purchase ledger application packages, due to the amount of detail involved — which can be seen by referring to the relevant software manual.

20.11 The sales ledger

The sales ledger is concerned with maintaining records of transactions with customers, in order to furnish the status of each customer's account. In effect, it controls accounts receivable by showing how much is owing by each customer and for how long. The sales ledger can be used in conjunction with the nominal ledger package or on a stand-alone independent basis. The application is set up in a similar way to that outlined for the nominal ledger. After the initial set-up of the application the package can be used operationally by selecting 'open' from the pull-down menu. A window then appears displaying the sales ledger icon, which is selected (opened) by pointing and clicking the mouse. All data is input by the data entry menu as shown in Fig. 20.8. The routine operation of the system includes the daily input of batches of customers' invoices (*see* Fig. 20.9) together with credit notes, remittances and adjustments. New customer records are added as and when required. An 'end of day' procedure ensures that all payments have been correctly allocated to customer accounts, and a day book is produced listing the transactions. When the sales ledger is integrated with the nominal ledger the day's sales ledger transaction data is transferred to the respective nominal ledger accounts. The customer account input window, as shown in Fig. 20.10, is accessed by selecting 'Customer account' from the data entry menu. Using the scroll bar displays a second window of information relating to the customer record, as shown in Fig. 20.11. Scrolling to a third window displays customer account data, as shown in Fig. 20.12. At the end of each accounting period the user selects from the menu and prints the required management reports, as shown in Fig. 20.13. The user then selects 'close period', which deletes the unwanted data from the sales ledger files and moves the accounting period on to the next. Back-up copies of files are made on to a different set of discs by selecting the utilities icon, which displays a screen for generating a security copy.

20.11.1 Open-item

In this system of record keeping each invoice is recorded on a customer's account and each remittance received is linked to specific invoices. Paid invoices and the payment transactions associated with them are automatically deleted after the periodic statement is printed. In this way only the outstanding invoices (the *open items*) are maintained on the files.

20.11.2 Balance forward

Invoices are recorded during the accounting period together with remittances received from customers. At the end of the accounting period after statements of account have been printed all transactions are deleted and replaced by one figure — the carried forward balance (*balance forward*). This becomes the brought forward balance at the start of the next period.

20.11.3 Benefits derived from a sales ledger package

The benefits of a computerised package include better management of cash flows by the earlier production of statements of account and greater control of outstanding balances; increased accuracy of records and quicker response to customer enquiries, so improving customer relations; the provision of management information; improved productivity of the accounting functions — a greater level of output with fewer staff and so on.

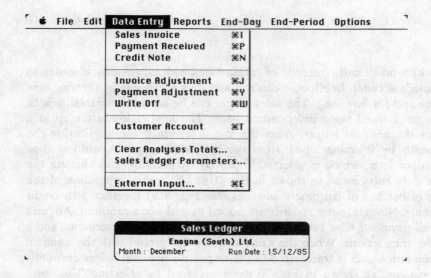

Figure 20.8 Data entry menu screen

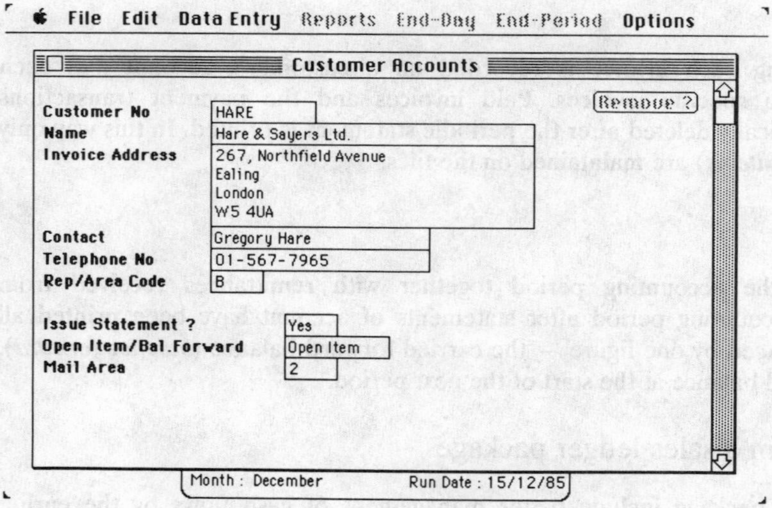

Figure 20.9 Sales ledger: customer account screen

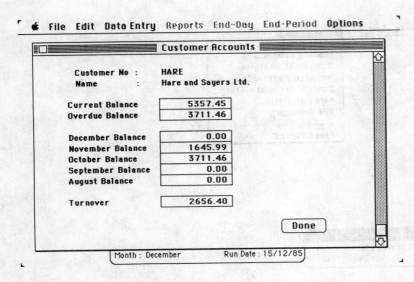

☀ File Edit Data Entry Reports End-Day End-Period **Options**

Sales Invoice

Customer Number	HARE	Hare and Sayers Ltd.
Transaction Date	31/8/85	**Branch No**	SP
Date Due	22/9/85	**Customer Ref.**	SW/44/E
Invoice Number	EN2531/1	**Description**	Part 3 of Order 23317/a

Ledger Code	Anal	Goods Amount	VAT Code	%	VAT Amount	Gross Amount
110-52		178.55	S	15.00	26.78	205.33
110-03		38.00	Z	0.00	0.00	38.00
110-51		49.60	E	0.00	0.00	49.60
Totals		**266.15**			**26.78**	**292.93**

Ledger Code Description   Sales – Retail Customers
Unit 4 Prodution Centre

[**Done**]

Month : December   Run Date : 15/12/85

Figure 20.10 Sales ledger: customer account screen

☀ File Edit Data Entry Reports End-Day End-Period **Options**

Customer Accounts

| Customer No : | HARE |
| Name   : | Hare and Sayers Ltd. |

Current Balance	5357.45
Overdue Balance	3711.46
December Balance	0.00
November Balance	1645.99
October Balance	3711.46
September Balance	0.00
August Balance	0.00
Turnover	2656.40

[**Done**]

Month : December   Run Date : 15/12/85

Figure 20.11 Sales ledger: credit control screen

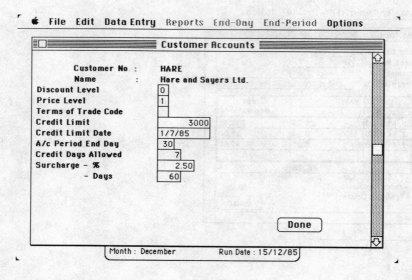

Figure 20.12 Sales ledger: customer accounts status

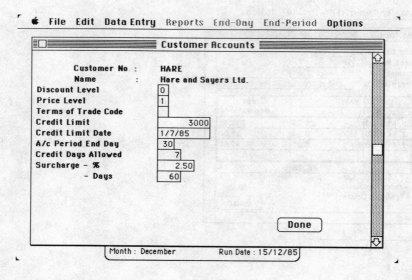

Figure 20.13 Sales ledger: report selection screen

20.12 The purchase ledger

The purchase ledger records transactions relating to a business's suppliers and maintains the status of each supplier's account. It can be used in conjunction with the nominal ledger package or used on a stand-alone basis. Purchase ledgers can be maintained for a number of companies by a multi-company facility and accounts may be maintained on an open-item or balance forward basis. After the initial configuration of the system, as shown in Figs. 20.14 and 20.15, and definitions of parameters, normal operations commence by selecting the 'open' icon from the file menu. A window is then displayed containing the purchase ledger icon, which is selected by pointing and clicking the mouse. All data input relating to purchase invoices, remittances, credit notes and adjustments is facilitated by the 'data entry' menu, illustrated in Fig. 20.16. The entry of a purchase invoice is accomplished by displaying the relevant screen, as shown in Fig. 20.17. The 'close day' routine creates a file of transactions on disc for transfer to the nominal ledger if the purchase ledger is integrated and prints transaction details into a day book. The 'close period' routine deletes those supplier records which have been deleted from the file during the period and increases the number of the next month/period. At the end of each accounting period reports are printed, which may be selected from the menu as shown in Fig 20.18. Back-up copies of files are made on to a different set of discs by selecting the utilities icon, which displays a screen for generating a security copy. Details relating to supplier accounts are displayed on various screens, as shown in Figs. 20.19–20.22.

20.12.1 Benefits derived from the use of a purchase ledger package

The benefits derived from using a purchase ledger package include better management of cash flows, increased accuracy of records and quicker response to supplier enquiries — which improve relations with suppliers; the provision of useful management information; improved productivity of the accounting functions — a greater level of output with fewer staff and so on.

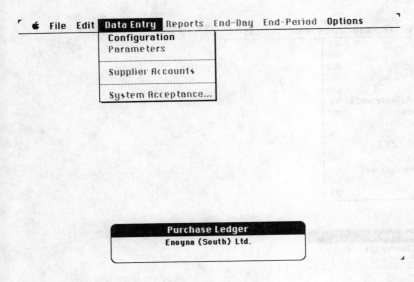

Figure 20.14 Purchase ledger: data entry selection

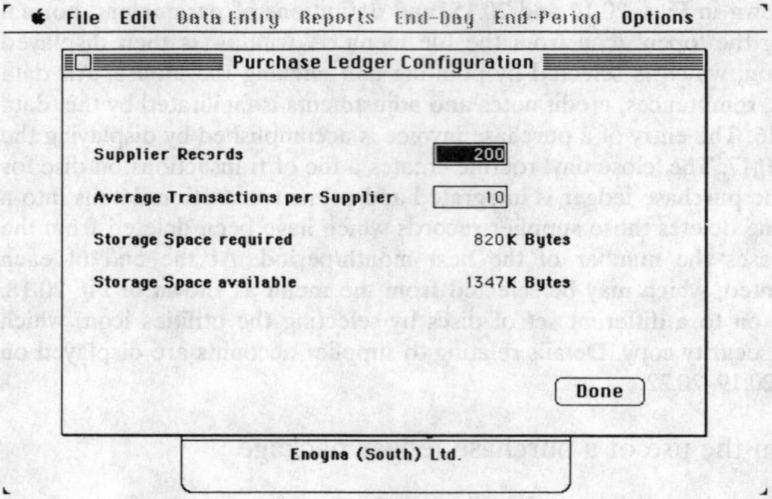
File Edit Data Entry Reports End-Day End-Period Options
Purchase Ledger Configuration
Supplier Records
200
Average Transactions per Supplier
10
Storage Space required
820K Bytes
Storage Space available
1347K Bytes
Done
Enoyna (South) Ltd.

Figure 20.15 Purchase ledger: configuration screen

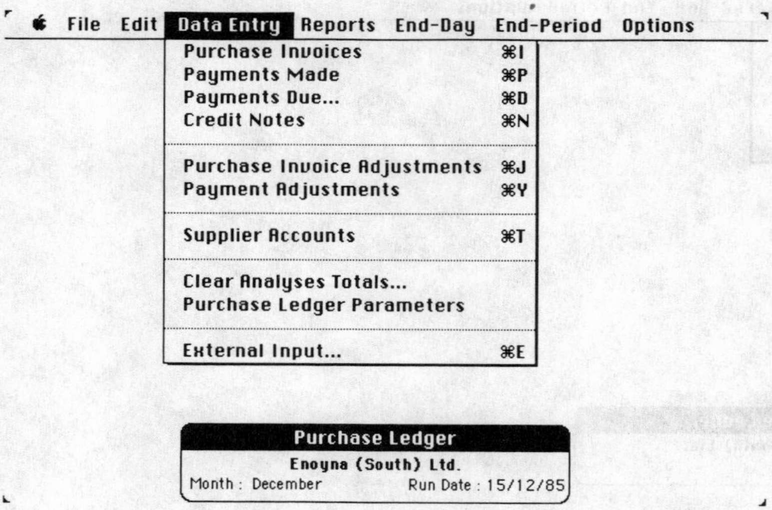
File Edit Data Entry Reports End-Day End-Period Options
Purchase Invoices ⌘I
Payments Made ⌘P
Payments Due... ⌘D
Credit Notes ⌘N
Purchase Invoice Adjustments ⌘J
Payment Adjustments ⌘Y
Supplier Accounts ⌘T
Clear Analyses Totals...
Purchase Ledger Parameters
External Input... ⌘E
Purchase Ledger
Enoyna (South) Ltd.
Month : December
Run Date : 15/12/85

Figure 20.16 Purchase ledger: data entry menu

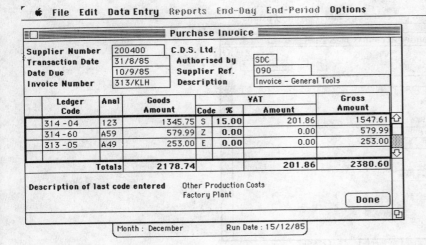

Figure 20.17 Purchase ledger: purchase invoice screen

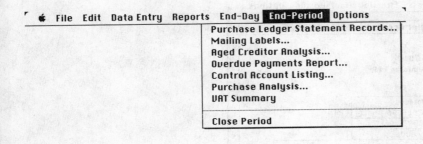

Figure 20.18 Purchase ledger: report selection screen

File Edit Data Entry Reports End-Day End-Period Options

```
┌─────────────────────────────────────────────────────────┐
│ ▢▤▤▤▤▤▤▤▤▤▤▤    Supplier Accounts    ▤▤▤▤▤▤▤▤▤▤▤▤     ⬆ │
│                                                           │
│   Supplier No        ┌──────────┐          [ Remove ? ]  │
│                      │ 010010   │                        │
│   Name               │ Alumform Ltd.              │      │
│   Payment Address    │ The Parade                 │      │
│                      │ Needham Avenue             │      │
│                      │ Glen Parva                 │      │
│                      │ Leicester LE2 9JW          │      │
│                      └────────────────────────────┘      │
│   Contact            │ Glynn Proxmire        │           │
│   Telephone No       │ 0533 384785           │           │
│   Category Code      │ 76   │                            │
│                                                           │
│   Open Item/Bal.Forward    │ Open Item │                 │
│                                                          ⬇ │
│  ┌──────────────────────────────────────────────────┐    │
│  │ Month : December       Run Date : 15/12/85        │    │
└──┴──────────────────────────────────────────────────┴────┘
```

Figure 20.19 Supplier account details screen1

File Edit Data Entry Reports End-Day End-Period Options

```
┌─────────────────────────────────────────────────────────┐
│ ▢▤▤▤▤▤▤▤▤▤▤▤    Supplier Accounts    ▤▤▤▤▤▤▤▤▤▤▤▤     ⬆ │
│                                                           │
│       Supplier No  :     010010                           │
│       Name         :     Alumform Ltd.                    │
│                                                           │
│                                                           │
│   Payment Method       │ Autopay        │                │
│   Bank A/c No          │ 342526678      │                │
│   Autopay Ref No       │ A7659          │                │
│   Bank Ledger A/c      │ 537 - 00       │                │
│   Bank Name            │ Lloyds Bank Ltd.         │       │
│   Bank Address         │ High St., Glen Parva.    │       │
│   Bank Sort Code       │ 783400      │                    │
│                                                           │
│                                      ┌──────┐             │
│                                      │ Done │             │
│                                      └──────┘            ⬇ │
│  ┌──────────────────────────────────────────────────┐    │
│  │ Month : December       Run Date : 15/12/85        │    │
└──┴──────────────────────────────────────────────────┴────┘
```

Figure 20.20 Supplier account details screen 2

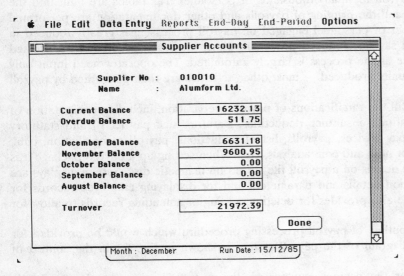

```
 File  Edit  Data Entry  Reports  End-Day  End-Period  Options
```

Supplier Accounts

```
Supplier No :    010010
Name        :    Alumform Ltd.

Current Balance              16232.13
Overdue Balance                511.75

December Balance              6631.18
November Balance              9600.95
October Balance                  0.00
September Balance                0.00
August Balance                   0.00

Turnover                     21972.39

                              [ Done ]
```

Month : December   Run Date : 15/12/85

Figure 20.21 Supplier account details screen 3

```
 File  Edit  Data Entry  Reports  End-Day  End-Period  Options
```

End-Day menu:
- Print Unallocated Payments...
- Allocations...
- Allocation Adjustments...
- Surcharges
- Print Day Books...
- Close Day

Sales Ledger
Enoyna (South) Ltd.
Month : December   Run Date : 15/12/85

Figure 20.22 Supplier account details screen 4

20.13 The payroll

Software for processing payrolls is readily available and affords many advantages. For instance, a payroll for 30 employees could be processed manually in approximately four to five hours; a computer with an on-line interactive payroll package would take 30 to 40 minutes. This time saving is extremely significant when processing a payroll for many thousands of personnel. Tax tables are built into the system and wages computations and the printing of payrolls and other documentation are performed at a very high speed. The number of personnel engaged on payroll processing is greatly reduced in larger companies providing cost savings; reduced processing time; increased accuracy of processed results and a reduction in fatigue as the process is largely automated. The operator need input only hours worked or the number of units produced — most other activities are then performed by payroll software.

Payroll packages provide for all the ramifications of payroll preparation, including computation of gross wages, tax calculations, national insurance deductions, statutory sick pay (SSP) and statutory maternity pay (SMP); printing pay advices, payrolls, list of deductions, payroll reconciliation, bank transfer list, cheques, giros and/or note and coin analysis, etc. When setting up a payroll package it is necessary to record all employee details on a payroll file stored on magnetic disc. Screen displays are provided for entering configuration details and parameters and for displaying employee records for data entry purposes. The package also provides for deleting, adding or amending records to allow for personnel changes.

There now follows a general outline of payroll processing procedure which would be provided for in typical payroll packages. A diagram of the payroll system is shown in Fig. 6.1 in the context of functional subsystems.

When preparing a payroll for the current pay period, the payroll department obtains details relating to each employee from the payroll file. The file contains details of tax code, NI contribution rate, and other deductions such as savings, loan repayments and pension payments where appropriate; it also contains details of earnings, tax deducted from earnings and NI contributions to date. What follows relates to the computation of wages rather than salaries. The current gross wages of employees are computed on the basis of attended hours or payment by results schemes, including bonus earnings. Gross wages for the current week are added to the earnings of the year to date up to the previous week, and the tax payable to date is then computed. The difference between tax payable to date and tax previously paid is either a refund or deduction for the current week depending on the level of gross wages earned. Details are recorded on a pay advice slip, which informs the employee of his or her earnings, tax and other deductions for the current week. The payroll records are updated with the current details to provide the latest 'year to date' status of the records. A summary of all details relating to each employee is recorded on a payroll, which is used for accounting and auditing purposes. Deductions are credited to appropriate accounts in the general ledger, including NI contributions for both employee and employer, standard deductions and tax deducted/refunded. Net wages are credited in the bank account and gross wages are debited to the wages account in the general ledger. Other statutory requirements are the preparation of P60s at the end of the tax year on 5 April. The P60 is a certificate of pay, income tax and national insurance contributions. A listing is produced of the P60s; P45s are provided to employees leaving the company, stating their 'year to date' earnings and tax in the current employment. A list of bank transfers or cheques is produced or a note and coin analysis as appropriate to the method of payment adopted (BACS perhaps?). An audit trail control list is also produced.

When evaluating a payroll package, general points to consider are those shown in the checklist (*see* 20.8.1)

20.13.1 Bankers' Automated Clearing Services

In practice, when systems are computerised the BACS system of payment may be used for making payments to employees and suppliers and for receiving remittances from customers. Bankers' Automated Clearing Services (BACS) is the clearing banks' computerised system for making payments on behalf of customers. It provides a means of making payments without recourse to cash, cheques or giro credits. The users' data is submitted on magnetic media such as 8-inch or 5 1/4 inch diskettes and is delivered to BACS City Reception, Bread Street, London or to the Edgware Reception. Delivery may be by means of users' messenger, security transport, the normal postal service or Datapost. Input from users via telecommunications is received at the Edgware centre.

20.14 Arguments for and against the use of packages

20.14.1 Arguments for the use of packages

These are summarised as follows:

(a) Programmers are able to concentrate their efforts on applications for which no suitable packages exist due to the special nature of a particular task.

(b) It is unnecessary to employ specialist programmers, particularly when using microcomputers, as packages are available for most requirements.

(c) Applications can be up and running (operational) much more quickly than would be the case when developing one's own computer systems, including the writing of programs.

(d) Expertise is *built-in* when using packages which, in effect, deskills the use of computers, particularly the use of micros.

20.14.2 Arguments against the use of packages

These may be summarised as follows:

(a) Package programs may take longer to run than specially written programs, but this depends on the relative skill of programmers and whether machine code is used rather than high level languages. Compiled programs usually take longer to run because they contain more instructions than machine code requires to achieve a specific task.

(b) It may be necessary to modify a package, as it may not be compatible with system requirements in all instances and this fact will increase the cost of the package.

(c) Purchased programs may cost more than internally written programs but this is dependent upon the expected volume of sales of the package since the larger the sales volume the lower the cost to the ultimate user, as the development costs are spread over a greater volume of sales.

Review questions

1   What is a software package?

2   From what sources are packages available?

3   Indicate the nature and purpose of vertical market applications software.

4 Specify the software requirements of:
  (a) accountancy practices;
  (b) estate agents;
  (c) solicitors;
  (d) stockbrokers;
  (e) insurance brokers.

5 What points would you check about software before making a selection?

6 What advantages do accounting packages provide?

7 Specify the nature and purpose of integrated accounting packages.

8 What is a chart of accounts?

9 Outline the features of the following packages:
  (a) nominal ledger;
  (b) sales ledger;
  (c) purchase ledger.

10 State the facilities provided by payroll packages.

11 What are the arguments for and against the use of packages.

21 Control software and utilities

21.1 Introduction

The most important element of control software is the *operating system*; without it a computer system cannot function. An operating system is a master control program which controls the functions of the computer system as a whole and the running of application programs. Many computers operate under the control of different operating systems making it imperative to assess the operating system used on a particular model before initial commitment. Some operating systems are adopted as 'industry standards', and these should be evaluated because they normally have a good software base. The reason for this is that software houses are willing to expend resources on developing application packages for machines functioning under the control of an operating system which is widely used. The cost of software is likely to be lower in such circumstances as the development costs are spread over a greater number of users. *Utility software* consists of programs which assist processing activities generally irrespective of the application being processed. They are in effect supporting programs designed to streamline and perform specific tasks to aid in achieving high levels of processing productivity. Precise details are included in the text.

21.2 Operating systems

21.2.1 General features of operating systems

Mainframe computers usually process several application programs concurrently, switching from one to another, for the purpose of increasing processing productivity. This is known as *multiprogramming* (*multi-tasking* in the context of microcomputers), and requires a powerful operating system (OS) incorporating work scheduling facilities to control the switching between programs. This entails reading in data for one program while the processor is performing computations on another and printing out results on yet another.

In multi-user environments (*see* 16.6) an operating system is required to control terminal operations on a shared access basis as only one user can access the system at any moment of time. The operating system allocates control to each terminal in turn. Such systems also require a system for record locking and unlocking to prevent one user attempting to read a record while another is updating it, for instance. The first user is allocated control to write to a record (or a file in some instances) and other users are denied access until the record is updated and unlocked.

Some environments operate in concurrent batch and real-time mode. This means that a 'background' job deals with routine batch processing while the 'foreground' job deals with real-time operations such as airline seat reservations, on-line booking of hotel accommodation or control of warehouse stocks, etc. The real-time operation has priority and the operating system interrupts batch processing operations to deal with real-time enquiries or file updates. The stage of batch processing attained at the time of the interrupt is temporarily transferred to backing storage. After the real-time operation has been dealt with the interrupted program is transferred back to internal memory from backing storage and processing recommences from a 'restart' point. The operating system also copies to disc backing storage the state of the real-time system every few minutes (periodic check points) to provide a means of 'recovering' the system in the event of a malfunction.

An operating system is stored on disc and has to be 'booted' into the internal memory (RAM) where it must reside throughout processing so that commands are instantly available. The operating system commands may exceed the internal memory capacity of the computer in which case only that portion of the OS which is frequently used is retained internally, other modules being read in from disc as required.

Many disc-based microcomputers function under the control of a disc operating system, known as DOS. An operating system performs many important tasks, which assists the activities of programmer and operator alike as many data handling and file organisation tasks are performed automatically by the operating system. The location of records, files or programs stored on disc is maintained by a disc operating system which, in respect of many microcomputers, is MicroSoft Disc Operating System (MS-DOS) or Personal Computer Disc Operating System (PC-DOS). The operating system calculates on which tracks of a disc to store records, files and programs and maintains a directory by file or program name. Disc directories are usually situated on tracks in the centre of the disc. The operating system stores text, records or programs wherever there is an unused sector. When a sector is filled the operating system searches for a free sector and continues recording at that location. When a file is stored on disc a track/sector index is compiled by means of a pair of bytes assigned to each file for specifying the index. One byte defines the track reference and the other the sector location. The first three tracks on a disc are often used for storing the operating system, which also controls the copying of files from one disc to another for file security purposes.

21.2.2 Typical tasks performed by an operating system

(a) Execute and monitor input and output operations.
(b) Monitor the status of hardware devices.
(c) Monitor and process hardware interrupts.
(d) Format new discs.
(e) Maintain disc directories.
(f) Execute disc reading and writing operations.
(g) Diagnose disc errors.
(h) Execute disc commands relating to the deletion, copying, renaming and dumping of files.
(i) Report on the status of disc usage and bytes available.
(j) Read-only file protection.
(k) Dynamic allocation of internal memory to software.
(l) Loading programs, chaining between programs and passing parameters.
(m) Receive, interpret and execute commands from the operator.
(n) Assigning logical input/output devices to the various input/output ports.
(o) Implementing the use of passwords.
(p) Provision of debugging aids.

21.2.3 Typical microcomputer operating systems

MS-DOS
An abbreviation for MicroSoft Disc Operating System, MS-DOS has a large software base and is a popular system, being used by Apricot, IBM and Amstrad among others.

This operating system is known as PC-DOS on the IBM PC. MS-DOS is an operating system designed for sixteen-bit computers, which are usually business-orientated machines. MSX-DOS is used in the MSX eight-bit machines and Concurrent DOS is used for multi-tasking machines.

UNIX and XENIX

UNIX was initially designed for minicomputers but is now being used on the more powerful models of microcomputers. It supports multi-tasking as well as multiple terminals connected to a single system. It is widely accepted as the main multi-user system available. XENIX is a multi-user system based on UNIX.

OS/2

This is the new IBM microcomputer operating system for use on the IBM PS/2 range of computers. It is to supersede PC-DOS. OS/2 was written by MicroSoft by and with IBM and, as with DOS, there will be a version marketed by IBM called IBM Operating System/2, and one from MicroSoft called MicroSoft OS/2. It is an advanced operating system that offers a micro the software facilities normally available only with a UNIX-based work station. It has multi-tasking abilities and provides methods by which multiple tasks can communicate.

Apple DOS

This operating system is used on the Apple series of computers and is an eight-bit system. It has a large software base as many programs were written to run on Apple machines. It occupies relatively little memory compared with other operating systems as it is not so sophisticated.

IBM Operating System/400

This operating system runs the IBM AS/400 family of minicomputers and has powerful facilities. In addition to normal operating system functions, changes made to data may be recorded automatically by a built-in *journalling* process, keeping track of what is happening to data on the system at all times. Should there be a failure while a transaction is being processed that results in it not being completed, it is restored when the system restarts to the state it was in before the transaction.

Mainframe computer operating systems

A number of operating systems exist for use on mainframe computers including VMS, VME, VAX.

21.2.4 Typical operating system commands

The commands listed below are a selection relating to MS-DOS.

CHKDSK

This command enables details to be obtained relating to disc usage and available capacity in terms of bytes for a specific floppy disc which is displayed on the screen. It also displays the number of files on each disc.

COPY

The COPY command enables a file stored on disc to be copied, as distinct from copying the whole of the contents of a disc, from one disc to another.   The format of the command to accomplish this is:
A > COPY ACC ACC/S.

If the file has an extension, e.g. .COM or .SYS, this must be typed in. A space must not be inserted, however, between the file name and the extension. A period (.) must precede the extension, otherwise a message will be displayed on the screen that the file is not found. The /S informs DOS that the system configuration has only one disc drive. The screen display is as follows.

Loading program . . .
Single DISK COPY
Insert Source Disk < CR >
Single Disk Copy
Insert Dest. Disk < CR >
Single Disk Copy
   1 File(s) copied
Strike a key to return to activities.

Note: CR means Carriage Return or Enter.

DIR

Typing DIR and then pressing the Enter key will produce a listing of all files on the disc showing their size and the date and time when they were last updated. If the disc contains a substantial number of files, they will zoom up the screen faster than the eye can read them. The scrolling is stopped by the STOP key.

The command is A> DIR

The screen goes blank and a message appears:

Loading program . . . .
   Volume in drive A is Apricot
   Directory of A:

COMMAND	COM	16437	7/09/85	10:16a
CONFIG	SYS	128	13/09/85	11:40a
AUTOEXEC	BAT	128	20/04/85	7:24p

.
.

After stopping and restarting SCROLLING by the STOP key the screen display continues:

B-W	EXE	10752	13/01/85	6:21p

   57 File(s) 122880 bytes free
Strike a key to return to activities

DIR/P

This command will fill up the screen with file details and then stop automatically. A message is provided at the bottom of the screen telling the user to 'Press any key' to resume for the purpose of viewing other file details. When the complete directory has been listed a message is displayed indicating the number of files on the disc and the available capacity on the disc for storing more files.

DIR/W

Produces an abbreviated list of the directory with the file names only.

CLS

Clears the screen except for the A> prompt.

REN

An abbreviation for RENAME, which allows the user to change the name of a file. The command takes the form: REN (old name) (new name). If the file has an extension, e.g. .COM or .SYS, this must be typed in. If a file already exists with the new name on the disc a message on the screen will state this and will not rename the file.

TYPE

Allows a text file to be displayed on the screen. TYPE will print text on the screen until the whole of the file is displayed but the process can be stopped with pressing the STOP key. Once stopped the process can be aborted by depressing the Control key and C, i.e. Control-C.

DELETE

Deletes files from a disc.

DISKCOPY

Makes back-up copies of contents of one disc to another.

DIR:SORT

Lists alphabetically sorted disc directory.

FIND

Searches for a specific string of text in a file.

21.3 Utility programs

21.3.1 General features

Utility programs are also referred to as *service* or *general-purpose* programs, as they are used for applications in general regardless of the nature of specific application programs. All processing activities require the support of utility programs to facilitate the activities required to attain a high level of performance in processing business information and in the development of business systems. This type of processing requires operations of a routine nature such as *sort/merge* for the purpose of arranging transactions into the sequence of the master file to which they relate prior to file updating; the conversion of data from one media to another, e.g. the conversion of data in floppy discs to magnetic tape or high speed discs after being validated. This arrangement enables data to be processed faster; copying of files for security purposes usually applies only to disc files which are copied to magnetic tape; reorganising disc files periodically to eliminate overflow conditions on the tracks; housekeeping routines including such tasks as the writing of header labels on magnetic files, the blocking and deblocking of records and zeroing memory locations to ensure garbage is eliminated.

It must be appreciated that many of the utilities are contained within the operating system for copying files from one disc to another; copying the complete content of discs to tape streamers or other discs; writing file details to directories and reorganising disc files; formatting discs; tracing routines which enable programs to be checked for errors by monitoring each step in a program as it is run; sub-routines for performing common series of instructions applicable to several applications, and so on.

21.3.2 Summary of utility programs

A number of programs falling into this category have been outlined above. Those and others are listed below:

(a) sort/merge routines;
(b) conversion of data from one media to another;
(c) copying of files (*see* 21.2.4);
(d) reorganising disc files periodically;

(e) writing of header labels on magnetic files;

(f) blocking and deblocking of records;

(g) zeroing memory locations to remove unwanted remnants of data from previous processing runs;

(h) trace routines for debugging;

(i) compilers (*see* 21.5);

(j) interpreters (*see* 21.6);

(k) assemblers (*see* 21.4);

(l) report generators (*see* Chapter 22);

(m) program generators (*see* Chapter 19);

(n) applications generators (*see* Chapter 19);

(o) CASE (computer-aided systems engineering) tools (*see* Chapter 28).

21.4 Assemblers

These are programs which translate a *source* program, written in an assembly or programming language, into a machine code *object* program. The translation process is performed by the computer itself, and this is known as *automatic programming*. The purpose is to simplify and speed up the task of programming by enabling the programmer to write programs in a language much simpler than machine code. Instead of writing a program which is immediately compatible to the computer, a program is written which is more compatible to the programmer for solving the problem. The computer is then used for the conversion of this program to machine code.

The assembler translates symbolic or mnemonic function codes into the equivalent machine codes and symbolic addresses into actual internal store locations. Each mnemonic instruction is normally converted into a machine code instruction on a one-for-one basis, but it is possible to use the technique of *macro-coding*, which enables a complete sub-routine to be incorporated into the object program by means of writing a single 'macro-instruction'. Once again, the objective is to simplify the task of programming.

The term 'object program' is used to define the program which is generated by the translation process and which is then used for processing the data of a specific application. The term source program is self-explanatory, as it is the original program written for processing the data of a specific application but which is not directly usable by the computer. After translation, the object program is retained on magnetic disc. In addition, a printout is produced by the line-printer of both the source and the object program instructions, for comparison and error checking. It is also possible to have a printout of diagnostics as an aid to error checking.

21.5 Compilers

These are programs which translate a source program, written in a high level language, into a machine code object program. A compiler performs the task of assembling the object program, but is generally more complex than an assembler because each source program instruction in a high level language such as COBOL generates a number of machine code instructions, i.e. a macro-instruction generates a number of micro-instructions.

As a result of the increased complexity, the compiler is larger in terms of the translation instructions it contains, and this produces a problem of internal storage capacity, as a large amount of storage is required to accommodate the compiler during the compilation run. It is sometimes necessary to compile a program on a computer which is different from that on which the compiled program will be run on account of this factor. As a matter of interest, this is the reason for stating the source computer and object computer in a COBOL program. Compiling is performed for similar reasons to assembling — to reduce the complexity and time involved in writing programs.

To give some idea of the amount of storage required for both assembling and compiling, it must be appreciated that during translation the internal store must hold the source program, the compiler or assembler and the resulting object program.

21.6 Interpreters

Interpreters are usually used by personal or small business computers, whereas mainframes utilise compilers. Interpreters and compilers are translation programs which, in respect of small computers, convert statements written in BASIC into machine code. When the command *run* is keyed in, each statement in the program is interpreted and if any statement does not conform to the rules or grammar (known as syntax) of the language then a syntax error is displayed on the screen. This can be a disadvantage as it slows down the execution of the program until the errors are removed. In addition, each statement is interpreted each time the program is executed and this also tends to slow down its execution.

Many small computers now have compilers available, which means it is only necessary to translate the program once, during the compilation run, and the compiled program is then stored on disc backing storage until the relevant application is to be run. As each statement does not have to be translated at *run time* the program runs faster than an interpreted program. An interpreter is more *firmware* than *software* as it is stored on a ROM (read only memory) chip.

21.7 Job control language

The purpose of job control language (JCL) is to control the running of jobs on a computer. Often on a large computer several jobs are run concurrently in multiprogramming mode. The JCL enables the names of jobs, the files to be used, the peripherals required, priorities of the various jobs and interrupt procedures to be specified. It enables a computer operator to communicate with the operating system by means of the keyboard/VDU for the purpose of controlling the processing of the various jobs.

Job control commands are written in a job control language. In batch processing applications the job commands are usually predefined and input with a source or object program with the relevant data, or are stored in a *command file*. Special symbols distinguish commands from program instructions. Examples of job control commands are listed in Table 21.1 below.

Table 21.1 Job control commands

Mainframe computers	BASIC for use with microcomputers	Timesharing systems
Compile	Run	Login
Execute	Load	Logout
Delete	Save	EOJ (End of Job)
Start	Verify	
Sort	Clr	
Dump	List	
Edit	New	

Review questions

1   State the nature and purpose of an operating system.

2   List typical tasks performed by an operating system.

3   Provide six examples of typical operating system commands.

4   State the nature and purpose of utility programs.

5   Define the difference between an assembler, compiler and interpreter.

Self-test question

21.1 What purpose do the following three categories of software serve?

(a) systems software;
(b) application programs; *and*
(c) utility programs.

Answer on pages 379–80.

22 Report generators

22.1 Introduction

Various types of software incorporate modules for producing reports. A spreadsheet screen, for instance, can be structured into report format and printed out. An example is provided in Chapter 8, outlining report requirements and how they are structured for printing. The format of a report can be changed by using a *setup* option. The screen changes showing the current settings for length of pages, width of lines and setup codes, etc (*see* Chapter 8 for further details). Databases also provide facilities for generating reports — dBASE II, for instance, allows the setting up of a command file using 4GL-type statements which transfers data to specific storage locations for use in subsequent processing, performs calculations on the contents of fields to be included in a report, computes totals and prints required details. Accounting packages also contain modules for different reports for production either on an *ad hoc* enquiry basis or as a matter of routine at the end of the period.

22.2 Report generators

A report generator is a programming language for extracting information from files. The input consists of report parameters defining the structure of a specific report and produces the appropriate report program to read the file, extract the information and format the output as required. The language used may be COBOL or RPG II. The input to an RPG must be information in respect of:

   (a) the input file containing the records;
   (b) the location of the fields to be included in the report file;
   (c) selection criteria — the conditions required in records to be selected for inclusion in the report;
   (d) details of calculations to be carried out on specific fields, perhaps to compute the average age or wages of specified personnel;
   (e) the columns to be totalled;
   (f) the main heading of the report, column headings, page headers and footers and page numbering, etc.

22.3 Reports from a nominal ledger package

As an example, the Macintosh nominal ledger software package allows users the option of designing their own reports and analyses. This enables the user to determine the information to be included in the report and its structure (format/layout). The option 'user-defined report formats' is selected by choosing 'Format NL reports' from the data entry menu. The report to be produced is selected by clicking on the required option by the mouse. If 'Define another report' is selected, the name of the new report will be typed into a specified box (*see* Fig. 22.1). The report name will appear in the nominal ledger's financial statements print menu. When the mouse clicks on 'Accept' (*see* Fig. 22.1) the screen shown in Fig. 22.2 is displayed. This display will be used for the layout of the desired report and instructions which control the report. The blank screen is a window on a part of the document which can be scrolled. The numbers on the horizontal axis are character positions; those on the vertical axis are lines. Fields can be located anywhere on the report and in any sequence. The fields can be 'dragged' to different positions by clicking on the field, holding down the mouse button, and dragging the image of the field to the new position. After completing the definition of a new report, or changing an existing one, the operation is terminated by clicking on the 'go-away' box in the top left corner of the report screen. This will write (save) the report definitions to disc where they are stored for subsequent use. Figure 22.3 shows the options which may be selected, including 'Description' and 'Analysis'. *Descriptions* are text fields to provide headings and descriptive information on the reports. 'Text' allows the user to enter any textual information required on the report. 'Account name' uses the contents of a description record as the text to put on the report. 'Analyses' are fields that are composites of other information; this includes provision for totals, percentages and arithmetic calculations.

The report's appearance can be improved by transferring it to a print file which can be read into a text (word) processing, or desktop publishing application and the structure and format amended to that required.

22.4 Easy*SQL

This is a software product marketed by Oracle Corporation UK Ltd. It increases the value of the ORACLE Relational Database Management System by extending its availability to novice and casual users. Among many other attributes it contains facilities for constructing queries to select data from a relational database to build and modify reports and graphs. The 'query' is the basic data retrieval tool for a relational database management system. A query panel is displayed on the screen as shown in Fig. 22.4. The query panel starts with the cursor on the first 'tables' name box, which allows up to three tables to be identified from which to display information. In this instance EMP table is selected. The cursor is then located at the first entry box for column names. The system does not expect the user to remember column names because a pop-up reference box is displayed on the right-hand side of the screen when moving to the column entry box. This lists the name of each column in the table selected. A down arrow highlights the column names to be included. The names of the columns to retrieve from the table are entered in the order to be displayed on the screen. This aspect is shown in Fig. 22.4. The cursor is now placed on the 'Format' line of the box, where the format for each column is defined. The cursor then locates on the third line of the first box where the user can enter a new heading instead of using the column name. The last entry box on the query panel is called a 'WHERE box' because it confines the query to those rows (database records) where certain conditions are met. In this case only the rows of employees whose salary is greater than £2,000 will be displayed.

Any entry can be corrected by returning to the relevant location. When the query is completed it is saved on disc and then displayed on the screen as shown by Fig. 22.5. When using some database software it is necessary to learn and use separate generation programs but Easy*SQL's report and graph options are built in and fully integrated with the software. Once the query has been defined the report option can be applied to add titles, sort rows, compute sub-totals and group totals and format the page. The report panel for designing the report is shown in Fig. 22.6, which displays a stylised representation of what the report will look like. When the name of the 'query' storing the information for this report is entered all the information will appear in the report. To the report is then added a top title, columns for sorting are selected, columns for totalling are selected, a bottom title is added and the page size is determined in respect of the number of lines required on each page and the number of characters per line. The report is then saved on disc and printed (*see* Fig. 22.7).

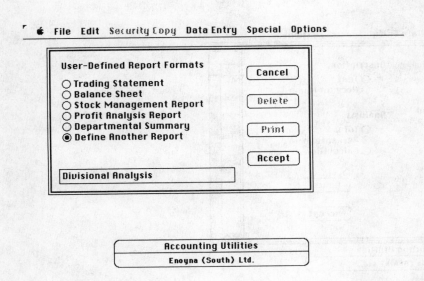

Figure 22.1 Nominal ledger: report selection menu

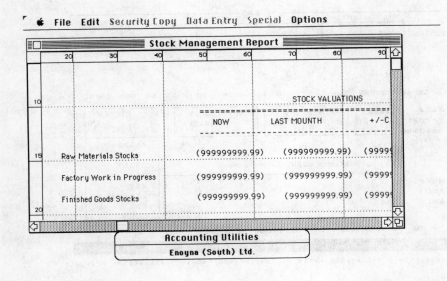

Figure 22.2 Nominal ledger: report structure

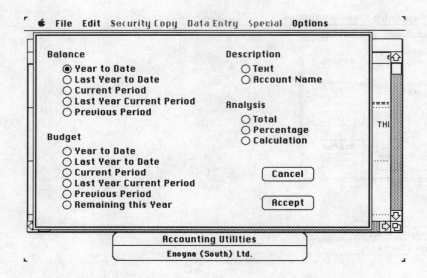

Figure 22.3 Nominal ledger information classes

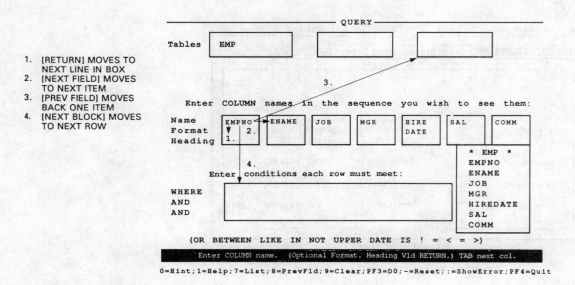

Figure 22.4 Query panel

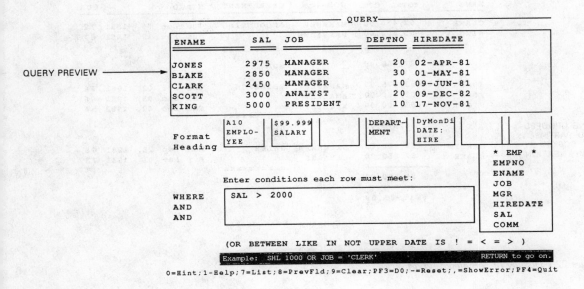

QUERY PREVIEW

Figure 22.5 Query preview screen

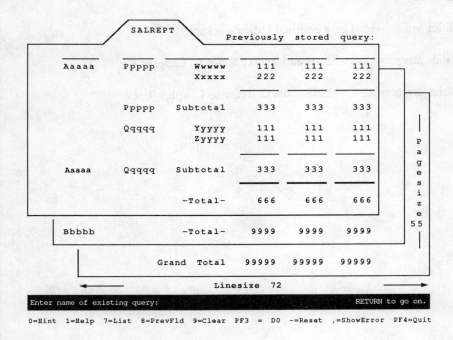

Figure 22.6 Report design screen

REPORT   ON   SALARIED   PERSONNEL
Personnel   Department

EMPLOYEE NAME	TOTAL COMP	JOB	DEPARTMENT	DATE HIRED				DUR
CLARK	$2,450.00	MANAGER	ACCOUNTING	Tue	Jun	09,	1981	72
KING	$5,000.00	PRESIDENT		Tue	Nov	17,	1981	67
			xxxxxxxxxx					
	$7,450.00		SUM					
JONES	$2,975.00	MANAGER	RESEARCH	Thu	Apr	02,	1981	74
FORD	$3,000.00	ANALYST		Thu	Dec	03,	1981	66
SCOTT	$3,000.00	ANALYST		Thu	Dec	09,	1982	54
			xxxxxxxxxx					
	$8,975.00		SUM					
MARTIN	$2,650.00	SALESMAN	SALES	Mon	Sep	28,	1981	68
BLAKE	$2,850.00	MANAGER		Fri	May	01,	1981	73
			xxxxxxxxxx					
	$5,500.00		SUM					
	$21.925.00							

ROWS GROUPED
BY DEPARTMENTS
AND SORTED BY
COMPENSATION ——————► BLAKE

Company   Confidential

Figure 22.7 Display of completed report

Review questions

1   What is a report generator?

2   What reporting facilities are provided by a nominal ledger package?

3   What reporting facilities are provided with spreadsheets? Refer to Chapter 8.

4   What reporting facilities are provided with databases? Refer to Chapter 9.

23 Organisational structures

23.1 Introduction

What follows outlines the organisational structures, functions, responsibilities and staffing considerations of a data processing department and of management services. Matters relating to information centres are also dealt with in this chapter. It is important to appreciate that standard organisational structures do not exist because the nature of business operations determines the type of structure required to attain optimum operating results. Much depends upon the geographical spread of businesses; those with dispersed factories, branch offices and warehouses will sometimes prefer centralised management services and independent centralised data processing functions for matters of economy. In other instances each group factory may have its own local management services function and separately structured data processing department. Sometimes the management services function will be structured to embrace systems development, data processing and information processing under the control of a management services manager. In many instances the data processing department may be centralised for corporate requirements with distributed processing functions throughout the group according to operational needs (*see* Fig. 16.6).

23.2 Management services

23.2.1 Management services defined

The term *management services* defines those activities which assist management to improve and control working practices. In the 1979 BSI *Glossary of Terms used in Work Study and Organisation and Methods* the term is defined as 'specialist groups or units established within organisations to assist and advise on improvements in executive management functions'. To this is added by way of explanation: 'These groups embrace one or more of the following disciplines: work study, O & M, operational research, data processing, ergonomics, economic forecasting, industrial engineering.'

23.2.2 The need for management services

Business operations take place in a highly complex and dynamic environment encompassing political, economic and social factors which cannot be influenced by a single business unit. The business must react to such influences, however, not only to remain in business but to attain defined productivity levels in pursuit of profit targets. This is the situation for which the advice of the management services function must be sought. Management services are not restricted to the industrial and commercial sectors of the economy but play an important part in varying types of organisation including hospitals, local authorities, central government, breweries and building societies. Even though some organisations are not profit orientated, such as local authorities, they do have a responsibility for providing cost-effective services in order to keep rates as low as possible. They need, therefore, to strive constantly for more effective use of resources to increase productivity. Wherever work activities take place problems will arise. The magnitude of the problem is often related to the size of the organisation — the larger the organisation, the larger and more diverse the management services department required to deal with them.

23.2.3 Responsibility for change

The prerogative of change lies with functional managers who are responsible for the effective use of resources in their area of responsibility. The specialists of change are management services personnel who have expert knowledge of many techniques from which to select for problem solving and/or improving productivity.

23.2.4 Development of systems

When a business changes course as a result of modified or new strategies it is often necessary to develop new systems or modify existing ones to contend with the new situation. This requires the services of systems analysts or O & M staff.

23.2.5 Inefficient systems and productivity.

Inefficient systems achieve low levels of productivity, which have the effect of increasing administrative costs in relation to the level of output. This is usually reflected in the price of the products or services offered to customers, which reduces the competitive advantage causing a reduction in market share. This can be corrected by systems analysts or organisation and methods staff, depending on the nature of the system whether predominantly manual, computerised, or — more likely — a combination of both.

23.2.6 Methods and techniques

Business systems and manufacturing systems need to be reviewed periodically to assess if their productivity can be improved by implementing more sophisticated methods and techniques. With factory-based operations this is a task for the methods engineer and in the office for the O & M practitioner or systems analyst.

23.2.7 Operational problem solving

When problem solving it is necessary to define the nature of the problem and then select a suitable technique for its solution. The next step requires the development of alternative solutions as a basis for selecting that which provides the most acceptable results, the optimum. Some problems require statistical or mathematical analysis to obtain a practical solution. This type of problem can be resolved by the application of quantitative techniques including linear programming, queueing theory and discounted cash flow computations. Quantitative analysis of this type is often performed by computerised problem solving packages. This is the province of the operational research specialist who is conversant with quantitative analysis, the application of logic to problems to find their root cause and their solution. Operational research staff are also conversant with simulating the operation of systems and defining system variables in order to understand the way in which they behave under varying operational conditions.

An example of this is the behaviour of *fixed* operating overheads, which vary per unit of output in inverse proportion to production volume — the higher the volume the lower the cost per unit, and vice versa. *Variable* overheads, on the other hand, vary in direct proportion to the volume of production — the total increases as production increases and vice versa, but the cost per unit remains constant irrespective of volume. Simulation requires the construction of a model defining system variables, their relationships and constraints such as limited production capacity preventing a volume of output beyond a stated value; and the behavioural aspects of variables when subjected to modified values such as when amending the re-order level and/or quantity in a stock control system, which can affect the number of occasions an item is out of stock or that excessive stocks are held. The results are used as a foundation for designing a more effective stock control system.

23.2.8 Staffing: functions and responsibilities of management services

A typical management services organisation structure does not exist, since it varies with the size, nature and needs of a specific business. Some organisations may have only a work study section dealing with changes of methods in the factory and the associated work measurement activity for establishing standard times for new or revised methods. Others may have a management services structure consisting of several specialisms including work study, systems development staff including organisation and methods and systems analysts; computing and information centre and operational research (*see* Fig. 23.1). Yet other businesses may have an industrial engineering function covering the design and implementation of systems comprising manpower, materials and machines viewed on the basis of an integrated system rather than as isolated elements. This type of function is orientated to production engineering in manufacturing companies and to process engineering in chemical-based businesses such as oil refining and paint manufacture, and so on.

Large companies have management services departments controlled by managers with a number of group or section supervisors reporting to them, each group consisting of several staff of the same specialism. A work study section may have specialists to deal with method studies and others with work measurement activity. A systems development section will probably be staffed by several analysts for the analysis and design of computer projects supported by organisation and methods staff for manually orientated operations. Indeed, very large companies undertaking many projects may be structured as project teams comprising a number of different specialist personnel. Operational research teams may be appointed for operational problem solving, each team being staffed on a multi-disciplinary basis — perhaps economists, engineers, accountants and statisticians — so that operational problems can be looked at from different viewpoints for the purpose of obtaining an optimum solution. Each of these disciplines would be under the control of a specialist manager reporting to a common superior, the manager of management services, or, in a very large combine, the director of group management services.

This form of structure recognises the importance of coordinating the interdisciplinary services at a high level in the organisation in order to gain the maximum benefit, for the corporate entity as a whole, by a planned use of skilled resources to optimise their use.

Requests for specific services from the different functions of the business would be channelled through a projects committee, in some instances, or directly through the management services manager in others.

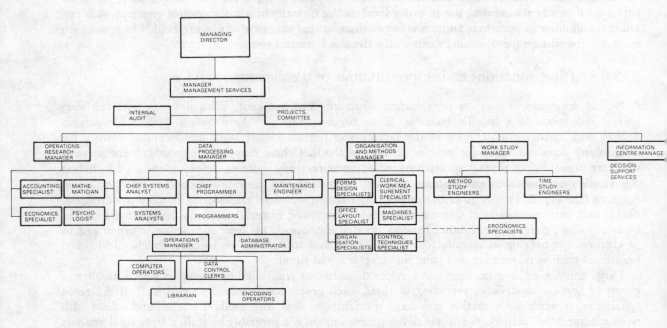

Figure 23.1 Management services organisation structure integrated with data processing

23.2.9 Job specification — management services manager

A typical job description is given below.

(a) Responsible to: managing director or director of group management services.
(b) Subordinates:

    (i)   work study manager;
    (ii)   operations research manager;
    (iii)   data processing manager;
    (iv)   organisation and methods manager.
    (v)   information centre manager

(c) Functional relationships: all departmental managers.
(d) Responsible for:

    (i)   coordinating all management services activities;
    (ii)   recruiting and training staff;

(iii)	assessing performance of staff;
(iv)	ensuring staff keep up to date with management and problem solving techniques;
(v)	investigating problems throughout the organisation in respect of operations, computing, data processing and systems;
(vi)	allocating assignments to relevant subordinates;
(vii)	controlling the use of resources and time spent on projects;
(viii)	resolving conflicts between staff and functional departments;
(ix)	optimising use of equipment, i.e. portable computers for capturing data relating to work study and operations research projects;
(x)	making recommendations to the board and advising functional departments of relevant courses of action in prescribed circumstances;
(xi)	monitoring performance of systems after new systems, methods or techniques have been implemented to ensure expected results are being achieved;
(xii)	authorising further study as necessary to remedy adverse situations.

(e) Limitations on authority; no direct authority over functional department staff unless specially delegated for a defined purpose. Direct authority only over management services personnel; otherwise advisory only.

23.3 Data processing department

The position of the data processing department is changing dynamically with developments in information centres (*see* 23.4). There will always be a need for 'traditional' DP staff in the larger business for systems development and running applications which require the processing of large volumes of data for payroll, stock control, invoicing, etc. Town halls require traditional DP departments to process the payroll for thousands of public employees and to process rates bills; the Vehicle Licensing Centre and electricity and gas boards have comparable requirements.

In the smaller business, staff in user departments have small computers for accounting routines, using software packages without the need for the services of a data processing (computer) bureau. The advent of small business computers and related applications software has allowed many small businesses to switch to doing their own computerised processing. It is advantageous to control their own processing and is now within their financial ability.

23.3.1 Organisation of a data processing department by function or activity

The functional organisation of a batch processing installation is shown in Fig 23.2, and may be summarised as follows.

Head of department — data processing manager:

(a) responsible to: director of administration, managing director or company secretary according to specific requirements;

(b) immediate subordinates: chief systems analyst, chief programmer, operations manager and database administrator.

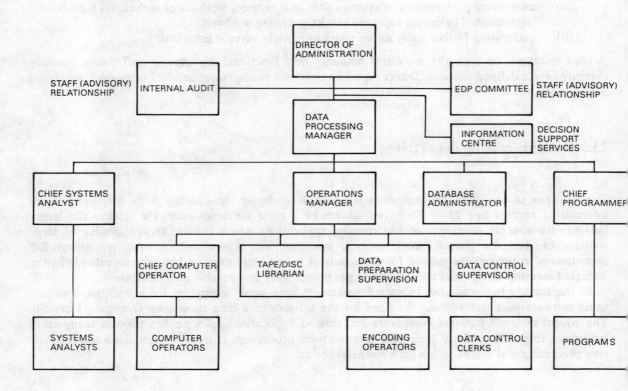

Figure 23.2 Organisation chart: by function or activity incorporating an information centre

23.3.2 Principal duties of data processing manager

The duties of a data processing manager may be summarised in the following manner:

(a) interpretation and execution of data processing policy as defined by the data processing steering committee or board of directors;

(b) controlling immediate subordinates in the attainment of project objectives;

(c) participation in policy formulation;

(d) liaison with user departments to ensure their interests are fully provided for;

(e) ensuring that company policy is adhered to;

(f) ensuring that computer operating instructions are updated when the need arises;

(g) assessing the effectiveness of the file maintenance procedures;

(h) assessing the suitability of file security procedures;

(i) ensuring that program modifications are applied effectively;

(j) monitoring test runs;

(k) post-implementation evaluation;

(l) ensuring that staff attend suitable training courses for their development;

(m) assessing performance of staff for salary awards and promotion;

(n) coordinating the whole of the data processing operations and ensuring that work flows smoothly;

(o) resolving conflict between subordinates;

(p) providing guidance on data processing problems;

(q) development and implementation of data processing standards.

23.3.3 Principal duties of chief systems analyst

The duties may be summarised as follows:

(a) liaison with user departments to ensure their requirements and problems are fully discussed before systems design and implementation;

(b) interpreting terms of reference before embarking upon systems investigations in order to establish the problem, areas of investigation and limits to the assignment;

(c) comparing the cost and performance of alternative processing methods and techniques;

(d) organising and coordinating the activities of systems analysts;

(e) reviewing performance of systems analysts;

(f) organising and reviewing systems documentation to ensure it complies with data processing standards;

(g) reviewing the progress of projects and reporting status to the data processing manager;

(h) presenting recommendations to data processing and user department management with regard to possible courses of action or design philosophy to achieve defined objectives;

(i) coordinating the implementation of new or modified systems;

(j) reviewing performance of implemented systems and assessing the need for amendments or additional training of staff;

(k) discussion of proposals with chief programmer.

23.3.4 Principal duties of chief programmer

These are summarised below:

(a) liaison with chief systems analyst to determine philosophy of proposed systems and establish the type of programming language to use — high level or assembly code (low level);

(b) review of systems specification to establish the details of systems requirements before discussing these with assigned programmers;

(c) defining test data requirements and monitoring test runs;

(d) reviewing programmers' performance;

(e) reporting status of program development to data processing manager.

23.3.5 Principal duties of operations manager

These are summarised as follows:

(a) control of all sections for which he or she is responsible, i.e. computer operations, data preparation and data control;

(b) development of operating schedules for all jobs to be run on the computer;
(c) ensuring that data is received on time from user departments;
(d) maintaining records on equipment utilisation;
(e) implementing standard procedures when appropriate to improve efficiency;
(f) controlling stocks of data processing supplies, tapes, stationery and discs, etc.;
(g) maintaining a log of computer operations;
(h) report to data processing manager of situations such as hardware malfunctions, staffing problems and other operational matters.

23.3.6 The database administrator

As the whole concept of a database is to rationalise business systems by the integration of such systems it follows that the data needs of an organisation must be coordinated at a very high level. This is basically the responsibility of a database administrator.

23.3.7 Organisation of a data processing department by purpose

It is sometimes found that a computer department is organised by 'purpose' (*see* Fig. 23.3) rather than by 'function' or 'activity' as shown in Fig 23.2. In this type of structure the various activities are grouped together to achieve a defined purpose. In the case of a computer department the 'purpose' may be multifold, i.e. to develop several systems for computerisation concurrently, in which case programmers and analysts would be combined into a project team for each project undertaken reporting to team leaders.

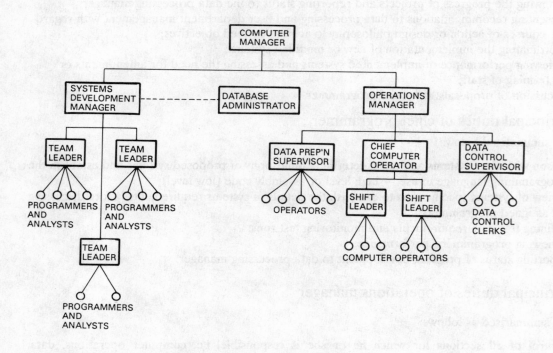

Figure 23.3 Organisation chart: by purpose

23.4 Information centres

The winds of change have led to fourth generation languages, which allow personnel other than professional computer staff to use computers on a personal basis. This is often for the purpose of accessing a database to make queries and generate reports and for developing spreadsheets for solving specialised types of problems related to their responsibilities. Such activities were formerly performed by DP specialists. With the advent of the silicon chip, which heralded the birth of the small computer, the situation began to change: the 'DIY' computer age had arrived. The term *information centre* may be defined in two different contexts.

23.4.1 Functional departments as information centres

When personnel in each department use computers for various tasks, as indicated above, they may be classed as information centres because they are generating and processing their own data to produce reports and solve problems on a DIY basis. This situation creates a number of problems, one of which is that information will be departmentalised to optimise the performance of an individual department (information centre). Other departments may require similar information but in a different format for a different purpose. This situation requires a database administrator or information coordinator to ensure data is precisely defined, redundant data eliminated and all data and its attributes formally recorded in a data dictionary. This is, of course, a standard facility in database management systems (DBMS).

23.4.2 Special section with information centre responsibilities

The second, and generally applicable, interpretation of an information centre is:

'A section of the organisation with special responsibilities for providing training and coordinating the use of personal computers and other office automation services throughout all business functions: the provision of problem solving aids, decision support services and facilities for making queries and generating reports.'

An information centre would not be under the control of the data processing manager but would report to, and be controlled by, a higher authority, a director of administration for instance, as shown in Fig. 23.3.

Review questions

1   What is the primary purpose of management services?

2   What techniques may be applied to operational problem solving?

3   Discuss the staffing and organisation of management services.

4   Specify the job specification for a management services manager.

5   Discuss the staffing and responsibilities of a data processing department.

6   Distinguish between organisation by function and organisation by purpose.

7 List the principal duties of a data processing manager.

8 List the duties of a chief systems analyst.

9 List the duties of a chief programmer.

10 List the duties of an operations manager.

11 What is the purpose of a database administrator?

12 What are the responsibilities of an information centre?

24 Systems development strategies 1: initial considerations

24.1 Introduction

Included in this chapter many important aspects of systems development are discussed which are essential to conducting system projects. This covers such topics as terms of reference, feasibility studies and feasibility study reports. Database design issues are dealt with in Chapter 9.

24.2 The need for systems development

The dynamic nature of a business requires the implementation of change to contend with the ever-changing factors influencing its activities. This is a time of intense technological development and it is necessary to harness the latest technology available to the functions and activities of a business to enable it to become or remain administratively efficient in comparison with its competitors. Change is often forced upon a business either because competitors develop their systems for greater productivity or efficiency, or as a result of business takeovers. Whatever the reason, it is usually necessary to reappraise the administrative systems in use, either to standardise them or to remove or replace those which are outmoded.

New technology in the form of computers and related electronic systems, such as on-line information processing systems, electronic mail and local area networks, etc., should before all else eliminate existing weaknesses within the organisation or function. Weaknesses may be due to outmoded practices, outworn machines, or equipment which is incompatible with current needs. When weaknesses are eliminated a business is in a better position to increase productivity, reduce operating costs, and increase the value of information produced.

It cannot be stressed too strongly that careful planning on the part of management, specialists and personnel is the key to a successful changeover. Plans can be made only on the basis of a *full* understanding of the company, its objectives and the ways in which each department currently operates. A detailed evaluation of present functions, costs, personnel and needs is the premise on which to base assessments of future requirements.

A business may have grown greatly both in its operations and information processing needs and may now be a widespread corporation with overseas branches resulting from takeovers and mergers. A major restructuring of the managerial, organisational, financial and information processing activities is inevitable. An increase in operating costs is here to be expected; this is especially true if the cost of the current system is low merely because it is not achieving the desired level of performance and is creating operational, administrative and managerial problems as a result. A manual sales accounting system may be so slow in dealing with customers' orders that orders are lost; invoices and statements of account may be so delayed after the end of the trading period that critical cash flow problems occur; or excessive errors may occur or the system may fail to produce the payroll on time because existing methods cannot cope with the increased number of personnel.

24.3 Problem analysis

Any new system should aim to solve the problems and remove the weaknesses inherent in the existing system. It is therefore important to identify and analyse what these problems are before commencing with the development of the new system. They may include:

(a) poor cash flow;
(b) unacceptable level of bad debts;
(c) dissatisfied customers;
(d) bad management decisions on stock levels and re-ordering.

Without identifying the causes of such problems it is impossible to solve them. It is pointless to implement changes which cannot solve fundamental problems and so may result in, for example:

(a) further delays in the production of invoices and issue of reminders and statements;
(b) failure to impose credit limit checks when customers place orders;
(c) delays in despatching goods to customers following the receipt of orders;
(d) failure to identify promptly that stock has fallen below re-order level;
(e) poor forecasting techniques for estimating demand.

Hence, from the moment computerisation is proposed it is essential to locate problem areas and trace their causes to ensure that the most effective system is chosen, that it caters to all needs, and that it successfully eliminates organisational weaknesses.

24.4 Project selection criteria

Projects for development may be selected on the basis of *key factors* which indicate areas of improvement and therefore the greatest potential for achieving the greatest benefits. Large cost savings on a low cost activity, for example, do not generate the required magnitude of benefits: a reduction of 50 per cent on operating costs of £5,000 is only £2,500. A 10 per cent reduction on operating costs of a £150,000 project is a saving of £15,000, which is of far greater significance.

Key factors for consideration include those listed below:

(a) systems with a high volume of errors;
(b) systems with a high volume of output;
(c) systems with a large number of operations;
(d) systems with a large number of personnel;
(e) systems with high operating costs;
(f) systems suffering from bottlenecks causing delays in the distribution of information for business control;
(g) systems functioning on outdated methods;
(h) systems which do not accord with current needs;
(i) systems which are too complicated for their primary purpose.

24.5 Systems competing for scarce development resources

What strategy should be adopted when several systems are being considered for computerisation and there is, for example, a shortage of systems development staff or of funds? Before it is possible to make a final decision it is advisable to prepare a summary of key factors which affect the running of the business. Only once these have been assessed and prioritised will it be possible to identify that system which would most benefit from computerisation. There are three basic steps:

(a) prepare a list of the important factors which will provide a basis for selecting one system for development;

(b) award points to each factor to a maximum of ten as a means of indicating the relative weighting (importance) of the individual factors to the improvement of the business as a whole;

(c) select the system with the highest points rating (score) for development.

The factors to include in the list are outlined below.

(a) *Cost effectiveness*: if staff savings are a necessity then the system that reduces the staff by the greatest number will score the highest number of points, or that which avoids increasing staff numbers by the highest number will score most points. An additional factor would be based on the reduction of total operating costs.

(b) *Operational efficiency*: the system which, if computerised, will achieve the highest level of operational efficiency will be the favourite contender. The accounting system, for example, may be assessed in terms of the number of days saved at the month-end to produce statements of account, the staff payroll or month-end accounts. An additional factor could, for instance, be based on the relative importance of achieving a greater degree of accuracy in the preparation of invoices. This has a bearing on customer satisfaction and goodwill. If the stock control system is a contender then it may be assessed on the value of the reduced level of stocks which will be possible due to improved stock management and control.

(c) *Development time and relative use of resources*: if time is crucial then the system which will take the shortest time to implement will score best. In addition, the system which utilises the lowest level of systems resources (i.e. the systems analyst's time) will score most points.

(d) *Simplicity*: the system which is the simplest to install may achieve both cost and time-saving results.

(e) *Company image:* the installation of a particular type of system may be a prestigious achievement for a company and may have a spinoff by way of an increase in the level of goodwill. This may apply to an automated purchase order system which provides suppliers with a forward supply schedule and which provides for prompt payment of supplies.

(f) *Improved flow of management information*: businesses must be controlled effectively to remain efficient or even to survive. A system which improves managerial performance by the provision of more timely information will tend to score well.

(g) *Improved problem solving and decision making*: any system which will provide management with facts on which timely decisions may be based or which can solve important strategic or tactical problems will tend to be favourably considered.

24.6 Overcoming shortages of systems development staff

Possible courses of action to overcome the shortage of systems development staff and permit the more rapid implementation of systems include the following.

(a) Employ a systems house to develop the systems.

(b) Use program generators and application generators.

(c) Use application packages.

(d) Employ freelance systems and programming personnel (from advertisements in computer journals and magazines).

(e) Enlist the services of a recruitment agency to obtain trained staff.

(f) Employ the services of a personnel agency for the hiring of temporary staff (similar to (d) above).

(g) Employ a training organisation for training suitable personnel on a short-duration external or in-plant course.

24.7 Traditional and structured systems development techniques

24.7.1 Systems development life cycle

The system life cycles for both traditional and structured techniques are similar, consisting of the following stages:

(a) define development strategy;

(b) systems analysis;

(c) systems design;

(d) develop the new system;

(e) prepare system and user documentation;

(f) system implementation;

(g) system testing;

(h) system maintenance.

As can be seen, the stages are very explicit but the traditional approach tends to suffer from an important disadvantage because it has a tendency to be 'technique'-orientated too soon. The 'physical' aspects of hardware and software tend to be considered, regarding 'how' to perform a task before the 'logical' requirements of a system have been thoroughly analysed. The traditional systems development life cycle approach uses the technique of flowcharting outlining the features of clerical and computer procedures including computer run charts. Flowcharts display the logical sequence of processing but tend towards thinking in terms of the physical, rather than the logical, requirements of users. On the other hand, structured techniques address the issues stated above by the development of models and diagrams representing the real world in which the system functions. Structured analysis defines in unambiguous terms *what* a system's requirements are. Structured design applies the same techniques specifying *how* a system will be built. The modern systems development methodology emphasises the solving of problems without technical constraints. A logical/conceptual model of a system is constructed specifying the requirements to achieve desired information flows and outputs to meet business objectives. These logical needs are subsequently matched to physical machines and equipment during the physical design stage of systems development. Logical models are constructed of data flows, processes and entities to obtain an appreciation of the nature of the elemental structure of a system as it now exists, and what changes are required to suit *what* system requirements are before determining *how* they are to be accomplished.

24.7.2 Advantages of an effective development methodology

An efficient systems development methodology is essential to reduce the risk of wasting resources and increase the productivity of development staff by providing a standard method of developing each project, and to provide the right tools and techniques for analysing and designing various elements of the system.

Structured system development techniques are discussed later (*see* Chapter 28), but there now follows a further discussion of the various stages of the traditional systems development life cycle listed above.

24.8 Extended stages of systems development life cycle

The stages of systems life cycle development methodology are summarised below. A number of the stages are dealt with in greater depth within the various topic areas, particularly those relating to feasibility study, terms of reference, systems analysis and design.

The stages are as follows.

(a) Define the problem.
(b) Management specify terms of reference.
(c) Conduct feasibility study:
    (i) *technical feasibility*: demands on the system regarding terminal enquiries or volume of data to be processed by batch or on-line processing; speed of system response required and the capability of hardware and software to meet these requirements.
    (ii) *economic feasibility*: matters relating to cost/benefit appraisal.
(d) Present report to management with recommendations.
(e) Management decision to abort or continue with project.
(f) Plan the project.
(g) Carry out systems analysis:
    (i) fact finding (collect the facts including environment and functional analysis);
    (ii) verify the facts;
    (iii) record the facts;
    (iv) procedure analysis.
(h) System design:
    (i) design philosophy:
        (1) establish design objectives and constraints;
        (2) design alternative systems;
    (ii) design activities:
        (1) prepare procedure charts (for clerical activities), block diagrams and system flowcharts;
        (2) determine actions to be taken in respect of specified conditions by means of decision tables or other methods of documenting procedure logic;
        (3) design input documents and output documents and reports;
        (4) design file structures and layout;
        (5) develop the structure of computer runs by means of run charts;
        (6) evaluate run times;
        (7) design screen layouts for on-line terminal operations;
        (8) develop dialogue to be used by terminal/work station operators;
        (9) develop fail-safe and restart procedures;
       (10) develop procedures for file security;
       (11) discuss with auditors and develop checks and controls to be incorporated.
(i) Prepare the system specification (system definition):
    (i) details of the system including clerical and computer procedures, block diagrams, system flowcharts, decision tables and a narrative providing a general description of the system;
    (ii) input, output and file specifications and layouts;

        (iii) schedule of equipment required by the system including new equipment needs and alternative equipment proposals;
        (iv) nature and use of use of passwords.
    (j) Present alternative proposals to management.
    (k) Discuss proposals with management.
    (l) Management decision — choice of proposals, if relevant.
    (m) Prepare program specification: statement of program requirements including initialisation, parameters, processing stages, input and output requirements, test data and testing procedure to be applied, checks and controls to be incorporated, exception routines, conditions and actions to be provided for and arrangements for test runs.
    (n) Programming:
        (i) determine validation checks and other controls to be incorporated into the system;
        (ii) prepare program procedure charts (flowcharts);
        (iii) prepare program coding sheets;
        (iv) prepare test data and testing procedures;
        (v) compile source programs;
        (vi) debug programs;
    (o) Convert files.
    (p) System testing:
        (i) prepare precalculated results;
        (ii) test programs with test data by dry runs, i.e. desk checking;
        (iii) compare results with precalculated results;
        (iv) report to management and discuss the results obtained from system testing. Decide on future course of action;
        (v) make appropriate modifications to system or programs and recompile as necessary.
    (q) Implementation:
        (i) plan system implementation;
        (ii) carry out parallel running of old and new system; implement direct changeover or pilot scheme as appropriate;
        (iii) prepare manuals for user departments and operation departments including data preparation and data control clerks.
    (r) Evaluate results with expectations:
        (i) monitor system performance in coordination with user department;
        (ii) report to management to discuss the situation and decide on appropriate action;
        (iii) make relevant adjustments to the system.
    (s) Maintain system:
        (i) develop, test and implement improvements;
        (ii) modify system to accord with changing circumstances;
        (iii) integrate related systems to improve processing efficiency.

24.9 Data, process and event-driven development

A number of approaches may be applied for developing business systems, three of which are *data*, *process* and *event-driven*. It is important to appreciate that whichever approach is adopted should reflect the nature of the problem under consideration and may require a combination of different approaches. Many business systems are data-driven and require a top-down, data-driven approach. There are instances, however, when the processes or devices to be used in a system are more predominant. It is a matter of choosing the relevant approach which will best suit the circumstances. It dosen't really matter as long as an efficient system results which achieves an acceptable level of performance at a reasonable cost.

24.9.1 Data structure-orientated

The philosophy of this approach is that design should be related to the structure of the data to be processed rather than the processes to be performed. Data may be organised on the basis of a hierarchical structure which takes the form of an inverted tree. Access to data starts at the top, proceeding downwards through the structure. This type of data structure often forms the basis of a database. A *network* is another method of structuring data, which is based on the concept of a *set* which is the relationship between record types, e.g. a customer's order and an order item. This type of structure is also used in the construction of databases and it simulates the logical data relationships existing in the real world of business, such as those which exist between customers, orders, products and order items. Relational data structures also form the basis of sophisticated databases whereby each record type is stored in a table, an array of rows and columns, the rows being the entities (records) and the columns the fields (*see* 9.10 and Fig. 9.11).

24.9.2 Data flow-orientated

The data flow approach portrays the elemental structure of a system including entities (subjects), processes, data flows and data stores (files). The approach can show high level data flows outlining the system in very broad terms, which may then be subjected to partitioning or levelling to portray data flows in increasing levels of detail, down to the ultimate level of what is known as a functional primitive. Refer to data modelling (*see* 28.3).

24.9.3 Process-driven

This approach initially defines the processes, sometimes referred to as functions, tasks or activities, which need to be done and the sequence in which they are to be performed. The system is designed to achieve the functional requirements, which also take into account the data flows and the structure of data.

Most modelling and structured design techniques use a form of hierarchical construction, known as *functional decomposition*, for breaking down (refining) a high level definition of a task, process or function into successively more detail.

Typical business functions or processes include recording transactions; computing the value of transactions; updating files and printing documents and reports.

24.9.4 Event-driven

Some systems need fast responses to events occurring in the environment, such as on-line systems being triggered by a request for a seat reservation in airline or theatre booking systems or package holiday enquiries in a travel agent. The events trigger specific processes which generate information flows in the system in response to events. The tour operator system has a number of events which trigger processes.

24.9.5 Other development strategies

Top-down approach
This approach initially considers management strategic needs and goals prior to specifying operational data requirements. The higher level functions are then progressively analysed into more detail (*functional decomposition*). It may be necessary to review the impact of lower level situations or operational needs on the higher level functions in order to determine whether it is necessary to revise the higher level goals.

Bottom-up approach

This approach is probably the most widely adopted (together with the output-to-input approach). The system is designed from scratch starting with the basic operational needs of the system and specifying the input documents and output requirements to deal with routine administrative needs. It is then built upon this foundation.

Total systems approach

The *total* systems approach requires a detailed analysis of all the business systems to identify the relationships which exist between them. This may relate to intercommunications and data flows which act as interfaces between the various subsystems. It is important to be aware of the effect on a system of the behaviour of a related system.

Piecemeal (functional) systems approach

This approach to systems design has a tendency to generate sub-optimisation as systems are developed in isolation from each other. The approach only considers the needs of specific functions in isolation from others.

Modular approach

A complex system may be analysed into a series of related subsystems, each being a *module* of the overall system. The approach achieves flexibility as a number of modules can be developed concurrently. Program debugging, testing and maintenance are facilitated by this approach. Modules may also be designed so that in the event of one module failing the others can continue functioning. This is known as *graceful degradation*.

Problem-driven approach

This approach commences by identifying the problems inherent in the current system. The problems are then resolved before proceeding with other elements of the system.

Database approach

The database approach requires the analysis of the data relating to the systems being designed for incorporation into a database to be controlled by a database management system (DBMS). As systems design progresses to other systems the data already resident in the database may be suitable for their use, thereby avoiding the need to duplicate common data in other files. This is what occurs if functional files are developed rather than developing a consolidated collection of data providing for the needs of the various functions.

24.10 Terms of reference

Terms of reference constitute the authority given to systems development staff to undertake a feasibility study of a system(s). Authority should preferably be in writing to avoid any misinterpretation or ambiguity at a later date.

Typical contents of the terms of reference include:

(a) boundaries to the assignment;
(b) purpose and objectives of the system under consideration;
(c) priority rating of the project.

24.10.1 Boundaries to the assignment

It is important for the boundary of an assignment to be clearly defined otherwise investigations will be needlessly pursued into the domain of systems other than the one to be computerised. Where close relationships exist between many subsystems this is even more important. If, for instance, the boundary stipulated is the stock control system then investigations should not overspill into the related area of purchasing.

24.10.2 Purpose and objectives

The purpose and objectives of the system(s) to be investigated must be stated at the outset, otherwise the project will have no defined aims. The purpose of a stock control system may be defined as: 'to record details of stock movements, i.e. stock transactions, on stock records so as to be aware of the latest status of each item in the stores for stock management requirements'.

The objectives may be defined: 'to control the level of stocks by means of stock control parameters, i.e. minimum, maximum and re-order levels, to avoid frequent stock shortages, to minimise stock levels and the cost of carrying stocks (storage costs) as a basis for achieving stock optimisation'.

24.10.3 Priority rating of project

The priority rating of the project must be clearly specified in relation to the other projects which are concurrently under review. This avoids any doubt in deciding the correct course of action in case of manpower absences, shortage of expertise or similar problems. Personnel may then be deployed as the situation dictates.

24.10.4 Modification of terms of reference

As investigations proceed the initial terms of reference may require modification either to eliminate an element of ambiguity, to incorporate new factors previously overlooked or to revise the boundary of a project to integrate several related subsystems, e.g. order processing, despatching, invoicing, sales ledger and stock control.

24.11 Feasibility studies

24.11.1 General considerations

A feasibility study may be defined as a preliminary survey of the business environment to establish if a business would benefit from using a computer for general business use, or for computerising specific accounting applications. Management decides on the basis of a feasibility study report. The correct decision is crucial, particularly if a mainframe or minicomputer is under consideration, due to the relatively high cost of hardware and the cost of the resources employed in developing systems. If management makes a decision not to implement a computer when one could be used to advantage, a 'competitive advantage' will be foregone because operational efficiency will be below that of competitors who have computerised. On the other hand, to use a large computer when it is not needed is likely to lead to administrative chaos: the smooth operation of systems will be disrupted needlessly due to systems development activities; the newly computerised systems may not operate smoothly and fail to achieve objectives because they did not need to be computerised in the first place. This can follow insufficient analysis of the business environment and the true needs of the systems in question. Some systems may need only a 'facelift' or to be 'retuned' to make them suitable for current needs, perhaps by redesigning forms, restructuring working groups and office layout, simplifying work or eliminating outmoded systems.

The success of any computerised system depends on the extent to which the inherent problems and weaknesses of current systems are identified. It is therefore essential to discuss problem areas with relevant managers and operations staff; to examine the forms and documents processed; the machines and equipment in use; the calibre of staff engaged on the various activities; policies covering such matters as discount rates in relation to value of sales orders; delivery charges in relation to value of orders and delivery distance; credit policy in relation to specific classes of customer and so on.

24.11.2 Human factors in systems development

The number and type of personnel required to perform the feasibility study depends upon the circumstances. If the study is to establish whether a large computer should be installed into the organisation, then it would be carried out by systems analysts or O & M staff. If systems analysts were not employed in the organisation at this time then it may be necessary to enlist the services of a computer consultancy. However, if O & M staff are already employed, then they may be utilised for the study because of their intimate knowledge of business systems. They often become the new systems analysts in the organisation.

In any event it is advisable to co-opt the services of personnel of the operating departments involved with the investigation, whether it is for the initial implementation of a computer or the transfer of a system to the existing computer. The reason for this strategy is that they have a detailed working knowledge of the relevant systems and are fully conversant with their strengths and weaknesses. This is invaluable information for the design of a successful computerised system. If stock control is under consideration then a member of that department should participate in the study. Similarly, a member of the accounting department should join the team if accounting systems are under investigation (*see* 25.16).

24.12 Feasibility study reports

24.12.1 Technical feasibility: performance criteria

The feasibility study report specifies the technical capability of the proposed computer system, stating its ability to satisfy the demands on it relating to batch processing applications and/or terminal operations dealing with on-line data entry requirements and random enquiries in respect of telesales applications, etc. It is also important to state the effectiveness of the proposed system for controlling real-time applications, such as for a warehouse with high velocity stock movements.

24.12.2 General factors

(a) Alternative types of computer configuration available which must be considered when initially assessing the use of a computer.

(b) The need for standby facilities in case of breakdown of the in-house computer.

(c) Information processing trends and their likely effect on the type and size of computer required.

(d) Availability of software packages for the systems under consideration.

(e) Additional hardware/software requirements for proposed systems.

Items (a) to (d) are relevant to the initial implementation of a computer in a business; items (d) and (e) are relevant when considering the computerisation of proposed systems on an existing computer configuration.

24.12.3 Staffing

The report should consider the following factors:

(a) The availability of experienced computer personnel for staffing the new computer.
(b) Incidence of redundancy of existing clerical personnel.
(c) Need for computer appreciation courses for management and staff.
(d) Need for retraining existing personnel to suit the needs of the computerised systems.
(e) Extent to which the organisation will need restructuring when systems are transferred to the computer. Some sections will be phased out, others will be depleted in numbers, a new computer department will come into existence and other sections of the organisation will be merged.

Items (a)–(e) are particularly relevant on the initial installation of a computer, but items (b)–(d) and some aspects of (e) also apply when transferring systems to an existing computer.

24.13 Economic feasibility

24.13.1 Capital expenditure

Expenditure incurred in the purchase of hardware and software may be classed as capital expenditure as it represents tangible assets which will appear on the balance sheet. Because the value of hardware is not used up in a single operation, it will be necessary to write it down each year as its value is reduced through wear and tear.

Expenditure incurred on computer accommodation, including the cost of converting an existing building or constructing a new building is also of a capital nature. Also included in this category is the cost of air conditioning equipment, storage racks for tapes and discs as well as desks and chairs. A larger computer will also require a standby generator in case of power failure and dust extraction equipment to avoid dust on the magnetic files which can corrupt the data they store.

24.13.2 Operating costs

This part of the report will take the form of a detailed profitability assessment, indicating both the cost of initial investment and the expected returns through increased profitability. The remainder of this chapter summarises the costing of different systems options.

One point to bring out in the report is that costs can be shared over the different user departments or the subsystems which benefit from the chosen installation. Each system run on the computer would be expected to carry a fair share of all costs incurred in operating the information processing (data processing) department as it provides a service to all participating functions. Such functions, by having data processed for them, are not incurring the cost of the processing resources directly but are using the resources of the servicing department.

The operating costs incurred in running the computer system include:

(a) leasing or rental charges of the computer or depreciation of machines and equipment if purchased;
(b) licensing charges for the use of proprietary software;
(c) establishment charges including rent of premises if not owned, rates, building insurance, heating, lighting and cleaning;
(d) electrical power for running the computer system;
(e) cost of leased lines;
(f) rental charges for modems;

(g) salaries of management and computer operations staff including data processing manager, operators, data control clerks, programmers, systems analysts and data encoders, etc.;

(h) payroll costs, i.e. national insurance paid by employer;

(i) holiday pay of staff;

(j) insurance premiums relating to computer systems;

(k) operating supplies including magnetic tapes, exchangeable discs and printout stationery;

(l) training course;

(m) telephone;

(n) travelling expenses;

(o) general supplies;

(p) subscriptions and publications;

(q) maintenance costs;

(r) cost of standby facilities;

(s) bureau charges.

24.13.3 Once-and-for-all costs

It is essential to take into account what may be classed as *once-and-for-all costs* which are incurred when developing a computerised system. Such costs include the cost of conducting feasibility studies, systems analysis and design, programming, and the costs incurred for running the two systems in parallel. Costs will also be incurred for changing over files from the current system to a form suitable for the computer when records are often converted from ledger cards to disc files.

It is important to consider the alternative financing methods available including purchasing, leasing or rental before arriving at a final decision. It will be necessary to ensure that the new system is performing satisfactorily and achieving the desired level of performance before discarding the current system. Such a *fail-safe* routine incurs additional costs.

24.14 Cost/benefit analysis

24.14.1 Investment in resources

Investment in computer systems or information technology in its widest sense must be recognised as being an investment in resources which must have an adequate return in the same way as any other investment. It is pointless incurring costs to produce information which serves no useful purpose and which therefore does not create benefits to the business.

Computer systems utilise resources in the same way as any other business activity because all activities in a business require manpower (personnel), machines, money and materials to accomplish tasks. The cost of the resources must be compared with what they accomplish. This is normally expressed in terms of benefits to the business.

Benefits are of two categories: tangible and intangible. Each of these categories is discussed below.

24.14.2 Intangible benefits

Many benefits are difficult to quantify. Cost savings or additional profitability cannot always be precisely defined. The following summary may help to put some sort of value on what may be described as intangible benefits.

Intangible benefits	Questions to ask
(a) More effective administration	How much more effective?
(b) Improved customer satisfaction.	Due to what factor and to what extent?
(c) More optimum solutions in operational problems.	What does this mean in terms of cost minimisation or profit maximisation?
(d) Improved forecasting techniques for strategic planning.	What will be the effect on sales?
(e) More timely information for the decision making process.	What will be the effect of this in terms of cost savings and/or contributions to total profit?

24.14.3 Tangible benefits

Tangible benefits can be evaluated in the following way:

(a) The streamlining of information flows reduces the output of redundant information thereby improving administrative effectiveness generating a saving in staff costs of £X p.a.

Customers' accounts are paid more promptly due to the provision of more accurate and timely data relating to invoices and statements of account. This has improved the inward cash flow by £Y p.a. which has the effect of reducing the interest on the bank overdraft by £X per month.

(b) As a result of implementing on-line enquiry systems customers are immediately informed of the information they require relating, for example, to product availability, availability of holiday accommodation and delivery dates, etc., and this enables them to respond accordingly without delay. This allows alternative choices to be selected, e.g. placing orders for alternative products or booking alternative holidays. This improves the profitability of the business by avoiding the prospective loss of profit as a result of not informing customers of available alternatives. This is assessed as an increase in profit in the region of £Y p.a.

(c) Due to the increased yield of material mix in the production of product X of Y per cent per week an additional profit of £X per week is achieved.

(d) Improved strategic planning as a consequence of improved forecasting techniques has generated additional sales of £Y p.a. and an additional profit of £X p.a.

(e) More timely information allows decisions to be taken in an acceptable time scale, i.e. response time, which has the effect of increasing operational efficiency in the use of resources thereby decreasing operating costs for £Y per week.

(f) More effective stock management reduces the level of investment in overall stocks by £X, in turn reducing interest charges on bank overdraft by £Y per month.

(g) More timely and accurate information relating to credit control improves cash flows and reduces debtors by £Y per month on average. This in turn has the effect of reducing interest on bank overdraft by £X per month.

24.14.4 Further considerations

Tangible benefits are more easily attainable at the operational level since control action taken to eliminate adverse situations or to take advantage of favourable conditions is very likely to have an acceptable pay-off. This is applicable in the following instances:

(a) reduction of excessive scrap to reduce production costs;
(b) reduction of excessive stock levels reducing the amount of money invested in stocks;

(c) improving the performance and efficiency of personnel by appropriate disciplinary measures;

(d) elimination of adverse expenditure variances by more effective control.

(*See* also 24.14.3 above.)

24.14.5 Dysfunctional effect

One way of establishing whether information is *paying its way* is to establish the effect on operations if the information ceased to be available. If its elimination has no detrimental effects on the results achieved then there is a case for its discontinuation thereby avoiding further costs. If, however, the elimination of specific information flows has a dysfunctional effect on the efficiency of performance then it should be possible to assess the cost or loss of profit resulting from it.

24.14.6 Economic viability

Cost savings are obviously essential for ensuring the economic viability of a computer. One common practice for assessing savings is to compare the annual operating costs for the new or proposed system with those of the old or current system. If the projected costs of the new system exceed those currently incurred then the decision may be to abort the project.

In certain instances, however, this inflexible approach, based on the evidence of operating costs alone, could be a mistake. All the expected benefits − the intangible factors − have not been taken into account. For example, one factor that has not been considered is the appraisal of weaknesses identified in the current system. A return to the old system will do nothing to solve these. Evaluation of a system's effectiveness must, therefore, take into account the general rule of thumb: if the value of the benefits of the proposed system exceeds the cost of obtaining them then it is a viable proposition.

24.15 Cost justification using the net present value technique

Net present value (NPV) is a technique used for investment appraisal, for example for a proposed computer system, and involves the computation of the present value of a series of future cash flows, i.e income or outlays, over a number of years. The technique enables the most profitable course of action to be established from a series of alternative investment proposals. It allows decisions to be made with regard to the cut-off point, i.e. the required rate of return on investments so that unprofitable investments are not made. The technique also recognises that future cash flows, including income, outlays or cost savings, are worth less than present cash flows. The reason for this is that current cash flows could be invested and earn interest. The further ahead the cash flows from investments, the lower their present values. One investment may appear to be more profitable than another, having greater cash flows, but on inspection the reverse may well be true because of their timing. See below for an example of this situation.

24.15.1 Computation of present value factors

Present value factors can be obtained from pre-printed tables, but may be computed using the formula:

$$\frac{1}{(1 + r)^n}$$

where r is the rate of interest and n the number of years ahead.

The computation takes the value of £1 at the end of each year, assuming an interest rate of 15 per cent, as follows:

(a) Year 1 — value at the end of the year $= (1 + 0.15)^1 = 1.15$
(b) Year 2 — value at the end of the year $= (1 + 0.15)^2 = 1.3225$
(c) Year 3 — value at the end of the year $= (1 + 0.15)^3 = 1.5209$
(d) Year 4 — value at the end of the year $= (1 + 0.15)^4 = 1.7490$

Present value factors are now computed using the reciprocals of the above computations as follows:

(a) Year 1 $= 1 \div (1 + 0.15)^1 = 1 \div 1.15 = 0.8696$
(b) Year 2 $= 1 \div (1 + 0.15)^2 = 1 \div 1.3225 = 0.7561$
(c) Year 3 $= 1 \div (1 + 0.15)^3 = 1 \div 1.5209 = 0.6575$
(d) Year 4 $= 1 \div (1 + 0.15)^4 = 1 \div 1.7490 = 0.5718$

24.15.2 Investment problem

The managing director wishes to be advised whether an investment in a proposed computer system is acceptable. The anticipated capital investment for a mainframe computer is £200,000, which it is hoped will create cost savings and/or increase profits, generating net cash flows in year 1 of £60,000; year 2, £120,000; and years 3 and 4, £40,000. The current criterion rate of return is 10 per cent. The discount factors are:

Present value factor
Year 0   1.0
Year 1   0.9091
Year 2   0.8264
Year 3   0.7513
Year 4   0.6831

The computations for the decision are outlined below:

Year	Net cash flows	Present value factor	Present value
	£		£
1	60,000	0.9091	54,546
2	120,000	0.8264	99,168
3	40,000	0.7513	30,052
4	40,000	0.6831	27,324
Present value of net cash flows			211,090
Less			
Capital cost of investment			200,000
Net present value of investemnt			11,090

The investment would be recommended as it yields in excess of the criterion rate of return of 10 per cent.

The managing director now wishes to be advised if the investment would be worthwhile if the cut-off rate of return was 15 per cent. The computations on which to base this decision are shown below:

Year	Net cash flows £	Present value factor	Present value £
1	60,000	0.8696	52,176
2	120,000	0.7561	90,732
3	40,000	0.6575	26,300
4	40,000	0.5718	22,872
Present value of net cash flows			192,080
Less			
Capital cost of investment			200,000
Net present value of investment			−7,920

When the cut-off rate is 15 per cent the net present value is a negative return and should not therefore be invested in.

24.15.3 Assessing profitability for alternative computer systems with similar cost savings/profit increases but with different timing of cash flows

Assume the discount factor is 10 per cent and the initial capital cost for either of computer systems A and B is £10,000, with cash flows over four years as shown below.

Investment (computer system) A

Year	Net cash flows £	Present value factor	Present value £
1	1,000	0.9091	909
2	2,000	0.8264	1,653
3	4,000	0.7513	3,005
4	5,000	0.6831	3,416
Present value of net cash flows			8,903
Less			
Capital cost of investment			10,000
Net present value of investment			−1,017

Investment (computer system) B

Year	Net cash flows £	Present value factor	Present value £
1	5,000	0.9091	4,546
2	4,000	0.8264	3,306
3	2,000	0.7513	1,503
4	1,000	0.6831	683
Present value of net cash flows			10,038
Less			
Capital cost of investment			10,000
Net present value of investment			38

The investment in computer system A generates a negative net present value, i.e. less than 10 per cent whereas the investment in computer system B has a positive NPV indicating that it achieves the cut-off rate of return of 10 per cent.

24.15.4 Further evaluation of investment in computer systems

The result of the computation in the first example is that the present value of cost savings and/or profit increases exceeds the cut-off rate of 10 per cent. This is a crucial computation, because it is possible to have a high net present value which generates a rate of return lower than the cut-off rate and is therefore not contributing the normal return required from an investment. All business investments should, so far as possible, achieve the target rate of return, otherwise the return to capital employed will deteriorate. Even though a project may show a high net present value it is necessary to take into account the magnitude of the investment and assess the risk factors involved. The cost savings or profit increases may be lower than anticipated in which case the return on the investment would be too. An ambitious project may hit snags and have to be abandoned due to unforeseen circumstances such as lack of cash flows to repay loans which funded the investment.

Review questions

1 Why is it necessary to implement change to business systems?

2 Why is it essential to identify problems within a system before developing a new system?

3 What criteria would you apply to the selection of projects for development?

4 List the stages in the systems development life cycle.

5 Describe the following approaches to systems development:

(a) data structure;
(b) data flow;
(c) process driven;
(d) event driven.

6 What are the nature and purpose of terms of reference?

7 What are the nature and purpose of a feasibility study?

8 What human factors should be considered when developing systems?

9 What information would you expect to find in a feasibility study report?

10 List the types of cost involved with systems development.

11 What tangible and intangible benefits would you anticipate when converting to computer-based systems?

12 Discuss the cost justification for proposed computer systems using the net present value technique.

Self-test questions

24.1 Give reasons why a project showing a high net present value is not necessarily of greatest benefit to a business.

24.2 A feasibility report presented to senior management must always contain details relating to costs and benefits. Categorise and give examples of the costs and benefits which would appear in such a report.

Answers on pages 380–1.

25 Systems development strategies 2: project management, systems analysis and design and implementation

25.1 Introduction

Systems analysis and design are integral elements of the systems development life cycle discussed in Chapter 24. They are included in this chapter together with other aspects of section 3. Before embarking on any project it is essential that it is well planned, using appropriate planning, evaluation and review techniques. These matters are discussed in the text as are matters relating to the tasks involved in the implementation of systems.

25.2 Steering committee

Implementation of computerised projects must be planned within the corporate framework as a whole rather than haphazardly within separate departments. Dysfunctional effects will otherwise be incurred because of fragmented uncoordinated projects. It is the responsibility of a *steering committee* to assess the viability of computer projects to ensure they are cost effective and create benefits to the business as a whole rather than merely to individual functions which can cause imbalance of subsystems creating sub-optimal results. The steering committee can also establish priorities for applications competing for development resources.

Membership of the committee should be representative of the organisation and should consist of personnel from the various functions which can be affected by future computerisation of systems. The interests of functions will then be considered as a whole and it will be possible to assess whether proposals are compatible with the future strategy of the business.

25.3 Planning and control

25.3.1 Analysis of project elements

A project should initially be analysed into primary activities for the purpose of assigning the most suitable systems staff to their investigation. Staff may be assigned to organisation or communication studies, forms, work flows, data flows, processing operations, file structures and systems outputs. In other instances individual systems personnel may be assigned to investigate the whole of a system depending upon the complexity of the project and the available manpower resources.

25.3.2 Setting targets

The next requirement of project planning is to formulate the project life cycle by deciding on the project start date. It is then necessary to estimate the duration time of each constituent component of the initial systems analysis stage. The time for developing a number of alternative proposals will also be required. Estimates should also be made of time taken in writing, compiling and testing programs; systems implementation, the evaluation of results and system maintenance.

It is then possible to assess the prospective completion date of the project. The target time is always difficult to achieve because of the many uncertainties which occur: problems are more difficult to resolve than expected; elements of a procedure critical to the effective operation of the system are not considered at the outset as they were not included in the procedure manual; unplanned staff absences, and so on. It is important to have a time schedule and a list of essential activities to be performed so that resources may be deployed from lower priority projects when necessary to achieve the stated completion deadlines.

The sequence in which tasks must be performed must be taken into account. Some activities are dependent upon the completion of others, for example it is not possible to write programs until the design of the system is finalised. In other instances various tasks can be performed concurrently — one investigator can study the organisation and communication structure of a system whilst others are looking into the forms, files and data flows, etc.

25.3.3 Planning techniques, evaluation and review

One project planning technique is the use of bar charts, known as Gantt charts, on which the various activities are listed in the form of a schedule. The length of a bar signifies the amount of time allocated to an activity. A more sophisticated technique is the *network analysis chart*. The various activities to be performed are mapped on to a diagram indicating which activities can be carried out concurrently and which must be processed in a set sequence. In this way different tasks and the time taken to perform each are charted. A *critical path* can thus be identified which consists of those activities which, if delayed, will have an adverse effect on the project completion time. It is this type of control information which provides the basis for project control as it can also provide for the deployment of resources to critical activities which are falling behind schedule. The analysis identifies activities which leave spare time available, i.e. *slack* time, and this enables resources to be deployed in the most effective way possible.

25.4 Structure of projects

A project may be structured in a number of ways depending on the scope and complexity of the system under review. A small project may be dealt with through all the constituent stages of analysis and design and perhaps programming, testing and implementation by one all-round systems and programming expert. This presupposes that the systems personnel possess a wide range of experience embracing the analysis of current systems and the design of inputs, records, files and outputs for proposed systems, including knowledge of processing and data capture techniques, etc.

25.4.1 Complex projects

Large complex projects covering a major business function, such as when changing over from manual operations in an accounting department to a fully integrated computerised accounting system, will need to be separated into smaller modules consisting of sub-projects, each of which is delegated to a project team under the control of a team leader. Each team leader would report to the project coordinator. The coordinator would take the necessary steps to ensure that all sub-projects were coordinated with overall system objectives and reallocate resources in emergencies to compensate for time lost on some stages of the project.

25.4.2 Pilot project

A project may consist of developing a pilot project in one section or operating unit of the business, such as a branch of a building society or a branch works. The results obtained from running the pilot system assist in evaluating its suitability for implementation in other locations in the business.

25.5 Systems analysis

Systems analysis provides details of the nature, characteristics, problems and weaknesses of a system to be used as a basis for designing a more effective computerised system. Systems analysis requires the coordination and cooperation of both specialist systems staff and the personnel of the department concerned with the system investigation, i.e. the user department personnel. Such personnel are seconded to the investigation so that they may participate in the analysis and subsequent design of the system of which they are an integral element.

Some projects may require a team of investigators depending upon the complexity of the system under review. This topic is discussed in more detail in 25.4.1.

25.5.1 Collect the facts

The fact collecting stage of an assignment is extremely important as it enables the systems staff to become familiar with the characteristics and features of the system under review. This is essential before it is possible to design a computerised version of the system. The specific facts to be collected depend upon the nature of the system and the terms of reference, but generally they will include details relating to the following matters.

Resources used
This requires details to be collected relating to the number of personnel engaged on the various tasks; the number and type of machines in use for specific operations; the number and type of forms and stationery used and other operating supplies; the use of computer bureaux; services provided by other departments, and so on.

Operational data
This data relates to the nature and volume of the various tasks and activities performed, the time taken to perform them and their volume and frequency. It also includes details of bottlenecks and delays in the system as well as other system strengths and weaknesses.

Operating costs
This data relates to the costs of running the system in respect of the resources used (*see* above). Such costs include salaries of staff, supervisors and management; the cost of electricity for heating and the supply of power to machines; machine and building maintenance and insurance costs; operating supplies, i.e. forms and stationery; inter-department service costs and computer bureau charges; depreciation of machines and buildings, etc.

Organisational data
This type of data relates to the number of personnel engaged on each activity, their job titles, superior/subordinate relationships and the span of control of the various supervisors.

Communication analysis

It is often necessary to establish the lines of communication which exist within a system, i.e. the incidence of intercommunications between personnel in the same department, within a section and between other subsystems and functions of the organisation. This is indicative of the nature of the communications which will be required by the proposed computer system. This may include the need for on-line terminals, electronic mail, access to a database, distributed processing for inter-communication between computers and random enquiry facilities, etc.

Company policy

It is essential to be aware of the various policies which exist and the manner in which they relate to the various systems. In respect of personnel policy, for example, this would embrace matters relating to long-service increments which must be provided for by the payroll system; within the sales system it includes matters relating to the level of discounts in relation to sales values, the credit limit and credit period allowed to specified customers and the policy in respect of delivery charges in relation to value of sales, and so on.

25.5.2 Fact finding techniques

Primary questions

Any person concerned with fact finding whether for normal work simplification or with a view to computerising a system must apply a methodical approach to ensure important facts are not overlooked. To this end a pre-prepared checklist may be used containing the main points to which answers are essential. The checklist is based on a framework of fundamental questions which are:

  (a) *What* is done?
  (b) *Why* is it done?
  (c) *When* is it done?
  (d) *How* is it done?
  (e) *Where* is it done?
  (f) *Who* does it?

If the answer to the question, 'Why is it done?' indicates that the system provides a useful purpose the fundamental questions outlined above may be expanded as follows:

(a) Purpose: *What* is done? This requires a definition of the activities performed which may be, for instance, the calculation of wages based on the hours worked by employees as recorded on time cards.

(b) Means: *How* is it done? Details are required of the resources and methods used to accomplish the defined activities including:

  (i) forms used;
  (ii) machines and equipment used
  (iii) method/technique used, e.g. three-in-one posting method using a writing board whereby three related documents are posted simultaneously, batch or on-line processing.

(c) Personnel: *Who* does it? Details of the personnel performing the activities are required which may include:

  (i) the number of personnel engaged on the activity both full-time and part-time;
  (ii) job titles and the skills required;
  (iii) type of staff — male or female.

(d) Location: *Where* is it done? The details required in this instance relate to the place where the activity is performed as follows:

  (i) which factory, branch, office or site?
  (ii) function;
  (iii) department;
  (iv) section.

(e) Time/sequence: *When* is it done? Details of the time period and the sequence in which the activity is performed are required on the basis of the following details:

  (i) day, week, month;
  (ii) sequence — before activity x;
  (iii) sequence — after activity y.

After completing the checklist based on the questions outlined it will be necessary to test the validity of the responses.

25.5.3 Methods of collecting facts

In addition to using the checklist approach a number of other methods of collecting facts may be used including:

  (a) interviewing;
  (b) questionnaire;
  (c) observation;
  (d) inspection.

Interviewing
This technique collects facts by interviewing personnel connected with the system under investigation as it is considered that they possess vital information relating to the systems with which they are concerned. The interviewer should encourage the staff to give their point of view of how they consider the system may be improved and accordingly the interviewer should be prepared to listen rather than dominate the interview. He or she should possess sufficient tact, however, to steer any discussion in the desired direction.

There should be no mystery surrounding an interview and the purpose of conducting it should be stated as it must be appreciated that personnel become very apprehensive of pending changes. An interview should be concluded amicably and in such a manner than any further assistance will be forthcoming freely.

Questionnaire
A questionnaire may be used as an aid to interviewing as it has the advantage of containing pre-formulated questions, answers to which are essential for the development of the system under consideration. This approach avoids the possibility of overlooking important facts. Questions should be framed as simply as possible to avoid ambiguity, should be asked in a logical sequence, should not be too numerous and leading questions should not be asked. The answers obtained may be verified by interviews after the questionnaire has been completed or it may be used during the course of an interview

Observation
This technique is used to obtain an overall visual impact of a systems environment. It takes into

account details relating to the movement of personnel and forms, types of machines and equipment being used, the speed of operations, working conditions, idle time, numbers of staff, bottlenecks and delays, etc.

Inspection

This entails the examination and inspection of documents regarding number of entries made, their general state, how they are filed and the effectiveness of the filing system. The state of machines and equipment will also be examined as will the general working conditions in the systems environment.

25.5.4 Recording the facts

Procedure charts

The systems analyst may record details of procedures on procedure charts which provide a pictorial representation of the procedure.

A procedure chart portrays the various activities in the procedure and by means of symbols indicates the type of activity performed. A typical procedure chart is illustrated in Fig. 25.1. Charts are normally prepared at the recording stage of system development when all the facts are assembled into order. It is at this juncture that facts may be further verified by requesting the operating staff to check the charts for completeness, absence of duplication and any inaccuracies. The verification of facts provides a number of important advantages including:

(a) establishing the reliability of facts;
(b) indicating omissions;
(c) eliminating ambiguity;
(d) avoiding duplication of activities;
(e) engendering valuable suggestions from operating personnel;
(f) highlighting matters for further investigation;
(g) increasing the effectiveness of proposed systems.

25.5.5 Recording techniques

Having collected the relevant facts of the current system it is necessary to marshall them into a form which will enable them to be fully understood and critically examined prior to designing a computerised version of the system. A number of techniques can be used depending on the type of facts to be recorded. These include:

(a) procedure chart (see Fig. 25.1);
(b) procedure narrative;
(c) procedure map;
(d) organisation chart;
(e) document analysis form — output;
(f) document analysis form — input;
(g) file analysis form;
(h) output analysis chart;
(i) flowcharting;
(j) decision tables.

Some of these will now be considered in detail.

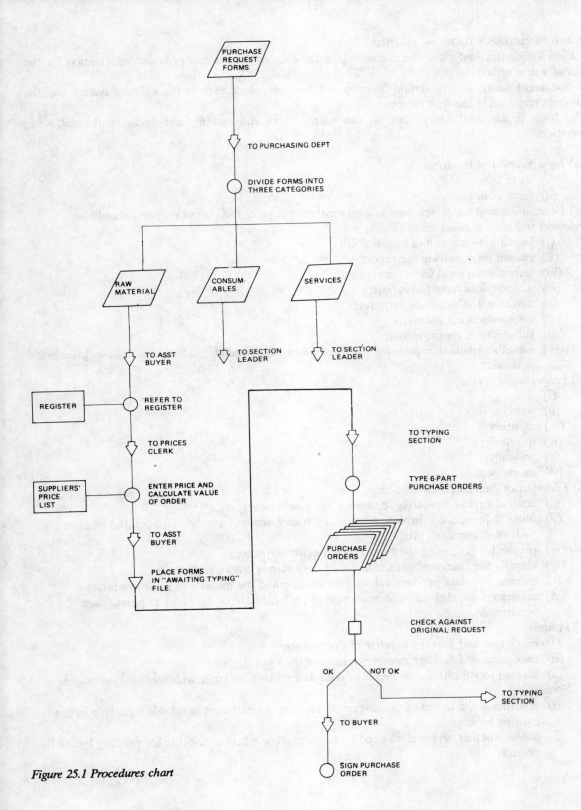

Figure 25.1 Procedures chart

Document analysis form — output

This form assists the analysis of the documents in the existing system and provides information for the design of a new system.

A document analysis form should be prepared for every document in the existing system and for documents required in the new system.

The form is essential for describing the output from the system, and includes the following information.

(a) *Identification* of the form:
- (i) form title;
- (ii) form number.

(b) *Distribution and use*. Each person who receives a copy of the output (report) should be interviewed and the following facts established:
- (i) job title, function and responsibility;
- (ii) reason for receiving the report;
- (iii) information used from the report;
- (iv) action taken from the report;
- (v) additional information required;
- (vi) information not required;
- (vii) suitability of report layout;
- (viii) establish whether copy is filed, passed on or destroyed (for subsequent follow-through if necessary.

(c) *Frequency of issue:*
- (i) daily
- (ii) weekly;
- (iii) monthly
- (iv) quarterly;
- (v) annually;
- (vi) on request.

(d) *Elements of data and their sequence*:
- (i) control keys or fields, e.g. customer account number, etc.;
- (ii) filing sequence, e.g. invoice number, customer account number, pre-printed number on pads of documents, etc.;
- (iii) reason for preparing the report in a specific sequence;
- (iv) identify the source of each element of data shown on the report;
- (v) elements of data produced during processing and the manner of their production;
- (vi) maximum, average and minimum size of each element of data and its percentage occurrence.

(e) *Volume:*
- (i) maximum and average number of documents;
- (ii) maximum and average number of lines of data per document;
- (iii) assess growth rate for elements of data and reports together with seasonal variations.

(f) *Format*:
- (i) consider if the layout of the document requires amendment or whether suitable in the existing format;
- (ii) assess whether all the data need be preprinted or whether suitable for printing by the line printer.

Document analysis form — input

This form is useful for describing the source documents within the system, that is those documents which contain basic data to be input for processing.

The information contained on the analysis form may consist of the following.

(a) *Identification:*
    (i) form title;
    (ii) form number.
(b) *Purpose* of the document.
(c) Where *originated* and by what means:
    (i) allows a check to be made for duplication of documents;
    (ii) determines the extent to which various similar documents may be combined;
    (iii) the contents of similar documents may be rationalised;
    (iv) enables an assessment to be made on the adequacy of the present methods of preparation;
    (v) an assessment is made to ensure if it is originated in the best possible location under the circumstances.
(d) *Elements of data and their sequence*:
    (i) description of each data field;
    (ii) sequence of each data field;
    (iii) pre-printed fields;
    (iv) fields which may be required but not presently included;
    (v) size of each of the fields indicated, specifying whether fixed or variable length, maximum, average and minimum size of each field;
(e) *Volume*:
    (i) maximum and average number of source documents;
    (ii) possible future changes in volume;
    (iii) seasonal variations in volume.
(f) *Frequency of preparation*:
    (i) at present;
    (ii) foreseeable or prospective changes in frequency.
(g) *Files affected* by the input:
    (i) determine the type of file affected by the input (transaction) and the applications concerned;
    (ii) assess the adequacy of the file organisation and content of records compared with the fields contained in the source document.

File analysis form

This form is used for defining the construction of files and may contain the following information.

(a) *Identification*
    (i) file name;
    (ii) application in which used.
(b) *Purpose* of the file.
(c) *Records constituting the file:*
    (i) maximum, average and minimum size of each record;
    (ii) names of different records contained in the file;
    (iii) percentage occurrence of each type of record in the file.
(d) *Volume* of records in the file:
    (i) maximum, average and minimum number of records contained in the file;
    (ii) maximum and average transaction volumes affecting the file;
    (iii) assess future size of file;

(iv) indicate future volumes of transactions affecting the processing of the file;

(v) indicate seasonal variations of transactions affecting the processing of the file.

(e) *File organisation:*

(i) sequence of records;

(ii) control key;

(iii) adequacy of present sequence;

(iv) suitability of present keys.

Output analysis chart

This chart assists in examining the outputs from the current system to establish the information content of reports, their source and the relationships which exist between source documents and reports. The chart is constructed as follows.

(a) Output documents are listed down the left-hand side of the chart.

(b) Information fields contained in reports are listed along the top of the chart.

(c) The type of character contained in files is classified as follows.

(i) N = numeric.

(ii) A = alphabetic.

(iii) A/N = alpha/numeric.

(d) Information fields derived from records are indicated by the designation R, and those derived from source documents by S.

(e) Information fields derived from calculations are indicated by the designation C.

(f) The maximum and average field size in characters is also indicated.

(g) Appropriate designations are entered in columns at the point of intersection of the document column and the appropriate information field.

(h) Fields marked R must be contained in master records.

(i) Fields marked S are the transaction details which must be contained in source documents.

25.6 Systems design

Once the analyst has documented the existing system, problem areas and future requirements, the next stage is to design the new system. When designing information systems a number of factors must be considered to ensure the new system is cost and operationally effective.

25.6.1 Design requirements

(a) Information must be produced at the right time, at the right cost, in the right format, at the right level of accuracy and by the right media.

(b) Routine decisions should be automated such as those relating to the automatic ordering of stock.

(c) Source data should be prepared in the most suitable manner.

(d) The system under review should not be considered in isolation from other subsystems.

(e) A system should be designed within the context of the requirements of the business as a whole, i.e. within the corporate framework, even though it is initially confined to a specific subsystem.

(f)Subsystems should be designed with future integration with other subsystems in mind.

(g) Checks and controls should be incorporated which are capable of detecting and reporting errors.

(h) Suitable coding systems should be incorporated for effective reference, comparison, sorting and validation.

(i) Computer runs should be efficiently structured.

(j) Effective safeguards should be incorporated for the prevention of fraud and for privacy and confidentiality.

(k) The time and cost of encoding data from source documents should be minimised.

(l) The direct input of source data should be considered in the context of on-line systems.

(m) Data should always be processed as efficiently as possible avoiding unnecessary complexity.

(n) File security measures must be adequate.

(o) Fail-safe and restart procedures should be incorporated as appropriate.

(p) Business policy matters should be incorporated in as much as they are relevant to a specific system.

(q) Relevant legislation should be provided for.

(r) Exception routines should be catered for.

(s) Screen layouts should be clear and unambiguous.

(t) Parameters should be clearly defined.

(u) Specific attention should be provided to the effective design of supporting clerical systems as well as computer operations.

(v) Systems should be as simple as possible keeping in view the requirements of the operating department staff, i.e. the users.

(w) Dialogue design should not be overcomplicated to facilitate ease of understanding by the work station/terminal operators.

(x) All forms should be designed for utmost simplicity of use.

(y) Systems documentation should be complete and standardised.

(z) The utmost cooperation and coordination are essential between all interested parties.

25.6.2 Design criteria and constraints

Apart from having to meet system objectives the systems analyst needs to establish criteria for the design process and be fully aware of constraints to any proposed strategy. A number of factors will be considered:

Portability
Portability enables programs written for one machine to be run on another without modification. This requires the formulation of a specific migration path keeping to one manufacturer to avoid reprogramming, or at least recompiling, which would be necessary if switching to a different manufacturer.

Integrity
This is the attainment of a specified level of service to achieve the desired level of system availability and the accomplishment of the required degree of privacy, confidentiality, security and reliability of data.

Efficiency of system performance
This refers to matters relating to minimising computer run time and optimising system response times for critical on-line applications.

Integration
This is the combination of separately structured systems to form a larger streamlined, fully automated system in the quest towards a *total system*.

Project life constraints

Constraints are necessary to control and minimise the time and resources utilised on the project, perhaps because of a scarcity of system development resources for competing projects.

Financial constraints

The projected costs of a project's development must be related to anticipated benefits to ensure it is an economically viable proposition.

Simplicity of design and user friendliness

Systems must always be designed with simplicity and user friendliness in mind, remembering that system design is a means to an end and not an end in itself.

Standardisation

Design standards should be considered but not to the extent of rigidity and inflexibility (*see* 25.17).

25.7 System specifications

A system specification is similar to any product specification, whether hi-fi unit, television set, refrigerator or radio, because it specifies the features and characteristics of the system. A specification provides the interface between systems analysis and systems design. The specific details contained in a system specification depend on the nature and complexity of the system but typically include a number of matters which are summarised below:

Introduction

This section includes details appertaining to:

    (a) name of the system;
    (b) glossary of terms used in the specification;
    (c) date of preparation;
    (d) statement of acceptance;
    (e) index to sections of the specification;
    (f) system relationships;
    (g) details of amendments to original terms of reference;
    (h) departments involved with the system;
    (i) standards of performance.

System objectives

Expected benefits, tangible and intangible (*see* 24.14).

System description

    (a) Procedure charts and narrative relating to clerical systems.
    (b) Data structure charts and data flow diagrams.
    (c) System flowcharts and computer run charts.
    (d) Decision tables.
    (e) System structure charts.
    (f) Coding system.
    (g) Auditing procedures.

Hardware

(a) Type of computer.
(b) Peripherals:
- (i) number and types of disc drive;
- (ii) number and types of printer;
- (iii) number and types of terminal, including point-of-sale terminals (if relevant);
- (iv) number and types of data encoding machines and/or key-to-disc systems;
- (v) type of input device: optical character/page reader, magnetic ink character reader.

Software

(a) Internally written programs: program names.
(b) Internally written sub-routines.
(c) Program generators.
(d) Operating system.
(e) Utility programs including program generators.
(f) Application generators.
(g) Applications packages.
(h) General purpose software; spreadsheets, executive information systems, report generators.
(i) Databases.

Input specification

(a) Name of system.
(b) Name of document.
(c) Source and method of origination.
(d) Details of data elements.
(e) Frequency of preparation.
(f) Volume.
(g) Validation checks to be applied.
(h) Details of screen layouts for input requirements.

Output specification

(a) Name of system.
(b) Name of report.
(c) Number of print lines.
(d) Maximum size of fields.
(e) Details of screen layouts for display of information.

File specification

(a) Name of system.
(b) File name.
(c) File medium: disc — floppy, fixed or exchangeable.
(d) File labels.
(e) Size of records.
(f) Record types.
(g) Number of discs.
(h) Block size.
(i) Field names.
(j) File security, privacy and confidentiality: use of password.

Program testing
Testing procedures: desk checking (dry runs).

System acceptance testing
(a) Test programs with test data.
(b) Comparison of pre-calculations with results obtained from testing.
(c) Procedure for system modifications.

System installation
(a) Method of changeover: direct, parallel running or pilot.
(b) Changeover timing.
(c) File conversion procedure.

System performance
(a) Estimated run timings.
(b) Estimated computer utilisation (proportion of down-time to planned operational availability).
(c) Estimated terminal utilisation (proportion of available time each terminal is in use).
(d) Types of error and remedial procedure.
(e) Response time requirements.

25.8 File design

25.8.1 File organisation

A number of methods are available from which to select the one best suited to a particular application. They include:

(a) serial;
(b) sequential;
(c) indexed sequential;
(d) inverted;
(e) random;
(f) direct;
(g) database:
    (i) hierarchical;
    (ii) relational;
    (iii) network.

25.8.2 Methods of file organisataion

Serial file organisation
With serial file organisation the records are not in any specific order and therefore access to records is time consuming and impracticable. The records are simply located physically next to each other on the backing storage media, regardless of numerical or alphabetical sequence.

If a customer file is organised serially on magnetic tape, the process of accessing a record is the same in principle as for an unindexed filing cabinet. The first record on the tape is read and checked to see if the required record, then the next record and so on until the right one is found.

Sequential files

Often, transaction files consist of unsorted records which are input to a sorting routine to place them in *sequential* order so that they are in the same sequence as the records to which they relate on the master file to facilitate speedy processing.

With this method of file organisation, records are normally organised in ascending order of key field. New records are added in sequence to facilitate quick and easy access. For example, assume we are looking for customer code A1234; if we pass on to A1235 first, we know immediately that A1234 is missing and so no time is lost in searching through the system for it.

With *magnetic tape*, new records must be added by insertion in the correct sequence on another reel of tape. It is also necessary to generate a completely new tape when applying file amendments, including adjustments, deletions and additions, because it is not possible physically to insert or delete them on the same tape.

With *disc files*, rather than magnetic tape, this problem is eliminated.

Thus, when files are stored on magnetic tape, serial and sequential access mean the same thing; disc files, because they can incorporate an effective overflow and retrieval system, are better organised and accessed sequentially.

Indexed sequential

This type of file organisation is widely applied for storage of records on magnetic disc. It allows records to be accessed *sequentially*, in ascending key field sequence, and also *at random* via an index. Records can be updated without needing to rewrite the whole file, as is necessary with simple sequential files.

When records are first loaded on to an indexed sequential file they are inserted on to the disc in sequence. Let us assume the blocking factor is 20 records and one block is stored in one sector or *bucket*. The block would initially contain, say, 15 actual records and five blank records. Thus records are stored in sequence and extra space is reserved in each block to add more records if desired. In this way the sequence of records on the file is maintained even when new records are added: the appropriate block is read into memory and the record is inserted in the correct place. When the number of new records exceeds five (i.e. the blank space allowed for new additions) even more records can be placed into *overflow* and an *address* is added to the block which points to where the records are located in overflow. When pointers are used to link records this is known as *chaining*. The last track or tracks in a disc cylinder are usually reserved for storing of overflow records. Further overflow space may be reserved at the end of the file.

Note that this is only one technique for dealing with indexed sequential files and overflow. Different disc operating systems will vary in the precise way in which they deal with indexed sequential files.

Random file organisation (directly organised)

Individual records are not stored in any particular sequence of key fields, i.e. they are stored randomly. It is not possible to apply a general rule for retrieving records from this type of file and it is necessary to develop an index which indicates the location of each record or, alternatively, the application of an address generation system.

Inverted files

This type of organisation is useful when no single key can retrieve a record because a combination of keys is necessary. The record has to be searched using some combination of keys known as *attributes*. Items possessing a specific feature are grouped together to form an inverted file. This reduces the time it takes to retrieve records as it eliminates the need for serial searching. The keys and data are organised so that the keys (attributes) can be accessed one by one and only the relevant keys referenced.

Direct access methods

(a) *Full index*. An index record contains the disc sector reference for every record in the file. The file is sorted initially into key sequence and the index is constructed as the records are transferred to disc. The index is sequential but the records may be stored randomly.

(b) *Partial indexing*. Two or more levels of index are stored on disc. One level consists of a rough index containing the key of the last record in a specific range, together with the bucket location (*see* below) of the fine index related to that range. The rough index contains a cylinder number while the fine index refers to a specific sector on a specified surface in that cylinder. The records need to be stored in ascending key sequence in each bucket. Comparison of the key of the required record against the rough index specifies the cylinder in which it is located. The cylinder contains the relevant fine index as its first record. Examination of the fine index indicates the surface within the cylinder. The rough index is usually transferred into internal storage during the time the file is in use.

Note: A bucket is a defined number of characters for data transfers from/to disc, to/from the processor. Some computers have discs with a bucket size of 512 characters which can be handled in ones or multiples to store records in bucket sizes of 512, 1,024, 2,048, or 4,096 character capacity.

(c) *Self indexing*. This type of organisation requires records to be stored in addresses that are related to their keys. File organisation is on the basis of:

    (i)   address = key
    (ii) address = key + constant
    (iii) address = (key + constant)/blocking factor

There are many variations of this type of equation because of differing disc starting addresses, different blocking factors and the structure of keys.

If storage locations are available from location 400, each location holding one record, then the address of the record would be obtained in the following manner:

Record keys
120   address = 120 + 399 = 519
141–180   address = 141 + 399 = 540–579
190–300   address = 190 + 399 = 589–699

Note: 399 is the 400th location as storage addresses commence at 0, therefore 0–399 = 400.

Some key sequences have too many gaps to be organised in this way as it is inefficient in the use of storage space, but when it is possible to link the address and key of a record directly self-indexing files are feasible.

(d) *Algorithmic address generation*. The basis of this method is a mathematical formula which is applied to the key of the required record which in turn generates the bucket reference containing the record. The bucket is then searched to access the specific record. It is possible for the formula to generate the same address for different keys which will create an overflow situation, necessitating several accesses to locate the desired record. Space is also wasted when records are deleted from a disc file as they will not be reassigned because of the nature of the algorithm. The formal manner of establishing a suitable algorithm is to examine the code number sequence in use or to be implemented. Code numbers should be numeric only. It is then necessary to establish a formula which will generate an even distribution of bucket addresses. Constants can be added to the formula to close large gaps in the sequence and so avoid wasting storage space. It is essential to determine that the bucket address is acceptable to the type of disc drive in use.

Algorithms are computed in a number of ways. For instance, random allocation of records is achieved by squaring the key, or part of it, and using some digits from the square, perhaps the centre digits, as an address. This technique can allocate more than one record to the same address and none to other addresses. The first record is stored in an address called a *home* record. If addresses can hold only a single record the subsequent records allocated to this address will have to be stored in overflow areas. These records are known as *synonyms*.

Example (i): Compute the address of the following keys by squaring the central two digits.

Keys	1111	1112	1113
Digits	11	11	11
Square	121	121	121

As can be seen, all records are allocated to the same address and are therefore synonyms.

Example (ii): Compute the address of the same keys by squaring the last two digits.

Digits	11	12	13
Square	121	144	169

As can be seen, gaps occur in the addresses of consecutive records.

Alternatively, divide the key by a prime number and use the remainder as an address. This method will generally provide a good distribution of records. Runs of keys produce remainders that do not generate synonyms as they each differ by 1. Constants can be added if necessary.

Example (i): Compute the address of the following record keys by dividing the keys by the prime number 13 and use the remainder as an address.

Keys	1111	1112	1113
Remainder	6	7	8

As can be seen a good spread of records is achieved.

Example (ii): Using the same record keys compute the address using prime number 11 and use the remainder as an address.

Remainder	0	1	2

This also generates a good distribution of records.

25.9 Implementation

25.9.1 Planning the installation

When preparing system installation plans it is necessary to take into account the complexity of changeover which will have a bearing on the time required. Other matters to build into time schedules will be the time needed for training of staff, preparing computer accommodation, obtaining pre-printed stationery, system testing, time for resolving problems, file conversion and take on (*see* 25.3).

25.9.2 File conversion and take on of opening balances

Many computer-based systems are of an accounting nature and so require speedy and efficient conversion of accounts files to magnetic media and the transfer of opening balances to the computer files. This task requires careful planning and control: the longer the transfer takes the more difficult it becomes to catch up with the current status of the system, leading to frustration and errors as personnel attempt to run both the current and computer system on a disjointed basis. While *catch-up* must be given priority, it is important to maintain the current system as effectively as possible.

Very often records are converted from ledger cards on which transaction details are recorded by hand or posting machine to magnetic media by suitable encoding methods. Before conversion it is essential that the balances on such records as stock record cards, suppliers' and customers' accounts and employee payroll records are reconciled to ensure only correct balances are transferred to the new system. This is a high volume activity and suitable arrangements must be made in advance to avoide unnecessary 'take on' delay.

25.9.3 Establish new working procedures

The proposed computer system will require supportive back-up facilities for the collection, control and checking of data. The collection of data may be effected by an internal messenger service, collecting batches of data from the various departments on the basis of a predefined timetable. Alternatively, if the computer is to be used as a central facility for the data processing needs of a locally dispersed group of companies then a data collection and distribution service may be provided by means of internal transport. If a group of companies is widely dispersed then data may be transmitted by telephone line from each of the companies to the central computer by means of remote job entry using a communications-based key-to-disc system.

Data received for processing should be recorded in a register by a batch control section. If the data is received as batches of source documents then it is necessary to check them to ensure the correct number of documents are in the batch and that obvious errors are corrected before being sent for data conversion by a key-to-disc system or other suitable method of conversion. After data has been processed arrangements should be made for its distribution either by messenger service, internal transport or data transmission

25.10 System, program and acceptance testing prior to changeover

Before an application goes live, i.e. before the new computerised system becomes operational and supersedes the previous system, it is necessary to check all parts of the application to ensure it will process data and produce the required outputs and update records efficiently.

25.10.1 System compatibility with system specification

Before programs are prepared for a specific application it is necessary to ensure the design of the system accords with the system specification with regard to input, output, files, screen layouts and processes, etc. Of particular importance is the need to check that adequate security measures are built into the system. This may involve the use of passwords to prevent unauthorised access to files and/or programs. Adequate measures must also be taken to ensure recovery procedures for real-time applications are effective. This may require the contents of the internal memory to be dumped to backing storage every few minutes to provide restart points in the event of a system malfunction. This type of application may require multiprocessing where one processor acts as a fail-safe back-up to the other. When operating in multi-user mode it is necessary to incorporate file or record locking so that one user is prevented from gaining access to a specific record while another user is updating it.

25.10.2 Program testing

Before an application goes live it is necessary to ensure the program will accomplish the desired results. This is done by the technique of *desk checking*, which is known as performing a *dry run*. It involves running through the program coding while making comparisons with flowcharts and decision tables. Any errors are corrected and the program is then converted into machine code by an assembler or compiler (*see* 21.4 and 21.5). This is followed by test runs using test data, the results of which are compared with precomputed values, totals and summaries to discover any anomalies which must be corrected before changeover. This is a fail-safe procedure requiring the current system to continue in operation during the period when the computerised system is being tested.

25.10.3 Input/output

The design of source documents which record details of transactions must be checked for simplicity of use, completeness and to ensure the data entry boxes are in the correct sequence and of the correct size for the details to be recorded. The forms should be discussed with the clerical staff who are to use them to make sure they are fully understood and are suitable for the required purpose. Screen layouts may sometimes be used for the entry of data from a document in which case the staff who are to use the work stations (terminals or microcomputers) need to become conversant with their use before live operations commence. They need to be conversant with the procedure for calling up operational and help screens, the sequence of entering data, error correction routines and file back-up procedures. Prototype screens should be used for this purpose so that the ultimate users have a say in the design of the screens. The users will then be in a position to indicate inconsistencies with system requirements.

The content and structure of information displayed on a screen as output are often directly related to the input screen as one generates the other after data has been entered, validated and subjected to mathematical computations. The output may then be stored on a disc transaction file for further processing in an on-line order entry system, for instance, or printed to provide a document such as an invoice or despatch note. The screen formats should be viewed objectively, as discussed above. In batch processing applications the output will be predominantly printed for such requirements as payrolls, payslips, despatch notes, invoices, statements of account, stock schedules and exception reports, etc. Such outputs must be viewed objectively by user department personnel to assess whether each document contains relevant information fields, that an appropriate number of copies are produced, that they are easily understood and will attain their required purpose.

25.10.4 Batch controls

The adequacy of the procedure for batch controls prior to data being input must be assessed and the control totals generated by the computer must be compared with those precalculated to ensure consistency. This is essential for controlling the flow of data through the system to avoid confusion as a result of lost data. (*See* 25.10.7.)

25.10.5 Data validation

Data validation routines in the programs must be checked out to ensure invalid data is rejected. The routines are outlined in 26.4.3, and they vary according to whether batch or on-line processing is being applied. It is necessary to verify the suitability of check digit verification tests for validating key fields such as stock codes, employee numbers, account codes and so on. Range and limit checks also need to be evaluated to assess their appropriateness to the magnitude of values pertaining to specified transactions. An order must be between £5 and £200, for instance: if it is less than £5 it is rejected because it is uneconomic to process; if greater than £200 it is checked because it is in excess of normal maximum order values, and so on. It should be observed that all invalid transactions are displayed or printed on an *invalid items report*, which should be used to check that corrected transaction data is re-entered.

25.10.6 Files

The files must be checked to ensure that file conversion has been carried out correctly and that all records contain relevant fields and correct brought forward balances. The file updating procedure should be tested to ensure correct account balances are produced in accordance with the transactions processed. The file organisation should be tested for its effectiveness, particularly when direct access to specific records is required to deal with enquiries. The response time should be checked with that stipulated in the system specification. In addition, the contents of files should be printed out to assess their integrity (accuracy and completeness).

25.10.7 Clerical procedures

Most computerised systems are supported by manual activities performed by clerical staff. They are concerned with the initial recording and collecting of data received for processing from various departments and/or branch works. Clerical staff are also involved with data control activities before and after processing to ensure all data recorded in a control register and that the printed documents and schedules produced are recorded and distributed. The procedures for these activities must be fully understood by the staff who are to administer them — not only is it essential that they understand them, but that they agree their suitability for the purpose (*see* 25.10.4).

25.11 System changeover methods

25.11.1 Direct changeover

This method may be relevant for relatively straightforward systems. All systems have inherent problems which do not always manifest themselves until the previous system has been dispensed with and so direct changeover should be contemplated only after detailed consideration of all the possible problems which can arise and their consequences. This is a high risk method but may be adopted when the system is straightforward, as stated, when user staff are confident in running the system and when time is short. This method may also be adopted when the current system and the new system are so dissimilar that parallel running is irrelevant. It may also be applied if the additional staff necessary for parallel operation are not available.

25.11.2 Parallel running

This method requires the running of both the current and new system side by side on a fail-safe basis. The current system is not dispensed with until the integrity of the new system has been proved. This is accomplished by comparing the results produced by the current system with those produced by the computer system. If they are in agreement the system integrity is assured. As this is a fail-safe method it is costly: it is necessary to engage staff for running both systems side by side. Parallel running also prolongs the testing period and delays system changeover. Therefore it is necessary to set a limit on the number of cycles for which the two systems will run in parallel.

25.11.3 Pilot scheme

This method restricts implementation to one location only and so resources are not fully committed. The results obtained from running the pilot scheme assist in determining its suitability for other locations in the business. As an example, it may be the basis of a pilot scheme to implement a system in one branch of a multi-branch business such as a bank or building society to assess its performance before implementing it on a wider basis. This applies when putting branches on-line to a centrally located computer for dealing with daily branch transactions.

25.12 Monitoring (follow-up)

After the system has gone live and proved to be performing satisfactorily it is still necessary to maintain a *watching brief* to ensure that no abnormalities occur and to remove the cause if problems arise. It may be found that although the system is achieving results as stipulated in the systems specification the system design itself does not provide for certain requirements. System modifications will then be necessary, involving program recoding, recompiling and retesting. Checks, for example to ensure that system security and privacy are maintained at the stipulated level or that there is no unauthorised access to confidential files, will also be carried out. Periodic review meetings should be arranged to discuss future development of the system, which may take the form of system integration or link-up to a database.

25.13 Auditing systems

It is essential for auditors to satisfy themselves that systems are suitable for their purpose and that they are achieving the objectives laid down in the systems specification. This is largely determined by running programs with test data representative of that to be processed when the system goes live. The results obtained are compared with precalculated values. Any differences are noted and these form the basis for program modifications or even major restructuring of the system (in circumstances when systems specifications have been misinterpreted). Trials should be incorporated to assess the accuracy with which transaction data is recorded on source documents prior to data conversion for input to the computer. Errors should be analysed to establish their nature and their cause. The effectiveness of built-in validation checks is tested in this way.

25.14 System maintenance

Systems in their original form often outlive their usefulness because of the need to change business practices to accord with changing economic circumstances and the introduction of new legislation. In addition, systems may be implemented initially on a stand-alone functional basis and management may later consider integrating related systems or implementing a database.

Batch processing applications may also be converted to on-line, multi-user or multi-tasking systems depending on the changing needs of the organisation.

25.15 User training

25.15.1 Retraining personnel

When manual systems are superseded by computerised applications existing personnel must be retrained or new staff recruited. Personnel should be carefully selected on the basis of aptitude and potential for specified tasks. This is very important when manual dexterity is essential for expert manipulation of a terminal keyboard or keyboard data encoder, as this determines the speed with which data can be input for processing, the efficiency with which terminal operations are conducted and the speed and accuracy with which data can be encoded.

25.15.2 Training schedule

It is important to prepare a training schedule sufficiently far in advance to ensure a smooth transition from one system to the other. Personnel should be released from their current duties to attend the specified training courses or training sessions. Careless planning can disrupt more than necessary the smooth functioning of the various departments concerned.

25.15.3 Mode of training

The mode of training provided will depend upon the nature of the activities. If the activity is concerned with preparing transaction data recorded on source documents into a form suitable for input to a computer, training on a key-to-disc or other data encoding system will be necessary. This type of training is often provided partly by the manufacturer and partly by the systems analyst.Training of clerical support staff in the collection and recording of transaction details on new source documents is likely to be the responsibility of departmental supervisors who receive instruction from the systems analyst. Alternatively, staff can be trained directly by the systems analyst. Similar considerations apply to the training of data control clerks who will be responsible for receiving, checking, recording and maintaining control of batches of work coming in from the operating departments. Training of computer operators is normally part of the manufacturer's preparatory course which provides direct operating experience of the type of configuration to be implemented. This will be supplemented by operating instructions from the programmer of the various applications. The chief programmer will receive guidance relating to the new systems from the program specification prepared by the systems analyst. When software packages are to be implemented, programmers, computer operators and systems analysts may attend seminars sponsored by the software marketing company to obtain first-hand knowledge as well as hands-on experience of such programs as integrated accounting packages, database management systems and spreadsheets.

25.15.4 Induction training

Apart from attendance at manufacturers' courses, on-site induction training may be arranged by systems staff to introduce the new technology to all relevant personnel, both departmental management and operating staff. Induction training may be presented in a number of ways including the use of slide projectors to project line drawings; photographs to provide details of hardware to be used; and simple system flowcharts to illustrate the structure of the proposed systems. Video films, prerecorded cassettes and lectures may supplement this training and a visit to see a similar system in operation at a local company may be arranged.

25.15.5 Monitor training effectiveness

An essential factor of the follow-up routine is the assessment of the effectiveness of training. If necessary, training can then either continue, change its focus or personnel can be replaced if they are found unsuitable for tasks after adequate training.

25.16 Human factors in implementation

25.16.1 Participation of users

It is advisable to co-opt the services of personnel in the departments concerned with the project under investigation because of their experience in operating the current system and the detailed working knowledge they possess. It is also important to maintain user involvement by emphasising the value of their specialised knowledge to the system. They alone understand the system's idiosyncrasies and are fully aware of its strengths and weaknesses. By incorporating strengths and eliminating weaknesses a more powerful and reliable system will emerge to suit current operational needs and practices. The extent to which users participate in the design of systems will vary with the type of business, management style, the role of trade unions, etc.

25.16.2 Cooperation

Users and systems analysts should consider that they both work for the same company and therefore should have common aims and interests in pursuit of operational efficiency. It is important that users appreciate that the project is for the purpose of improving the performance of the particular function. Operating staff should be informed at the outset that it is not their performance which is in question. It should be explained in clear terms that the system has been overtaken by new technology which if implemented will help the company to withstand competition and remain economically viable. It is important too that user department personnel are aware of the nature of the proposed system and the ways in which it differs from the current one.

After initial implementation subsequent proposals may recommend further computerisation which will again alter the work environment. For example, an on-line order-entry system to streamline the order handling procedure and speed up the input of order details to the computer may be proposed, or the system may be integrated with other related subsystems to speed up the preparation of invoices and optimise stock levels, so minimising stock shortages and avoiding excessive investments in stocks. It is therefore necessary to advise the operating personnel of new jobs to be created and this should create job enrichment and make the work more interesting (*see* 24.11.2).

25.17 Standards and documentation

The purpose of standards is to guide staff in the general rules, conventions and code of practice relating to the development, design, programming, implementation and operation of systems. The project control system will be structured to be compatible with the various stages of development, thereby providing a standard way of controlling all projects on the basis of a standardised schedule which should enable the highest possible level of project productivity to be achieved.

25.17.1 System and program documentation

System and program documentation standards outline the way in which systems should be structured and the manner in which they should be documented. This factor relates to the method employed and the style adopted for the construction of procedure charts, system flowcharts, data flow diagrams, data structure charts, system structure charts, decision tables and run charts. Standards also embrace programming methodology in respect of the use of standard coding sheets and the application of structured or modular techniques of program design.

25.17.2 Detailed design of system inputs, files and output

Documentation standards specify the way in which documents should be structured and compiled. Such documents contain details and specifications relating to the design of computer input which refers to the design of source documents and screen displays; output from the computer either as a screen display or a printed report; and the structure of master files. The primary purpose of such standards is to adopt a uniform, effective method of documentation which enables systems to be designed in the most efficient way.

25.17.3 System continuity

The application of system and program documentation standards assists in attaining system continuity as it removes complete dependence on system details in which only the system designer will be expert. It is imperative that all details of the current system and the proposed system be committed to paper, i.e. document layouts and specifications as well as diagrammatically in the form of flowcharts, etc. If design staff are ill or leave the company then newcomers or replacement staff can pick up the details of the project at the stage it has reached without much difficulty. This ensures continuity in the development of systems so avoiding disruption.

25.17.4 Operations standards

The implementation of operations standards requires the compilation of a standards manual. Reference to the manual on points of procedure by operations personnel will ensure adherence to laid down standards. The standards should typically encompass details relating to the flow of work in respect of: handling procedures, batches of source documents when received from the user departments in respect of batch control and data conversion; security measures to be applied to the files after updating; work scheduling activities; archiving procedures; purging procedures in respect of files retained for security purposes; error control routines; output distribution routines, and so on.

25.17.5 Performance standards

Performance in a data processing environment is essential and standards are required for effective control of output in order to ensure scheduled completion time; input schedules should be prepared to ensure input is received on time and prevent delays and the build-up of work. The cost of operations should be controlled to ensure operations are performed economically. This may be accomplished by the implementation of cost standards or the use of budgets. Run timings should enable the time spent on different jobs to be effectively controlled and provide the means of compiling job schedules.

25.17.6 Standards officer

The implementation of and effective adherence to standards should be under the control of a standards officer. The duties and responsibilities include advising management and staff, both in the data processing department and user departments, in the use of the various standards. The results attained and methodologies practised should be monitored to ensure they accord with the relevant standards. Staff suggestions for modifying established standards, should be implemented if they provide the means of improving results and working practices. All modifications to existing standards and the application of new standards should be recorded in a standards manual to ensure all details are fully up to date. The meaning and underlying philosophy of standards should be discussed with appropriate personnel.

25.17.7 Communication and coordination

The major benefit of standardisation of systems methodology and documentation is the provision of a medium for discussion. Discussion of system details should be encouraged between designers and users, designers and programmers and designers and management. Such discussions enable misconceptions to be removed and system features to be more fully understood. When personnel from the different functions affected by systems development are able to communicate then many of the inherent problems are more easily dealt with. It is always good practice to compile a *glossary of system terminology* which further aids understanding of the language of system designers and eliminates ambiguity in the understanding of terms being used during discussions.

Note
The National Computing Centre has developed a comprehensive set of standards embracing systems documentation, programming and operating.

Review questions

1 What are the purpose and membership of a steering committee?

2 What are the nature and purpose of project management?

3 What are the nature and purpose of systems analysis?

4 What techniques may be applied to fact finding?

5 What are the primary objectives of systems design?

6 What is a systems specification?

7 What information is contained in a systems specification?

8 Discuss file design issues.

9 What factors need to be considered for system implementation?

10 What system changeover methods may be applied?

Self-test questions

25.1 Describe staff training issues to be considered prior to the changeover to new computer applications.

25.2 Why is it essential to record system changes in a manual?

25.3 Why is it advisable to co-opt the services of the personnel who are concerned with a new system being implemented?

25.4 Describe the issues to be considered under file conversion prior to changeover to a new computerised application.

25.5 Describe various installation strategies that may be selected for changeover to computerised applications. Give reasons for each strategy.

25.6 List the various tests on system inputs, files, output, programs and clerical and computer procedures which would be carried out prior to changeover.

25.7 One of the primary elements of system documentation is a systems specification. State the purpose and list the contents of a typical systems specification.

25.8 What role is played by standards in the control of the design and development of a computer-based system?

Answers on pages 382–8.

26 Control and security

26.1 Introduction

That business systems function correctly is not left to chance. Because of the highly automated nature of computerised applications, various checks and controls are built into the software. The first part of this chapter covers administrative controls which address the need for the division of responsibility to prevent fraudulent practices. This topic is also included in computer audit techniques (*see* 26.5). Administrative controls also embrace physical installation security matters, including access controls requiring adequate security measures to prevent unauthorised access to data, to the computer room and to files and software stored in the library. Passwords, to prevent access to files and programs, and datakeys (special electronic keys) for gaining access to restricted areas are also necessary. This type of control also incorporates back-up and standby facilities, normally via a computer bureau or a similar computer installed in a local company, in case of a system malfunction.

Development controls include project reporting stages, which address the ways in which effective reporting, written and verbal, may be achieved. Matters relating to documentation are also discussed. Operational controls include those which detect data encoding (conversion) errors, which are dealt with by data verification. Data recording errors are detected by the process of data validation. Controls relating to the accuracy of transmitting data are also included as well as file controls, check point and recovery provisions relating to real-time operations and control totals and access controls. This chapter also outlines the various aspects of computer audit techniques and when they need to be effected.

26.2 Administrative controls

26.2.1 Personnel, division of responsibility

(a) The data processing department in the larger organisation should function through a policy-formulating steering committee in order to ensure that only those projects are undertaken which will provide maximum benefit to the business as a corporate entity. This does not preclude the data processing manager gaining direct access to an immediate superior, the managing director for instance, as this is often essential during the course of day-to-day operations to resolve immediate problems.

(b) The data processing manager, as a functional manager, should report to a higher authority than the functional level. It is necessary for the manager to report to, and receive instructions from, a superior such as the managing director, so that overriding authority may be implemented in conflicting circumstances.

(c) The various activities of a data processing department should be organised to allow for the implementation of *internal check* procedures to prevent fraudulent conversion of data and master files, regarding the transfer of funds to fictitious accounts for instance. This course of action necessitates a separation of duties, as in the accounting function, but in this case instead of separating cash handling from cash recording it is necessary to separate systems development from systems operation. It also necessitates the independence of a data control section even though it is normally structured within the operations section under the control of the operations manager. The preparation of input should be shielded from the influence of operations staff as data must maintain the utmost integrity. There must also be independence of the computer file library, as in a large data processing complex chaos can occur if stringent controls are not applied to the movement of master files and program files. Strict control procedures are required to ensure *purge* dates are adhered to, to avoid premature overwriting or prolonged storage.

26.2.2 Physical installation security

(a) Access to data relating to business transactions should be restricted to functional and data preparation staff in the data processing department.

(b) Access to the computer room, if a centralised department, must be restricted to authorised personnel only.

(c) Master files and programs must be released from the library only on the presentation of an authorisation slip and they must not be allowed to leave the data processing department unless by special authority for processing at a bureau in the event of a systems breakdown.

(d) Adequate security measures must be incorporated to prevent fraudulent entry of data to perpetrate fraud, by the use of passwords and datakeys.

26.2.3 Back-up and standby facilities

Back-up facilities are outlined below (*see* 26.4.9). Standby facilities often take the form of a reciprocal arrangement between local companies, each having similar computer configurations, to use each other's system in the event of a malfunction. The facilities would probably be available during off-peak times, say in the evening or even during the night, depending on local circumstances. Alternatively, a computer bureau may be employed for the same purpose in which case the data can be processed by the bureau staff or on a do-it-yourself basis.

26.3 Development controls

26.3.1 Project management reporting stages including modification and enhancement

It is important for a systems analyst to receive and disseminate information on a variety of subjects throughout the life cycle of a project. Several different types of written communication are received or prepared by a systems analyst during the development of a computer-based system. It will be recalled that the stages of the systems development life cycle (*see* 24.8) include a number of reporting stages, one of which is terms of reference (*see* 24.10) provided by management to systems development staff as authority to undertake a feasibility study. Subsequently, the systems analyst prepares and submits to management a feasibility study report (*see* 24.12) specifying the findings of the study and reporting the technical and economic feasibility of the project set out in the terms of reference. A further report is prepared to inform management of various alternative proposals for its deliberation and to decide on its choice of system, processing technique or computer configuration. Progress reports from time to time keep management informed of the stage reached. After the system has been implemented a report is provided to inform management of actual compared with anticipated results. Management then discusses the situation with systems analysts to determine a plan of action to resolve unwanted situations or to modify or enhance the system.

26.3.2 Documentation

Systems documentation includes a detailed summary of the proposed system (a systems specification — *see* 25.7). A further important document is the *program specification*, which provides the programmers with all the details they require for writing the relevant programs to accomplish the defined processing tasks (*see* 19.4). Other systems documentation includes various analysis documents relating to input, output and files, providing detailed information relating to current documentation which is invaluable as a basis for the design of input documents, file organisation and output reports (*see* 25.5.5). In addition, documentation includes systems and program flowcharts, screen layouts, data flow diagrams, procedure charts, decision tables, data structures and testing procedures, etc.

26.3.3 Manuals

Various operating manuals are written by systems analysts for the guidance of clerical and computer operations staff in the operational features of the system. They are written to cover such matters as data validation and error correction procedures, data preparation and data control procedures and computer operating instructions. The instructions relate to file back-up procedures, system recovery routines and start-up and loading procedures. In addition, manuals are provided relating to the content, origination and destination point and time and frequency of preparation of forms.

26.4 Operational controls

26.4.1 Data conversion controls

This topic relates to data verification procedures, which are dealt with in Chapter 15 (*see* 15.3.1).

26.4.2 Operational controls in data transmission systems

In most data transmission systems redundancy checking is used for the detection of errors which are then corrected by retransmission of the blocks in which errors have been found. Redundancy checking detects errors by computing additional bits from the data which are then added to the original blocks. The receiving terminal performs checks by comparing bit patterns in the data blocks, thus identifying bits which have been lost or corrupted during transmission. Blocks containing errors are then automatically retransmitted.

Parity checking is also possible. An additional bit is added to the frame of bits forming a character before transmission. Parity checking can be either odd or even parity: the count of bits is either odd or even according to the mode of parity selected.

Errors may also be detected by retransmitting signals received back to the transmitting terminal on a separate channel. The signals are then compared with the original transmission and differences indicate transmission errors.

26.4.3 Data validation

A computer is quite adept at processing data at an extremely high speed — unfortunately it will process incorrect data at the same speed as error-free data! It is therefore necessary to ensure data accuracy by implementing routines for the detection of errors before they are submitted for processing.

It is important to distinguish between data validation and verification:

Data verification is concerned with detecting and eliminating transcription (encoding) errors as data is transferred from one medium to another, e.g. a sales invoice document to disc.

Data validation is a technique used to assess the accuracy of data from a more subjective viewpoint and should eliminate obvious illogicalities.

The initial run in a batch processing application is for the purpose of detecting and reporting on errors. This ensures that data is corrected and resubmitted before it is processed, as the processing routine contains an error control loop, as shown in Fig. 26.1.

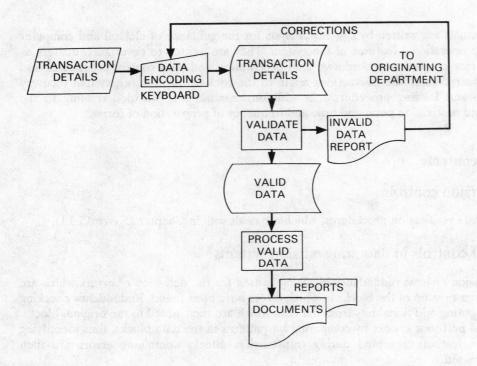

Figure 26.1 Batch processing: data validation

26.4.4 Typical data validation checks

(a) Check to ensure that data is of the *correct type* in accordance with the program and master file.

(b) Check to ensure that data is for the *correct period*.

(c) Check to ensure that master files have the *correct generation indicator*.

(d) Check digit verification detects transposition errors when recording *key* fields on source documents in respect of customer account codes, stock codes or expenditure codes, etc. (*see* 26.4.5).

(e) Check to ensure that each character has the *correct number of bits* — parity check (hardware check).

(f) Check to ensure that records and transactions are in the *correct sequence and all are present*.

(g) Check to ensure that fields contain the *correct number and type of characters of the correct format* — format (or picture) check.

(h) Check to ensure that data *conforms to the minimum and maximum range of values*, for example stock balances, gross wages and tax deductions, etc. As the range of specific items of data may be subject to fluctuation, the range limits may be input as parameters prior to a run instead of being incorporated in a program.

(i) In a nominal ledger computer application the validation of nominal ledger codes would be accomplished by reference to a nominal description file as an alternative to using check digits.

(j) In an order-entry system product codes would be validated by reference to a product file and customer account codes by reference to a customer file as an alternative to using check digits.

(k) Some errors may be detected by various types of check, e.g. a five-digit product code being used instead of a six-digit salesman code could be detected by a check on the type of transaction (*see* (a)). The difference in the number of digits could be detected by a field check (*see* (g)).

(l) An error in the quantity of raw material being recorded in tonnes instead of kilograms could or should be detected by visual inspection rather than a computer validation program. The unit of weight is normally pre-recorded on transaction data and weight designations are pre-defined in the program.

(m) Compatibility checks are used to ensure that two or more data items are compatible with other data items. For instance, discounts to customers may be calculated on the basis of order quantity but a discount may only apply if a customer's account balance is below a stated amount.

(n) Probability checks are used to avoid unnecessary rejection of data as data can on occasions exceed normal values in a range due purely to random causes. If this arises with an acceptable frequency (probability) at a defined level of confidence (normally 95 per cent), then the data need not be rejected. This would tend to reduce the level of rejections and the time expended on investigating causes of divergences.

(o) Check to ensure *hash* and other control totals agree with those generated by the computer. A hash total may be the total of account numbers, which is meaningless for accounting purposes but useful for control, as it indicates missing transactions.

26.4.5 Check digit verification

Check digit verification
It is important to appreciate that the accuracy of output from data processing can only be as accurate as the input from which it is produced. Errors often occur in the initial recording and transcription of numerical data, such as stock numbers and account codes, frequently through transposition.

Check digit verification is a technique designed to test the accuracy (validity) of such numerical data before acceptance for processing. The data vet program performs check digit verification as part of the editing routine. Data is rejected as invalid when the check digit is any other number than the correct one. The data must then be re-encoded and represented for processing.

Check digit
A check digit is a number which is added to a series of numbers (in the form of a code number for stock or customer identification) for the purpose of producing a *self-checking* number. Each check digit is derived arithmetically, and bears a unique mathematical relationship to the number to which it is attached. The check digit is normally added in the low-order position.

Modulus
Before indicating the way in which a check digit is calculated, it is necessary to understand what is meant by a *modulus*. A modulus is the figure used to divide the number for which a check digit is required. Moduli in common use are 7, 10, 11 and 13.

Check digit calculation

(a) Assume modulus 11 is selected for the purpose of calculating a check digit.

(b) Assume the number for which a check digit is required is 2323.

(c) Divide 2323 by 11 and note the remainder. Remainder is 2.

(d) Obtain the complement of the remainder and use as the check digit. $11 - 2 = 9$ (complement = check digit).

(e) The number including its check digit now becomes 23239.

Calculation of a check digit using weights

A weight is the value allocated to each digit of a number according to a specified pattern, to prevent acceptance of interchanged digits. A more refined method of obtaining a check digit is achieved by the use of weights.

(a) Assume the same number and modulus as in the above example, i.e. 2323 and 11 respectively.

(b) The selected series of weights is 5, 4, 3, 2.

(c) Multiply each digit of the number by its corresponding weight as follows:

		Weight	Product
Units digit	3	2	6
Tens digit	2	3	6
Hundreds digit	3	4	12
Thousands digit	2	5	10
Sum of products			34

(d) Divide sum of products by modulus 11 and note the remainder. Remainder is 1.

(e) Obtain the complement of the remainder and use this as the check digit: $11 - 1 = 10$ (assigned the letter x).

(f) The number including its check digit is 2323x.

A check may be applied to confirm that 10 or x is valid as follows:

Sum of the products	34
Add calculated check	10
	44

Divide by modulus 11 and note any remainder. As there is no remainder, the check digit is valid.

26.4.6 Examples of data validation

Limit check

For on-line processing data validation is performed interactively (*see* Fig. 26.2).

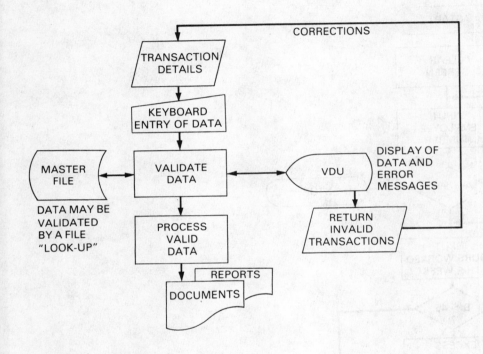

Figure 26.2 On-line data verification

Example 1: Validation demonstrating a limit check

The example chosen here is a limit check routine on excess hours and hourly rate which could be built into a payroll system. The flowchart given in Fig. 26.3 is designed to trap employee hours in excess of a stated minimum and an hourly rate which does not conform to a specific value.

The interactive nature of this application is demonstrated by messages on the screen of the terminal (monitor/VDU) as follows:

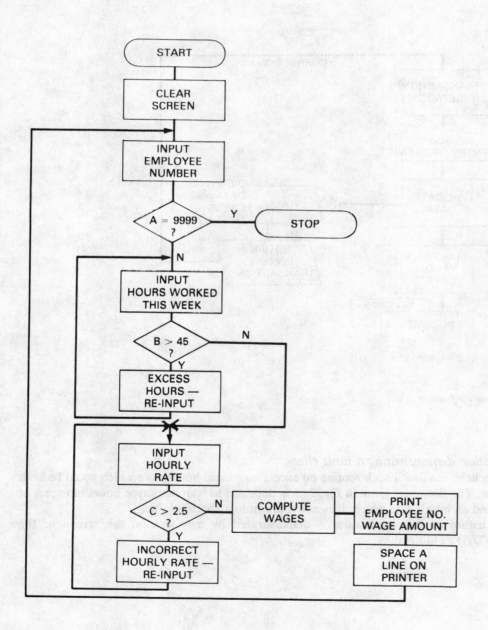

Figure 26.3 Limit check routine on excess hours and hourly rate

*Screen display User respon*se
Employee number? Keys in employee number.
Hours worked this week? Keys in hours worked.

If the hours worked are greater than 45 the program displays a message on the screen:

Excess hours — re-input Keys in correct hours.

If the hours worked do not exceed 45 the program does not display this message but does display:

Hourly rate? Keys in hourly rate.

If the hourly rate exceeds £2.50 the program displays a message on the screen:

Incorrect hourly Keys in correct rate.
rate — re-input

If the hourly rate does not exceed £2.50 then the program continues with the normal routine.

Example 2: Validation demonstrating a range check

The example chosen here is a range check to detect order quantities above or below a specified value (*see* Fig. 26.4). Such a check could be necessary in a company in which orders less than, say, 5 need to be rejected on the grounds that the value of the order would be insufficient to cover handling costs, whereas orders over, say, 20 would be unusual and worthy of special treatment.

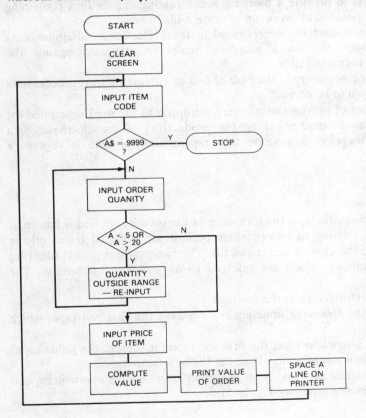

Figure 26.4 Order quantities: range check

The interactive nature of this application is demonstrated by messages on the screen of the terminal (monitor/VDU) as follows:

Screen display User response
Item code? Keys in item code.
Order quantity? Keys in order quantity

If the order quantity is less than 5 or greater than 20 then the program displays the message:

Quantity outside Keys in correct quantity
    range — re-input

Of course quantities in excess of 20 may be correct on occasions but this is validated to ensure the integrity of the data before processing commences. The program then continues with the processing routine.

Interactive processing often incorporates 'descriptive read-back' in which a description of a part or names of customers are displayed on the screen to validate the integrity of the code numbers entered.

26.4.7 File controls

The purpose of a file security system is to provide a basis for reconstituting master files containing important business information, as it is possible to overwrite or erase a file in error.

It is essential that file security precautions be incorporated in those electronic computer data processing systems which store master files on a magnetic media to safeguard against the consequences of loss of data, errors or corrupted data.

Without such precautions, it would be necessary in the case of loss or corruption to reprocess data from the last run when the file was known to be correct.

The reprocessing of data for a number of previous runs is very disruptive to the work scheduled for the computer and consequently has an adverse effect on the productivity of the electronic data processing (EDP) department. It is therefore imperative that reprocessing of data is kept to a minimum.

Generation technique
In respect of master files recorded on magnetic tape, the technique of file security applied is known as the *generation* technique because files relating to two previous periods are retained transiently in addition to the current updated file and the current movement file. The two previous period files plus the current file comprise three generations, which are referred to as *grandfather-father-son*. The technique operates as follows.

(a) The first master file produced is referrred to as the *son* tape.

(b) The *son* tape produced during the following updating run replaces the first *son* tape, which becomes the *father* tape.

(c) The next updating run produces a new *son* tape, the first *son* tape (at present the *father* tape) becomes the *grandfather* tape. The previous *son* tape now becomes the new *father* tape.

(d) On the next updating run, the original *son* tape (now the *grandfather* tape) is overwritten, and can in fact be used for producing the new *son* tape (*see* Fig. 26.5).

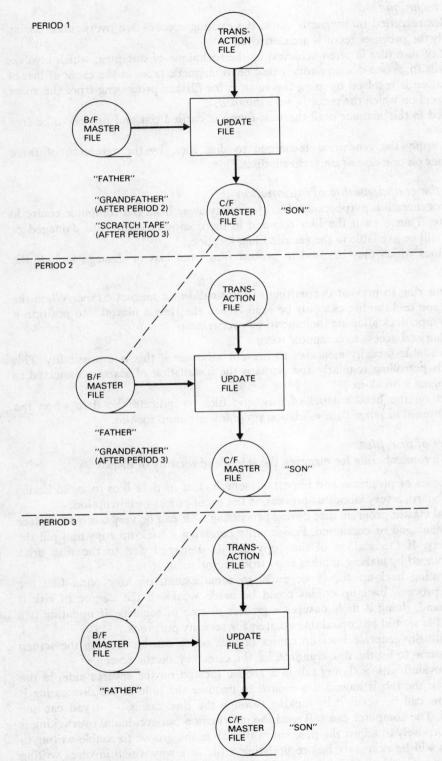

PERIOD 1

TRANS-
ACTION
FILE

B/F
MASTER
FILE

UPDATE
FILE

"FATHER"

"GRANDFATHER"
(AFTER PERIOD 2)

"SCRATCH TAPE"
(AFTER PERIOD 3)

C/F
MASTER
FILE

"SON"

PERIOD 2

TRANS-
ACTION
FILE

B/F
MASTER
FILE

UPDATE
FILE

"FATHER"

"GRANDFATHER"
(AFTER PERIOD 3)

C/F
MASTER
FILE

"SON"

PERIOD 3

TRANS-
ACTION
FILE

B/F
MASTER
FILE

UPDATE
FILE

"FATHER"

C/F
MASTER
FILE

"SON"

Figure 26.5 Generation technique of file security

The dumping (copying) technique

With regard to master files recorded on magnetic discs, the existing records are overwritten during updating, and consequently the previous records are destroyed.

File security in respect of disc files is often achieved by the technique of dumping, which involves copying the updated records from one disc to another disc or to magnetic tape. In the event of loss of data on one disc, the situation is resolved by using the records for further processing from the spare disc or the magnetic tape reel on which the records were *dumped*.

The records are retained in this manner until the next dump is carried out and proved to be free of errors and corrupted data.

It is also possible to apply the *generation* technique to disc files, by the retention of three generations of records either on one disc or on separate discs.

File safety and ensuring the confidentiality of information

The records retained for regeneration purposes are filed for safety away from the computer centre in case of damage by fire, etc. Thus even if the files retained in the computer centre are damaged or destroyed the records will still be available in the remote filing location.

Other physical precautions which may be used to protect files from loss or damage include the following.

(a) Use of a write-permit ring to prevent overwriting of information on magnetic tape. When the ring is removed from the tape reel the file can only be read. When the ring is placed into position it depresses a plunger on the tape deck allowing the tape to be overwritten.

(b) Prevention of unauthorised access to computer room.

(c) Implementation of suitable security measures to prevent sabotage if this is a possibility. This may require security guards patrolling regularly and perhaps the installation of alarms connected to the local police station to signal a break-in.

(d) File labels encoded on the header label of magnetic files to indicate the date when the information may be overwritten. The *purge* date validation programs are used for this.

Rules for ensuring security of disc files

A number of rules are worth remembering for ensuring the safety and security of discs.

(a) Maintain back-up copies of programs and important, lengthy text or data files to avoid having to re-enter them by the keyboard, a very laborious process, in the event of loss or corruption.

(b) Never use the original master program disc during processing — it can be very costly to replace if the disc drive or disc is damaged or corrupted. For security construct a back-up copy and put the original in a place of safety. If the surface of the copy disc is damaged due to the disc drive malfunctioning it can be replaced by making another copy from the original.

The frequency of generating back-up copies depends, to some extent, on how often files are updated. If this is a daily process, back-up copies could be made weekly if the degree of risk is acceptable. On the other hand, doing it daily ensures a greater degree of security. If updating is a weekly routine the updated file should be copied immediately for security purposes.

Some computers automatically generate back-up copies of files which can be seen on the screen after asking the operating system to list the disc contents, i.e. the directory, on the screen.

(c) 3.5-inch discs are provided with a sliding tab in a groove located on the reverse side, in the lower left-hand corner. When the tab is moved downwards to uncover the hole in the disc casing it 'write-protects' the disc. This can be verified by looking through the disc casing — if you can see daylight it is write-protected. The computer can still read the information but accidental overwriting is prevented. It is necessary purposely to adjust the position of the tab in the groove to enable writing to take place on the disc. This will be necessary before updating a file in a way which involves writing new data to the disc and overwriting the previously recorded data.

Overwriting destroys the previous contents of the disc at a specific location, hence the need to make back-up copies. The larger discs have a notch near the bottom left-hand corner which, when covered by sellotape, prevents accidental overwriting.

General rules for handling discs

(a) Avoid touching the recording surface of a disc.

(b) Ensure the disc is placed in the disc drive the correct way round.

(c) Do not bend the disc.

(d) Do not expose the disc to dust as this can corrupt data on the tracks.

(e) Do not remove a disc from the drive while the disc light is glowing.

(f) Never leave discs in the disc drive while the computer is switched on or off as the disc can be corrupted by doing so.

(g) Do not place discs near magnetic fields such as on the top of the computer or hi-fi unit or even near a telephone when in use.

26.4.8 Security of databases

Alterations to a database are only possible by the database software, i.e. the database management system (DBMS) which prevents data being altered by applications software. Databases often incorporate a number of security measures; for example, a user may be required to enter a user name before access is authorised. In addition, a password (as with file security) may be required to gain access to confidential information and access to some parts of the database can be restricted to specified terminals. Each information owner must specify the names of users allowed to access data and other information owners who can look at, but not amend, parts of the database. Individual pages can also be restricted by specifying user names.

Data Protection Act 1984

With developments in database technology and electronic mail the need to protect the privacy of personal data is increasingly urgent. The Data Protection Act 1984 provides legislation to curb unauthorised access and maintain data security.

Schedule 1 of the Act requires both individuals and computer services bureaux who are in control of personal data to register with the Data Protection Registrar and comply with the *data protection principles*. The most important of these are listed below.

Data protection principles

(a) The information to be contained in personal data shall be obtained, and personal data shall be processed, fairly and lawfully.

(b) Personal data shall be held only for one or more specified and lawful purposes.

(c) Personal data held for any purpose or purposes shall not be used or disclosed in any manner incompatible with that purpose or those purposes.

(d) Personal data held for any purpose or purposes shall be adquate, relevant and not excessive in relation to that purpose or those purposes.

(e) Personal data shall be accurate and, where necessary, kept up to date.

(f) Appropriate security measures shall be taken against unauthorised access to, alteration, disclosure or destruction of, personal data and against accidental loss or destruction of personal data. Regard shall be had:

    (i) to the nature of the personal data and the harm that would result from such access, alteration, disclosure, loss or destruction as are mentioned in this principle; and

    (ii) to the place where the personal data are stored, to security measures programmed into the relevant equipment and to measures taken for ensuring the reliability of staff having access to the data.

(g) Personal data held for any purpose or purposes shall not be kept for longer than is necessary for that purpose or purposes.

(h) An individual shall be entitled at reasonable intervals and without undue delay or expense to be informed by any data user whether he or she holds personal data of which that individual is the subject; and to access any such data held by a data user and where appropriate, to have such data corrected or erased.

Application and exceptions

The principles included in the Act apply to all users who operate from the UK and thus overseas branches using data held in the UK are equally compelled to follow the legislation. The Act does not, however, cover data held, controlled and processed wholly outside the UK by an overseas branch.

Legislation covers not only computer mainframes, minis, micros and software but applies to any equipment which can be used to hold data, such as telephone logging systems or electronic flexi-time systems (flexible time-logging systems). The Act defines the term *equipment* in the following way:

'. . . Equipment operating automatically in response to instructions and applies where the program is in the form of hardware or software.'

Note, however, that the Act does not provide for data processed on a once-only basis, for example a single word processor (or typewriter) printout which is not stored in a memory or retrieval system.

Data user

The term *data user* as specified in the Act includes any individual, company, corporate or unincorporated body that holds data. The Act gives a detailed definition of the term but the main points are as follows:

(a) a data user has control of the data;

(b) the data has been or will be processed by the user;

(c) an individual or company that processes on behalf of the person who controls the data is also classed as a data user.

26.4.9 Checkpoint and recovery provisions

Real-time systems are designed to deal with dynamic situations in order to control critical operations which must be continually updated as events occur. Such systems accept random input at random time intervals and the status of files changes accordingly making it necessary to implement security measures. These take the form of dumping all relevant restart and audit information periodically, say every two to three minutes, to tape or disc. The dumped data can then be used to restart the system in the event of a malfunction. Such operations are also provided with a second processor which is automatically switched into the real-time system in the event of the first machine ceasing to function for any reason.

26.4.10 Control totals

These are dealt with in 26.5.7, below.

26.4.11 Access controls: identification, authentication, authorisation

(a) Particularly in time sharing systems it is normal practice for each authorised user to be provided with a password which is entered on the keyboard of the terminal and transmitted to the computer. The password is not printed or displayed on the terminal, however, so that it cannot be observed by anyone in the vicinity. The password allows access to specific files related to the user of the system.

(b) Information on a file may be stored in a scrambled format which can only be decoded by providing the system with the decoding key to unscramble the information.

(c) Specific terminals may be prohibited from receiving transmitted information by lock-out procedures. In this way only designated terminals will actually receive file information.

26.5 Computer audit techniques

26.5.1 Auditors and computerised systems

The most effective time for auditors to review the checks and controls which have been incorporated in a computerised system is immediately after the systems specification has been completed. It is then possible to observe the controls which have been provided and to rectify omissions before the system is implemented. Other factors to consider include the need to prevent unauthorised access to the computer room and to information stored in files. The adequacy of program amendment procedures and back-up arrangements in case of system failure also need to be reviewed. The effectiveness of communications between other installations and local area networks should be looked at to ensure the required level of service is being attained. This takes into account the response time of the system — often related to the traffic density, which often varies with the time of day. Branch offices may transmit transaction data to head office at the end of the day, for instance. Checks should also be applied to ensure that computations have been calculated correctly and that facts obtained from the audit trail are suitable for their purpose and so on.

Auditors should review the design philosophy relating to specific applications, necessitating an assessment of the relative merits and demerits of the processing technique applied. This contrasts batch with on-line processing and centralised with distributed processing, for instance. Whether a database would suit the needs of the application as a basis for systems integration better than the use of separate functional files should also be assessed. Auditors should ensure that, wherever possible, systems are designed to be self-checking and self-correcting. Auditors also need to know if invalid data is rejected before being subjected to processing: if not, processing time is wasted and the results obtained will be unreliable and worthless. This is accomplished by inbuilt data validation checks, including range and limit checks and checks to ensure data is complete, of the correct type and is for the correct period, etc.

26.5.2 Auditors and systems documentation

Systems documentation produced by the systems designer should be routed to the audit department as a matter of routine. Auditors then have the opportunity to assess the effectiveness of their recommendations and see that important checks and controls are incorporated. The documentation normally includes the detailed description of the system, i.e. the system definition, and decision tables which outline the conditions to be tested for and the actions to be taken when they are present. In addition, the documentation includes system and program flowcharts, data flow diagrams, a printout of the program coding, error handling routines and test data to be used, etc.

26.5.3 Internal check

The staffing of any large computer installation system should incorporate the principles of internal check. This ensures that duties are separated, rendering fraudulent practices that much more difficult.

It is necessary to simulate the operation of the computer application before it becomes operational to detect the presence of errors, or bugs as they are called. This is accomplished by the technique of desk checking, or dry running. It involves running through the program coding as the computer would do when processing data. This may be done in conjunction with related flowcharts and decision tables. Checks should be made to assess the accuracy with which transaction data is recorded on source documents prior to data conversion for input to the computer. Errors should be analysed to establish their nature and their cause so that appropriate remedies may be applied.

26.5.4 Auditing and accounting packages

Some accounting packages facilitate the work of an auditor by printing out a checklist indicating balances on a specific ledger, a sales ledger for instance, and the corresponding balance in the debtor control account in the nominal ledger. The printout may also specify the number of the last invoice, credit note and similar details relating to the payroll and purchase ledger. Copies of source documents can also be stored for future reference.

26.5.5 Audit packages

Audit packages allow selected records to be printed from master files so that they can be subjected to further scrutiny to determine if all transaction details affecting the record are shown. By this means it is also possible to examine control parameters to ensure they accord with current needs. This applies to stock control levels in a stock control system and credit limits in a sales ledger system.

26.5.6 Computer operations and test data

Prior to implementing an application it is necessary to prepare and run test data with relevant programs to obtain satisfactory evidence that the system is suitable for its purpose and will achieve the objectives laid down in the systems specification. This ensures that no abnormalities occur and indentifies the cause of problems when they arise. The results obtained are compared with precalculated values. Any differences are noted and form the basis for implementing program modifications or even major restructuring of the system in circumstances when system specifications have been misinterpreted. The effectiveness of the built-in validation checks is tested in this way. This is a feature of parallel running (*see* 25.11.2).

26.5.7 Audit trail and control totals

During the operation of a computer system auditors need to ensure that the control totals generated during processing agree with precomputed control totals in respect of both document number counts and values, in order to assess whether all the transactions are accounted for. An audit trail is also facilitated by the provision of a printout listing all the transactions processed during the run or period. A sales ledger application would include a list of all invoices, credit notes, remittances and journal adjustments. Details of VAT charges would also be listed.

Review questions

1   Why is it necessary to divide responsibility in business systems?

2   What physical installation security measures may be applied to computerised systems?

3   What back-up and standby facilities may be required for computerised systems?

4   List the project management reporting stages required when developing computerised systems.

5   What does systems documentation consist of?

6   What is the purpose of operating manuals?

7   What operational controls are included in data transmission systems?

8   List a number of essential validation checks.

9   What is check digit verification?

10   What controls are required for file security pruposes?

11   What measures are taken to ensure security of data in databases?

12   What are the purpose and nature of checkpoint and recovery facilities?

13   Write notes relating to computer audit techniques.

Self-test questions

26.1 How might a system designer ensure the accuracy of data entering the system?

26.2 What methods and techniques may be applied to prevent unauthorised access to files, databases and computer centres?

26.3 It is important for a systems analyst to receive and disseminate information on a variety of subjects throughout the life cycle of a project. Describe several types of written and verbal communication that a systems analyst may use.

Answers on pages 388–91.

27 Traditional design tools and techniques

27.1 Introduction

This chapter covers details relating to system flowcharts, run charts and decision tables which may be classified as traditional as distinct from structured techniques which are separately dealt with in Chapter 28. Matters relating to file design are included in Chapter 25, and in respect of database design in Chapter 9. Procedure or systems specification is also dealt with in Chapter 25.

27.2 System flowcharts

A flowchart is a pictorial or diagrammatic representation of a system prepared on the basis of flowchart symbols. The term is used in its widest sense to describe any type of diagram showing the functions, data flows and the sequence of events or activities in a system. It is important to appreciate the nature of a system flowchart as distinct from a run chart. It is necessary to be aware that a systems flowchart portrays both non-computer and computerised operations whereas a run chart is restricted to computer activities only.

27.3 Computer run chart

Computer run charts are a specific type of flowchart for portraying the different elements of a system including system inputs, processing operations and outputs from each run. A run chart provides useful information to a computer operator as it conveys the nature of the hardware devices required for each run by means of appropriate symbols. Each run is shown separately with a brief narrative specifying the activities performed and its relationship with other runs.

27.4 Block diagram

A block diagram, sometimes referred to as a 'system outline' or 'system function' diagram, is a low level flowchart which portrays the whole of a system in simple terms. It indicates the inputs, files, processing and outputs independent of operation details (*see* Fig. 27.1).

27.5 Flowchart symbols

A number of standard symbols are used in the construction of flowcharts (*see* Fig. 27.2). These symbols represent various types of hardware device and/or processing activity, including input devices/type of input, an action box specifying the nature of the computer activity, storage devices using disc and/or magnetic tape, and symbols which indicate the nature of the files used in each run.

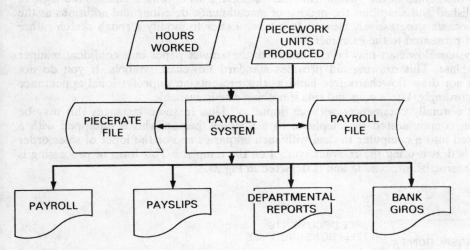

Figure 27.1 Block diagram of a payroll system

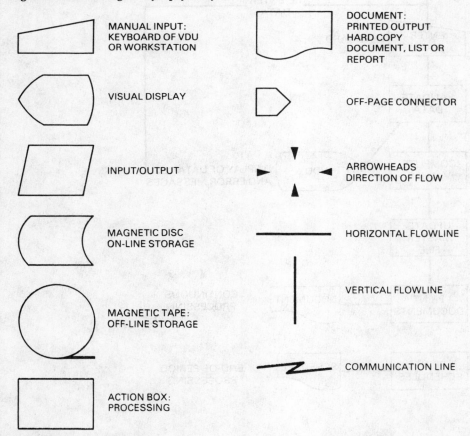

MANUAL INPUT: KEYBOARD OF VDU OR WORKSTATION	DOCUMENT: PRINTED OUTPUT HARD COPY DOCUMENT, LIST OR REPORT
VISUAL DISPLAY	OFF-PAGE CONNECTOR
INPUT/OUTPUT	ARROWHEADS DIRECTION OF FLOW
MAGNETIC DISC ON-LINE STORAGE	HORIZONTAL FLOWLINE
MAGNETIC TAPE: OFF-LINE STORAGE	VERTICAL FLOWLINE
	COMMUNICATION LINE
ACTION BOX: PROCESSING	

Figure 27.2 Flowchart symbols

27.6 Constructing system flowcharts

It is good practice to prepare initially a rough sketch of the system flowchart on a sheet of scrap paper whilst reading through the details of the system from the question. This approach enables the logic of the system to be established and simplifies the making of amendments, deletions and additions as the details of the system became progressively clearer. It is much easier to modify a rough sketch rather than the final flowchart presented to the examiner.

Subsequently, the system flowchart may be committed to the answer paper in a confident manner using a flowchart template. This drawing aid provides standard flowchart symbols. If you do not possess a template do not draw flowcharts free-hand as this presents an unprofessional appearance and will lose marks accordingly. Use a coin and rule if nothing else is available.

A system flowchart normally commences with an 'input' of data. In some instances this may be details of a transaction communicated by telephone to a telesales person who is equipped with a terminal keyboard linked into a computer to deal with such enquiries and/or the input of sales order details. The keyboard is drawn using the relevant symbol on the template. This form of processing is referred to as on-line interactive processing and is depicted in Fig 27.3.

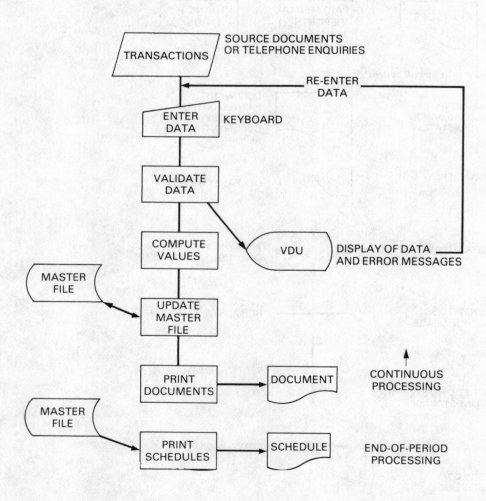

Figure 27.3 System flowchart: interactive (on-line) processing

For batch processing systems the initial data relating to business transactions may be in the form of batches of 'source' documents which may be portrayed by the input/output symbol. Data may then be encoded either to magnetic disc or magnetic tape. The keyboard symbol may be used for this purpose. If data is recorded on disc a 'key-to-disc' data preparation system may be used for converting the data to magnetic disc. This approach enables data to be input at high speed thereby saving time. It would take much longer to input the same volume of transactions by keyboard and cause the processor to be inactive for a considerable proportion of the total processing time. Figure 27.4 outlines the structure and activities relating to a batch processing system, including data preparation activities.

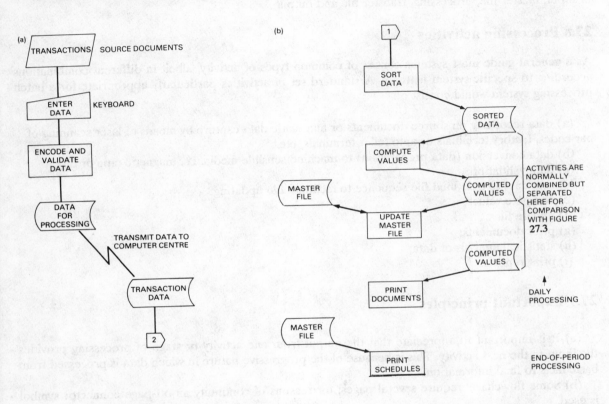

Figure 27.4 System flowchart: (a) batch processing – off-line activities – key to disc encoding and validation; (b) batch processing activities

Processing steps are shown by the action box symbol, which specifies the 'activity' or 'operation' to be performed by the computer at that specific stage of processing. After data is processed an 'output' is produced which is depicted by the relevant symbol, e.g. magnetic disc or magnetic tape symbol if the output is to a file such as a work file or master file. Alternatively the output may be visually displayed on the computer monitor (visual display unit) either in text or graphics mode, or output may be printed, in which case either the input/output symbol or report symbol may be used.

If data is transferred to the processor from a file or from the processor to a file this activity is shown by the relevant magnetic tape or disc symbols. All inputs and outputs to and from the processor, represented by the action box, are connected by a horizontal or vertical flowline with arrowheads showing the direction of flow, i.e. in or out of the processor. Each action box should contain a brief 'legend' defining the nature of the activity and each file symbol should be labelled with the name of the file. The nature of the output should be specified, whether, for instance, it is an error report (i.e. invalid items), audit trail consisting of a list of the transactions posted, a business document such as a payslip, a schedule such as a payroll, or a management report such as a list of items out of stock, or customers whose credit limit is exceeded.

27.7 An alternative method of constructing a flowchart

More meaningful flowcharts or run charts may be constructed on the basis of the columnar analysis, as illustrated in Fig 27.5. The different aspects of processing are shown in separate columns in respect of input, master file, processing, transfer file and output.

27.8 Processing activities

As a general guide most systems consist of common types of activity, albeit in different combinations according to specific system features. A standard set of activities particularly appropriate for a batch processing system would consist of:

(a) data recording on source documents or automatic data capture by means of laser scanning of bar codes, factory terminals or auto teller terminals, etc.;
(b) data conversion (data preparation) to machine-sensible media, i.e. magnetic tape or disc;
(c) data validation;
(d) sort data to a defined file sequence to facilitate file updating;
(e) compute values;
(f) update files;
(g) print documents;
(h) statistical analysis of data;
(i) print reports.

27.9 Important principles

(a) It is important to appreciate that the output from one activity or stage of processing provides the input to the next activity. This is because of the progressive nature in which data is processed from basic facts to final information.

(b) Some flowcharts require several pages; for reasons of continuity an off-page connector symbol is used.

(c) A flowchart must be identifiable and authenticated. For this reason it must show clearly the *name of the system*, the *date* the chart was constructed so that it is possible to assess its status (i.e. whether it is portraying the current system, a future system or an earlier version of the present system), and the *author* of the chart or system.

(d) Some parts of a system are processed daily, weekly, monthly or annually according to circumstances and requirements. A factory payroll system may have daily data capture procedures relating to jobs worked on in the factory with a weekly wages calculation and statistical routine. This may be supported by monthly statistics for management accounting needs. The system must also incorporate the annual preparation of certificates of pay, tax deducted and national insurance contributions (P60s). In some instances the preparation of sales invoices may be performed daily or weekly according to volume, but statements of account are prepared monthly at the end of the trading period. In other instances, some parts of a system are performed on-line interactively, as in the instance of inputting sales order details. This is referred to as on-line order entry and is often supported by daily processing of the orders in batch mode. These aspects are illustrated in Fig. 27.6 which shows a simple flowchart of both on-line and batch processing activities.

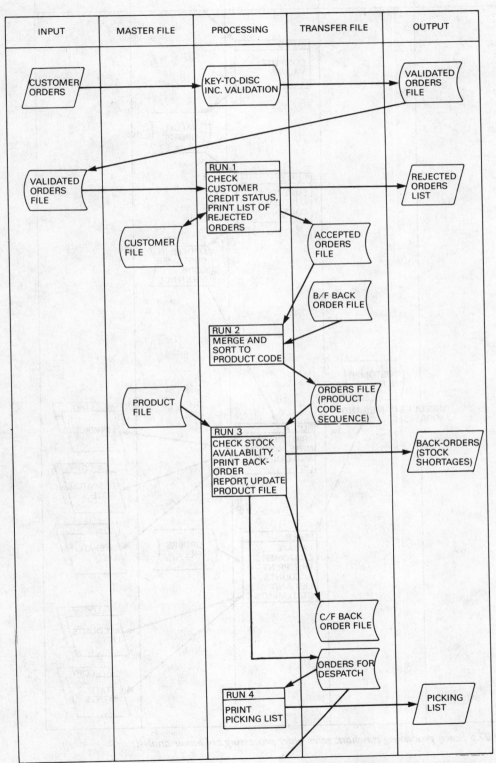

INPUT	MASTER FILE	PROCESSING	TRANSFER FILE	OUTPUT

CUSTOMER ORDERS

KEY-TO-DISC INC. VALIDATION

VALIDATED ORDERS FILE

VALIDATED ORDERS FILE

RUN 1
CHECK CUSTOMER CREDIT STATUS, PRINT LIST OF REJECTED ORDERS

REJECTED ORDERS LIST

CUSTOMER FILE

ACCEPTED ORDERS FILE

B/F BACK ORDER FILE

RUN 2
MERGE AND SORT TO PRODUCT CODE

PRODUCT FILE

ORDERS FILE (PRODUCT CODE SEQUENCE)

RUN 3
CHECK STOCK AVAILABILITY, PRINT BACK-ORDER REPORT, UPDATE PRODUCT FILE

BACK-ORDERS (STOCK SHORTAGES)

C/F BACK ORDER FILE

ORDERS FOR DESPATCH

RUN 4
PRINT PICKING LIST

PICKING LIST

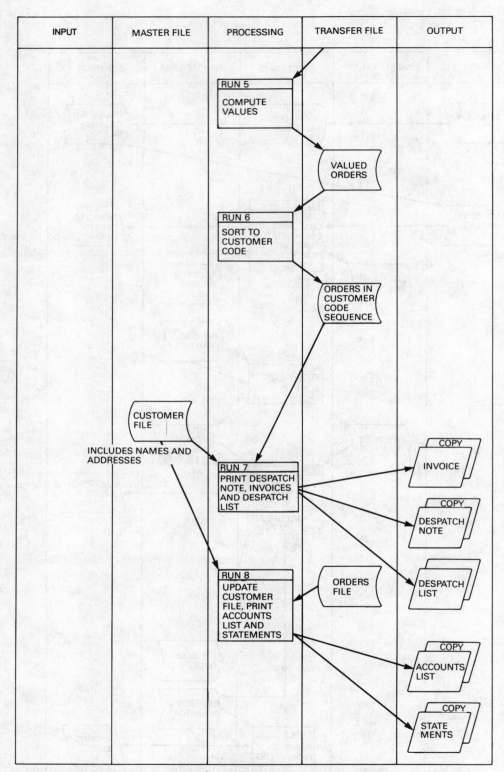

Figure 27.5 Batch processing runchart: sales order processing columnar analysis

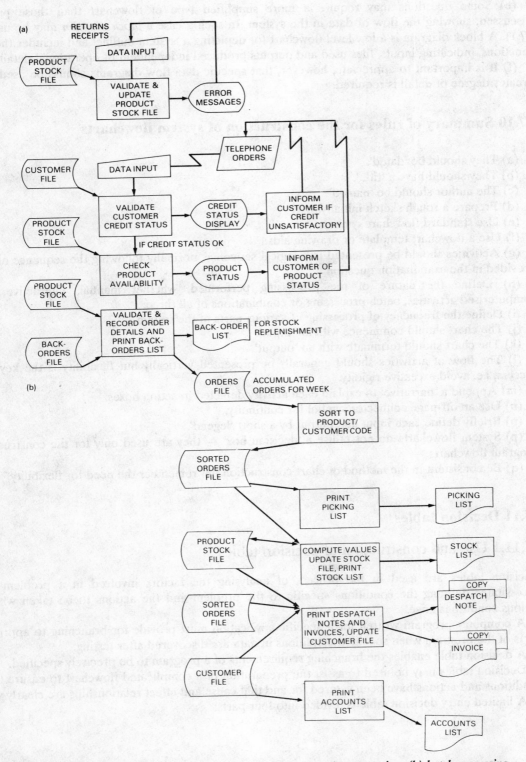

Figure 27.6 Combined on-line and batch processing activities: (a) interactive processing; (b) batch processing

(e) Some questions may require a more simplified type of flowchart than those previously discussed, showing the flow of data in the system. In such a case a *block diagram* may be used (Fig. 27.1). A block diagram is a low level flowchart for depicting a 'system outline' and includes the system functions, indicating inputs, files used and outputs produced independent of operational details.

(f) It is important to appreciate, however, that specific data flow diagrams should be used when a greater degree of detail is required.

27.10 Summary of rules for the construction of system flowcharts

(a) They should be 'dated'.

(b) They should have a 'title'.

(c) The author should be 'named'.

(d) Prepare a rough sketch initially.

(e) Use standard flowchart symbols.

(f) Use a flowchart template or drawing aids.

(g) Activities should be presented in a logical sequence, normally following the sequence of details provided in the examination question.

(h) Define the nature of the processing performed, whether manual, interactive on-line computerised activities, batch processing or combinations of all three.

(i) Define the frequency of processing of various parts of the system.

(j) The chart should commence with an 'input'.

(k) The chart should terminate with an 'output'.

(l) The flow of activities should generally be presented vertically but flexibility is the keynote of success, i.e. avoid excessive rigidity.

(m) Append a 'narrative' to explain each activity depicted in action boxes.

(n) Use an off-page connector symbol for continuity.

(o) Briefly define each input and output by a short 'legend'.

(p) System flowcharts do not utilise a 'decision box' — they are used only for the construction of program flowcharts.

(q) Be consistent in the method of chart construction but remember the need for flexibility.

27.11 Decision tables

27.11.1 Use and construction of decision tables

Decision tables are used in the process of analysing the factors involved in a problem which necessitates defining the conditions specific to the problem and the actions to be taken when the various conditions arise.

A computer program written for a specific application must provide for branching to appropriate parts of the program when specified conditions in data are discovered after testing.

A decision table enables the branching requirements of a program to be precisely specified.

Decision tables may be used to assist the preparation of a complicated flowchart to ensure that all conditions and actions have been catered for and that cause and effect relationships are clearly visible.

A limited entry decision table is divided into four parts:

(a) condition stub

(b) condition entries ⎫ condition statement

(c) action stub

(d) action entries ⎫ action statement

The condition stub and condition entries define the conditions to be tested.

The action stub and action entries define the actions to be taken dependent upon the outcome of the testing.

The 'rules' consist of a set of outcomes of condition tests, together with the related actions.

A decision table may be prepared from a procedure narrative by underlining all conditions present with a solid line and all actions with a broken line. The conditions and actions are then recorded on the decision table.

The features of a decision table are as follows.

(a) Each condition and action stub contains a limited entry, that is to say an entry complete in itself.

(b) The entry part of the table in respect of the condition stub indicates if a particular rule satisfies the condition.

(c) The entry part of the table is respect of the action stub indicates the action required in respect of the condition entry.

(d) Three symbols are used in the condition entry part of the table:

    (i) Y (yes) if the condition is satisfied;

    (ii) N (no) if the condition is not satisfied;

    (iii) - (hyphen), if the condition is not relevant to the rule.

(e) In the action entry part of the table an x is recorded to signify a required action. If no action is required the column is left blank.

27.11.2 Extended entry decision table

An extended entry decision table only partly records conditions and actions in the stub. The remaining details are recorded in the entry sections. This type of table is more compact and less complex to understand than a limited entry decision table but is less easy to check for completeness. Compare Fig. 27.7 with 27.8 for an indication of the difference between a limited entry and extended entry table.

27.11.3 When to prepare and use a decision table

A decision table may be used to assist the preparation of a program flowchart when the detailed logic involves a number of complex decisions. This ensures that all possible combinations and actions are met. The program flowchart is then prepared on the basis of one rule at a time working through the decision table. Decision tables may be used when programmer time is limited and the available software permits the direct input of decision tables.

		RULES			
		1	2	3	4
CONDITION STUB		CONDITION ENTRY			
SALES REGION CODE ⩾ £50		Y	Y	N	N
INVOICE AMOUNT ⩾ £1000		Y	N	Y	N
ACTION STUB		ACTION ENTRY			
DELIVERY CHARGES					
ADD £15 TO INVOICE TOTAL				X	
ADD £20 TO INVOICE TOTAL		X			
ADD £30 TO INVOICE TOTAL					X
ADD £40 TO INVOICE TOTAL			X		

Figure 27.7 Limited entry decision table

SALES REGION CODE	⩾ 50	⩾ 50	< 50	< 50
INVOICE AMOUNT £	⩾ 1000	< 1000	⩾ 1000	< 1000
DELIVERY CHARGES	£20	£40	£15	£30

Figure 27.8 Extended entry decision table

27.12 Decision tables and program flowcharts

27.12.1 Decision table and flowchart exercise 1

Stockists Ltd calculates discounts allowed to customers on the following basis:

Order Quantity	% Normal discount
1 – 99	5
100 – 199	7
200 – 499	9
500 and over	10

These discounts apply only if the customer's account balance is below £500 and does not include any item older than three months. If the account is outside both these limits, the above discounts are reduced by 2 per cent. If only one condition is violated, the discounts are reduced by 1 per cent. A customer who has been trading with Stockists Ltd for over five years and conforms to both of the above credit checks is allowed an additional 1 per cent discount.

You are required to:

(a) construct a limited entry decision table illustrating the above situation; and
(b) draw a flowchart illustrating the above situation.

Solution: The solution to this question is illustrated in Figs. 27.9 and 27.10

CONDITION STUB	RULES																			
	1	2	3	4	5	6	7	8	9	10	11	12	13	14	15	16	17	18	19	20
	CONDITION ENTRIES																			
ORDER QUANTITY 1–99	Y	Y	Y	Y	Y	–	–	–	–	–	–	–	–	–	–	–	–	–	–	–
ORDER QUANTITY 100–199	–	–	–	–	–	Y	Y	Y	Y	Y	–	–	–	–	–	–	–	–	–	–
ORDER QUANTITY 200–499	–	–	–	–	–	–	–	–	–	–	Y	Y	Y	Y	Y	–	–	–	–	–
ORDER QUANTITY 500 AND OVER	–	–	–	–	–	–	–	–	–	–	–	–	–	–	–	Y	Y	Y	Y	Y
ACCOUNT BALANCE < £500	N	N	Y	Y	N	N	N	Y	Y	Y	N	N	Y	N	Y	N	N	Y	N	N
ANY ITEM OLDER THAN 3 MONTHS	Y	N	Y	Y	N	Y	N	–	–	Y	N	–	–	–	Y	N	–	–	Y	N
TRADING FOR OVER 5 YEARS	–	–	–	Y	N	–	–	–	–	Y	N	–	–	–	Y	N	–	–	–	N
ACTION STUB	ACTION ENTRIES																			
NORMAL DISCOUNT 5%	X	X	X	X	X															
NORMAL DISCOUNT 7%						X	X	X	X	X										
NORMAL DISCOUNT 9%											X	X	X	X	X					
NORMAL DISCOUNT 10%																X	X	X	X	X
NORMAL DISCOUNT −2%	X					X					X					X				
NORMAL DISCOUNT −1%		X	X				X	X				X	X				X	X		
NORMAL DISCOUNT +1%				X					X					X					X	

Figure 27.9 Solution to decision table and flowchart exercise 1: decision table

27.12.2 Decision table and flowchart exercise 2

A soft drinks manufacturer sells to three sales outlets:

(a) supermarkets and large departmental stores;
(b) retailers;
(c) hotels and catering establishments.

Dependent upon the sales outlet and the value of sales, the following chart indicates the discounts allowed to customers.

Supermarkets and large departmental stores:	*Discount Allowed %*
For orders less than £50	5
For orders £50 and over but less than £100	8
For orders £100 and over	10

Retailers:	*Discount Allowed %*
For orders less than £50	3
For orders £50 and over but less than £100	7
For orders £100 and over	10

Hotels and catering establishments:	*Discount Allowed %*
For orders less than £50	4
For orders £50 and over but less than £100	7.5
For orders £100 and over	10

(a) From the information given, construct a 'limited entry' decision table and flowchart.
(b) What advantages are there from the use of decision tables?

Solution: The solution to the question is outlined in Figs. 27.11 and 27.12

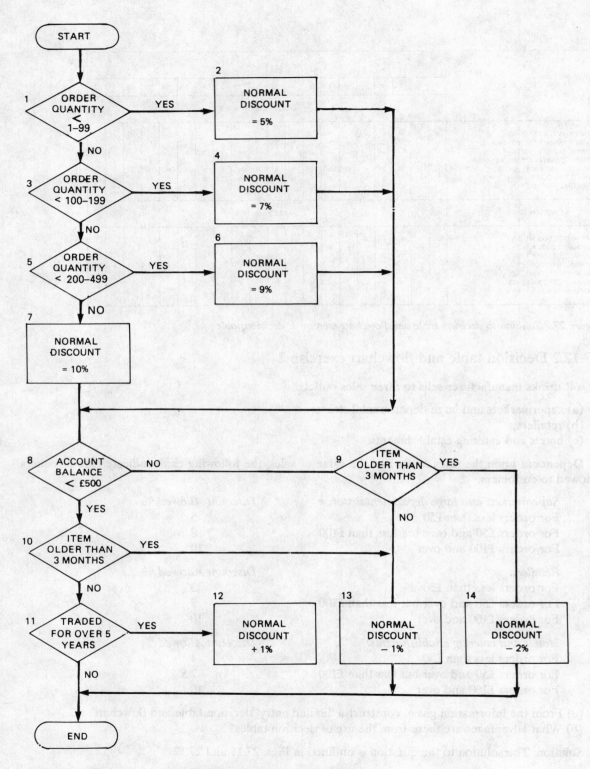

Figure 27.10 Solution to decision table and flowchart exercise 1: flowchart

	1	2	3	4	5	6	7
CONDITION STUB	CONDITION ENTRY						
ORDER ≥ £100	N	N	N	N	N	N	Y
RETAILER	Y	Y	N	N	N	N	–
HOTEL & CATERING	–	–	Y	Y	N	N	–
S & L	–	–	–	–	Y	Y	–
ORDER < £50	Y	N	Y	N	Y	N	–
ACTION STUB	ACTION ENTRY						
DISCOUNT							
3%	X						
4%			X				
5%					X		
7%		X					
7½%				X			
8%						X	
10%							X

Figure 27.11 Solution to decision table and flowchart exercise 2: decision table

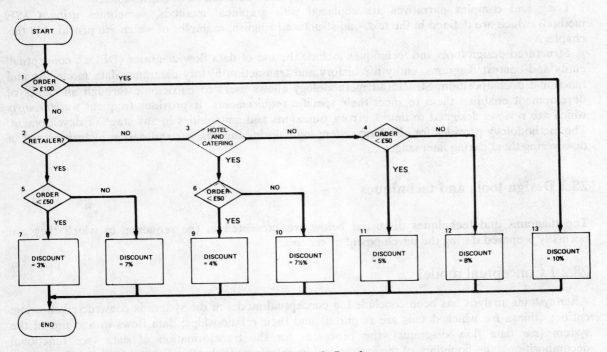

Figure 27.12 Solution to decision table and flowchart exercise 2: flowchart

Review questions

1   What are the nature and purpose of a flowchart?

2   How are system flowcharts constructed?

3   What are the nature and purpose of decision tables?

28 Structured design tools and techniques

28.1 Introduction

Structured methodology allows the system developer to accurately identify user information needs. It also provides management with a check list for reviewing project progress and for assessing both completed tasks and those which are due to be completed, referred to as deliverables.

Long and complex narratives are replaced with graphical methods, sometimes using CASE methods, which are defined in the text, and structured English, examples of which are provided in this chapter.

Structured design tools and techniques include the use of data flow diagrams (DFDs), conceptual, entity and context diagrams, entity life history and transaction history diagrams, data modelling and functional decomposition. Structured methodology allows users to participate through all stages of development enabling them to meet their specific requirements. It provides frequent *walkthroughs* which are reviews designed to detect errors, omissions and ambiguities in any stage of development. The methodology provides for checking system logic during the analysis and design phases instead of discovering them during later stages.

28.2 Design tools and techniques

The diagrams and techniques discussed below are presented in the sequence in which they are normally prepared during the development of systems.

28.2.1 Conceptual model

After systems analysis has been concluded, a conceptual model of the system is constructed showing: entities (things for which details are required) and their relationships; data flows in and out of the system (*see* data flow diagrams); the processes for the transformation of data (*see* functional decomposition); the boundary of the system and its interfaces with other related systems. Figure 28.1 portrays a conceptual model of a holiday booking system.

28.2.2. Entity life history diagram

An entity life history diagram specifies for each entity the events which modify or update its data. It is important to know what event (logical transaction) will trigger the creation of an entity. Such transactions may include a new record added to a file (insertion), an event that will change the status of the entity (modification), an event that will require an entity to be amended (updated) or one which will eliminate it (deletion). Figure 28.2 shows an entity life history in respect of a holiday booking system.

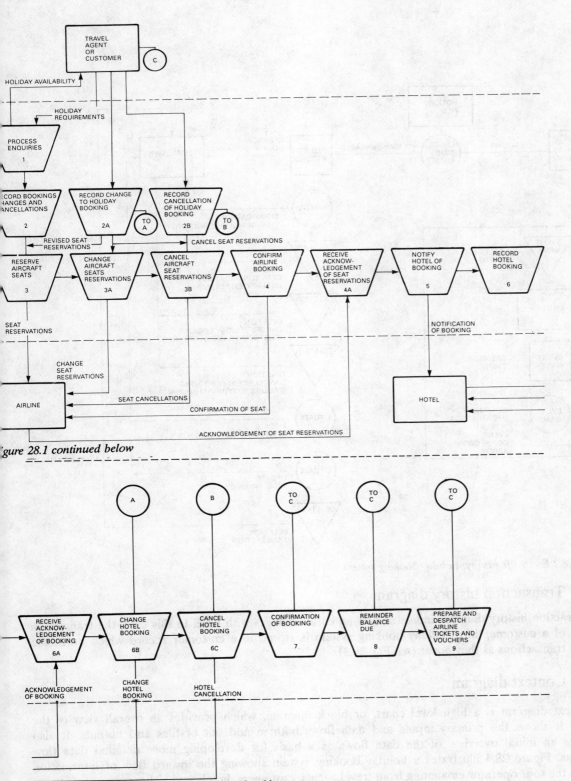

Figure 28.1 continued below

Figure 28.1 Conceptual model for holiday booking system.

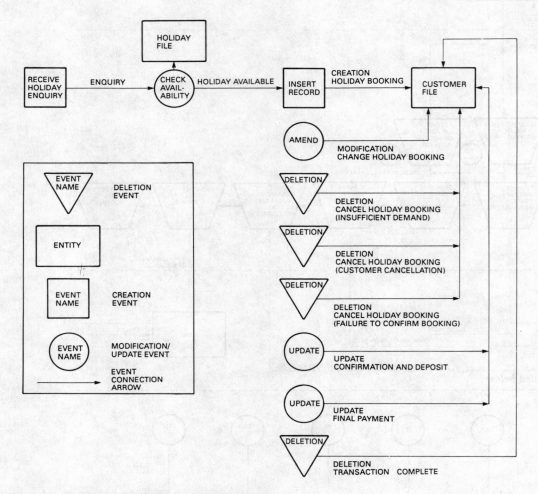

Figure 28.2 Entity life history: holiday booking system

28.2.3 Transaction history diagram

A transaction history diagram indicates how an entity changes with time. In this case, the transaction history of a customer in a holiday booking system is stored in a customer record which notes the various transactions as they occur (*see* Fig. 28.3).

28.2.4 Context diagram

A context diagram is a high level chart, or block diagram, which provides an overall view of the system. It shows the primary inputs and data flows both in and out of files and outputs. It also provides an initial overview of the data flows as a basis for developing more detailed data flow diagrams. Figure 28.4 illustrates a holiday booking system showing the inward flow of information to/from the tour operator emanating from travel agents, customers, hotels and airlines.

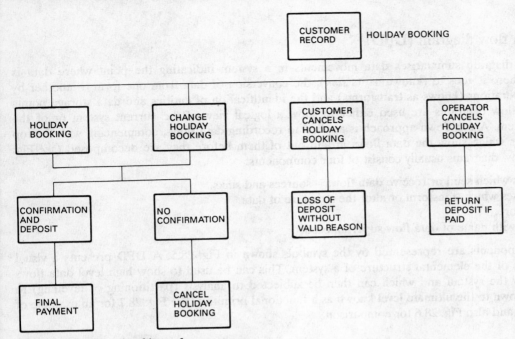

Figure 28.3: Transaction history for a customer

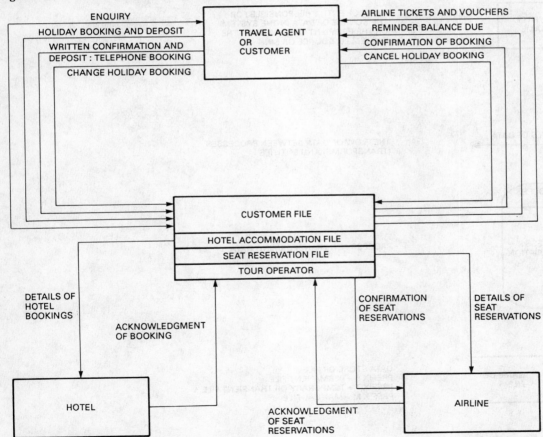

Figure 28.4 Context diagram: holiday booking system

28.2.5 Data flow diagram (DFD)

A data flow diagram summarises data movements in a system indicating the point where data is originated; where it goes to (known as its *sink*); the conversion of data from one form to another by processing operations (knows as transforms) and the identification of entities and data storage points (files). Data flow diagrams are used either to show a logical view of the current system or of the proposed system. A top-down approach is applied to recording data flows, commencing with the top level functions which show the data flows in and out of them before they are decomposed (*see* Fig. 28.6). Data flow diagrams usually consist of four components:

(a) Entities which send or receive data flows – sources and sinks.
(b) Processes which transform or alter the structure of data.
(c) Data store.
(d) Arrow with name of data flow superimposed.

These components are represented by the symbols shown in Fig. 28.5. A DFD presents a visual representation of the elemental structure of a system. This can be used to show high level data flows which simplify the system and which can then be subjected to analysis (partitioning or levelling) to define them down to the ultimate level known as a functional primitive. *See* Fig. 28.7 for an example of levelling-refer and also Fig. 28.6 for comparison.

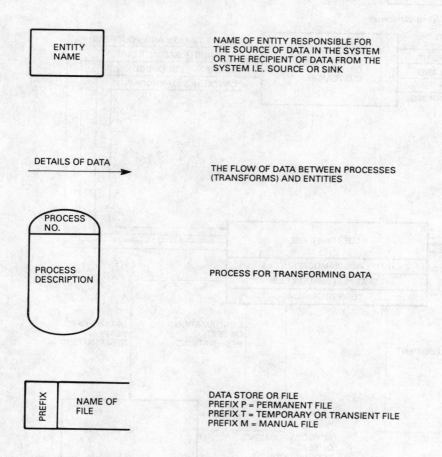

Figure 28.5 Symbols for constructing data flow diagrams

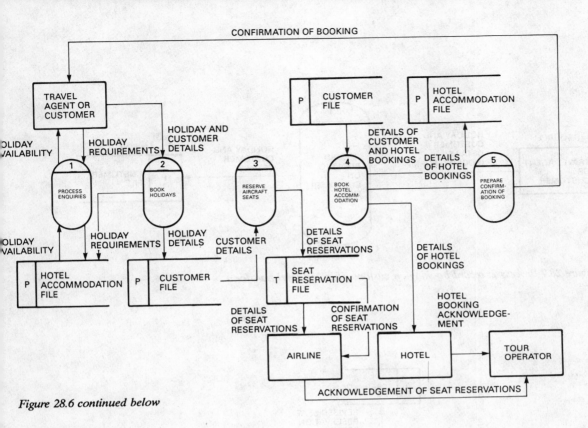

Figure 28.6 continued below

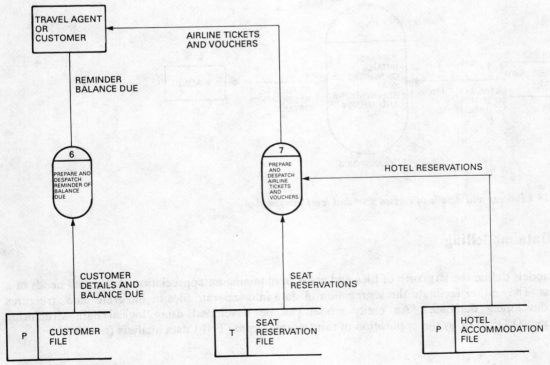

Figure 28.6 Parent data flow diagram: holiday booking system

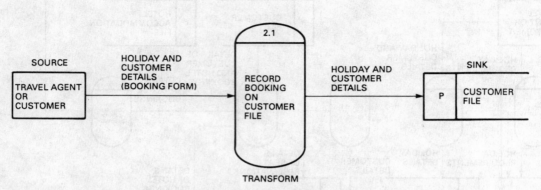

Figure 28.7 Process 2: record booking on customer file 2nd level transform

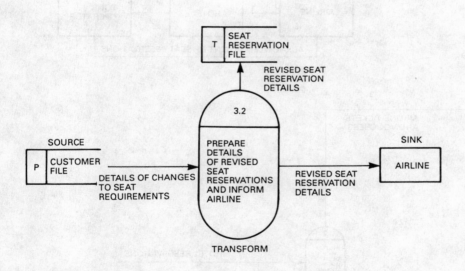

Figure 28.8 Process and details of revised seat 2nd level transform

28.3 Data modelling

Data models define the structure of files and assist in obtaining an appreciation of the data needs of a business. They either facilitate the segregation of data into separate files or integrate data structures when developing databases. An entity model can be developed using logical data structuring techniques (LDST) or by the application of third normal form (TNF) data analysis (*see* 28.3.2).

28.3.1 Logical data structuring

An entity diagram is a logical data model which identifies the principal entity types involved in running a business. In respect of a holiday booking system entities include travel agents, customers, hotels and airlines (*see* figure 28.9). An entity diagram specifies the relationships which exist between entities and the type of data flowing between them. It is necessary to analyse the system under development to identify those items which represent data groups forming a record or entity.

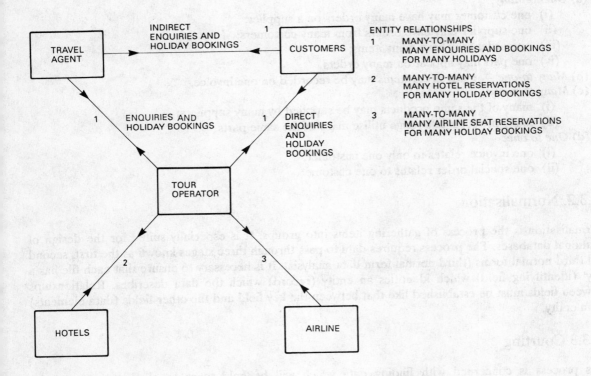

Figure 28.9 Entity diagram – (logical data model): level 1, holiday booking system

Entity diagrams (models)
These consist of three basic components:

    (a) entities,
    (b) attributes,
    (c) relationships.

Entity relationships

Referring to Fig. 28.9 of the holiday booking system it will be observed that all relationships are many-to-many:

(a) Many enquiries are received from many customers by the tour operator for many different holidays.
(b) Many hotel reservations are made to many hotels by the tour operator for many customers.
(c) Many airline seat reservations are made by the tour operator for many customers.

The various entities which exist in an application environment will be interrelated either directly or indirectly. In order to show which entity is dependent upon another the convention is to define one data group as a master and another as a detail. Figure 28.9 uses arrows pointing from the master entity, the tour operator, to the detail entities, travel agent, customers, hotels and airlines.

Examples of other entity relationships

(a) *One-to-many*:
    (i) one customer may have many orders on a supplier;
    (ii) one supplier may have orders from many customers;
    (iii) one order may have many items;
    (iv) one part may appear on many orders.
(b) *Many-to-one* — many order items may be recorded on one invoice.
(c) *Many-to-many*:
    (i) many of the same products may be supplied by many suppliers;
    (ii) many products in a range utilise many of the same parts.
(d) *One to one*:
    (i) one invoice relates to only one customer;
    (ii) one special order relates to one customer.

28.3.2. Normalisation

Normalisation is the process of gathering items into groups. It is especially suited for the design of relational databases. The process requires data to pass through three stages known as the first, second and third normal forms (third normal form data analysis). It is necessary to ensure that each file has a 'key' (identifying field) which identifies an entity (record) which the data describes. Relationships between fields must be established like that between the key field and the other fields (data elements) of an entity.

28.3.3 Courting

This process is concerned with finding data which will be held twice to eliminate unnecessary redundancy. This could apply in a stock control system whereby one data structure stores 'basic stock data' and another stores 'usage history data'. They would both contain common fields, i.e. item code and description. In addition, when items are issued from the stores it affects the field 'quantity in stock' in the 'basic stock data' store and the 'usage to date' field in the 'usage history data'. Both could be merged which would avoid inputting the same unit of data twice. When common keys occur in data structures, as in this case, it is probable that the same entity is under consideration from two points of view. This indicates that the structures should be reviewed with an eye to merging. The important point to consider is 'relationships', i.e. courting.

28.4 Functional decomposition

A decomposition diagram analyses high level definitions of a function into more detailed functions for further analysis. The decomposition diagram of this process forms an inverted tree structure. Figure 28.10 illustrates the first level of functions for a holiday booking system and Fig. 28.11 outlines the functions after being decomposed to the second level, providing more detail of the data transforms (processing operations) required by the system.

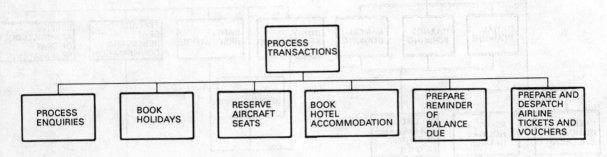

Figure 28.10 Functional decomposition; level 1: holiday booking system

28.5 Data dictionary

A data dictionary provides textual support and gives a precise definition of all data represented in the various models. It does this by defining the meaning (semantics) composition (syntax) and important characteristics of flows and stores on data flow diagrams and objects and relationships on entity diagrams. The dictionary serves as a central definition catalogue that provides uniformity of expression among analysts and simplifies future analysis and revision. A dictionary can be compiled by computer-aided systems engineering (CASE) tools automatically when preparing diagrams or by direct entry to dictionary screens, etc. The data dictionary is expanded throughout system design to include new or modified record structures and their relationships including reference keys, size of data elements, data validation requirements and a description of data items. Most dictionaries are computerised forming an element of database management systems.

28.6 Automated approach to systems development

Businesses today must take every opportunity to develop efficient and effective information systems to accomplish a defined level of performance, quality assurance, speedy access to information and cost effective system operation. In order to achieve these goals and improve the productivity of systems development automated methodology should be implemented using CASE tools, i.e. computer-aided systems engineering. The use of such tools reduces the time required for systems development. The detailed preparation of diagrams, charts and data dictionaries are delegated to the computer resulting in superior quality computer systems produced much more quickly than by less sophisticated techniques. These factors ensure that the user has quality and acceptable outputs whereas the management and systems developers obtain the benefits of increased productivity. CASE tools generate increased profitability and a short pay-off period as more projects can be undertaken in a given time than by using traditional methods.

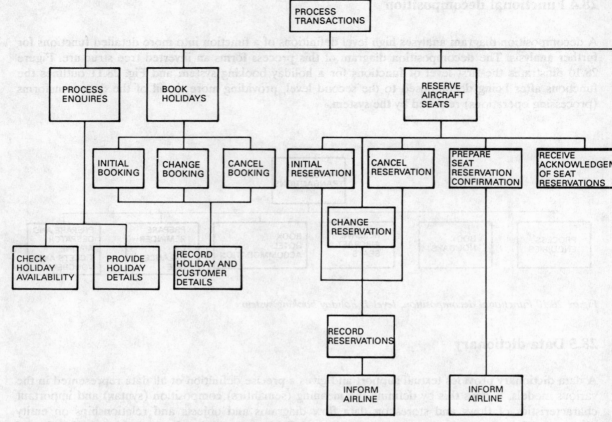

Figure 28.11 Functional decomposition: level 2: Holiday Booking System

General benefits of case tools

   (a) Development productivity increased.
   (b) Development costs have a shorter pay-back period.
   (c) Quality assurance improved.
   (d) Deliverable outputs in a shorter time period.

Review questions

1   What is a conceptual model?

2   What is an entity life history diagram?

3   What is a transaction history diagram?

4   What is the purpose of a context diagram?

5   What is the purpose of data modelling?

6   What is a functional decomposition diagram?

7   What are CASE tools?

8   What is the purpose of data analysis?

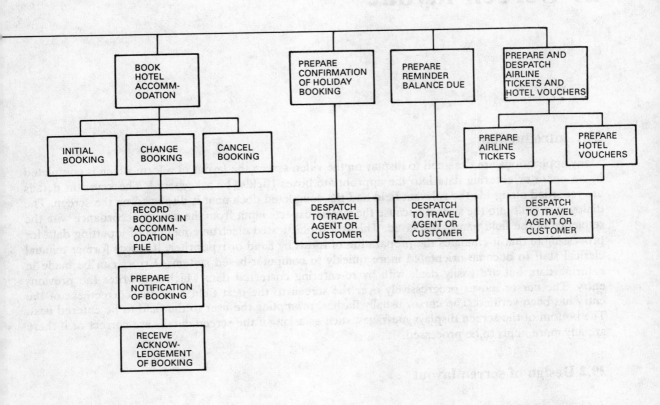

9 What is a data flow diagram used for?

10 What is the purpose of an entity diagram?

11 What is normalisation?

12 What is courting?

13 What information is contained in a data dictionary?

14 What is a system definition?

Self-test question

28.1 Give a brief outline of the nature and purpose of structured design methodology and indicate how it differs from the traditional systems life cycle approach to systems design.

Answers on pages 392–4.

29 Screen layout

29.1 Introduction

Many applications are designed to display on the video screen the layout of a form which is completed by an operator entering data into the appropriate boxes (fields) by a keyboard. The keyed-in details are recorded alongside the relevant field and the completed document is displayed on the screen. The dialogue is built into the system because the system expects input from the user in accordance with the sequence of the field names displayed. This is a sophisticated electronic method of inputting data for processing in that it emulates the preparation of forms by hand or typewriter. It assists former manual clerical staff to become orientated more quickly to computer-based systems. Errors can be made in entering data but are easily dealt with by re-entering corrected data which overwrites the previous entry. The cursor moves progressively over the screen to the next field after the correctness of the entry has been verified. The cursor usually flashes, prompting the user to the field to be entered next. The bottom of the screen displays messages, such as asking if the screen details are correct or if there are any more items to be processed.

29.2 Design of screen layout

A form to be displayed on a video screen should be designed on a screen layout form and should be authenticated as follows:

(a) title of the screen, e.g. order-entry screen;
(b) name of the program activating the screen, e.g. ORDS;
(c) author;
(d) date of compilation.

The layout form should take into account the screen width, measured by the number of characters which can be displayed on a line — typically 80 — and the screen depth, measured by the number of lines which can be displayed, typically 24. Data fields should be located in a logical sequence. The left-hand side of the screen can be designed to display fixed data fields such as names, addresses and account/code references which need to be validated. On the right-hand side of the screen may be structured transaction details, such as quantities, and item details as in the case of an order-entry screen (*see* Fig. 29.1). The use of screens normally commences with the display of menus for the selection of alternative routines. This aspect is outlined below.

29.3 Menu selection

Many business applications display a menu for selecting alternative options, which serves the same purpose as a dialogue but avoids the need to type in messages or commands to inform the system of the type of processing to be done.

Menus are explicit and simple to understand because the user is able to follow the details displayed on the screen without difficulty. This leaves little to be learned by the user in order to operate the system efficiently as it is unnecessary to learn complex commands.

29.3.1 Option selection

Options can be selected in several ways:

(a) locate the cursor adjacent to the required option and press the *enter* or *return* key on the keyboard;

(b) key in *number* specifying the required option;

(c) use a *mouse* to point to the desired option on a pull-down menu;

(d) a touch-screen facility enables the user to point with a finger to the desired option on a pull-down menu.

Menus may list the various applications such as sales, purchase ledger or stock control, or routines within an application from which a choice may be made. A menu listing various routines of a stock control system is shown below.

Stock control
Main menu

Stock transactions	1
Stock enquiries	2
End of day processing	3
Reports	4
Product file maintenance	5
System maintenance	6
Exit	Carriage return

Please select required option

Menus are organised hierarchically with options grouped according to function or sub-routine.

Sales order processing
Main menu

Transaction entry	1
Order processing	2
Order reporting	3
End of session	4
Sales analysis reporting	5
Product maintenance	6
System maintenance	7
Exit	8

Please select a function

If a sales office clerk needs to process orders, option 2 is selected by pressing the relevant key on the keyboard for access to the order processing routine. This causes the order processing sub-menu to be displayed as shown below:

Please select a function

In this instance, the sales office clerk presses the '1' key to select 'process orders by customer', which then displays the screen as shown in Fig. 29.1.

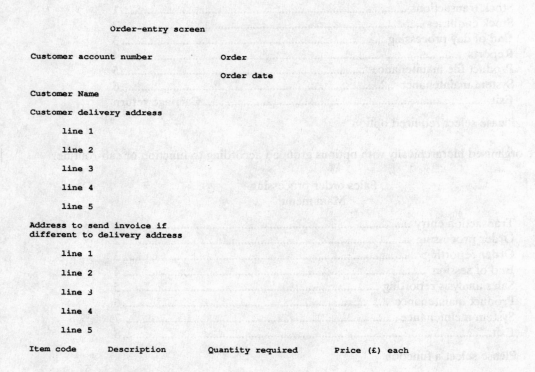

```
            Order-entry screen


Customer account number              Order

                                     Order date

Customer Name
Customer delivery address

      line 1

      line 2

      line 3

      line 4

      line 5

Address to send invoice if
different to delivery address

      line 1

      line 2

      line 3

      line 4

      line 5

Item code    Description      Quantity required     Price (£) each
```

Figure 29.1 Order-entry screen

Data is input via the keyboard for each field and the completed order appears as shown in Fig. 29.2.

```
                Order-entry screen

Customer account number 6754        Order No    12345

                                    Order date  31/12/88

Customer Name A B Smith plc

Customer delivery address

     line 1       Monarch Way Factory Estate

     line 2       Unit 1

     line 3       Hadlington Street

     line 4       Anywhere

     line 5       YT7 9FD

Address to send invoice if
different to delivery address

     line 1

     line 2

     line 3

     line 4

     line 5

Item code     Description      Quantity required      Price (£) each

  876         Volmeter                5                    10
  877         Ammeter                 2                    12
```

Figure 29.2 Completed order-entry screen

As each field is entered validation checks are performed, one of which requires the product file to be accessed to check that item codes are correct and match the description. Checks will also be made to ensure that the type of data being entered is correct, e.g the customer name field should be alphabetic characters whereas the item code and price fields should be numeric characters. Errors are signalled by reverse video (characters are displayed in the opposite background and foreground colours to normal displays — white characters on a black background instead of black on white, for instance) or flashing the field in error.

The bottom of the screen displays messages such as asking if the screen details are correct or if there are any more items to be processed. It is important to appreciate that the system may incorporate inbuilt credit checking, triggered when the customer account number is entered, which causes the customer's account to be accessed in the sales ledger.

When orders are prepared in this way the details may be printed out as an internal order document instructing the warehouse as to the items to despatch to customers. It is more likely, however, that once the details have been input and validated they will be recorded on an orders file stored on magnetic disc for batch processing prior to sorting the items into product code (item code) for checking stock availability. If on-line transaction processing is applied then after order details have been input, validated and corrected they are transmitted to the processor for further processing, bypassing disc storage which is unnecessary for this type of processing.

Review questions

1   How would you set about designing a form to be displayed on a video screen?

2   Menu options can be selected in several different ways. Outline details of four such ways.

3   What are sub-menus?

4   Outline the layout of an order-entry screen.

Self-test question

29.1   Give details of the type of screen dialogue that could be appropriate for a senior manager who needs summarised information occasionally from a system.

Answer on pages 394–6.

30 Dialogue design

30.1 Introduction

Dialogues need to be user friendly, guiding the user through the routines with the aid of HELP facilities, which display explanations on the video screen or provide references to the system manual in response to the user pressing the HELP key. Dialogues can be selected at several levels to suit the experience of the user and can take a variety of forms, listed below. A dialogue provides the interface for the interactive processing of data by responding to prompts from the computer or a means of extracting information from expert systems or databases.

30.2 Command selection keys

A dialogue may consist of abbreviated commands, which speeds up their entry to the computer. When using spreadsheet software, for instance, a series of options may be shown at the bottom of the screen. Details of the options are contained in the manual but, as an example of their use, if the S key (an abbreviation for SAVE) is pressed, the spreadsheet is saved on disc. If it is required to clear the worksheet from the workspace Z, an abbreviation for ZAP, does this.

30.3 Fourth generation languages and expert systems

The knowledge of experts is contained in the knowledge base of an expert system and is available to the non-expert by responding to questions asked by the system. The dialogue is targeted or addressed by the user directly to the problem to be solved. Such a facility provides everyone in an organisation with expert knowledge simply by sitting at the keyboard of a terminal, small business computer or work station. Expert systems may provide details of company procedural and policy matters for granting credit to customers, handling customers' orders, rules for computing corporation tax and granting loans to employees, etc. For further details refer to Chapter 10.

30.4 Searching a database using keywords

A database has searching facilities which allow related facts to be extracted, via the keyboard, by searching using a keyword. This provides the means of obtaining from a large volume of data useful facts which could not possibly be found by physical search methods in sufficient time on which to base a decision.

30.5 Extracting information from a database by commands or menu selection

Information can be extracted from a database by use of commands or menu selection. A DBMS is software for database management activities including updating, deleting, adding, amending, validating, sorting, searching and printing selected records from the database. This is accomplished by selecting the required option from a menu displayed on the video screen or by keying in the relevant command from the keyboard.

30.6 Retrieval of information by keypad or keyboard

Public databases such as Prestel provide valuable business information relating to particular subjects such as share prices, travel information, weather and general information relating to business, finance, economics, engineering, technology and science, etc. Information can be retrieved by terminals linked to the host computer supporting the database via the telephone network or the packet switched stream (PSS) network, which allows users to access distant databases more economically. To obtain information from Prestel the user telephones his or her nearest Prestel computer by pressing a single button on the keypad. Information selection is accomplished by using either a keypad or a keyboard to key in the page number. The pages of information are linked together so that each page can lead to other pages.

30.7 Natural language systems

30.7.1 Accounting applications

You should refer back to Chapter 19: *see* 19.13.1.

30.7.2 Database query systems based on natural language

A natural English language database query and retrieval system is used for query and *ad hoc* reporting. It provides easy and instant access to information: when a user asks a question the system retrieves the data, computes and presents the information in a sophisticated columnar display on the video screen. This type of system requires English conversion of the data dictionary describing the database into a lexicon which lists alphabetically all the words and phrases used. The lexicon is used for reference purposes during the processing of natural language queries. This type of query language responds to questions phrased, for example: How many cars of each model did we sell last week compared to target?

The system retrieves from the database the target and actual sales for each model and displays them on the screen together with the actual and planned sales and percentage deviation from the planned sales for each model.

30.8 Fourth generation languages

Fourth generation languages are covered in Chapter 9 (*see* 9.6 and 9.10.3) and Chapter 19 (*see* 19.13).

Review questions

1   A dialogue may consist of the use of command keys for selecting options. Discuss.

2   A dialogue may consist of using keywords for extracting facts from a database. Discuss.

3   Menus may be used for database management activities. Discuss.

4   A dialogue may take the form of pressing buttons on a keypad to retrieve information from a public database. Discuss.

5   Dialogue may take the form of a natural language. Discuss. (*See* Chapter 19.)

6   Fourth generation languages are designed to assist the manipulation of a database by way of a query language. Discuss.

Self-test question

30.1   A sales office entry clerk enters orders into an on-line order processing system. Describe the type of screen dialogue that might be suitable for such work.

Answers on pages 396–7.

Answers to self-test questions

4.1   *Strategic planning*

Business strategy is concerned with how a company proposes to achieve its objectives from various options. Establishing a suitable strategy depends on information relating to the company's strengths and weaknesses so that future plans can incorporate major strengths and minimise the effects of its weaknesses. Strategy must also take into account an assessment of risk and constraints to specific courses of action. Strategic decisions often have long-range consequences, especially when concerned with developing new products, building new factories and warehouses or extending existing premises. In these instances information is required on the available or potential market for new products, trends in building costs and development grants available for specific areas of the country and so on. Information is also required on product life cycles so that plans can be made to change over products at the most opportune time in order to maintain or increase profits and overall profitability. The degree of competition is always of paramount interest and information relating to market intelligence is essential. In addition, information is required in relation to developments in the economic, technological, financial, sociological and legislative spheres so that strategy can be formulated within the framework of company policies which take these factors into account.

Tactical planning

Information for tactical planning is obtained by analysing the strategic plans into greater detail in respect of production, sales, expenditure, stocks, purchases, personnel and plant and machinery. The tactical planning activity needs to consider planning in a number of spheres, notably planning an effective organisation structure for achieving corporate objectives; product-market development planning; resource development planning; capital expenditure project planning and operational planning. Such plans establish the *tactics* to be employed in pursuit of strategic objectives. They are prepared by functional managers responsible for defined objectives as a means of achieving the overall objectives of the business.

Business control

Control information emanates from well-structured, standard, routine systems including quality, budgetary, cost, credit, stock and production control systems. They all incorporate a common feature, that is, management by exception, as they function on the basis of variances, i.e. deviations from a specified target or standard of performance.

4.2   (a) Top management

As a general guide, or rule of thumb, information density and volume vary according to the position of the recipient in the hierarchical management structure. For example, at chairmanship level information must be very broad in scope enveloping the key factors which pinpoint the economic and financial health of the business. These include profit comparisons with previous periods to obtain an appreciation of current trends as a basis for taking remedial action when necessary and in the most relevant way. The state of the order book is also of extreme importance as it indicates the possible level of future profits or losses which assist in pinpointing the need for strategic decisions.

The trend of cash flows is an important key factor as it indicates the financial health of the business and assists in determining the extent to which *lines of credit* must be drawn upon and whether the situation indicates a need for short-term finance by way of overdraft facilities, or whether a share flotation is more appropriate for long-term growth and development.

Current share prices are also of great concern, reflecting as they do the financial standing of the business, which has a bearing on future share flotations and the value of the business on a going concern basis. Share prices also provide an indicator of possible takeover overtures.

The managing director requires similar information, but also needs details of functional achievements covering the main operating areas of the business. Such information includes details of budgeted and actual income and expenditure, the latter embracing both capital and revenue; progress of contracts, jobs or projects; sales trends; level of production against targets; extent of competition measured by market share, and other information for use in corporate strategic planning and policy determination. Much information is derived from the use of forecasting techniques and spreadsheets and other modelling techniques using micros as part of decision support facilities on an end-user basis. Such techniques provide the means for assessing the viability of a number of alternative, mutually exclusive, options having inbuilt factors for assessing uncertainty and risk on a defined probability basis.

(b) Middle management

This level of management requires information summaries relating to the departments comprising their functional responsibilities in sufficient detail to enable them to apply whatever measures are required to bring situations into line with requirements. Information is required for tactical planning, including the planned use of resources to achieve specified objectives, and information relating to operations as they are taking place, rather than afterwards, so that appropriate action is taken to control events while they are current and not historic – what has happened cannot be remedied for past periods but can of course be used as a basis of modifying future actions on a *feedforward* basis. Depending upon the nature of the business middle (functional) management require details appertaining to operating expenses, manpower levels – current and projected – plant capacity, spare capacity, amount of capital expenditure incurred on various projects and the level of productivity being attained, the cost per unit of output and the incidence of scrapped production and so on. Information is often provided on an exception basis in the form of operating statements showing budgeted and actual results together with variances for both the current period and for the year to date. Such statements may also include comparative figures for the same period of the previous year to indicate trends.

(c) Supervisory management

This level of management requires information of a very detailed nature relating to specific orders, operations, personnel, materials, parts and costs, etc., as they are needed to pinpoint entities that require some action on the part of management to rectify adverse situations. Accordingly, management need to know about the efficiency of individuals so as to take direct positive action to improve it as it is not possible to do this on a global basis. Similarly, it is necessary to know cost variances on specific items rather than in total for all costs in order to control them. It is also necessary to know the stock position of each item in the stores to avoid unfortunate stock out situations on the one hand and overstocking on the other. In the same context credit control can be effective only by being aware of the account status of individual customers.

4.3   Individual businesses require information according to the nature of their operations. A car manufacturer is particularly interested in the extent of competition from overseas manufacturers and, to a lesser degree, from home-based manufacturers. A tour operator is concerned about purchasing power and its effect on holiday bookings, and the political situation prevailing in various countries. The following summary will highlight the key facts required by a cross-section of typical businesses to enable them to operate intelligently:

Car manufacturer
(a) Extent of competition from overseas manufacturers.
(b) Technological developments.
(c) Current styling trends.
(d) Success of productivity packages.
(e) Share of market achieved compared with that required.

Tour operator
(a) Status of hotels in various countries and resorts.
(b) Medical facilities and health hazards in various countries.
(c) Political unrest in countries and its likely repercussions on holiday centres.

(d) Expected level of future costs of package holidays in the light of inflationary trends and the cost of fuel for aircraft operations.

(e) Availability of holiday accommodation at all resorts at all times.

Stockbroker

(a) Movement of share prices.

(b) State of money market.

(c) Economic climate.

(d) Climate in particular industries.

Building society

(a) Clients overdue with mortgage repayments.

(b) Balances on customer investment, share and mortgage accounts.

(c) Likely trend in interest rates and its effect on building society funds.

(d) Trend in house prices.

(e) Government policy relating to mortgage levels.

5.1 Data may be defined as the details relating to business transactions which are collected and input to a data processing system to produce a defined output. Data can therefore be identified immediately as being *input* to a data processing system which produces *output*. Output, providing it serves a useful purpose in the decision making process, is classed as *information*.

Examples of business data include hours worked by employees; number of units of specific items ordered by particular customers; number of items received of a particular commodity from a specific supplier, and so on.

The result of processing data into a meaningful form is, as stated, classified as information. Information is the lifeblood of business and plays an ever increasing part in day-to-day management. Information may be output from a data processing system in printed form, displayed graphically on a video screen or plotted in the form of graphs by a graph plotter. Printed output may take the form of exception reports or complete lists of entities, such as items in stock or orders in progress on the shop floor, etc. All types of printed output are classified generally as *reports*.

The term information processing is probably more appropriate than the term data processing. Information processing recognises that the end product of processing data is information, whereas the term data processing apparently signifies that processing data is an end in itself. Information processing includes all those activities concerned with the transition of a set of uncorrelated facts into a meaningful correlated whole, in the form of a report. The preparation of the report may involve subjecting the data to various operations including: verification, validation, sorting and merging, computing, comparing, updating and printing.

Desirable properties of management information are that it:

(a) must serve a useful purpose;

(b) must be relevant to the responsibilities of specific managers to enable them to control operations effectively;

(c) must contain an appropriate level of detail for the level of management;

(d) must relate to current circumstances as outdated information is not only useless but dangerous as wrong decisions may be made; dynamic information systems rather than static systems are essential;

(e) must have an acceptable level of accuracy – not necessarily complete accuracy;

(f) must be available at the right time to comply with the response time needs of the system being controlled;

(g) must be based on the exception principle when appropriate;

(h) must be produced at an acceptable level of cost;

(i) must be easily understood;

(j) must avoid unnecessary redundancy.

There are three different types of information system: the traditional data processing system, the office support system and the end-user system, an integral element of the *information centre* concept.

The traditional data processing system primarily consists of accounting applications for updating files and printing business documents. When the operations are extended to embrace analysis of the primary data and its comparison with budgets, standards or targets then it becomes an operational control system enabling management to control their sphere of responsibility by the provision of exception reports.

As the name implies office support systems support the day-to-day functions of office personnel, executives and managers as well as other professional personnel and secretaries. These systems incorporate facilities for increasing administrative productivity by such means as electronic mail for speeding up inter-office communications; electronic filing for speeding up the retrieval of information; efficient document copying facilities for image processing and the effective processing of text by word processing, etc.

End-user systems are also referred to as *decision support systems*, *executive support systems* and *professional support systems*. The end-user system has a primary objective of providing professionals, managers and executives with computing facilities to improve the performance of their work. This facility is provided within the concept of the *information centre* which enables users to gain access to their data from a database directly without the need to learn computer programming: software is user friendly allowing the use of English-style statements. By this means data can be downloaded from a database to the user's small computer for further processing, for forecasting, planning and modelling, using the tools provided. These include: a query language for accessing the database; a tool for extracting data from the computer files for transfer to the user's computer; a tool for defining new records; a report writer and a decision support system including electronic spreadsheets, modelling programs, statistical analysis programs, graphic display subsystems and data manipulation languages.

10.1 An expert system stores knowledge relating to a specific subject (field of knowledge) in a database which can be accessed and processed by software. Expert systems are also known as knowledge-based systems (KBS), which themselves form part of that branch of knowledge relating to artificial intelligence. They may be defined as computerised systems which simulate human knowledge by making deductions from given facts using the rules of logical inference. Rules define relationships between facts and may be defined as representations of human reasoning which in combination with an antecedent specify an inference on which to base a specified action. Details are input to the knowledge base in the form of 'production rules', each representing an individual item of knowledge. Expert systems may be used on a stand-alone basis or may be embedded into routine accounting applications.

Applications

Everyone in an organisation can be provided with expert knowledge, obtained from experts, by sitting at the keyboard of a small business computer using the expert system for the particular subject on which knowledge is required. The system asks the user questions as a means of obtaining information on which to base an answer by the process of inferencing from inbuilt rules. Expert systems can be designed to provide details of company procedures and policies for such matters as granting credit to customers, handling customers' orders, computing corporation tax, and granting loans to employees, etc. This is very useful to the efficiency of a business because it allows non-experts to obtain expert knowledge without consulting an expert personally. The knowledge of an expert relating to a particular domain (subject area) is built into the computer software for access by anyone needing such knowledge during the course of their business activities. Expert systems can be interfaced with routine data processing tasks performed by the batch or transaction processing applications, which call the inference engine when required. This may be performed when an expert system is required for determining discount based on the value of customers' orders and the delivery distance, for example, in an order processing system. An expert system may also be applied to determine sales strategy from information stored in the customer history file.

The elemental structure of an expert system consists of three primary elements:

(a) an inference engine, which acts as a rule interpreter;
(b) a knowledge base, which stores the specialised knowledge of human experts in the form of rules;
(c) a database containing facts relating to the status of a system of a particular domain, i.e. subject area.

Inferencing is the process of reaching a solution or decision by reasoning. An inference engine is an element of an expert system which functions in combination with the knowledge base. It is a program that directs the search for knowledge and determines the sources required for input: responses to questions from users, databases or spreadsheets to infer a conclusion to a problem.

The knowledge base stores knowledge of a specific subject in the form of rules consisting of facts and relationships. The inference engine questions the user and interprets the rules of relationship. It matches rules in the knowledge base with the information in the database. As each rule is examined and fired the resulting actions may amend the content of the database, which changes the status of the problem. The inference engine can communicate with the existing corporate database, programs or files in the process of seeking its goal.

The initial conditions of the problem to be solved are stored in the database from which the starting point of the search process is derived. It may ask questions of the user, to which answers are typed in, or it may display options in a menu from which the user can select the one required. In effect, the database is part of the working memory, storing information relating to the current status of the problem being solved, which may be altered by the inferencing process as stated above. Initially, known facts are stored in the database to which are added new facts as they are generated by the inference process.

11.1 The term 'office automation' relates to the harnessing of electronic technology, in all its different forms, to office activities. The term 'convergence' is used to define the integration of the various aspects of information technology: embracing the use of microcomputers for information processing and storage, including the use of software in the form of electronic spreadsheets and business modelling programs; word processors for preparing standard reports and other correspondence at high speed; electronic mail for the transmission of information from one office or site to another (without the use of paper) by means of data transmission lines linking microcomputers, word processors or work stations.

Silicon chips and the advances made in telecommunications have had a profound effect on the nature of office activities, which include all of those administrative activities concerned with the handling of information for the efficient conduct of business operations. Communications is the essential catalyst for integrating all the various office activities and functions. Teletex, the international text communication service, will play an important part in office automation as it will enable text transmissions to take place thirty times faster than telex. It will also provide the necessary standardisation to enable interworking of terminals from any manufacturer on a number of different networks.

Electronic technology enables documents, as well as normal business data relating to business transactions, to be stored on magnetic media in binary code generated by electronic signals. Filing cabinets, index cards and 'in' and 'out' trays may soon be redundant, due to advances in electronic storage techniques in the form of text filing and retrieval systems.

Multi-purpose work stations will generally replace those previously performing dedicated tasks because work stations incorporating the latest technology are capable of performing a number of different functions, and this enables them to handle data and information in the form of text, graphics or video displays. They also provide electronic mail facilities.

Digital PABX telephone exchanges are likely to have a great impact on office automation because of their ability to handle both voice and data transmissions and to function as message switching centres for terminals and other devices. They will also control the routing of data or text from work stations.

Information technology embraces the use of interactive 'viewdata' such as British Telecom's Prestel, and private internal viewdata systems such as ICL's Bulletin. These systems support a database for information retrieval requirements and operate in an interactive manner because, after information has been accessed, it is displayed on the screen of a television. The user can then, for example, book hotel accommodation or order goods from a supermarket by means of a keypad which transmits the required information to the relevant computer. This is accomplished by what is known as a 'response' page.

Local area networks consisting of combinations of work stations, word processors or microcomputers provide high data transmission speeds between the various devices on the network and allow printing and storage facilities to be shared.

Information technology also includes the technique of COM which allows computer output to be stored on microfilm or microfiche, which can be accessed by a viewer displaying images on a screen. Using this technique avoids the need to print all the output from a computer, thereby saving stationery costs and computer printing time. Facsimile document transmission allows detailed images such as drawings and graphs to be transmitted from one place to another at high speed.

Historical note. The idea of the electronic office was mooted in 1947 by Lyons, the British catering company, when they assessed the viability of computers for performing office activities. They did in fact build their own computer known as 'LEO', an acronym for Lyons Electronic Office, which became operational in 1951.

Notes to answer

1. Other terms broadly synonymous with 'electronic office' are 'office automation' and 'information technology'. It is important to be aware of this because questions may use either term in the context of office technological developments.

2. As can be seen from the details contained in the answer the electronic office is more than data processing by computer but in fact relates to electronic spreadsheets and modelling programs, teletex, electronic filing, multi-purpose work stations, digital PABX, interactive databases, local area networks, computer output on microfilm and facsimile document transmission, etc.

11.2 It must be appreciated that all personnel in a business will not readily accept change because many, particularly those approaching retirement age, are quite content to continue with the status quo. This is due to the fact that they feel comfortable with their duties and do not need to stretch their mind because the tasks they perform have become second nature to them over the years. Consequently they do not feel inclined to learn new ways of doing things with 'new fangled gadgets'. In addition, an element of laziness exists in some people who are decidedly not anxious to learn new ways of performing old tasks or modern ways of performing new tasks. Both groups may be defined as 'stick-in-the-muds'.

Personnel may become more enlightened if they are invited to attend informal technology meetings or participate in technology committees. In-house education and training programmes may also assist in overcoming resistance to change, particularly if personnel can see for themselves that their own area of work will benefit from the implementation of hi-tech facilities.

A number of situations and problems arise due to opposition to change, including:

   (a) overmanning;
   (b) inefficiency;
   (c) low productivity;
   (d) failure to meet objectives;
   (e) out-of-date methods, procedures and systems creating high processing costs;
   (f) uncompetitiveness due to all of the above factors.

There are a number of ways in which personnel may be encouraged to accept technological change, some of which are listed below:

   (a) inform personnel affected by pending changes of the reasons for such changes;
   (b) enlist the cooperation of personnel by friendly persuasion;
   (c) allow staff to participate in the development of systems, implementing their practical ideas when appropriate;
   (d) discuss objections to change and provide genuine reasons for such change – it must not be overlooked that any changes envisaged may be to the direct benefit of personnel due to the elimination of tedious tasks;
   (e) do not con people, be sincere;
   (f) provide prestigious examples of similar changes being implemented in well-known companies;
   (g) show concern for the interests of personnel;
   (h) avoid criticising past performance;
   (i) aim at a mutually acceptable solution;
   (j) discuss, do not argue;
   (k) attempt to overcome prejudices, real or imaginary;
   (l) attempt to dispel rumours at the outset by adequate communications.

12.1 The three main types of computer are mainframe, mini and micro, in descending order of size, power and cost. In the past the distinction between micro, mini and mainframe computers was quite well defined but is now becoming increasingly indistinct. Minicomputers are tending to rival all but the largest mainframe computers in power while PCs (microcomputers) are becoming increasingly more powerful. It is important to appreciate that all types of computer consist of a combination of devices including the processor and its supporting (or surrounding) devices, which are called peripherals.

Mainframe

A mainframe computer is the largest type of computer used for business and accounting applications. Large businesses ususally require large computers for the efficient processing of large volumes of accounting and other types of data. Mainframes are usually sited at the head office of a large company, such as a large manufacturing or chemical organisation or at the headquarters of banking organisations, insurance companies or building societies; or in town halls for municipal accounting and administrative applications. Mainframes require to be operated by expert DP professionals because of the complexity of commands to the operating system, etc. They can be used as stand-alone computer systems or to support a large network of terminals, facilitated by their telecommunications, distributed data processing and systems network architecture (SNA) capabilities. Input is usually by keyboard, including remote terminal keyboards for on-line processing applications, but transaction files for batch processing may be encoded on discs by key-to-disc equipment. A powerful operating system provides for multiprogramming, allowing the interfacing of multiple VDUs, industrial, retail and financial terminals both locally and remotely. Printer output is by means of various models of printer, including laser printers, and graph plotters for graphical output. Modems are required for communication-orientated configurations for linking terminals to the computer via a multiplexor. Backing storage consists of banks of disc drives each with a capacity in the region of 100+ MB or, in some instances, a gigabyte (1,000 million). The discs may be fixed or exchangeable but would need to be fixed for on-line operations from remote locations to allow for demand processing needs. Mainframes support a large database for servicing the needs of major operations such as order processing, airline reservations and banking operations, etc. They also facilitate report generation, on-line program development and applications relating to accounting and information processing.

Minicomputer

In many cases the minicomputer fills the gap between the larger PC and the smaller mainframe. Minis are produced by a number of manufacturers including DEC (Digital Equipment Corporation), Hewlett Packard, IBM, ICL and GEC. They tend to be used by medium-sized organisations which cannot justify a mainframe. Applications processed on a mini include accounting routines, databases and other management information systems. They are also used for numerical control of machine tools in the factory and for monitoring various types of processes. When the capacity of a mini is exceeded it is often necessary to switch to a mainframe to attain a more powerful processing capability and larger internal memory. Specialist DP staff are required to operate a mini, like a mianframe, due to its complexity compared to a PC. When management considers the implementation of distributed processing, a strategy which provides computing power where it is most useful in a dispersed organisation, a minicomputer is often installed in each of the various locations. Typically, it is used for local accounting routines, payroll, stock control and order processing, etc. It may be connected to other minis in a network for data interchange or for gaining access to information, such as budgets, in a corporate database. On the other hand it may function as a stand-alone system with its own database.

Transaction data is usally input by keyboard and output by a printer. The processor is based on 32-bit technology with a memory capacity in the region of 4 – 16 MB. The processor has a built-in Winchester hard disc drive with a capacity between 80 – 320 MB which may be supplemented by an integral tape spooler for backing up files (taking copies). In addition, backing storage may be further complemented by exchangeable and floppy disc drives.

A stand-alone mini does not need expensive communication equipment and does not have to rely on the corporate database for accessing information or records for processing because it supports its own. The cost of a mini is less than a mainframe but much more than a PC.

Microcomputers – personal computers (PCs)

Manufacturers of microcomputers for business use include IBM (the IBM PC), Apple (Apple Macintosh), Amstrad and Compaq, who market a range of models. Micros are normally stand-alone machines operated by end-users for their own particular processing needs such as payroll, stock control and general accounting routines. They are also widely used by accountants for problem solving using spreadsheets. They can, however, be linked into a network consisting of mainframes, minis and other micros for the purpose of interchanging data between operating units and accessing a corporate database. They can also be connected to facsimile systems which transmit and receive images, drawings and diagrams, and telex systems which transmit and receive textual messages They may also share the resources of high speed printers and high capacity disc storage. They are smaller than minis and much simpler to operate – the non-professional can become quite proficient in a short space of time.

12.2 (a) Specify the applications being considered for computerisation together with details of the number of records in files and the number of characters in each record to give some idea of backing storage needs.

(b) Assess which operating systems are used on the alternative systems. Standard operating systems provide access to a wide range of applications packages, which avoids the need to have programs specially written by software houses or by internal programmers.

(c) Invite manufacturers or dealers to demonstrate their models to obtain an appreciation of their operating features. If a mainframe is required, then selected manufacturers' representatives should assess the client's needs and specify a *proposal* for a defined model of computer system. It is then possible to assess performance and price more specifically.

(d) Benchmark tests may provide some guidance for appraising the performance of various models. Such tests establish the time taken to perform specific types of operation relating to arithmetic computations, sorting of data, calling sub-routines and handling of arrays, and so on. The results of these tests provide information on features of particular significance to individual users.

(e) The users of computer systems can be consulted to obtained unbiased opinions of their strengths and weaknesses.

(f) Turnkey services may be used for the initial identification of the type of computer system best suited for the needs of the business. The service also embraces systems design, programming, system testing and implementation. A business with little data processing experience would find this a very useful service.

(g) The services of computer consultants may be employed to assess the needs of the business thereby avoiding a computer system too large and expensive on the one hand, or one which would soon be inadequate for its purposes on the other.

(h) It is also necessary to determine the effectiveness of after-sales service and support from specific suppliers or dealers.

(i) When dealing with subjective assessments it is good practice to list all the important features: storage capacity required for records; internal memory capacity required related to software sophistication and the volume of data to be input; speed of the processor; whether single-user or multi-user facilities are required; peripherals which can be supported such as terminals, serial or parallel centronic printers; soft or hard discs (Winchesters as they are called); high resolution graphics; programming languages supported; operating system used, and so on. Points may be awarded to each factor and the highest scoring system may be the one most suitable subject to general considerations such as reliability of hardware, quality of software, cost of the system, availability of peripherals and effectiveness of maintenance agreements, etc.

14.1 (a) Digital PABX telephone exchanges are an essential communication catalyst for the electronic office of the present and future. Digital voice and data communication systems provide the foundations for extending office automation. The digital exchange translates voice analogue signals into digital signals, which are the common language of computers and electronic equipment such as work stations, word processors and terminals in general. This technology will widen the horizons for developing automated offices as it makes it possible to access all electronic devices comprising the electronic office. This includes access to local area networks, mainframe computers, terminals, word processors, electronic mail stations, telexes, microcomputers and electronic printing equipment. The devices are connected to the wiring of the digital switchboard at no additional cost. PABX systems can also act as message switching centres for terminals and other devices. They also control the routing of data or text from workstations.

(b) Packet switching is a technique whereby the terminal or computer in a data transmission system collects data into a block which is allocated an address. The block is sent to the local packet switching exchange which transmits it to its destination exchange. The communication lines between exchanges are only engaged when a packet is being transmitted. During lapses in transmission, lines are available to other users. If data is transmitted by the normal telephone network a charge is incurred for the length of time the line is used, even for the time when no data is being transmitted. Packet switching is designed to eliminate this. In the UK this applies where telephone calls or data transmissions on public switched telephone lines are charged on a time used basis.

(c) Teletex is the international text communication service embracing a set of internationally agreed standards, which ensures the interworking of terminals from any manufacturer on a number of different networks. Communication between various equipment models cannot be achieved without standardisation. Teletex represents an automatic text transmission system thirty times faster than telex. Business correspondence, documents, data and messages can be transmitted between terminals, which may be work stations or word processors, in around ten seconds a page. Letters can be typed and sent automatically. Other work can continue while documents are being transmitted or received. Copies of documents can be stored electronically or printed for filing in the normal office filing cabinets.

14.2 Local area networks, referred to an LANs, comprise typically microcomputers connected to one another and sharing resources. There are three main topologies (ways of structuring the connection); these are ring, star and bus (see Figs. 1, 2 and 3).

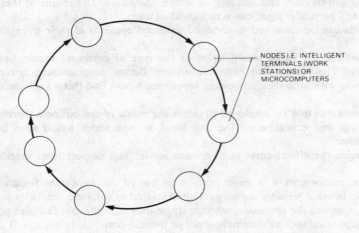

NODES I.E. INTELLIGENT TERMINALS (WORK STATIONS) OR MICROCOMPUTERS

Figure 1 A ring network

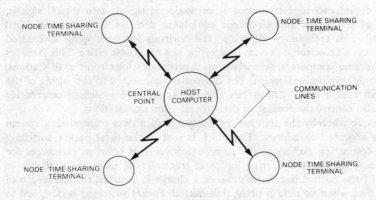

NODE: TIME SHARING TERMINAL

NODE: TIME SHARING TERMINAL

CENTRAL POINT

HOST COMPUTER

COMMUNICATION LINES

NODE: TIME SHARING TERMINAL

NODE: TIME SHARING TERMINAL

Figure 2 A star network

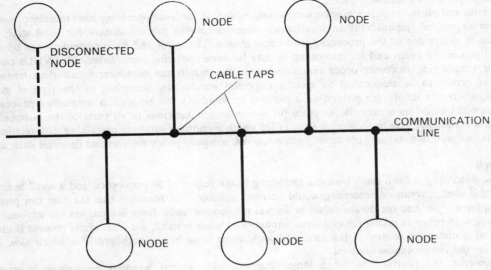

WORK STATION/MICROCOMPUTER

NODE

NODE

DISCONNECTED
NODE

CABLE TAPS

COMMUNICATION
LINE

NODE

NODE

NODE

Figure 3 A. bus network

Typical network protocols (access methods) are *carrier sense multiple access with collision detect* (CSMA/CD), which is used on a bus network, and the token ring method, which is used on a ring network. IBM currently markets a token ring network. A token is passed around the network and unless a device has the token it cannot transmit on the network. This avoids any collision of messages. Devices are addressed so messages can be directed. There are three main carriers used: twisted pair wires, co-axial cable and fibre optic. Twisted pair is that cable traditionally used in telephone communications and is cheap and easy to install. It has limited range and is a baseband medium. Co-axial cable is rather like a television aerial and is a broadband medium (it can carry a number of messages on different frequencies at the same time). Co-axial cable can carry messages over longer distances than twisted pair. Fibre-optic cable is a more recent development: it is a glass-based substance which uses light to transmit information. Local area networks allow micros to share expensive resources, such as hard discs and laser printers. They can offer multi-user applications if programmed to provide record locking. Electronic mail is a popular application for local area networks.

16.1 Centralised data processing utilises a mainframe computer for processing the data of the whole organisation. In such instances the computer is used for processing routine accounting data relating to such applications as payroll, invoicing, sales ledger, stock control and purchase ledger, etc.

The computer is usually located at the head office of the group; in the data processing department of a single operating unit or at a data processing centre servicing the needs of the group. The main objective is economy of scale and standardisation of processing routines. This was particularly applicable in the early days of computers in the 1960s and early 1970s due to the enormous cost of computers. Only the larger organisation could financially justify the use of such a facility and it was often necessary to adopt a three-shift working system so as fully to utilise the costly hardware.

In the past, if the central computer serviced a number of local companies, then a data collection and delivery service was often provided on a daily basis. Data was collected by a van and processed by the computer. The printouts were also distributed by the van. Nowadays the trend is towards the use of terminals to transfer data speedily to and from the computer. Key-to-disc facilities are often used on a remote job entry basis for transmitted batches of data, often for processing overnight. The processed results can then be transmitted back and printed on a local printer thereby avoiding delays in the post.

The underlying philosoply of distributed processing is the provision of computing power within the organisation where it can be most effective, as distinct from concentrating all computing power at a single centrally located computer as outlined above.

A distributed system can consist of many different types of hardware facility, typical examples of which are minicomputers and microcomputers.

The mini and microcomputers may be used autonomously at the local operating level thereby providing a greater degree of responsibility to local management; increased job enrichment for local staff; and reduction in delays due to the processing load being shared. The minis and microcomputers can be used for local processing needs and for interchanging data between operating units. Sales office VDUs can be used for transferring customer order requirements to the mainframe computer which then transmits details of orders to be despatched to specific dispersed warehouses, according to the type of goods required, where the details are printed on a printing terminal. As can be seen, a distributed processing system is often based on a network structure for speedy communications to all parts of the business. In addition, a mainframe may be located at head office which supports a database containing data relating to corporate budgets, sales targets, production achievements, company policy matters and financial data, etc.

16.2 (a) Payroll
If payroll processing is for a small business employing in the region of 50 employees, and a small business computer is used, interactive processing would be more suitable. The reason is that the user can process each employee's pay and tax details on an individual transaction basis. Data is input via the keyboard in accordance with prompts asking for employee number and hours worked, etc. The whole process is menu driven and is under the control of the user. Although direct input by the keyboard is relatively slow it is suitable for the circumstances outlined.

If, however, the payroll was for a larger business with several hundred employees, interactive processing would be unsuitable because a fast, automatic input of transaction data is required. This situation is more suitable for batch processing whereby all the details of employees' earnings are stored on a transaction file on magnetic disc. Transactions stored on a disc file are input to a mainframe computer under program control and matched with the relevant payroll record on the master file.

(b) Customer invoicing
The same considerations apply as for the payroll discussed above. If few invoices are required each day interactive processing would be a suitable method using menu-driven invoicing software to process each invoice on a transaction basis on a small business computer. Details of items to be invoiced would be entered by keyboard and the software would prompt the user through the various processing stages. If a large volume of invoices is required batch processing on a mainframe should be selected to take advantage of high speed, automatic input of transactions relating to customer sales stored on magnetic disc.

(c) Airline seat reservations
Real-time, interactive, conversational mode transaction processing is the only method suitable in this instance. A terminal in a travel agent's office can be connected to a master file storing the seat availability on various airlines, to different destinations on specific dates. This type of system enables seats to be booked immediately, so avoiding double bookings due to inaccurate information. It is a random enquiry system requiring fast access and immediate updating of files storing the current status of seats available.

(d) Credit checking
An interactive system is required in this case for dealing with random enquiries occurring at random time intervals. An on-line order processing system has an inbuilt routine for the on-line checking of customers' accounts to ascertain whether an order can be accepted, which depends on their credit standing. If their account balance exceeds the credit limit, or payments are outstanding, the order will not be accepted. This may be accomplished using a stand-alone small business computer or by a terminal linked to a mainframe or minicomputer. It is a file 'look-up' procedure which accesses a specific customer's account from the customer master file and displays the account details on the monitor screen of the PC or on the screen of a terminal.

Credit card companies such as VISA now have on-line credit checking facilities by means of special devices located in retail shops. The credit card is passed through a device linked to the credit card company's computer. An instant response is provided on the credit card status of the customer. The sale will not be accepted if the customer has exceeded the credit limit. If accepted the value of the sale is automatically updated on the customer's account. For less sophisticated systems, the customer's account is checked by the retailer telephoning the credit card company. The updating of customers' accounts could be done weekly on a batch processing basis from batches of sales vouchers submitted by the retailers

19.1 Program specification

A program specification is a formal directive from the system designer to the programmer defining the requirements of a program to attain the purpose and objectives of a specific system. The specification is an important element of system documentation and provides an interface between the system design and programming. The specification identifies the program(s) and the name of the analyst(s) who designed the system. The logical requirements of the system are indicated in great detail specifying the validation checks to be incorporated; the type of processing required – batch or on-line (transaction) processing, multi-tasking or multi-user, centralised or distributed and so on; the name of the files to be updated and how often, the organisation of the files and the file media to be used – fixed or exchangeable discs, for instance. It also specifies the data to be input for processing, the content and layout of reports and documents and auditing requirements.

The specification should also indicate that programming methodology and documentation should accord with programming standards. The specification should provide information relating to priority interrupts, when operating in a multiprogramming environment, recognising that specific jobs have a higher priority for the use of input and output devices than others. These factors are defined in the job control language. The processing procedures for dealing with abnormal situations such as error conditions and when to abort a program must also be included; error detection and correction procedures; utility programs to be employed; library sub-routines to be incorporated and the use to be made of open and closed sub-routines; dump and restart procedures, etc. It is imperative that back-up requirements are implemented to ensure files can be reconstituted in the event of loss or corruption.

21.1 (a) Systems software

This category of software is for the purpose of aiding programmers to develop application programs or a type of program which interacts with application programs whilst running on the computer. This naturally includes operating systems and data management systems.

An operating system is the primary element of software as it is a master control program which controls the running of all other programs. It is a powerful unit of software without which the hardware is inanimate. This type of software controls multiprogramming on the larger mainframe and minicomputers and assigns control to the various programs on a priority basis. It controls data transfers between the various peripherals, and generates system messages on the video screen and reacts to commands input by the keyboard, etc.

It is important when considering the purchase of a computer for business use to know what operating system it runs under as the more efficient the operating system, the more effective is the computer. Many manufacturers have their own operating system but others adopt specific operating systems.

A *bootstrap loader* is a small program which facilitates the loading of the operating system from backing storage into the internal memory on some of the larger computers. Without a bootstrap loader it would not be possible to load the operating system, and processing could not be activated. Some small computers have the operating system built into a ROM chip, which is located on the main circuit board so that the operating system is available immediately the power is switched on.

The primary tasks performed by an operating system depend upon the type of computer because the larger mainframes are capable of processing several jobs in multiprogramming mode and others are used for real-time processing tasks, all of which are controlled by the operating system.

The normal tasks performed by an operating system include:

(a) communicating with computer operator by means of the console unit or typewriter;
(b) loading and unloading of programs;
(c) supervising multiprogramming operations, including:
    (i) supervising the running of each program;
    (ii) allocating control to each program according to its priority and the operating state of its peripheral units;
    (iii) protecting each program's working store from overwriting;
(d) allocating peripherals to programs and checking their availability;
(e) controlling and monitoring all information transfers;

(f) warning the operator when peripheral units require attention;

(g) automating the logging of time relating to computer operations.

A program generator is a type of software which creates program code automatically using standard functions. Programs developed in this way include data entry and editing facilities. Apart from being easy to use by non-specialists for developing relatively simple application programs, they can also be used by experienced programmers as a foundation on which to develop more complex programs, thus minimising the time required for the normal input, processing, updating and reporting routines. The program which generates a program is of a much higher level than the programming language it generates as it is highly orientated to people.

A program generator also requires a data dictionary for specifying the content and format of data files and also high speed retrieval facilities.

Other types of system software include:

(a) debugging and trace routines;

(b) text and link editors;

(c) assemblers and compilers.

(b) Application programs

These are programs prepared for specific applications either in-house or from external sources (application packages), and include those for payroll processing, stock control, purchase ledger, order processing, sales invoicing and sales ledger; nominal ledger and fixed asset accounting, etc.

Each application requires a suite of programs which typically contains programs for validation, sorting, calculating, updating, comparing and printing, depending on the particular requirements of a defined application.

A program consists of all the relevant instructions for the processing of transactions. Each instruction defines the operation to be performed and the location of the data to be processed.

In a business environment application programs actually perform the processing needs of the business automatically and may be classed as the automation of clerical activities. Systems software, particularly the operating system, interacts with application programs while they are being processed to attain defined results. Also included are word processing, spreadsheet diaries, databases.

(c) Utility programs

Utility programs, also referred to as service programs, are general-purpose software as they are used for all applications whether stock control, payroll or invoicing, etc. The reason for this is that all application programs, particularly those processed in batch mode, require specific routine tasks performed such as *sort/merge* routines; *conversion* from one media to another, e.g. magnetic tape to disc to take advantage of the faster access speed to records; making *copies* of files for security back-up needs; *reorganisation* of disc files periodically to eliminate overflow conditions, i.e. where records stored on tracks are not in sequential order because the relevant tracks are fully utilised. In addition, *housekeeping* routines covering such tasks as the *writing of header labels* on magnetic tape files, *blocking* and *deblocking* of records stored on magnetic tape; attending to data transfers, i.e. *input/output* routines and *clearing of registers*, i.e. internal memory locations in readiness for new data.

24.1 Net present value (NPV) is a technique used for investment appraisal and involves the computation of the present value of a series of future cash flows, i.e. income or outlays, over a number of years. The technique enables the most profitable course of action to be established from a series of alternative investment proposals. It allows decisions to be made with regard to the cut-off point, i.e. the required rate of return on investments so that unprofitable investments are not made. The technique also recognises that future cash flows, including income, outlays or cost savings, are worth less than present cash flows. The reason for this is that current cash flows could be invested and earn interest. The further ahead the cash flows from investments, the lower their present values. One investment may appear to be more profitable than another, having a greater net present value, but on inspection the reverse may well be true because of the timing of the cash flows, or cost savings, which may be too far ahead to be a feasible proposition.

All business investments should, so far as possible, achieve the target rate of return, otherwise the return to capital employed will deteriorate. Even though a project may show a high NPV it is necessary to take into account the magnitude of the investment and assess the risk factors involved. The cost savings or profit increases may be lower than anticipated in which case the return on the investment would be lower.

An ambitious project may hit snags and have to be abandoned due to unforeseen circumstances such as lack of funds to pay interest on loans and/or loan repayments which financed the investment. In addition, many benefits derived from a computerised system may be of an intangible, but very important nature, which cannot be included in NPV computations, which provide only the means for evaluating tangible financial factors (cash flows) relating to competing investments. Even so these are purely 'guesstimates' which may not be achieved.

24.2 Capital expenditure

Expenditure incurred in the purchase of hardware and software may be classed as capital expenditure as it represents tangible assets which appear on the balance sheet. This is because their value is not immediately used up but depreciates through use during the course of business operations. Accordingly, it will be necessary to write down the value of all hardware each year as its value is reduced due to the effluxion of time and wear and tear.

Expenditure incurred on computer accommodation, including the cost of converting an existing building or constructing a new building, is also of a capital nature. This category also includes the cost of air conditioning equipment, storage racks for tapes and discs as well as desks and chairs. A large computer will also require a standby generator in case of power failure and dust extraction equipment to avoid dust on the magnetic files which can corrupt the data they store.

Revenue expenditure: operating costs

This class of expenditure relates to operating costs incurred in running the computer system and includes:

(a) leasing or rental charges of the computer or depreciation of machines and equipment if purchased;

(b) licensing charges for the use of proprietary software;

(c) establishment charges, including rent of premises if not owned; rates, building insurance, heating, lighting and cleaning;

(d) electrical power for running the computer system;

(e) cost of leased lines;

(f) rental charges for modems;

(g) salaries of management and computer operations staff, including data processing manager, operators, data control clerks, programmers, systems analysts and data encoders, etc.;

(h) payroll costs, i.e. national insurance paid by employer;

(i) holiday pay of staff;

(j) insurance premiums relating to computer systems;

(k) operating supplies, including magnetic tapes, exchangeable discs and printout stationery;

(l) training courses;

(m) telephone;

(n) travelling expenses;

(o) general supplies;

(p) subscriptions and publications;

(q) maintenance costs;

(r) cost of standby facilities – bureau charges.

Once-and-for-all costs

It is essential to take into account what may be classed as 'once-and-for-all costs', which are incurred when developing a computerised system. Such costs include the cost of conducting feasibility studies, systems analysis and design, programming, and the costs incurred for running the two systems in parallel. Costs will also be incurred for changing over files from the current system to a form suitable for the computer. Records are often converted from ledger cards to magnetic tape or disc files.

Abnormal operating costs are incurred initially because of the need to employ additional staff and/or retain displaced existing staff for running the two systems.

Investment in resources

Investment in computer systems or information technology in its widest sense must be recognised as an investment in resources which must have an adequate return in the same way as any other investment. It is pointless incurring costs to produce information which serves no useful purpose and which therefore does not create benefits to the business. Computer systems utilise resources in the same way as any other business activity because all activities in a business require manpower (personnel), machines, money and materials to accomplish tasks. The cost of the resources must be compared with what they accomplish, which is normally expressed in terms of benefits to the business.

Benefits are of two categories, namely tangible and intangible. Each of these categories will now be discussed.

Intangible benefits

Many benefits are difficult to quantify and they are referred to as being intangible because cost savings or additional profitability cannot be precisely defined. The following summary lists general areas in which such benefits arise:

  (a) more effective administration;
  (b) improved customer satisfaction;
  (c) more optimum solutions to operational problems;
  (d) improved forecasting techniques for strategic planning;
  (e) more timely information for the decision making process.

Tangible benefits

It may be possible to convert the intangible benefits listed above into tangible benefits it they can be evaluated in the following ways:

(a) The streamlining of information flows has reduced the output of redundant information thereby improving administrative effectiveness, which has generated a saving in staff costs of £X p.a.

Customers' accounts are paid more promptly due to the provision of more accurate and timely data relating to invoices and statements of account. This has improved the inward cash flow by £Y p.a., which has the effect of reducing the interest on the bank overdraft by £X per month.

(b) As a result of implementing on-line enquiry systems, customers are immediately informed of the information they require relating to such factors as product availability, availability of holiday accommodation and delivery dates, etc., which enables them to respond accordingly without delay. This allows alternative choices to be selected, such as placing orders for alternative products or booking alternative holidays. This improves the profitability of the business by avoiding the prospective loss of profit as a result of not informing customers of available alternatives. This is assessed as an increase in profit in the region of £Y p.a.

(c) Due to the increased yield of material mix in the production of product X of Y per cent per week an additional profit of £X per week is achieved.

(d) Improved strategic planning as a consequence of improved forecasting techniques has generated additional sales of £Y p.a. and an additional profit of £X p.a.

(e) More timely information has allowed decisions to be taken in an acceptable time scale, i.e. response time, which has had the effect of increasing operational efficiency in the use of resources, decreasing operating costs by £Y per week.

Other tangible benefits include more effective stock management which has reduced the level of investment in overall stocks by £X and interest charges on bank overdraft by £Y per month.

More timely and accurate information relating to credit control has improved cash flows as evidenced by an average reduction in debtors of £Y per month. This has the effect of reducing interest on bank overdraft by £X per month.

Tangible benefits are more easily attainable at the operational level because corrective control action taken to eliminate adverse situations or to take advantage of favourable conditions is very likely to have an acceptable pay-off. This is applicable in the following instances:

  (a) reduction of excessive scrap to reduce production costs;
  (b) reduction of excessive stock levels, reducing the amount of money invested in stocks;
  (c) improving the performance and efficiency of personnel by appropriate disciplinary measures;
  (d) elimination of adverse expenditure variances by more effective control.

25.1 When manual systems are superseded by computerised applications there is a need to retrain existing personnel or recruit personnel from external sources for the new types of task which have been created as a result of implementing new technology. Before training can commence, however, it is necessary to select suitable personnel with the required aptitude and potential for specified tasks, to avoid the 'square pegs in round holes' syndrome. This is very important when manual dexterity is essential for expert manipulation of a terminal key board or keyboard data encoder, as this determines the speed with which data can be input for processing, the efficiency with which terminal operations are conducted and the efficiency with which data can be encoded. Hamfisted personnel should not, of course, be selected for these tasks.

Training schedule
It is important to prepare a training schedule sufficiently far in advance of the date set for system changeover to ensure a smooth transition from one system to the other. It will also be necessary to arrange for personnel to be released from their current duties to attend the specified training courses or training sessions. This can disrupt the smooth functioning of the various departments concerned, but must be accepted as a necessary requirement – there is always a price to pay for future efficiency.

Mode of training
The mode of training provided will depend upon the nature of the activities. If the activity is concerned with preparing transaction data recorded on source documents into a form suitable for input to a computer, it may require training on a key-to-disc or other data encoding system, which will be undertaken partly by the manufacturer and partly by the systems analyst. The training of clerical support staff in the collection and recording of transaction details on new source documents is likely to be undertaken by a supervisor after receiving instruction from the systems analyst. Alternatively, direct training may be provided to staff by the systems analyst. Similar considerations apply to the training of data control clerks who will be responsible for receiving, checking, recording and maintaining control of batches of work coming in from the operating departments. The training of computer operators will probably require their attendance at a manufacturer's training course for the purpose of providing direct operating experience of the type of configuration to be implemented. This will be supplemented by operating instructions provided by the programmer of the various applications. The chief programmer will receive guidance relating to the new systems from the program specification prepared by the systems analyst. This document specifies the requirements of the program to achieve the objectives of the system. When software packages are to be implemented, programmers, computer operators and systems analysts may attend seminars sponsored by the software marketing company to obtain first-hand knowledge of the *modus operandi* as well as hands-on experience of such programs as integrated accounting packages, database management systems and spreadsheets.

Induction training
Apart from attendance at manufacturers' courses, on-site induction training may be arranged by systems staff to introduce the new technology to all personnel concerned with the new systems. This would include departmental management as well as operating staff. Induction training may be presented in a number of ways, including the use of slide projectors to project line drawings and photographs to provide details of hardware to be used; and the structure of the proposed systems by means of simple systems flowcharts; lectures may be pre-recorded on cassette to provide a general background before embarking on matters specific to the object system. Video films may also supplement slides and cassettes and initial impact for induction purposes may be achieved by arranging a visit to a similar system in operation at a local company.

Monitor training effectiveness
It will be an essential factor of the follow-up routine after a system has been implemented to assess the effectiveness of training and either supplement it with further training if necessary, or replace personnel if they are unsuitable for the tasks assigned to them. The importance of an effective selection procedure was indicated previously to avoid this situation.

25.2 After a system has been implemented and ostensibly proved to be performing satisfactorily, it is still necessary to ensure that no abnormalities occur and to remove the cause if any problems arise. It may be found that although the system is achieving results as stipulated in the systems specification, the system design does not provide for certain requirements. This situation will, of course, require changes to the system – referred to as modifications. Such changes will involve rewriting programs, recompiling and retesting. Checks will also be required to ensure that system security and privacy are maintained at the stipulated level and that there is no unauthorised access to payroll and customer files, for instance. All such changes should be recorded in a 'System changes manual', a copy of which should be given to the internal audit department so that it may inspect the changes. Any anomalies will be referred to the systems development staff for discussion and further amendment if necessary. It is essential for auditors to satisfy themselves that systems are suitable for their purpose and are achieving the objectives laid down in the systems specification.

25.3 It is advisable to co-opt the services of personnel in the user departments concerned with the system being implemented, because of their knowledge and experience in operating the current system. It is essential to incorporate their specialised knowledge into the new system since they alone understand the system's idiosyncrasies and are aware of its strengths and weaknesses. Strengths need to be built on and weaknesses eliminated. In this way a more powerful and reliable system will emerge to suit current operational needs and practices. The extent to which users participate in the design of systems will vary with the management's outlook and style, whether autocratic or democratic for instance, and the viewpoint of trade unions regarding the interests of their membership.

Communicate purpose of project

Users and systems analysts should consider that they both work for the same company and therefore should have common aims and interests in pursuit of operational efficiency. It is important that users appreciate that the purpose of the project is to improve the performance of the particular function as the current system is outmoded for current demands. It is important to consider the feelings of the operating staff and essential to inform them that their performance is not in question – the system has been overtaken by new technology, which it is important to implement to become more efficient, to withstand competition, and to remain (or become) profitable. User department personnel should be aware of the nature of the proposed system and how it differs from the current one.

Subsequent proposals may recommend implementing an on-line order-entry system to streamline the order handling procedure and speed up the input of order details to the computer to achieve a 24-hour turnround time, which is not possible with the present system. The system may also be planned to be integrated with other related subsystems to avoid entering data more than once, to speed up the preparation of invoices and optimise stock levels to minimise shortages and avoid excessive investment in stocks. It is necessary to advise the operating personnel of the new jobs to be created, which will create job enrichment and make the work more interesting.

25.4 Many computer-based systems are of an accounting nature necessitating the conversion of files to magnetic media and the transfer of opening balances to the computer files. The time taken to accomplish this task requires careful planning and control. The longer the transfer takes the more difficult it becomes to catch up with the current status of the system. This leads to frustration as personnel attempt to run both the current and computer system on a disjointed basis. 'Catch-up' must be given priority while maintaining the current system in an up-do-date condition.

Very often records are converted from ledger cards on which transaction details are recorded by hand or posting machine (if they still exist) to magnetic media by suitable encoding methods. Before conversion it is essential that the balances on such records as stock record cards, suppliers' and customers' accounts and employee payroll records are reconciled to ensure only correct balances are transferred to the new system. This creates a high volume activity and suitable arrangements must be made sufficiently in advance to avoid unnecessary 'take on' delay.

25.5 When preparing system installation plans it is necessary to take into account the complexity of changeover which will have a bearing on the time required. Other matters to build into time schedules will be the time needed for training of staff, preparing computer accommodation, obtaining pre-printed stationery, system testing, time for resolving problems, file conversion and take on. After data has been processed arrangements should be made for its distribution either by messenger service, internal transport or data transmission.

Direct changeover

This method may be relevant for relatively straightforward, simple systems. However, even the simplest systems have inherent problems which do not always manifest themselves until the previous system has been dispensed with – and then the trouble starts. Direct changeover should be contemplated only after considering all the possible problems which can arise and the consequences if they do. This is a high risk method but may be adopted when the system is straightforward, as stated, when user staff are confident in running the system and when time is short. The method may also be adopted when the current system and the new system are so dissimilar that parallel running is irrelevant. It may also be applied if the additional staff necessary for parallel operation are not available.

Parallel running

This method requires the running of both the current and new system side by side on a fail-safe basis. The current system is not dispensed with until the integrity of the new system has 'been proved beyond reasonable doubt'. This is accomplished by comparing the results produced by the current system with those produced by the computer system. If they are in agreement the system integrity is assured. As this is a fail-safe method it is costly because it is necessary to engage staff for running both systems side by side.

This usually prolongs the testing period and delays system changeover; consequently time must be allowed for this factor. It is necessary, however, for a limit to be set on the number of cycles for which the two systems will run in parallel.

Pilot scheme: staged implementation

This method also adopts a cautious approach by not fully committing resources to a corporate implementation but restricting implementation to one location only. The results obtained from running the pilot scheme assist in determining its suitability for other locations in the business. As an example, it may be the basis of a pilot scheme to implement a system in one branch of a multi-branch business such as a bank or building society to assess its performance before implementing it in all branches. This applies when putting branches on-line to a centrally located computer for dealing with daily branch transactions.

25.6 Before an application goes live, i.e. before the new computerised system becomes operational and supersedes the previous system, it is necessary to check all parts of the application to ensure it will process data and produce the required outputs and update records efficiently.

System compatibility with system specification

Before programs are prepared for a specific application it is necessary to ensure the design of the system accords with the system specification with regard to input, output, files, screen layouts and processes, etc. Of particular importance is the need to check that adequate security measures are built into the system . This may involve the use of passwords to prevent unauthorised access to files and/or programs. Adequate measures must also be taken to ensure recovery procedures for real-time applications are effective. This may require the contents of the internal memory to be dumped to backing storage every few minutes to provide restart points in the event of a system malfunction. This type of application may require multiprocessing where one processor acts as a fail-safe back-up to the other. When operating in multi-user mode it is necessary to incorporate file or record locking so that one user is prevented from gaining access to a specific record while another user is updating it.

Program testing

Before an application goes live it is necessary to ensure the program will accomplish the desired results. This is done by the technique of desk checking, which is known as performing a 'dry run'. It involves running through the program coding while making comparisons with flowcharts and decision tables. Any errors are corrected and the program is then converted into machine code by an assembler or compiler. This is followed by test runs using test data, the results of which are compared with precomputed values, totals and summaries to discover any anomalies which must be corrected before changeover. This is a fail-safe procedure requiring the current system to continue in operation during the period when the computerised system is being tested.

Input/output

The design of source documents which record details of transactions must be checked for simplicity of use, completeness and to ensure the data entry boxes are in the correct sequence and of the correct size for the details to be recorded. The forms should be discussed with the clerical staff who are to use them to make sure they are fully understood and are suitable for the required purpose. Screen layouts may sometimes be used for the entry of data from a document in which case the staff who are to use the work stations (terminals or microcomputers) need to become conversant with their use before live operations commence. They need to be conversant with the procedure for calling up operational and help screens, the sequence of entering data, error correction routines and file back-up procedures. Prototype screens should be used for this purpose so that the ultimate users have a say in the design of the screens. The users will then be in a position to indicate inconsistencies with system requirements.

The content and structure of information displayed on a screen as output are directly related to the input screen as one generates the other after data has been entered, validated and subjected to mathematical computations. The output may then be stored on a disc transaction file for further processing in an on-line order entry system, for instance, or printed to provide a document such as an invoice or despatch note. The screen formats should be viewed objectively, as mentioned above. In batch processing applications the output will be predominantly printed for such requirements as payrolls, payslips, despatch notes, invoices, statements of account, stock schedules and exception reports, etc. Such outputs must be viewed objectively by user department personnel to assess whether each document contains relevant information fields, that an appropriate number of copies are produced, that they are easily understood and will attain their required purpose.

Batch controls

The adequacy of the procedure for batch controls prior to data being input must be assessed and the control totals generated by the computer must be compared with those precalculated to ensure consistency. This is essential for controlling the flow of data through the system to avoid confusion as a result of lost data.

Data validation

Data validation routines in the programs must be checked out to ensure invalid data is rejected. The routines vary according to whether batch or on-line processing is being applied. It is necessary to verify the suitability of check digit verification tests for validating key fields such as stock codes, employee numbers, account codes and so on. Range and limit checks also need to be evaluated to assess their appropriateness to the magnitude of values pertaining to specified transactions. An order must be between £5 and £200, for instance: if it is less than £5 it is rejected because it is uneconomic to process; if greater than £200 it is checked because it is in excess of normal maximum order values, and so on. It should be observed that all invalid transactions are displayed or printed on an invalid items report, which should be used to check that corrected transaction data is re-entered.

Files

The files must be checked to ensure that file conversion has been carried out correctly and that all records contain relevant fields and correct brought forward balances. The file updating procedure should be tested to ensure correct account balances are produced in accordance with the transactions processed. The file organisation should be tested for its effectiveness particularly when direct access to specific records is required to deal with enquiries. The response time should be checked with that stipulated in the system specification. In addition, the contents of files should be printed out to assess their integrity (accuracy and completeness).

Clerical procedures

Most computerised systems are supported by manual activities performed by clerical staff. They are concerned with the initial recording and collecting of data received for processing from various departments and/or branch works. Clerical staff are also involved with data control activities before and after processing to ensure all data received is recorded in a control register and that the printed documents and schedules produced are recorded and distributed. The procedures for these activities must be fully understood by the staff who are to administer them – not only is it essential that they understand them, but that they agree their suitability for the purpose.

25.7   A system specification specifies the features and characteristics of a system and provides the interface between systems analysis and systems design. The specific details contained in a system specification depend on the nature and complexity of the system and provide an important list of the features of a system. A specification typically includes a number of matters which are summarised below.

Introduction

This section includes details appertaining to:

    (a) name of the system;
    (b) glossary of terms used in the specification;
    (c) date of preparation;
    (d) statement of acceptance;
    (e) index to sections of the specification;
    (f) system relationships;
    (g) details of amendments to original terms of reference;
    (h) departments involved with the system;
    (i) standards of performance.

Systems objectives: expected benefits, tangible and intangible.

System description

(a) Procedure charts and narrative relating to clerical systems.
(b) Data structure charts and data flow diagrams.
(c) System flowcharts and computer run charts.
(d) Decision tables.
(e) System structure charts.
(f) Coding system.
(g) Auditing procedures.

Hardware

(a) Type of computer.
(b) Peripherals:
   (i) number and types of disc drive;
   (ii) number and types of printer;
   (iii) number and types of terminal, including point-of sale terminals (if relevant);
   (iv) number and types of data encoding machines and/or key-to-disc systems;
   (v) type of input device: optical character/page reader, magnetic ink character reader.

Software

(a) Internally written programs: program names.
(b) Internally written sub-routines.
(c) Program generators.
(d) Operating systems.
(e) Utility programs including program generators.
(f) Application generators.
(g) Application packages.
(h) General purpose software: spreadsheets, executive information systems, report generators.
(i) Databases.

Input specification

(a) Name of system.
(b) Name of document.
(c) Source and method of origination.
(d) Details of data elements.
(e) Frequency of preparation.
(f) Volume.
(g) Validation checks to be applied.
(h) Details of screen layouts for input requirements.

Output specification

(a) Name of system.
(b) Name of report.
(c) Number of print lines.
(d) Maximum size of fields.
(e) Details of screen layouts for display of information.

File specification

(a) Name of system.
(b) File name.
(c) File medium: disc – floppy, fixed or exchangeable.
(d) File labels.
(e) Size of records.
(f) Record types.
(g) Number of discs.
(h) Block size.

(i) Field names.

(j) File security, privacy and confidentiality: use of password.

Program testing

Testing procedures: desk checking (dry runs).

System acceptance testing

(a) Test programs with test data.

(b) Comparison of pre-calculations with results obtained from testing.

(c) Procedure for system modifications.

System installation

(a) Method of changeover: direct, parallel running or pilot.

(b) Changeover timing.

(c) File conversion procedure.

System performance

(a) Estimated run timings.

(b) Estimated computer utilisation (proportion of down-time to planned operational availability).

(c) Estimated terminal utilisation (proportion of available time each terminal is in use).

(d) Types of error and remedial procedure.

(e) Response time requirements.

25.8 The purpose and objectives of standards in the context of the question are for guiding staff in the general rules, conventions and code of practice relating to the design and development of systems.

Methods standards relating to project control

The application of standard methods to the development of systems must stipulate whether the 'system life cycle' or the 'structured' approach is to be implemented. The project control system can then be structured to be compatible with the various stages of development thereby providing a means of controlling all projects on the basis of a standardised schedule, which should enable the highest possible level of project productivity to be achieved.

System and program documentation

System and program documentation standards outline the way in which systems should be structured and the manner in which they should be documented. This factor relates to the method employed and the style adopted for the construction of procedure charts, system flowcharts, data flow diagrams, data structure charts, system structure charts, decision tables and run charts. Standards also embrace programming methodology in respect of the use of standard coding sheets and the application of structured or modular techniques of program design.

Detailed design of system inputs, files and output

Documentation standards specify the way in which documents should be structured and compiled. Such documents contain details and specifications relating to the design of computer input which refers to the design of source documents and screen displays; output from the computer either as a screen display or a printed report; and the structure of master files. The primary purpose of such standards is to adopt a uniform, effective method of documentation which enables systems to be designed in the most efficient way.

26.1 A computer is quite adept at processing data at an extremely high speed, and it will process erroneous data at the same speed as error-free data. It is therefore necessary to ensure data integrity by implementing routines for the detection of errors before they are submitted for processing. It is important to appreciate that data validation is concerned with detecting recording errors on source documents and keyboard input errors in on-line applications, including transposed digits in reference fields, i.e. key fields. Data verification is concerned with detecting encoding errors.

The initial run in a batch processing application is for the purpose of detecting and reporting on errors. This ensures that data is corrected and resubmitted before it is processed as the processing routine contains an error control loop. Typical data validation checks include those listed below.

Limit check

To detect hours worked in excess of standard working hours and hourly rates in excess of normal rates.

Range check

To detect an order quantity outside a specified range of values. It is sometimes necessary to detect an order quantity below or above a specified value. This is for the purpose of complying with company policy which requires the rejection of any order below a stated minimum because the value of the order is insufficient to cover handling costs. It is also necessary to check for quantities in excess of a defined maximum because they must be validated before the order is despatched. Otherwise an excessive manufacturing order may be placed on the factory, causing capacity and cash flow problems; or additional supplies may be obtained from external suppliers at excessive cost. There could also be extra storage space needs when the excess quantity is returned by the customer. Of course, quantities may be correct on occasions, but they are validated to ensure the integrity of the data before processing commences. The program then continues with the processing routine.

Other types of validation check

(a) Check to ensure that transactions are compatible with the program.

(b) Check to ensure that data is for the correct period.

(c) Check to ensure that master files have the correct generation indicator.

(d) Check digit verification to detect transposed digits.

(e) Check to ensure that records and transactions are in the correct sequence and all are present.

(f) Check to ensure that fields contain data with the correct number and type of character.

(g) Compatibility checks to ensure that two or more data items are compatible. For example, a discount may apply only if a customer's account balance is below a stated amount.

(h) Probability checks are used to avoid unnecessary rejection of data. Data can on occasion exceed normal values in a range due purely to random causes. If this occurs at an acceptable frequency the data need not be rejected.

Definition of risks

It is important to define the risks attaching to the various types of error which can occur in accounting sytems. A number of typical errors and the risks they create are outlined below. Some of the examples apply to clerically based routines, which apply even though accounting routines may be generally computerised.

Risk 1: Payment for goods/services not received.

Cause: Fraudulent conversion because of a failure to apply normal clerical checking procedures.

Consequences: Financial insolvency if practice continues undetected.

Type of control to be implemented: Ensure that authorised cheque signatories, e.g. the chief buyer, are provided with related documents appertaining to the transaction including a copy of the purchase order, goods received note, delivery note and invoice(s) in order that the transaction can be validated.

Risk 2: Cash payments recorded in wrong account.

Cause: Incorrect classification.

Consequences: Problems of reconciliation of suppliers' accounts.

If the payments are also made to the incorrect supplier, then suppliers not receiving payment will become irritated and may stop supplies.

Type of control to be implemented:

(a) Reconcile with suppliers' statements and remittance advice slips.

(b) Apply check-digit verification to reduce the risk of transposition errors when inputting account codes by on-line terminal or when writing the code on a source document. This type of control will not, however, trap the incorrect recording of a valid account code. This will require the procedure outlined in (a) above.

Risk 3: Incorrect amount of cash payment.

Cause: Transposed digits when writing a cheque or other payment document. It may also be the result of fraudulent conversion.

Consequences: Problems of reconciliation of suppliers' accounts. Financial insolvency if due to fraud and remains undetected. Irate suppliers if payments are for a lesser amount than the value of goods or services supplied. This could also cause the cessation of future supplies or services.

Type of control to be implemented: Prevent unauthorised access to suppliers' accounts to prevent fraudulent conversion. Ensure cheque signatories inspect relevant document such as an invoice to verify the amount.

26.2 To prevent unauthorised access to confidential files a password is provided to bona fide users of the applications. The password when input to the system is compared with that stored in the software. Access is barred if the password is incorrect. When entered the password is not printed or displayed on the video screen to prevent unauthorised personnel viewing the password and using it illegally.

It is essential to protect highly sensitive information against unauthorised access. In addition to the use of passwords, terminal identification codes may be used to accomplish terminal lockouts, thereby preventing unauthorised access to files by specific terminals. Voice prints may also be used so that individuals with authority to access files are directly identified by voice patterns. Keys to sensitive data should be held only by relevant authorised personnel. Data encryption may also be applied for converting standard ASCII code into a special code which is transmitted by the information channel. The code is then converted to its original form at its destination point.

Databases often incorporate a number of security measures. Users are required to enter a *user name* before access is authorised, a password may be necessary to gain access to confidential information and access to some parts of the database can be restricted to specified terminals. Each information owner must specify the names of users allowed to access his or her data and other information owners who can look at, but not amend that part of the database. Individual pages can also be restricted by specifying user names.

Real-time systems are designed to control critical operations which must be continually updated. Such systems accept random input at random time intervals and the status of files changes accordingly, making it necessary to implement security measures. All relevant restart and audit information is periodically *dumped,* say every two to three minutes, to tape or disc. The dumped data can then be used to restart the system in the event of malfunction. Such operations are also provided with a second processor which is automatically switched into the real-time system in the event of the first machine ceasing to function.

An electronic device known as a *datakey* may be issued to personnel with authority to enter the computer centre. The datakey is an electronic memory circuit embedded in plastic and moulded into the shape of a key. It is a personal, portable information device with alterable semiconductor memory. It can be coded with data for identification purposes. A device known as a *keytroller* incorporates the intelligence for interchange of information between the datakey and the host system. Various voice recognition techniques are available for converting the spoken voice into digital signals. Authorised personnel wishing to gain access to a computer centre can state their name which is compared with a dictionary of prerecorded digital voice prints. When voice prints match, access is allowed.

26.3 Written communications
Terms of reference
The stages of the systems development life cycle include a number of reporting stages one of which is the terms of reference, which is provided by management to systems development staff as authority to undertake a feasibility study.

Feasibility study report
Subsequently the systems analyst prepares and submits a feasibility study report to management specifying the findings of the feasibility study. This reports the technical and economic feasibility of the project stated in the terms of reference.

General reports
Subsequently a report is prepared by the analyst to inform management of various alternative proposals for their deliberation and to make a decision on their choice of system, processing technique or computer configuration. Progress reports are provided from time to time to keep management informed of the stage of system development attained. After the system has been implemented a report is provided to management informing them of the results attained compared with those anticipated. Management then discuss the situation with systems analysts to determine a plan of action to resolve unwanted situations.

Systems documentation

Systems documentation includes a detailed summary of the proposed system, known as a systems specification. A further important document is the program specification, which provides the programmers with all the details they require for writing the relevant programs to accomplish the defined processing tasks. Other systems documentation includes various analysis documents relating to input, output and files, providing detailed information relating to current documentation which is invaluable as a basis for the design of input documents, file organisation and output reports. In addition, documentation includes systems and program flowcharts, screen layouts, data flow diagrams, procedure charts, decision tables, data structures and testing procedures, etc.

Manuals

Various operating manuals are written by systems analysts for the guidance of clerical and computer operations staff in the operational features of the system. They are written to cover such matters as data validation and error correction procedures, data preparation and data control procedures and computer operating instructions. The instructions relate to file back-up procedures, system recovery routines and start-up and loading procedures. In addition, manuals are provided relating to the content, origination and destination point and time and frequency of preparation of forms.

Minutes

A formal record of all meetings would be made during the various stages of system development so that they may be referred to as necessary to establish the authority for specific actions to be taken. The minutes would also state the personnel present, the time and place of the meeting and the nature of discussions, the conclusions reached and decisions made regarding the execution of a specific course of action.

Internal memos

Written memos may be used to convey brief messages to specific personnel for particular purposes. On the other hand, with the advent of electronic technology, the written memo may be dispensed with and electronic mail used instead.

Verbal communications

Sometimes face-to-face discussions or telephone conversations may be adequate for conveying or requesting *ad hoc* information needs.

Meetings

Face-to-face communications are best pursued by arranging systems meetings to discuss future systems development proposals and policy deliberations. Meetings may also be arranged at various stages of systems development to discuss progress and action required to remedy the situation when cost and time targets are not being attained.

Presentations/demonstrations

One of the best ways to get the message across, as it were, is to demonstrate a practical situation. This may be achieved when discussing proposals with user department staff, when the technique of prototyping may be used to advantage. This enables user staff to view the operation of the system on the screen and provide suggestions for its improvement.

Tuition

Tuition is necessary for the purpose of instructing personnel how to load and run a spreadsheet, desktop publishing program or a database management system. These situations are of a practical nature requiring hands-on experience and knowledge of the hardware and commands to run the relevant software. When an initial 'walk-through' of this type is provided prospective users gain confidence because actually seeing the system in operation and its 'user-friendliness' will probably dispel any premature misgivings as to their proficiency in running the applications.

Interviews

This is the most widely used method of collecting facts relating to the current system. Facts are obtained by the analyst interviewing personnel engaged on various parts of a system. The knowledge of staff actually performing tasks is invaluable to the subsequent design of an improved computerised version of the current system.

28.1 Structured design is a method applied to the development of a new computer system, which creates a detailed description of the logical features of the system without taking into account any physical hardware and software factors. It is a logical approach to systems analysis and design based on the identification of objectives, i.e. 'what' is required before attempts are made to define 'how' they can be accomplished. it requires the use of conceptual models, entity diagrams, data flow diagrams, data modelling and functional decomposition. This detail provides the means of preparing a first sketch of the proposed system outlining the logical system to which physical hardware devices and appropriate software may be applied for the achievement of system objectives.

The traditional approach is very systematic but relies heavily on detailed narratives describing the features of the system, which can be very difficult to interpret particularly by non-systems experts. In addition, the traditional approach has a tendency to think prematurely in terms of how a task can be accomplished before the logical aspects are fully assessed. Flowcharts are used to show the processing stages of a system but they tend to be 'hardware'-orientated rather than emphasising the logical aspects of the system.

Logical system design

The stages of structured logical methodology vary according to circumstances and the nature of business activities. Initially the terms of reference are obtained from management, specifying the problems, strengths and weaknesses of the current system and what is required from the proposed system. The current system is then analysed to become familiar with its characteristics. After the preliminary analysis stage a conceptual model, a high level flowchart, is constructed showing each entity and its relationships; the boundary of the system and its interfaces with other related systems; data flows in and out of the system and the processes for the transform of data.

Systems analysis defines in unambiguous terms *what* a system's requirements are whereas logical design specifies a system which achieves user requirements without considering *how* it will be physically accomplished. These logical needs are subsequently matched to physical machines, equipment and software during the physical design stage of systems development. Logical models are constructed of data flows, processes and entities to obtain an appreciation of the nature of the elemental structure of a system as it now exists, and what changes are required to suit *what* a system requirements are before determining *how* they are to be accomplished. A data-driven, top-down structured approach is often applied, which emphasises the use of data flow diagrams (referred to as DFDs), data analysis, data modelling and definition of processes by functional decomposition. The logical approach to system design allows the system developer to identify user information needs accurately. Long and complex narratives and complex flowcharts are replaced with graphical methods and structured English. Structured methodology allows users to participate through all stages of development, enabling them to meet their specific requirements. It provides frequent walk-throughs, i.e. reviews designed to detect errors, omissions and ambiguities in any stage of development. The methodology provides for checking system logic during the analysis and design phases instead of discovering logical errors during the later stages of physical design. Some proprietary systems of structured methodology, such as LSDM, also cover physical system design including definitions of files or databases, programs and computer runs, resource usage estimation and optimisation.

The stages of the structured logical approach to system analysis and design may be summarised as:

(a) obtain terms of reference and conduct feasibility study;

(b) analyse current system in respect of:

    (i) operational details;

    (ii) entities;

    (iii) data;

    (iv) events;

(c) construct conceptual model;

(d) construct entity life history diagram;

(e) construct transaction history diagram;

(f) construct context diagram;

(g) specify data elements (attributes) relating to each input data flow;

(h) specify data elements (attributes) of output data flows and the origin of each output data flow;

(i) prepare data flow diagram specifying input and output data flows and an outline of processing activities;

(j) transform analysis – levelling of data flows;

(k) data modelling using an entity diagram to depict the relationship between data items, their entry points and access paths;

(l) functional decomposition of processes;

(m) construct flowchart portraying logical model of the system.

Physical system design

Once an idea has evolved during the logical design stage of the requirements of the new system it is necessary to determine how the system will work in broad terms. This involves the consideration of response times, volumes of data to be processed, frequency of processing, processing techniques to be applied, hardware and software requirements including accounting packages, spreadsheets and databases. These factors influence the physical design of the system and enable the system designer to construct a 'first sketch' of the physical system. Some designers may consider there is no need for a 'first sketch' as matters relating to processing methods together with the other considerations may have evolved during the various stages of system development. When a 'first sketch' is developed it is reviewed to ensure it is compatible with the system specification.

It is essential to establish how quickly a system must respond to events in the environment. In critical operating areas of a business this may be of extreme importance for the effective control of operations, particularly in large distribution warehouses which require on-line updating of files to record the current status of stocks as transactions occur, i.e. shipments to customers and deliveries from suppliers. The activities are essential for the effective operation of this type of business. Not only is it important to update transactions speedily but also to deal with random enquiries expeditiously. The faster the response time needs of the system the more costly the system will be in terms of both hardware and software.

A hierarchy of priorities must also be established to enable parts of the system with a low priority to be interrupted to deal with real-time requirements. In some circumstances multiprocessing may be adopted using two processors in tandem (incurring high hardware costs) to allow batch and real-time processing to proceed side by side but with the batch procesor programmed to switch immediately to the real-time operation in the event of a malfunction. This is a fail-safe routine to protect the integrity of the data and to avoid 'system downtime', which would be chaotic in an operation such as an airline seat reservation system having terminals located in booking offices throughout the country.

The nature of the processing activities is also indicative of the processing technique to be applied: batch, on-line, interactive, real-time, multi-tasking or multi-user. The processing technique will also determine the type of file medium required, for example large capacity Winchester hard discs perhaps organised on an indexed sequential basis or other direct addressing method.

A front-end processor or multiplexor would also be required to control the communications from the various lines. Modems and terminals will be needed at each location in the network.

Highly sophisticated software will be required for controlling the real-time operation including interrupt facilities, as appropriate, with provision for controlling background tasks such as the processing of routine applications in batch mode. The software takes the form of a powerful operating system. Communications software will also be required to handle enquiries from the various terminals. Cluster controllers may also be necessary to control groups of terminals at specific locations.

Data relating to business transactions is generally recorded on source documents, which must be clear and concise, readily identifiable and serve a useful purpose. A number of important requirements which the system designer must ensure are accomplished are listed below:

(a) Define the title of the document.

(b) Identify the nature of the transaction.

(c) Identify the document by a unique reference number.

(d) Identify the subject of the document, i.e. tour reference number, catalogue number, item code, insurance scheme number and so on.

(e) Describe the entity by means of a short description.

(f) Specify the date of the transaction.

(g) Quantify the transaction.

(h) Price the transaction (when appropriate).

(i) Value the transaction (when appropriate).

(j) Define the entity to be charged, e.g. customer, job, contract or department, by an appropriate reference such as a code or account number.

(k) Authenticate by means of an officially authorised signatory.

(l) When designing documents it is necessary to describe each of the data elements, known as fields. Some systems are designed to display on a video screen a form outline, to which details are entered by an operator using a keyboard. This activity is very similar to entering details on a form by means of a typewriter. Each screen must be separately designed for specific needs such as preparing invoices or entering order details.

29.1 Methods and techniques for accessing summarised information

Any manager wishes to obtain information in the most expeditious and simplified manner without first having to become a computer expert. The solution to this is to provide information retrieval methods which are easy to use and which do not involve learning commands. To this end there are various types of information system, including executive information systems, spreadsheets, internal databases, public databases such as Prestel, and information from accounting packages. The screen dialogue methods which may be applied in the various circumstances include the use of menus, a mouse, touch screen, pointers, keypads and the application of query and natural languages.

(a) Use of menus, mouse or touch screen in an executive information system.

Executive information systems (EIS) provide a solution to the need to obtain summarised information in the form it is required (the user view), when it is required. The EIS is software designed to provide electronic delivery of critical information in the form of reports and charts without the need for executives to learn the technical aspects of computers. Provision is made for using a mouse or touch screen either for performing functions or for pointing to the type of report required. A mouse is used to direct a pointer to the type of report required. With a touch-sensitive screen, it is necessary only to touch with a finger the point on the screen specifying the nature of the summarised information required. It is possible in this way to obtain information stored in multidimensional spreadsheets containing data which may be viewed in many different ways, e.g. information relating to product sales by geographical area, by division and product group, distribution channel, customer group and, at the corporate level; divisional and corporate income, expenditure, profits and losses etc. Any one of these views may provide the best perspective on a problem or opportunity requiring executive action.

(b) Searching a database by means of keywords entered via the keyboard.

A database has searching facilities which allow related facts to be extracted, via the keyboard, by searching using a keyword. This provides the means of obtaining from a large volume of data useful facts which could not possibly be found by physical search methods in sufficient time on which to base a decision.

(c) Menu selection.

(d) Retrieval of information by keypad or keyboard.

Public databases such as Prestel provide valuable business information relating to particular subjects such as share prices, travel information, weather and general information relating to business, finance, economics, engineering, technology and science, etc. Information can be retrieved by terminals linked to the host computer supporting the database via the telephone network or the packet switched stream (PSS) network, which allows users to access distant databases more economically. To obtain information from Prestel the user telephones his or her nearest Prestel computer by pressing a single button on the keypad. Information selection is accomplished by using either a keypad or a keyboard to key in the page number. The pages of information are linked together so that each page can lead to other pages.

(e) Commands as normal sentences in natural language:

Accounting software is being developed which enables the computer to recognise commands input in a natural language, so simplifying their use. Natural language lets users omit the need to select options from menus and fill in boxes on the screen because the computer performs these tasks automatically under control of software. Commands are entered as normal sentences; for example, it is possible to type in 'enquire account 33011' and the system identifies the verb 'enquire' as a command, the item name as 'account' and the item reference as '33011'.

(f) Database query systems based on natural language.

A natural English language database query and retrieval system is used for query and *ad hoc* reporting. It provides easy and instant access to information: when a user asks a question the system retrieves the data, computes and presents the information in a sophisticated columnar display on the video screen. This type of system requires English conversion of the data dictionary describing the database into a lexicon which lists alphabetically all the words and phrases used. The lexicon is used for reference purposes during the processing of natural language queries. This type of query language responds to questions phrased, for example: How many cars of each model did we sell last week compared to target?

The system retrieves from the database the target and actual sales for each model and displays them on the screen together with the actual and planned sales and percentage deviation from the planned sales for each model.

(g) Fourth generation languages.

Fourth generation languages are designed to assist the manipulation of a database by way of a query language providing facilities for creating, retrieving, updating, appending, deleting or amending data. The query language is an element of the database management system. When designed to access a database from a terminal keyboard it is classified as an interactive query language. The primary purpose of query languages is to provide non-computer specialists in the various business functions (the end-users) with the means to do their own information processing without having to become programming experts. A fourth generation language translates the user's requests into procedural steps to produce the desired output. In this way user views of an application are separated from the mechanics of the system – the end result is important to the user, not how it is accomplished. Fourth generation languages enable personnel changing from clerical to computerised database applications to understand the new working procedures more easily. For example, a database may contain a plant register of machines located in the factory, which includes fields (items of information) for machine type, cost, location, depreciation and book value. If the cost of a particular class of machine is required the query language allows the question to be asked in the following way:

LIST COST, MACHINE, FOR MACHINE = 'PROFILER'

This is interpreted by the database management system as: List the cost of the machine type 'PROFILER'. The response provides the record number containing the specific machine and its cost as follows:

00005 8500 PROFILER.

A query to retrieve information relating to which function a particular model of car is allocated may be phrased as LIST FUNCTION, FOR MODEL = 'SIERRA': the response would be ACCOUNTS SIERRA. A list of the registration numbers of each model can be obtained by phrasing a query as, for instance, LIST REGNO, MODEL. The screen would then display, for example:

E255 REA METRO
B360 BEA CAPRI
D890 CEE SIERRA
C450 DAC CHERRY
A125 JAG ESCORT

(h) Query by example.

Some databases provide the technique of 'query by example' so that the need to learn a formal query language to retrieve data is dispensed with. To enter a query it is necessary to press an 'Enter query' function key and type the selection criteria into the appropriate columns. For example, to obtain a list of cars which cost more than £6,000 all that is necessary is to type 6000 in the initial cost column. The list would then be displayed as, for example:

CAPRI B360 BEA 6500 PRODUCTION
SIERRA D890 CEE 7500 ACCOUNTS

Multiple selection criteria can also be performed by typing the condition into each column. For example, purchasing records stored in a database may consist of columns containing supplier, part number, description and price. If a list is required of parts from a specific supplier with a price greater than a stated amount it would be necessary only to enter the supplier's name into the supplier column and the amount into the price column.

(i) Menu selection of reports generated by an accounting package:

information relating to transactions, which can easily be accessed by selecting the required option from those displayed on the screen. A nominal ledger enquiry screen, for instance, provides for displaying account balance details and a reporting screen provides for printing the nominal ledger. The printout may contain a summary of all nominal ledger accounts, including such details as:

- (i) account name;
- (ii) transaction date;
- (iii) serial number of journal entry;
- (iv) narrative;
- (v) debits;
- (vi) credits;

30.1 General background information to menu/screen-based on-line order-entry systems.

Many on-line applications display a menu for selecting alternative options, which serves the same purpose as a dialogue but avoids the need to type in messages or commands to inform the system of the type of processing to be done. Options can be selected in several ways, one of which is to locate the cursor adjacent to the required option and press the enter or return key on the keyboard. Others require a particular number to be keyed in specifying the required option, followed by pressing the enter key; or the use of a mouse to point to the routine required, which is selected when the button on the mouse is pressed.

After selecting the required routine from a menu, form-orientated systems display on the video screen a replica of the form which would be completed by hand in a clerical system. The operator completes it by entering data into the appropriate boxes (fields) by the computer keyboard. The keyed-in details are recorded adjacent to the relevant field and the completed document is displayed on the screen. The dialogue is built into the system because the system expects input from the user in accordance with the sequence of the field names displayed. This is a sophisticated electronic method of processing documents in that it emulates the preparation of forms by hand or typewriter. It assists former manual clerical staff to become orientated more quickly to computer-based systems.

Errors can be made in entering data but are easily dealt with by re-entering corrected data which overwrites the previous entry. The cursor moves progressively over the screen to the next field after the correctness of the entry has been verified. The cursor usually flashes, prompting the user to the field to be entered next. The bottom of the screen displays prompts and messages.

On-line processing of orders

Before orders can be processed it is necessary to load the sales order processing software. If it is a menu driven, form-orientated, application the main menu will be displayed on the screen listing the varous routines from which to select the one required. The main menu will appear as shown below:

Sales order processing
Main menu

Transaction entry 1
Order processing 2
Order reporting 3
End of session 4
Sales analysis reporting 5
Product maintenance 6
System maintenance 7
Exit 8

Please select a function

In the context of the question the sales office clerk would select option 2 by pressing the relevant key on the keyboard for access to the order processing routine. This causes the order processing sub-menu to be displayed as shown below:

Please select a function

In this instance, the sales office clerk presses the '1' key to select 'process orders by customer', which then displays the screen as shown below:

Data is input via the keyboard for each field and the completed order appears as follows:

As each field is entered validation checks are performed, one of which requires the product file to be accessed to check that item codes are correct and match the description. Checks will also be made to ensure that the type of data being entered is correct, e.g. the customer name field should be alphabetic characters whereas the item code and price fields should be numeric characters. Errors are signalled by reverse video (characters are displayed in the opposite background and foreground colours to normal displays – white characters on a black background instead of black on white, for instance) or flashing the field in error.

The bottom of the screen displays messages such as asking if the screen details are correct or if there are any more items to be processed. It is important to appreciate that the system may incorporate inbuilt credit checking, triggered when the customer account number is entered, which causes the customer's account to be accessed in the sales ledger.

When orders are prepared in this way the details may be printed out as an internal order document instructing the warehouse as to the items to despatch to customers. It is more likely, however, that once the details have been input and validated they will be recorded on an orders file stored on magnetic disc for batch processing prior to sorting the items into product code (item code) for checking stock availability. If on-line transaction processing is applied then after order details have been input, validated and corrected they are transmitted to the processor for further processing, bypassing disc storage which is unnecessary for this type of processing.

Index